How Fascism Ruled Women

A CENTENNIAL BOOK

One hundred books
published between 1990 and 1995
bear this special imprint of
the University of California Press.
We have chosen each Centennial Book
as an example of the Press's finest
publishing and bookmaking traditions
as we celebrate the beginning of
our second century.

UNIVERSITY OF CALIFORNIA PRESS

Founded in 1893

How Fascism Ruled Women

Italy, 1922–1945

VICTORIA DE GRAZIA

University of California Press

BERKELEY   LOS ANGELES   LONDON

University of California Press
Berkeley and Los Angeles, California

University of California Press, Ltd.
London, England

© 1992 by
The Regents of the University of California

First Paperback Printing 1993

Library of Congress Cataloging-in-Publication Data
De Grazia, Victoria.
  How fascism ruled women : Italy, 1922–1945 / Victoria de Grazia.
    p.   cm.
  "A Centennial book."
  Includes bibliographical references (p.   ) and index.
  ISBN 0-520-07457-2
    1. Women—Italy—History—20th century.   2. Women—Government
policy—Italy—History—20th century.   3. Italy—Politics and
government—1922–1945.   4. Fascism—Italy—History—20th century.
I. Title.
HQ1638.D4   1992
305.42'0945—dc20   91-8901
                                                                                      CIP

Printed in the United States of America
9 8 7 6 5 4 3 2 1

For my mother, Jill,
and my daughter, Livia

Contents

Preface

In the gruesome light of Nazi Germany, Benito Mussolini's dictatorship over Italy looks benign. This image holds true for Italian fascism's treatment of women as for so many other of its features and undertakings. The Nazis thrust women back into the home as custodians of race, culture, and sentiment, and they mobilized totalitarian organizations to penetrate deep into society and home life. The Third Reich unabashedly promoted eugenicist precepts, and its programs culminated in a frightful race war whose paramount goal, to wipe out the "Bolshevik menace" and extirpate European Jewry, meant systematically killing off women and children too. By contrast, the Duce's regime fell back on the traditional authority of family and religion to enforce biologically determined roles as mother and caretakers. Further, fascist eugenicism was tempered by Catholic Church opposition and never debated in councils of state until Mussolini came under Hitler's influence in the late 1930s. Nonetheless, the antifeminist zeal of the two dictatorships, their laws relegating women to the home, and their public cult of motherhood in the name of building national-state power were similar enough to justify speaking of a common fascist politics toward women.

My goals in this book have been threefold: first, to explore the experience of women under Mussolini's dictatorship: second, to study the creation and impact of fascist sexual politics in the light of broader changes in Italian society during the first part of this century; and, last, through comparisons with other European nations, to highlight how an avowedly fascist regime handled the entry of women into the age of mass politics in the wake of World War I and during the hard times of the 1930s. This book thus proposes a double scope, as a synthesis and an interpretation. More than an exhaustive account of all of the multifarious patterns of state meddling, social custom, and sexual behavior, it is intended to provoke questions, invite comparisons, and stimulate research.

This is a project I came to slowly and, initially, reluctantly. Several years ago, I completed another history of Italy between the wars, one treating the impact—mainly on lower-class men—of the dictatorship's welfare and cultural policies. Long before drawing up the index and tabulating how many times I had explicitly referred to women, I realized that the female subjects of the regime had not been dealt with adequately. At the time, however, there was so little work on most aspects of twentieth-century Italian social history, and the resources to study women seemed so skimpy and inaccessible, that the problem perforce was set aside. But I resisted approaching the subject as well; for writing about victims is saddening, and I had already dwelt so long and in such detail on the dictatorship's torment of working people. To probe reactionary legislative texts for meaning, to evaluate misogynist propaganda, and to decipher more pamphlets touting good deeds seemed only to lead me once more to confront the attitudes of fascism's male officialdom rather than to comprehend the experience of Italian women.

Several circumstances caused me to overcome this reluctance. The first was the rapid maturing of women's studies in the United States during the last decade. My American colleagues, both those studying Europe and those working in a great range of other fields, provoked me to treat Italian women not as mere victims of dictatorship and patriarchy, but as historical subjects and actors, whose experience of fascist rule was enormously varied and might be explored in ways I had never before considered. More important, changes in my own life strengthened and made more intimate my connections with Italian society. Raising a child partly in the United States, partly in Italy, I came to see how diversely Italian women of various generations relate to each other around questions of motherhood and child nurture and how different some of their attitudes were from my own. As a historian, I wanted to find out more concretely and dispassionately how such differences arose.

Not least of all, I was prompted by two strong obligations. One is to American colleagues and friends, in particular John Gillis, Temma Kaplan, Jan Lambertz, Robert Moeller, Abigail Solomon-Godeau, and Christine Stansell, whose considerable knowledge about related issues provoked me to reflect on the condition of women in Italy. I am also the grateful beneficiary of the women's history program of Rutgers University. My other major obligation is to researchers in Italy who have braved Byzantine library systems, underfinanced archives, and an unresponsive publishing world—often while employed outside the university system or in precarious positions at its margins—to produce pioneering studies in women's history and related fields. These have been invaluable to finishing my own work. My friend Michela De Giorgio was an unstintingly generous intellectual companion. I also want to thank Annarita Buttafuoco, Bruno Wanrooij, Stefania Bartoloni, and Barbara Curli for sharing with me their work-in-progress, Angelo Gaudio and Pierre Lanfranchi for reading sections of the book pertaining to their fields of expertise, Monica Miniati for research assistance, and Lando Bortolotti, who lent me the late Franca Pieroni Bortolotti's notes and inventories. Gisela Bock, now of the University of Bielefeld, both debated with me the book's arguments and enabled me to finish writing it by inviting me to be a Jean Monnet Fellow attached to the European Culture-Research Center of the European University Institute in Fiesole; special thanks to the staff of the Center and of the EUI library. The German Marshall Fund of the United States generously supported the extension of my stay there. In Rome, Carla Pasquinelli was unflaggingly hospitable, while in New York, my dear friend Bena Frank Mayer made me the gift of a room of my own in which to write. Finishing up the manuscript, I was aided by Adrian Lyttelton's prudent reading, by the precise editing of my mother, Jill de Grazia, and by the calm professionalism of Sheila Levine and her staff of the University of California Press. At home, in the United States as in Italy, my husband, Leonardo Paggi, was generous with sound if severe advice on intellectual as well as family matters.

New York City
January 1991

1 The Nationalization of Women

The generation of Italian women that came of age in the 1930s, as Irene Brin saw it, was "noisy, ingenuous, and sad." Although "frightfully self-conscious about itself," it was a generation "ignorant of being subject to constraints unprecedented in their absoluteness." So exalted was it by "a sense of freedom from all moral, sentimental, and physical bonds that it didn't realize until too late that it had lost its liberty."[1] Brin, an emancipated, rapier-witted journalist who moved easily between Rome, Milan, London, and Paris, was mainly referring to women whom she knew from her own social circles. By and large, they were the offspring of propertied families that had comfortably accommodated themselves to the dictatorship. Born to privilege, they lived insulated from the troubles of Italian working-class women. Nor were they familiar with the existence of rural women, whose habits of life they would only have shrugged off as dismally dull and backward.

Still, Brin's remarks are relevant to the experience of young women of all backgrounds coming of age in Italy during the long years of Mussolini's dictatorship. Their lives were a disconcerting experience of new opportunities and new repressions: they felt the enticement of things modern; they also sensed the drag of tradition. Mussolini's regime stood for returning women to home and hearth, restoring patriarchal authority, and confining female destiny to bearing babies. To be sure, these constraints were not as overtly violent as other state actions in peacetime, including stifling political freedoms and smashing the free trade unions, not to mention the persecution of Italian Jews in the wake of the racial laws of November 1938. It was indeed the apparent normalness of the constraints on women that made them all the more mystifying, insidious, and demeaning. At the same time, the fascist dictatorship celebrated the

Nuova italiana, or "New Italian Woman." Fascism stood just as visibly for the camaraderie of volunteer organizations and for recognizing rights and duties for women in a strong national state. Not least of all, the dictatorship was identified with the physical freedom and more emancipated behaviors associated with the spaces and occasions of modern leisure pastimes. Why a regime that is usually associated with totalitarian repression and utter patriarchal reaction should have been experienced so ambivalently is the subject of this book.

From the start, then, this book tells of the deep conflict within the fascist state between the demands of modernity and the desire to reimpose traditional authority. Benito Mussolini, like Hitler in Nazi Germany, vaunted his ability to promote economic change in order to build up national strength. At the same time, he condemned and sought to forestall the social fallout that, at least since the nineteenth century, had accompanied rapid economic transformations. This conflict was especially visible in the regime's attitudes toward women. On the one hand, fascists condemned all the social practices customarily connected with the emancipation of women—from the vote and female participation in the labor force to family planning. They also sought to extirpate the very attitudes and behaviors of individual self-interest that underlay women's demands for equality and autonomy. On the other hand, fascism, in an effort to build up national economic strength and to mobilize all of Italian society's resources—including the capacity of women to reproduce and nurture—inevitably promoted some of the very changes it sought to curb. Mobilizing politics, modernizing social services, finally, the belligerent militarism of the 1930s, all had the unintended effect of undercutting conservative notions of female roles and family styles. In the process, fascist institutions ordained new kinds of social involvement and recast older notions of maternity and fatherhood, femaleness and masculinity. As in other areas of society, the dictatorship claimed to be restoring the old, when, in spite of itself, it established much that was new.[2]

Because Italian fascism's positions on women were not merely of its own invention, nor were they, in the last analysis, that distant from the attitudes, policies, and trends prevailing in nonauthoritarian states, they need to be studied in a wider time frame and in comparative context. Mussolini's sexual politics crystalized deep-seated resentments against broader changes in the condition of women in Western societies. These, in turn, were bound up with the final crisis during the Great War of what John Maynard Keynes described in 1919 as the Victorian mode of capital accumulation.[3] Reinforced by an ideology of scarcity, Europe's pre–World War I liberal order had progressed by demanding of its subjects strict social discipline and puritanical sexual mores. The exercise of public power was relatively limited, political participation was restricted, and the demands on most subjects were rudimentary, namely that they labor hard, consume minimally, and refrain from making excessive demands on government resources. This order was challenged not least of all by the great emancipatory movement among European women. Already evident in the prewar suffrage movements, the trend toward female emancipation had deeper wellsprings in the demographic revolution and the spread of liberal ideas in the latter half of the nineteenth century. It became irreversible once millions of women were mobilized in wartime economies and partook thereafter in the manifestly freer sexual and social customs of 1920s mass culture.

At the same time, Western governments were confronting the complex concerns which policymakers addressed under the rubric of the "population problem" or "demographic crisis."[4] These ran the gamut from fertility decline and what social workers now call "problem families," to male-female job competition and unpredictable consumer behaviors. Practically all of these issues bore on the multiplicity of sometimes incompatible roles women performed in contemporary society—as mothers, wives, citizens, workers, consumers, and clients of social welfare services. The proposed solutions inevitably presented policymakers with a conundrum, which the Swedish sociologist and social reformer Alva Myrdal summed up in an incisive phrase: "One sex [women] a social problem."[5]

In the interwar decades, all Western governments reacted to this double challenge of democratization and demographic crisis. They responded at first by sanctioning female suffrage, and then by developing new public discourses about women, legislating about their place in the labor market, and recodifying family policies. A restructuring of gender relations thus went hand in hand with the recasting of economic and political institutions to secure conservative interests in the face of economic uncertainty and the democratization of public life.[6] In no previous period did state action focus so intensely on institutionalizing what Michel Foucault has called "the government of life."[7] Never before was the sphere of gender relations more explicitly the focus of reformist zeal. However, both the scope and outcome of policies differed from country to country. In the state-interventionist capitalism which emerged everywhere in Western societies during the two decades between the World Wars, decisions were made about whether government policies would take an authoritarian or democratic cast, repress labor or coopt it, allow women greater freedom or impose more restrictions on them. By and large, the outcomes varied according to the character of the class coalitions in power and their stands on broad issues of social welfare and economic redistribution.

In fascist Italy (and, later, arguably, in Nazi Germany as well), government addressed the double issue of population politics and female emancipation by exploiting longstanding traditions of mercantilist thinking. These traditions had acquired renewed currency from the 1870s onward as European elites, reacting to heightened international competition and growing class conflicts, sought to protect domestic markets from foreign goods and build up export capacity. Like their eighteenth-century forebears, who theorized the need for a "multitude of laborious poor," neo-mercantilists worried about optimizing population size to supply cheap labor, satisfy military needs, and keep up home demand.[8] By the turn of the twentieth century, these concerns became complicated by additional worries: declining fertility rates, ethnic minorities whose racial characteristics and nationalist strivings allegedly undermined national-state identity, and, finally, internal fertility differentials that threatened the proliferation of the least fit while the elites dwindled away. By the eve of the Great War, a new biological politics was emerging, permeated with social Darwinist notions of life as a deadly struggle for existence. Eugenicist and social welfare programs were proposed to serve two principal ends of state policy: to buttress declining power in the international field and to secure control over home populations. Insofar as ethnic diversity and female emancipation were identified as obstacles to success, biological politics was easily fused with antifeminism and anti-Semitism.

The integrally authoritarian and antifeminist character of Italian fascism's response to the population question becomes clearer when contrasted to what contemporary observers saw as its virtual opposite, the population policy formulated by Sweden's social democrats. Having won the 1932 elections, the social democrats established the Royal Commission on the Swedish Population Problem in 1935; after consolidating its majority in both houses of parliament in 1936, the party set the agenda for the "mothers and babies session" of the national legislature the following year. Sweden's social democrats were at least as conscious as the Italian fascist elite of the importance of population to maintaining state power, Sweden itself having just 6.2 million inhabitants in 1933. And to overcome the "crisis" caused by declining fertility rates, the Swedish state was just as willing to overrule the distinctions between public power and individual interest and between state rule and family authority that had guided liberal conceptions of politics and gender relations in the nineteenth century.

Beyond that, there was little similarity. The Swedish social democrats, backed by a broad-based liberal coalition that included farmers and feminists as well as labor, tied the goal of population stability and fitness to a broad program of social and economic reform. Swedish population politics presumed a "mild form of nationalism," as was consistent with Sweden's openness to the international economy. But as the chief architects of policy Gunnar and Alva Myrdal explained, the government had to find non-coercive ways "to get a people to abstain from not reproducing itself."[9] Reforms were the main means by which the Swedish government sought to persuade its people to reproduce. With the same spirit of redistributive justice that inspired higher wages and tariff protection for farmers, the government socialized certain important aspects of consumption in order to equalize the burdens of bringing up children. The chief provisions were services in kind, from low-cost housing to free school lunches. The state also affirmed its interest in replacing patriarchal family structures with more rational, efficient, and equitable means of helping women to balance weighty and sometimes incompatible burdens as wives, mothers, workers, and citizens. Social policy thus implied that women still bore the main burden for bearing and rearing children, but the state would help women make the choice to have children less arbitrary and the task of raising them less onerous. Hence, women were encouraged to work as well as to have children, abortion was legalized, and birth control and sex education were widely promoted on the grounds that births be neither "undesired" nor "undesirable."[10]

By contrast, fascist Italy cast the population issue in terms of quantity rather than quality. Citing the overriding national interest, the state declared itself the sole arbiter of population fitness. Hence, on principle, it denied women any role in decisions regarding childbearing. Indeed, on population issues, women were presumed to be antagonists of the state, acting solely on the family's interest without regard for the nation's needs. Seeking to compel women to have more children, the state banned abortion, the sale of contraceptive devices, and sex education. At the same time, the fascist state favored men at the expense of women in the family structure, the labor market, the political system, and society at large. It did so by exploiting the vast machinery of political and social control that had made it possible in the first place to shift the burden of economic growth to the least advantaged members of society. In sum, by foreclosing reforms and by aggravating economic insecurity and social inequalities, fascist policy may actually have increased deterrents to childbearing and heightened fertility differentials between urban and rural areas.

In the context of these broader changes, this book addresses how the Duce's regime sought to define the rights and duties of Italian women in

relation to the national state. My contention is that Mussolini's government sought to nationalize Italian women, much as during the previous
century, in Italy and elsewhere, bourgeois governments sought to nationalize men. At least until the second half of the nineteenth century, most
Europeans remained marginal to the political process, even those in societies with liberal constitutions. Excluded from the formal political system,
they were nonetheless socialized through the civic culture to fulfill their
duty to the state.[11] Through schooling, military training, and public rituals, the political elites, entrepreneurs, and social reformers sought to
impress on their compatriots the civic obligations, collective virtues, and
personal values required for citizenship in nation-states embattled in an
increasingly competitive world system. Up until the early twentieth century, however, "nationalizing the masses" largely referred to *male* subjects: the creation of hardened soldiers, dutiful taxpayers, disciplined
workers, thrifty consumers, and, ultimately, of course, predictable voters.
By and large, women were excluded from those domains of concern, especially in Europe's peripheral areas.

Indeed, the effort to involve men in the duties of bourgeois nationhood
was everywhere premised on institutionalizing the separateness of wom-
en's domain of action. In the high Victorian model of late nineteenth-
century Europe, the destiny of nations was considered to rest on manly
skills and the virtues of the soldier-citizen, whereas women nurtured the
values of privacy. The male purview was the public, and the man's voice
articulated political sentiment; the female was the pillar of the household,
and her voice expressed intimacy. Virility was publicized and glorified;
femaleness was castigated and idealized. As the family was singled out to
uphold distinctions of rank and status, women—middle-class women in
particular—were removed from active life outside the household and entrusted with the constitution and care of the home.[12]

This tidy assignment of gender roles, if never more than a historical
tendency, became harder to sustain everywhere by the turn of the twentieth century. Faced with sharpening rivalries abroad and growing social
conflicts at home, liberal states demanded more from their citizens, becoming less tolerant of diversity and deviance. Sexual conduct hitherto
unremarked upon was now classified as normal or deviant; if suspected to
be the latter, it was treated as a source of social disturbance, hence subject
to surveillance and to political repression. The pressures on the family to
uphold respectability intensified. The female networking which, in Catholic countries especially, underlay suspect social movements and religious
traditions appeared less manageable.[13] The suffrage movement that cropped
up in Italy as well as in more advanced nations after the turn of the cen-

tury clashed with male common wisdom about the natural political order of society. Finally, declining birth rates, which seemed to undercut national strength in an imperialistic world system, became the focus of apprehensive comment.[14]

That women performed an absolutely central, yet strikingly complex role in sustaining state power became manifest in the course of the Great War. In Italy, as in other belligerent nations, women were mobilized to an unprecedented degree. In urban areas they filled the munitions industries and staffed government bureaucracies and commercial offices. In rural communities they worked the fields, tended the animals, and managed relations with a more intrusive and helping national government. Upperclass women volunteered for service in the Red Cross or joined the patriotic-emancipationist National Council of Italian Women. During the war's course, Italian women built up networks, acquired professional self-confidence and work skills, and grew knowledgeable about the operations of state institutions. After the war, it seemed that in compensation for their services and sacrifice, they would acquire citizenship status equal to men, including parity in the labor market, the right to vote, and public recognition of their myriad contributions to Italian society.

As it turned out, the "nationalization" of women in Italy occurred under authoritarian, not liberal, terms. Fascism took as axiomatic that women and men were different by nature. The government politicized this difference to the advantage of males and made it the cornerstone of an especially repressive, comprehensive new system for defining female citizenship, for governing women's sexuality, wage labor, and social participation. Every aspect of being female was thus held up to the measure of the state's interest and interpreted in light of the dictatorship's strategies of state building. In this system, recognition of women's rights as citizens went hand in hand with the denial of female emancipation; reforms on behalf of the welfare of women and children were bound up with brutal restraints.

To argue that the dictatorship "nationalized" Italian women is not to say that the fascist movement itself had any ready-made stance on "the woman question" when Mussolini became prime minister in 1922. Policies on women's issues coalesced much more haltingly than policies on culture or policies on labor. Not until its third year in power did the government make its first reform in the area of women's concerns: the establishment of the national agency ONMI (*Opera nazionale per la maternità ed infanzia*) to oversee maternal and infant welfare. And not until two years later, in 1927, did the Duce launch his campaign to increase Italian birthrates. The first significant effort to establish a range of special political organizations for women occurred only in the course of the early 1930s, as fascism "reached out to the people" to still unrest caused by the Great Depression. The rallying of phalanxes of black-shirted women, the laws against miscegenation, the persecution of non-Aryans, and the publication of draconian statutes to drive women from the workforce were all measures taken after 1935, as the Italian military machine geared up for war and the example of Nazi sexual and racial politics became well known to fascist leaders.

This is not to say that there was no system to fascist rule. Ultimately, the various actions the fascist regime took to consolidate its power determined the overall patterns of how Italian women were treated in interwar society. During the first half of the 1920s, fascism grew from a splinter social movement in search of a constituency into a single-party government. An authoritarian regime with shallow roots in civil society through the late 1920s, it became a mass-based state with totalitarian pretensions in the 1930s. Laissez-faire at the outset, the dictatorship's economic policy became neomercantilist in the late 1920s; later, in the wake of the Depression and the Ethiopian war in 1936, it pursued full-fledged autarchy. This evolution was premised on and confirmed the dictatorship's alliances with big business, the large landed proprietors, the military establishment, the monarchy, and the Catholic Church. In turn, the dictatorship subjected the Fascist party to the central state bureaucracy. Mussolini then used the PNF *(Partito nazionale fascista)* to reach out to social groups—workers, peasants, and small entrepreneurs—whose interests were either ignored or systematically violated in the economic realm, seeking to integrate them into a broad if superficial political consensus.

To secure this conservative alliance, the dictatorship put unremitting pressure on wages and consumption. The Italian economy was especially vulnerable to the vicissitudes of the international economy: Italian agriculture was backward, and the industrial sector imported raw materials and producer goods while exporting textiles. By squeezing wages and curbing purchasing power—steps made possible only by the suppression of the socialist labor movement in the early 1920s—the dictatorship was able to revalue the currency in 1927. A stronger lira, along with other measures, lowered the costs of imported goods, made Italy an attractive place for foreign (especially U.S.) lenders, promoted industrial restructuring, and boosted state-backed electrification and land-reclamation programs. Development proceeded in the 1930s, accentuating the dualistic nature of the Italian economy. At one extreme, it was characterized by inefficient agriculture and a broad strata of small businesses, the precarious status of which was belied by official paeans to antiurban ideologies;

at the other, by a highly concentrated industrial establishment, bailed out by state aid and stimulated by rearmament after 1933. Meanwhile, labor's share of national income continued to shrink. One indicator of fascism's "low-wage" economy was that in 1938 real incomes for industrial workers were still 3 percent short of their 1929 level and 26 percent lower than their postwar peak in 1921. As late as 1938, over one half of the average family's income was spent on food (compared to 25 percent in the United States). All told, Italy was the only industrialized country in which wages fell continuously from the start of the 1920s through the outbreak of World War II. The standard of living, as measured by food budgets, purchase of consumer durables, and availability of public services, put Italy well behind other industrialized nations.[15]

Mussolini's strategies of regime building inevitably had far-reaching repercussions on the situation of Italian women, in particular on the working-class and peasant majority. To pursue its population politics, fascism sought to establish more control over female bodies, especially female reproductive functions, at the same time that it sought to rehabilitate older patriarchal notions of family and paternal authority. To sustain its pressure on wages and consumption, the dictatorship exploited household economic resources to an unusual degree for a country well advanced on the path of industrialization: it demanded that women act as careful consumers, efficient household managers, and astute clients to squeeze services out of an ever-stinting social welfare system, in addition to being part-time, oftentimes concealed wage earners who rounded out family incomes. To curb the use of cheap female labor in the face of high male unemployment, yet maintain Italian industry's reserve force of low-cost workers, the regime devised an elaborate system of protections and prohibitions regulating the exploitation of female labor. Finally, to make women responsive to the increasingly complex claims on them, as well as to exploit women's pent-up desire to identify with and serve the national community, the regime walked the thin line between modernity and emancipation. Thus it devised new kinds of organizations to satisfy the desire for social engagement, while repressing the female solidarities, individualist values, and political freedoms once promoted by feminist associations.

To know the intentions of fascist sexual politics is not necessarily to know its outcome. Mussolini's state was a totalitarian regime to the extent that he, like his nationalist counselors, believed in obliterating the distinction between public and private and between central government and civil society. However, national identity is a complicated construction, and no regime, not even an avowedly totalitarian one, exists in a social vacuum such that it can implement programs as it sees fit. In Italy, fascist policies toward women were at every moment conditioned by the legacy of institutions the dictatorship inherited from the liberal state, as well as by the economic, social, and cultural environments in which its own strategies of rule were designed and put into effect.

On coming to power, the fascists faced a society in which the benefits of growth were unevenly distributed. If the economy was to grow, changes had to be made in the labor market. Work-force participation tended to acquire a more typically modern face, which meant that women would move from agriculture and light industry into heavy manufacture, commercial establishments, and government offices. Economic development also entailed urbanization and the separation of the worksite from the home. Some women would become more isolated in domesticity, but many more would be drawn into the freer sociability of urban life. Finally, economic development was accompanied by the rise of mass consumption, associated with American models of consumer culture. Radio, cinema, department stores, women's tabloids, and fan magazines offered new styles of group and individual expression, new models of living, and new outlets for disposable income. The fascist regime could try to forestall these trends. Or it could attempt to exploit the unevenness of their impact on a society in which there were acute differences in sexual mores and cultural habits between city and countryside and between north and south. But ultimately the regime was unable to stop their advance. How the fascist regime sought to interpret and manipulate the meaning of the habits and pastimes associated with the rise of mass culture is an important theme of this study.

Italian Catholicism was another major force with which fascism had to contend. The once-atheistic Duce's attempts to pacify the Church are well known, as are the sometimes furious rivalries between local Catholic groups and fascism's own party organizations. But in the lives of many Italian women, the renascence of Catholicism in public life signified something more profound than conservative compromise between church and state. From the early 1920s, and particularly after 1926, when ceremonies in honor of the seventh centennial of the death of Saint Francis occasioned a huge mobilization of Church forces, Italian Catholicism mounted a veritable counterreformation. Sensitized to the allure and dangers of modern fashion, the mass media, and urbanized sexual behaviors, Church institutions shaped new female role models and new moral codes. To do so, they drew on zealous professionals, congregations of the faithful, and a far-flung, well-established press. They also benefited from the considerable social-scientific skills of experts who gathered around Father Agostino Gemelli, rector and founder of the Catholic University of Milan. After 1929, following the Lateran Accords between the Vatican and the Italian state, Catholic propagandists pursued their work through the state school system. Always, Church positions on women had the coherence of dogma and tradition. They were indeed formidable ideological fallbacks when fascism's own secular logic supporting the subordination of women failed to convince.

To rule its female subjects, the regime, of course, had also to contend with the attitudes of women themselves. Some female views were clearly articulated by urbane and cultured women in published accounts of their political involvement, intellectual enterprises, and social undertakings. Italy's middle-class feminist associations, though not especially cohesive or widely supported before the fascists' March on Rome in 1922, survived for over a decade after Mussolini came to power. Forced to give up on the issue of suffrage after 1925, one-time feminists redoubled their activities as social volunteers or turned to cultural pursuits, building up a new national women's subculture. Throughout the West, World War I had caused a social earthquake, dividing older and younger women. Fascism only accentuated this division by its incessant denunciations of the "demo-liberal" past, by its exaltation of youth, and by its censure of female emancipation as démodé, spinsterish, and foreign-born. Italian emancipationists, like those elsewhere, had had to come to terms with postwar society's "new" women. More difficult still, Italian feminists then had to come to terms with Mussolini's regime in all of its bluster, manipulativeness, and complication. They had to learn how to relate to its male hierarchies and militaristic posturing; how to respond to its biological determinism and narrowly conceived maternalist ideology; how to link the voluntary work they practiced under the aegis of feminist or Catholic networks to intrusive new state social welfare bureaucracies and the allegedly scientific practices of professional social workers.

The attitudes of the unorganized, insofar as they can be determined, likewise illustrate that Italian women were not passive subjects, much less hapless victims, of the dictatorship. They were protagonists; they made choices. True, these were limited choices. Women were constrained not only by market pressures and by the dead hand of tradition—which even in freer societies weighed so heavily on women's freedoms—but also by the flagrant legal discrimination imposed by the dictatorship. How women negotiated these choices is harder to document than the fact that they made them, for the preponderance of written sources echo male anxieties rather than voice women's concerns.

All of this is to preface one key point: how fascism ruled Italian women is also the story of how Italian women experienced fascist rule. At one level, the ways in which Italian women related to their families, to their society, and to each other were the outcome of the myriad policies which shaped family planning, the labor market, educational opportunities, and public attitudes. At another level, they were the result of women's own actions: in particular, how they responded collectively and individually to enticing new habits of mass consumption, to changing standards of family and child care, and to the novel occasions of sociability offered by the fascist auxiliaries, as well as by Catholic women's groups, informal neighborhood networks, and the several surviving feminist clubs. As we come to see how Italian women shared information among themselves—about sentiments, sexuality, family, and work—their responses to fascist rule appear more complex than the attitudes commonly ascribed to them, namely, passive subordination or delirious enthusiasm. Among Italian women there was disquiet, rebelliousness, dissimulation, and shrewd manipulation, together with a newly arising consciousness of their rights as women and as citizens of Italy.

To speak of all Italian women with a single voice is of course to oversimplify, just as it would be to speak of a coherent fascist program toward women. There were differences of class and custom: in Florence, one might encounter young companionate couples in the Anglo-American style, whereas in rural districts barely outside of the city limits, the sharecropper *capoccia* ruled his female family members in the manner of an absolute patriarch. At newspaper kiosks in Turin, newly urbanized servant girls were buying American-style fan magazines, while their staunchly Catholic *padrone*, accompanied by their elder daughters, were absorbed in devotionals of the Cult of the Sacred Heart of Jesus. Loquacious, cosmopolitan women gathered in the refined salons of Milan and Rome. Speeding over country roads, the Fiat *Ardita* roadsters advertised as the car of these elegant "new women" blasted dust over mute, prematurely aged peasant women.

Italian women had enormously different experiences of maternity as well. The black-swathed rural proletarians; the dazzling writer Margherita Sarfatti, social doyenne of Rome's most powerful intellectual salon; or a chief supervisor of fascist feminism, the Genoese aristocrat Olga Medici Del Vescello, seemed to have had only their sex in common. Yet, they were divided even by that. The emancipated city dweller with two or three children or even none was separated from the peasant woman with a family of six or more not only by class, education, and tradition, but more profoundly by the single fact of life that ostensibly bound them together—the act and consequences of childbearing. Generational differences were at least as important. As one cohort of women reached midlife in the 1930s and another came to adulthood, their mutual incomprehension was accentuated by their different experience of mass culture and by the fascist dictatorship's cult of youth.

Still, these distinctions pale in the face of fascism's gender-based system of exploitation and the misogyny it sanctioned. Class differences among women were as sharp as ever under the fascist regime, and the fascists exploited the diversity of social mores and sexual behaviors to isolate upper- and lower-class women from one another. The regime's social provisions mainly affected women of the lower classes; for abnormalities in the condition of their families were most likely to attract busybody social workers, and they were the most needy and had the fewest alternative sources of aid. But no matter how highly placed the women were, or how personally secure, none were impervious to the antifemale policies of the regime. Keeping in mind class distinctions, along with differences of age and geographical provenance, I have sought here to document how official policies, reinforced by stereotypes circulated through the mass media, standardized public discourse about women. Yet this tendency should not prevent us from underscoring what might seem its opposite: the very effort on the part of the dictatorship to nationalize its female subjects eventually caused the proliferation of alternative identities, in particular those associated with Catholic, youth, and left-wing oppositional cultures.

To capture the diversity of female experience, while suggesting how fascism overtly and subtly shaped new notions of womanhood and citizenship among its female subjects, means breaking with certain conventions common in the study of Mussolini's rule. Take the question, "Did women back the fascist dictatorship?" If support is intended to mean consensus, the question is moot, for under an authoritarian government, people were not free to express their opinions.[16] Fluctuations of outlook were of course registered in police and other official records and by the ebb and flow of membership in mass institutions, as well as by means of the rough registers of opinion compiled by clandestine resistance groups. But unlike the male working class, for whom the fascist trade unions and labor courts acted as sounding boards of sorts, women had no special grievance mechanisms through which to signal their interests or register their complaints. And whereas officials were attentive to working-class opinion, and they claimed to listen to the rural voice, they never solicited information about female opinion. Moreover, in their relations with central authority, fascist women affected a conspicuously stoical attitude, either to win praise for silent self-sacrifice or to stave off interference from male officialdom.

In the absence of evidence, one might conclude that the overriding majority of women respected the regime. Even further, it might be argued that by the mid-1930s, female constituencies were especially susceptible to the quasi-religious cult of Ducismo. Yet what did this signify more concretely? Did such attitudes preclude a distaste for demographic politics, a horror of war, or antipathy to fascism's anti-Semitic legislation? Were these the same women who later refused to end hoarding, volunteer sons for the draft, or outfit their men for wartime labor service in the German camps? Gramsci's notion of "contradictory consciousness" usefully underscores the complexity of belief systems and the difficulty of probing the way subaltern groups come to terms with the dominant order.[17] Honor for the Duce could go hand in hand with the ridicule of official prescriptions on female conduct. Sacrificing gold and silver marriage rings in the huge scrap-metal collections organized to further the Ethiopian war effort went along with the outright flouting of the regime's demographic programs. The family could be more permeable to state interference at the same time that its behavior became more privatized in order to resist the mounting pressures of a bellicose regime.

The second convention called into question regards the modernity of fascism. Propagandists boasted that fascism's treatment of women was both "modern" and "traditional"; indeed, the fusing of the past with the present, the old with the new, was bruited to be among the new era's most magnificent achievements. It is tempting to accept these particular fascist claims, and many have done so. The fact that women went to public rallies, young girls were massed in calisthenics on Fascist Saturday, and rural housewives paraded their hens and rabbits in photographs would seem to document the regime's modernity. Likewise, the fact that the regime recognized that women were important to the state, defining their rights and duties within it, might be interpreted as a signal of progress. Yet the argument that fascism modernized female roles—an argument common to both liberal and Marxist interpretations of the dictatorship's impact on women—rests on three wrong assumptions. First, it presumes that before fascism, women were unorganized. This of course was not the case: large numbers of women were involved in Catholic, socialist, and bourgeois feminist organizations, not to mention informal solidarities of all kinds. Second, it identifies modernity with presence in the public sphere, treating the private sphere as ipso facto backward. Under this misconception, the presence of women publicly organized under fascism is viewed as a progressive measure, regardless of its reactionary ends. Third, it presumes that involvement in political organizations, even fascist ones, is more influential than other modes of socialization in shaping perceptions of social order.[18]

Instead, the transformation of women's political culture must be understood more broadly, in order to consider not just what fascism wanted from its women's groups, but how women related their individual goals, family needs, and social commitments to the dominant political beliefs and institutions. Mussolini's dictatorship redefined the boundaries between public and private, thereby altering the relations between state intervention and individual initiative and between collective engagements and private lives. In response, intellectual women sought new outlets of self-expression, for example, in writing fiction or embellishing their homes. In fascist Italy, we thus find that the changes in women's lives derived as much from the novel ways in which women experienced feelings, needs, and pastimes normally identified with the private sphere as from their more visible presence in the public world of commercial pastimes, sports events, or mass rallies. Viewed in this light, Italian women's lives in the interwar years were akin to those of women elsewhere. The signal difference was that the fascist dictatorship sought as systematically as possible to prevent Italian women from experiencing these occasions as moments of individual, much less collective, emancipation.

Finally, there is the convention of periodization. The history of the dictatorship is now customarily divided into two broad periods: the 1920s, with the seizure of power, and the 1930s, during which the fascist state extended outward to build up a wide base of popular support.[19] This dating follows naturally from the rhythms of the economy and political society and provides a necessary framework for identifying turning points in state policy toward women. Other significant changes, however, proceeded at a slower pace, beginning and ending outside the Duce's reign: such were structural changes in labor markets, long-term shifts in demographic rates, the seeming immobility of national customs and character, and the decades-long transition in models of family life. From the perspective of these changes, fascism itself at times seems almost an irrelevant factor, as if we were telling the story of a repressive system that was ordained well before the Duce seized power and came to an end well after his catastrophic fall. Yet fascism was no mere political postiche to top the balding patches of age-old patriarchy. As a system of rule, it both responded to and determined profound changes in the condition of Italian women and society in the first half of this century.

In the last analysis, the question of how fascism ruled Italian women is more than the history of the half left out. The crisis of the gender order in liberal Italy was part and parcel of the crisis of the liberal system as a whole. For the prescient liberal social theorist Vilfredo Pareto, the readiness of the Italian political elite to capitulate to what he called in 1914 the "virtuist myth" was a sure sign of the frailty of its rule.[20] By caving in to private notions of virtue, having even considered passing laws that treated a "pathological sense of shame" as if it were a universal moral value, Italy's liberal government was repudiating the laissez-faire principles that had hitherto been its strength. The target of court rulings, proposed obscenity laws, and government circulars was sexual behavior, and the major offenders were women. Some twenty-four years later, in a book that would be widely quoted, an ambitious young fascist ideologue named Ferdinando Loffredo contended that the Duce needed a coherent sexual politics to perfect his totalitarian rule.[21] Loffredo cheered the dictatorship for having brought order out of economic chaos, lauded it for having forced Italians to respect the sovereign authority of the nation, and praised it for having inculcated a fervid love of country; but he was perplexed that the dictatorship seemed at an impasse before the intractable individualism of family life and moral conduct. The best evidence was the regime's inability to ban women from the workforce and thrust them back into the household. Indeed, its measures on behalf of economic development and political mobilization fostered an individualist reaction against state interference that accentuated notions of private interest. By Loffredo's account, the gender of that resistance was female.

The order of this book's subsequent chapters is intended to reflect how the dictatorship impinged on women's lives and to single out the numerous ways in which the various moments of their existence, from maternity to political involvement, interacted and changed during the interwar years. Chapter 2 speaks to the liberal legacy, in particular to how the newly emerging fascist movement exploited the liberal state's neglect of issues regarding women and motherhood. Chapter 3 deals with motherhood and maternity, how the dictatorship redefined the meaning of childbearing in a time of rapid demographic change and how, in turn, Italian women, responding to government, professional, and Church pressures, redefined for themselves what it meant to be a mother. Chapter 4 focuses on family life, how it was experienced as families were stripped of old responsibilities and acquired new duties toward the state. Chapter 5 is about growing up; it highlights the new ideals of girlhood at a time in which Catholic, fascist, and commercial models of conduct competed intensely to shape young women's perceptions of themselves and their society. Chapter 6 discusses work in a period in which women's roles in the labor force were being recast both by fascist politics and major shifts in the job market. Chapter 7 looks at women's new public presence, at how commercial culture aroused desires and caused frustration, while fascism and the church contested how women should interpret modern leisure pastimes. Chapter 8 takes up the issue of political culture, how women managed their relations with the fascist state and how female notions of political engagement fit in with fascism's virilist politics. The final chapter, on militarization and resistance, explores the effects of warmongering in the late 1930s and the role women played during the war in delegitimizing the dictatorship.

In large measure, these experiences during the fascist period determined how Italian women entered into national political life after the final defeat of the dictatorship in 1945: how they finally exercised the suffrage; how they experienced the coming of mass consumption during the economic miracle starting in the 1950s; how they related to work and to homelife. In many respects, this legacy of change would endure until the "silent revolution" of the late 1960s. The economic miracle turned rural society topsy turvy and drew huge numbers of women into jobs in industry and commerce. At the same time, new models of mass consumption shook loose the hold of conservative sexual and social values. It was then that Italian women began to acquire the social and individual identities they have today. The 1970s saw the rise of neofeminist movements and significant challenges to the prewar legal system, and Italy's "new" women began to rediscover the long-suppressed heritage of turn-of-the-century feminism. Perhaps only then did women's long voyage through fascism come to an end. But that is another, more joyous, if no less complicated, history.

2   The Legacy of Liberalism

Today, whenever women hear political leaders call their sex
important, they grow suspicious. In the importance of the sex
too often has lain the unimportance of the citizen, the worker,
and the human being.

> Winifred Holtby, *Testament of a Generation* (1934)

A Legacy of Neglect

In peacetime no public leader in liberal Italy ever spoke of Italian women
as "important." Women were mothers and workers. They might be soldiers' widows. They taught in elementary and middle schools and volunteered for charity causes. They were frequently taxpayers as well. But the
state accorded women no special recognition for these services. It didn't
grieve with them for kin mutilated or lost in war. Nor did it welcome
their newborns with birth prizes or little layettes. In that respect liberal
Italy was not much different from other European states before the Great
War.

Nevertheless, early-twentieth-century Italy's treatment of women
presented certain anomalies that the fascist regime was later to exploit.
Liberal Italy was laissez-faire to an unusual degree, a feature much com-
mented on in reference to its impact on Italy's male subjects. In the wake
of the country's patched-together unification in 1859–60, the conservative founders of the new Kingdom of Italy spoke of their commitment to
"making Italians," but they, along with their more liberal successors,
pursued that commitment in a desultory way. Consequently class, regional, and civic-cultural splits were as great as ever at the turn of the
century. These were aggravated not only by the lagging development of
Italy's south and islands, but also by the patent inequality of tax levies, a
stunted educational system, and the near absence of measures of social
reform. Until the liberal prime minister Giovanni Giolitti broadened the
electoral franchise in 1912 to include all literate men over thirty and those
over twenty-one who had completed military service, most male Italians
could not vote. On the eve of World War I, nearly a half-million people,
mostly men, emigrated abroad each year in search of employment. As

industrial growth picked up in the 1890s, especially in the more prosperous northwest of Italy, labor protest grew widespread. The Italian Socialist party, founded in 1892, was Italy's first mass-based political party. As such, its following was unusually broad; not only did it include industrial and craft workers and peasant laborers from the Po Valley, Apulia, and Sicily, but it also included members of the middle class such as teachers, municipal employees, lawyers, doctors, and journalists, whose interests were not represented in the narrowly based political system.[1]

Liberal Italy's neglectful treatment of its subjects was compounded when they were female. By law at least, men enjoyed economic and civil rights denied to women—a circumstance reflected in Italian family law, which since 1865 had been ruled by the Pisanelli Codes. Inspired by Napoleon's *Code Civil*, the Italian legislation affirmed the state's interest in the good order of the family by delegating all authority to male heads of household.[2] Accordingly, wives were obliged to take their husbands' names and to reside with them. Without their spouses' consent or "marital authorization," women were barred from most commercial and legal acts and from contracting debts or writing checks. The law also prevented them from acting as children's guardians and even excluded them from the "family councils" that until 1942 were legally empowered at the father's death or incapacitation to dispose of family patrimonies, inheritances, and dowry settlements. In the interest of keeping the family property intact, the state disinherited the offspring of adulterous and incestuous unions, made adultery a crime for women only, and prohibited all forms of paternity suits. At the same time, liberal Italy recognized only civil-law marriages. The offspring of the thousands of Italians who contracted their unions with religious rites only or without any official imprimatur were not legitimate in the eyes of officialdom.

Liberal Italy's hands-off policy was perhaps nowhere so remarkable as in the realm of social policy. The economy industrialized at least a generation later and far more unevenly than in northern European states. When Italy's industrial revolution started in the last decade of the nineteenth century, the accompanying social problems already familiar in northern Europe accumulated rapidly, including the exploitation of child and female labor, which because of the importance in Italy of textile manufacture, played a greater role in the industrial labor market than it did abroad. Elsewhere governments became more paternalistic, passing factory laws and pension reforms in the name of women's and children's welfare, albeit with the ulterior purpose of safeguarding male wages and promoting racial fitness. In Italy, at the turn of the century, women accounted for half of the total industrial labor force. However, because of

Italy's relative backwardness, Italian industrialists insisted they needed cheap female and minor labor to compete abroad. Hence no factory laws spoke to the issue of women's work until the Carcano law was passed in 1902. This set a twelve-hour maximum workday for women and minors and barred working mothers from returning to their jobs for a month after childbirth. Like other social legislation passed after 1900, it was riddled with exceptions and its provisions were hard to police.[3]

Italian liberalism's insouciant treatment of motherhood, family, and female labor was all the more striking in view of the paternalistic values of Italy's pervasive and well-entrenched Catholic culture. The Papacy, offended by the loss of its dominions, had refused to recognize the new kingdom. In 1864 Pius IX decreed that Italian Catholics should be "neither elected, nor electors," and up until 1904 Catholics did not participate officially in the political system. Their reentry then was to combat the advance of socialism. In the meantime, notwithstanding strong secularizing trends, the Catholic Church sank deep roots into important areas of Italy's northeast, while cultivating its age-old influence in many rural zones. In a country in which the benefits of industrialism were so unevenly distributed, the Church drew strength from denouncing modernity and the market while advocating social reconciliation; the reforming tenets of Leo XIII's *De Rerum Novarum* (1891) resonated in the company paternalism of leading Catholic entrepreneurs and the philosophy of good works of Christian democrats. Moreover, the Church had a special message for women. Although intolerant of individualist philosophies generally, and especially hostile to female emancipation, it applauded motherhood—its mysteries, duties, and obligations—in a papal encyclical (*Arcanum*, 1880), in pastoral letters, and in Sunday sermons. The Church thus became the chief champion of so-called family values against the corrosive effects of modern existence.

Peculiarities of Italian Feminism

In the light of this legacy, it is easy to see how the Italian women's movement—and perhaps women generally—developed an ambivalent, if not antagonistic relationship to liberal ideology and institutions. As one might expect of a relatively backward country, in which economic growth, occasions of civic participation, and widespread female literacy were lacking, the women's emancipation movement developed tardily.[4] When it did indeed finally grow during the 1890s, it was linked to the major protest movement of the time, that spearheaded by Italian labor organizations. The first to speak on behalf of emancipation were thus working-class and lower-middle-class women, mainly factory workers, clerks, and teachers

of northern Italian towns. Most were inspired by the radically
views of Anna Maria Mozzoni, the founder in 1881 of the *Le
trice degli interessi femminili.*[5] In the prosperity of the Giolittian ... (1901–
14), emancipationist ideas spread, fed by the great surge of feminism in
more advanced nations. It was characteristic of the Italian movement that,
being weak and isolated at home, it cultivated its ties with women's associations abroad. These links to more visible, often more militant movements, like that of the British suffragists, inevitably exposed Italian feminists to the criticism that feminism was alien to Italian soil. When these
ties were weakened in the face of rising nationalism, the cause of women's
rights suffered.

As emancipationist strivings grew after the turn of the century, it also
became apparent that there were at least three currents of feminism responsive to them. The first derived from the growing groups of working
class and salaried women committed to socialism. Catholic women also
organized, to separate themselves from secular women's groups after 1908.
The points of difference were divorce, the suffrage, and the Church's influence over schooling. Finally, there was the lay-bourgeois movement:
the National Council of Italian Women, or CNDI, founded in 1903, together with the Milan-based *Unione femminile nazionale,* the *Associazione per la donna* of Rome, and several other smaller groups, comprised
what critics in the fascist era derided as the "old" feminism. Present-day
feminists speak of the movement as "historic feminism," making ironic
reference to its affinities with the "historic right," Italy's honest, if stod-
gily conservative, founding fathers.[6] The three movements had a common
goal, civil rights for women, however much they differed in their purposes, tactics, and attachments to male-dominated parties and associations. This sense of commonality lasted at least until the beginning of
World War I, when the intensification of class conflict and nationalist zeal,
by accentuating the differences among them, cast doubt on any shared
unity of interests.

By 1910 the socialist women's movement had acquired the character
that would prove to be both its strength and its eventual undoing. From
the start the solution to the "woman question" was bound up with the
solution to the "social question." Female emancipation seemed inconceiv-
able unless there was a thoroughgoing political and economic democratization of the nation; according to Second-International Marxist canons
this was to be led by the factory proletariat. In Italy, under pressure from
their female constituents, the socialists were relatively supportive of
women's economic issues. Unemployment was such an intractable problem that it was politically worthwhile to support unionizing women on

equal terms with men. Socialist party support for the vote was more guarded. Anna Kuliscioff, the Russian émigré who became a major figure in the Italian Socialist party (PSI), sought to place the suffrage at the very center of party policy. But her comrade, the party's leader Filippo Turati, equivocated. Uncertain whether such a radical proposition would undo working-class men's chances of getting the vote, he also saw it as favoring Catholic interests in the short run. Ultimately, the emancipationist movement within the party was beset by conflicts between civil rights and labor rights. As the PSI became more militant after 1910, renouncing reformist positions for a head-on confrontation with Italian capitalism, it forced its local organizations to renounce cooperation with bourgeois groups. Socialist women, some of whom occupied key positions in the labor movement, persisted in their fight for women's rights; since the party was still little bureaucratized, and most local activity still occurred in tight-knit community institutions, women maintained a stronger voice than might be expected given the masculinism of socialist political culture. Still, the goal of female emancipation was inevitably subject to the vicissitudes of the labor movement in its entirety. When socialism came under attack from the fascists after the war, demands made in the name of sexual equality deferred to demands made on behalf of the survival of the worker community. When the whole of the opposition was outlawed in 1925–26, the voices of socialist women too were silenced.[7]

The Catholic movement was, by contrast, a relatively late starter, but with the support of the Church, it quickly put down powerful roots. The first national meeting of Italian women, convoked by the National Council of Italian Women in Rome on April 24–30, 1908, was an occasion for Catholic women to be made more aware of their differences with respect to liberal, not to mention socialist, women. It also made the Church hierarchy appreciate the value of a countermovement. At first Pius X responded begrudgingly to Princess Maria Cristina Giustiniani Bandini's request to head up this cause, citing an old Venetian saying, "La donna . . . che la piasa, che la tasa, che la staga in casa" ("Woman . . . that she be sweet, silent, and stay at home"); soon after, however, he gave it his blessing. The Union of Catholic Women in Italy was not a fully unified movement, being divided between a Milan-based Christian-social wing associated with the modernists Giuseppe Toniolo and Romolo Murri and conservative groups of Roman charity women.[8] However, the Catholic hierarchy had now definitively reversed the nineteenth-century Papacy's position that women should not exist outside family life. In 1909 on the occasion of the beatification of Joan of Arc, Pius X urged women to undertake "duties outside the family circle that regard others." What is more, the Church, together with conservative statesmen such as Sidney Sonnino, supported women's suffrage for unabashedly conservative reasons, namely, to offset the socialist advance and as "a means of struggle to preserve and defend the family's integrity."[9] These positions, articulated with ever more emphasis and clarity by Benedetto XV in the wake of World War I, made the Catholic movement a novel blend of modernity and traditionalism. The combination would allow Italian Catholicism to be at once a powerful supporter of the fascist system and a vigorous competitor for female allegiances.

From the turn of the century to the mid-1920s, the lay-emancipationist current dominated Italian feminism, not least of all because its projects were similar in many ways to those of the emancipationist movements hegemonic elsewhere. By 1900 Italian middle-class feminists were becoming more moderate, forsaking the radical egalitarianism of Anna Maria Mozzoni for the principles of what sometimes has been called "maternalist" or "social" feminism. In Italy emancipated women spoke of a "practical feminism"; this philosophy advanced their claims to be recognized as citizens not in the name of some abstract natural right, or because they were equal to men in the conventional sense, but because, as mothers, they were indispensable to the social order. Like their contemporaries in Great Britain and the United States, whose faith in liberal government was shaken as they witnessed its impotency in the face of social catastrophes, Italian feminists renounced laissez-faire tenets to seek governmental recognition for women's special mission in public life.[10] But unlike their Anglo-American sisters, Italian middle-class feminists had little invested in social-contract notions of personal and social relations, the principles of formal equality, or the distinction between private and public that lay behind liberal notions of citizenship, the family, and social institutions. Unlike the Anglo-Americans who emphasized equal rights, the bourgeois feminists of Italy did not trust that economic progress and universal suffrage would lead to their emancipation.

In a backward society it often happens that the subaltern, in their effort to obtain social justice, are thrust into the position of being state builders. In keeping with a traditional vision of maternal self-sacrifice, practical feminists interpreted citizenship as requiring a hard course of duty. They promised to be especially fit and dutiful subjects: in their capacities as modern household managers, well-informed mothers, and capable and service-oriented professionals, they would act as agents of progress, voices of moderation, and fonts of moral strength. In this commitment to regenerating Italian society, they were akin to reformist socialists. However, Italian working-class politics, unlike the women's movement, was bound up with an eschatological vision of labor's ultimate victory, and it fostered a powerful sense of rights and claims. Moreover, socialist radicalism was buttressed by the tightly knit oppositional subculture around the people's houses *(case del popolo)*, cooperatives, and municipal chambers of labor. By contrast, practical feminism, to quote its foremost historian, Annarita Buttofuoco, "propelled women to integrate themselves into the state, educating them—or trying to educate them—to 'citizenship.' "[11] This powerful desire to obtain recognition of a special female mission in modern public life would cause many middle-class women seeking emancipation to rally to nationalist causes during the war. Not long after, they would prove susceptible to Mussolini's resounding claims that female citizenship in a reconstructed national society was soon to be achieved.

That the never large, little unified, and rarely militant movement described so far should have incited widespread antagonism would be inexplicable unless we reflected further on liberal society's lack of cohesiveness. Nowhere, to be sure, was feminism welcomed by male public opinion. But in Italy public opinion was especially uncomprehending of modern female roles. This was partly because emancipated behaviors were highly conspicuous in this half-industrial, half-rural society—one that boasted the modern industrial center of Turin and a truly European city, Milan, but still had over half its population living off agricultural undertakings. The liberal elites also abetted antifeminist attitudes, most prominently by denying women the vote. Prime Minister Giovanni Giolitti expediently asserted that female suffrage constituted a "leap in the dark," implying that Italian women, if enfranchised, would fall under the influence of conniving priests or socialist firebrands. The real danger was that a vastly expanded electorate, overgrown with newly enfranchised female as well as male voters, would spring the narrowly opened door of the liberal political system, wrecking the carefully arranged coalitions of "transformative politics." At the same time, liberal governments little appreciated the social services rendered by women who, guided by the belief that their "maternal sensibility" was indispensable to "temper and complete the political order," sought to cure social ills and calm working-class unrest through philanthropic undertakings. Failing to act in this domain themselves, liberal elites missed the opportunity not only to recognize women's volunteer work but also to subject working-class mutualism as well as centuries-old corporative and religiously inspired charity to central state authority. These were opportunities that the fascists would not fail to seize and exploit: to excoriate liberal "neglect," outlaw oppositional associations, and enlist support from thousands of female volunteers.

Italian feminism's unsettling impact on public opinion would still not be fully comprehensible without some further mention of the discontents of Italy's male citizenry. The discordant voices of underemployed degree holders, liberal professionals, and opinion makers of various ilk, raised in the name of building a "New Italy," reverberated within the ranks of revolutionary syndicalism, around the recently constituted Nationalist Association, as well as among the followers of the Florentine journals *La voce* and *Lacerba*, the poet Filippo Tommaso Marinetti's futurist movement, and the decadentist writer Gabriele D'Annunzio. A whole study might be devoted to the social-psychological origins of their virilist posturing and its myriad literary manifestations—whether in D'Annunzio's grand erotic sensibility, Giovanni Papini's antifeminist metaphor, or Marinetti's notorious "scorn for women." In Italy, even before the war, old-fashioned "Latin sexism" had degenerated into an exasperated masculinism.[12] This was compounded by men's frustration at being closed out of the narrowly based liberal "gerontocracy" and by embarrassment at Italy's modest international stature at a time when male honor was staked on the outcome of imperialist exploits. Fears about demographic exhaustion added another worry, although a groundless one; Italy's birth rate of thirty per thousand at the turn of the century was the highest in Europe after Spain and Romania. However, several factors peculiar to Italy exaggerated anxiety about sexual disorder and racial decline. In addition to the disturbing influence exercised by French worries about demographic catastrophe, these included the draining off of Italian men as more and more were forced to emigrate, the importance attributed to sheer numbers of people in a capital-scarce environment, the startling diversity of sexual behaviors and social mores in an unevenly developing society, and, finally, the pervasive influence of positivist scientific hypotheses and Catholic doctrine in matters regarding fertility. "Maternity is the patriotism of women," as the nationalist Scipio Sighele aphorized.[13] Doubts that society could control population decline were fed by fears that Italian women, their individualistic propensities encouraged by feminism, would withhold vital reproductive services from the nation.

By the eve of the war, what we might call a "neopaternalistic politics" had begun to emerge in liberal Italy. From around 1910 moral zealots launched campaigns against the degeneration of family life, joining forces with Catholic leagues to blame declining birth rates on urbanization, women's emancipation, and radically inspired neo-Malthusian practices. Liberal elites, although ever reluctant to intervene in social policy, were inclined to abandon laissez-faire and anticlerical principles to legislate against obscenity and blasphemy, prostitution, and juvenile delinquency. With Marinetti's futurist manifesto of 1909, modernist culture also rallied against individualist conceptions of female emancipation: "We seek to glorify war—the only hygiene of the world—militarism, patriotism, the destructive act of the anarchist, the mighty ideas that kill—and scorn for women. We want to tear down museums and libraries, to fight against moralism, feminism, and all the opportunistic and utilitarian forms of cowardice."[14] To be sure, the interests behind this neopaternalistic politics were so varied, the ideas themselves so diverse, and the means to implement them so wholly lacking that it hardly added up to a new program for ruling women. It suggested, however, that there was a legacy of outlooks and institutions ready to be exploited, as would happen in the second half of the twenties, when the dictatorship tapped widespread antiemancipationist sentiment to legitimate its antifemale politics.

The Disorienting Impact of War

Ultimately, it was the Great War that made women "important." The Italian state needed their labor, their volunteer work, and their courage to hold up the home front. For the first time, then, Italian political elites were outspoken about the need to mobilize women in the national interest, even to the point of condemning the "ridicule, reproof, scandal-mongering, (and) disdain" to which women, especially middle-class women who had started to work, were subjected. By 1916–17, the government had begun to call attention to women's sacrifices. It even coined medals to reward their heroism. At the same time, women were empowered as never before. The Lombard nationalist writer Paola Baronchelli Grosson, better known by her pen name, Donna Paola, perhaps exaggerated when she argued that middle-class women "had obtained more from three years of war than from several decades of feminism; the opportunity finally to advance in life, to take in the air of freedom, to taste the heady nectar of command, of higher rank, and in no few cases, economic independence." Because of war orders, the working woman too "found herself sought out and fought over for positions in offices, banks, and state bureaus." Now that women were out in public life, Donna Paola was sure they would never go home again. Working-class women would never put up with the "heavy [economic] sacrifice" caused by going back to their old jobs or, worse, of being unemployed. Middle-class women would no longer abide lives filled only with "foreign fiction, embroidery, going on about fashion, idle gossip, the *via crucis* past store windows and through cinema halls." They wouldn't again put up with being considered "last place both in the family and society" and "incompetent as regards everything outside the domestic walls." Never again would they tolerate the worst of all humiliations, namely, each day "holding out their hands, subject to the good or bad humor of father or husband, to satisfy a desire or purchase some necessity."[15]

Though the war prompted government to conceive of women as a special category and heightened women's own consciousness of their separate interests, it divided women socially and politically. Several thousand middle-class volunteers staffed Red Cross stations, military hospitals, postal relays, and soldiers' canteens. In such capacities, upper-middle class and aristocratic women were exposed to the operations of government and grew confident that at the war's end the nation would respond favorably to their claims for representation and parity. Many of the groups they had founded to help veterans, widows, and orphans and to fight against luxury expenditure, along with the ethos of "battles" and "sacrifice," would be resurrected under the dictatorship. Moreover, many well-known feminists, including Paola Baronchelli Grosson, Teresa Labriola, and Margherita Sarfatti, split from the feminist mainstream during the war to push the interventionist cause. At the same time, tens of thousands of working-class women were thrust into factory jobs; sympathetic to the antimilitarism and maximalist programs of socialism, they harkened back to the radical egalitarianism of late-nineteenth-century feminism, with its demands for the vote, political representation, and social leveling. Desperate to fulfill their traditional obligations as mothers, wives, and family members, they joined their sense of entitlement to a minimum subsistence to the demand for a just social order.[16] Frightened by working-class radicalism, middle-class feminists turned their backs on the half-million or so women soon to organize themselves in socialist leagues and cooperatives. Instead, they intensified their volunteer service in the cause of the nation, busying themselves on behalf of the war-wounded, displaced persons, widows, and orphans. The sad paradox was that just when women's associations seemed unanimous in demanding equal rights—including the vote, work opportunities, and the revamping of family law—their forces were on the point of being irreversibly divided.

Indeed, coming out of the war, the feminist movement grew apace, rallied by social protest and the demand for the vote, the concession of which seemed imminent in 1919. The groups that promoted "female social action"—which was perhaps the only common denominator of the movement—were as diverse as ever. They included several national lay groups, the largest being the CNDI, the leading Catholic women's organization, now called the *Unione donne cattoliche italiane* under the leadership of Maddalena Patrizi, as well as about 115 socialist women's groups, loosely organized around the weekly journal *Difesa delle lavoratrici* and intermittent national congresses. In 1921 Silvia Bemporad's annual *Al-*

manacco della donna italiana also began listing the newly formed nationalist and fascist women's groups. How many women this multiform activism embraced is hard to estimate: perhaps 25,000 were involved in the old lay groups, considering that the two or three largest, including the CNDI, had several thousand members each, and at least twenty-nine associations had some national following. Tens of thousands of other women belonged to the socialist and Catholic groups. At the time, just a few hundred belonged to the fascist organizations.

The movement's mainstay in the struggle for equal rights continued to be the middle-class lay groups, namely, the CNDI; the *Unione femminile*; the National Women's Pro-suffrage Federation; and the newest edition, FILDIS, or *Federazione italiana fra laureate e diplomate degli istituti superiori*. This last was founded in 1920 as an offshoot of the London-based International Federation of University Women to bring together "cultivated women" to defend their common interests and build international sympathy for the League of Nations. The crisis of these groups between 1920 and 1925 showed how difficult it was for the bourgeois women's movement to sustain its autonomy, much less maintain political momentum under the conditions of near civil war which prevailed as the fascists fought their way to power. Their crisis also demonstrated the susceptibility of middle-class "practical feminists" to the appeals of "a government of national unity," one that promised at once to recognize women, promote social solidarity, and undertake national reconstruction.

On its own, the Italian right's aggressive nationalism was not attractive to most feminists because of its virulent militarism, elitism, and antifeminism. Yet as early as Italy's war to win Libya from the Ottoman Empire in 1912, many well-known supporters of female rights, including Paola Baronchelli Grosson, had begun to translate the nationalist program into terms emancipationists might find congenial. By 1917 Italy's best-known feminist intellectual, Teresa Labriola, had endorsed the Nationalist Association's program. In some respects, her political shift from left to right was similar to that of Mussolini and other members of the Front Generation. Marxist socialism had come as second nature to Labriola, whose father, Antonio, was the distinguished Neapolitan social activist and political philosopher. However, Teresa's volatile café-society intellect latched on to little of Marxist philosophy. Like Mussolini, she was an elitist. She was also imbued with the voluntaristic notions common to an entire intellectual cohort. Like them, Labriola admired the idealist philosophy of Giovanni Gentile, with whom she studied, and preferred the iconoclasm of Georges Sorel and Friedrich Nietzsche to the inexorable laws of Second

International Marxism. Fresh vanguards, abandoning the bumbling reformism of the Italian socialist movement, would build a new Italy; they would repudiate liberal "agnosticism" to infuse the Italian people with a new "ethicity." However, Labriola's elite was female: as early as 1908, she referred to "the capacity of sacrifice peculiar to woman" as a quality that made them uniquely able to reconcile "the contrast between the needs of the individual and those of the species."[17] Her position that Italian women would champion a new order based on "reform of the conception of race, nation, and state" was captivating if paranoid. That it resonated with familiar feminist motifs and was well-tolerated in feminist circles should not be surprising.

Such rhetoric would have acquired little credibility as a program without the more general crisis of the liberal state. After 1919 feminists were more and more taxed to keep faith with the liberal political system. In June 1920 the cabinet of the proemancipationist Francesco Saverio Nitti fell before it was able to bring the suffrage issue before the Senate. As a result, the overwhelmingly positive vote of the Chamber was nullified, and the measure was postponed for consideration pending the election of a new legislature. As it turned out, the next legislative elections produced no solid majority. However, the liberals' electoral alliance with Mussolini and other right-wing groups brought fourteen Fascist party deputies into parliament, giving it a powerful leg up in national political life. The successive cabinets formed by the liberals were more precarious and ineffectual than ever. Down to the autumn of 1922, they were unable to muster support for electoral reform, much less pass measures to aid the huge numbers of war orphans and widows, assure respect for the war dead, or defend public order against the alleged "strikomania" of Italian workers.

With no existing party to their liking, some advocates of women's rights pressed for a party of a new kind—"social not socialist, national, and not nationalist," to recall the words of the Roman Paola Benedettini Alferazzi, who in 1918 had founded the *Giornale della donna* to rally support for the suffrage campaign. It was possible to see such a movement in fascism, if not in the new ministerial cabinet which Mussolini claimed he would form in the name of national reconstruction. After all, as the politically seasoned socialist feminist Laura Cabrini Casartelli observed, the women's movement had never achieved "much self-awareness . . . always living through other's experiences." This left it unprepared to contend with "the great and overwhelming movement that was the fascist revolution." Indeed, as Cabrini Casartelli, who despised fascism, remarked, it was middle-class emancipationists' very "love for their country, broad humanitarianism, and strong social sentiment" that led them to sympathize with fascism's "program to valorize the victory, exalt the national war, and oppose men and methods" appearing to damage the nation and public life. If still wary of fascism's "exaltation of force" they were at the same time attracted by its "strong spirit of sacrifice."[18]

Fascist Women of the First Hour

To argue that feminists were favorably disposed to Mussolini's promise to build a government of national reconstruction is not to imply that initially even bourgeois women were especially or broadly sympathetic to fascism as a political movement. Quite the contrary—only nine women have been identified as veterans of the movement's first gathering at Piazza San Sepolcro in Milan on March 23, 1919, and female followers did not exceed several hundred until close to fascism's March on Rome on October 28, 1922. Nor did the so-called fascists of the first hour make any special gestures to reach out to a female constituency, except such as were in keeping with the movement's opportunistic tergiversations. True, the *fasci*'s June 1919 program called for full voting rights for all women over twenty-one. It also called for their equal right to hold office. But since the women's suffrage bill was before parliament at the time and was expected to pass in both the Senate and the Chamber, this measure did not notably distinguish the fascist movement from other political groups, except perhaps to underscore that, from birth, it displayed unusual mimetic talents. Indeed, other conservative parties would soon take more significant steps. By 1922 both the Nationalist Association and the liberals, who under Giolitti's leadership had long opposed women's suffrage, espoused the vote for women. They also sponsored their own women's groups, fearing that the legalization of women's suffrage would exclusively benefit the Catholics and the left. By contrast, the foundation of the first women's *fascio* at Monza on March 12, 1920, was strictly a female initiative, largely ignored by the movement leadership.[19]

Nonetheless, fascism of the first hour had certain potentially attractive features. Or so they might be regarded by middle- and upper-class women who styled themselves as being eminently modern and emancipated, yet who were hostile to the feminism of the bourgeois women's movement because of its liberal sympathies, its high-mindedness, and its unlikely chances of success. One of these features was Dannunzianism: The poet Gabriele D'Annunzio, *commandante* of the March on Ronchi to claim Fiume for Italy on September 12, 1919, was master of the beau geste, as renowned for his romantic maneuvers as for his military heroics. Unlike the brusque-mannered Mussolini, D'Annunzio's erotic sensibility was on display in his art and personal life. In politics, too, he catered to women:

the Charter of the Carnaro, with which he defiantly ruled Fiume until forcibly routed after the treaty between Italy and Yugoslavia at Rapallo in November 1920, called for full civil and political rights for all citizens in their twenty-first year "without distinction of sex." His most important legacy, however, was the mobilization of female philanthropy on behalf of the rebellious troops of the Fiume adventure. The National Association of the Sisters of the Legionnaires of Fiume and Dalmatia, founded on June 13, 1920, was one of several support groups for nationalist causes promoted by women after the war. The sight of the well-born, elegantly blue-shirted *Fiumane*, parading through central Milan with hundreds of little children "rescued" from the beleaguered Regency of Carnaro, rallied public opinion to D'Annunzio's "holy cause" and further undermined support for the liberal state's endeavors to resist right-wing disorders.

Another attractive feature of early fascism was Italian futurism, which, with its mix of activism and antiauthoritarianism, was compatible with the emancipationist yearnings of young women. Unquestionably, futurist ideology, with its violent attacks on the torpid provincialism of the Giolittian era, was the product of a militaristic and profoundly antifeminist mentality. Yet in Marinetti's ambition to forge a new male citizenry, he endorsed a gender revolution. The futurist poet's hero Mafarka was a man who could do without women, and his notion of "scorn for women," first used in the 1910 pamphlet *L'amore e parlamentarismo*, was invented to castigate the despicably effeminate qualities preventing virile modernity from triumphing in Italian public life. He also denounced "horrible and heavy Love which obstructs mankind's march forward." Marinetti's paeans to a "futurism of the species"—according to which "Woman belongs to no man, but to the future and development of the race," declared females freed from the domination of any single male, only to subordinate them to the interests of the race. Still, futurism's iconoclastic views on free love and on marriage—which Marinetti despised as an "occasion for legal prostitution tricked up with moralism"—were refreshing for young intellectuals, women and men alike.[20] Following the war, futurism offered women a place in the forefront of the movement. Or at least it allowed a few especially urbane and articulate young women to be as vocal as their male comrades in denouncing the senescent patriarchalism of the bourgeois ruling class.

That early fascism was construed as a modern and liberatory force for some women, if not for all, was manifest in the various types of women who joined the movement before 1925. Thereafter, as the dictatorship firmed up, enrollment became both a safe and an opportune step for more conventional figures. To a degree, all the early joiners might be regarded as eccentric: they had some prior political experience; they joined a movement of which they constituted a tiny minority; they received little or no prompting from men and earned no approval from other women. Some were old comrades-in-arms of the socialist Mussolini, including Margherita Sarfatti, Regina Terruzzi, and Giselda Brebbia. Others were recruits from the ranks of D'Annunzio's *Fiumane*, such as Elisa Majer Rizzioli, the founder of the women's *fasci*; Angiola Moretti, the secretary of the fascist women's groups from 1927 to 1930; and Rachele Ferrari del Latte, widow of the *sansepolcrista* Guido del Latte and a longtime functionary. A small number were camp followers of the first men's squads, like the fiery Fanny Dini of Florence. Perhaps all that these women shared was a disgust at the alleged lack of values of liberal society, an abhorrence for reformist socialism, a belief in an orderly and strong state, and a good measure of personal willfulness, without which they could not have defended their often idiosyncratic life-styles and what at first seemed a bold political choice. At the same time, they were remarkably diverse figures, in personality and in social provenance, as well as in prior political experience. In that sense, they resembled the fascist movement of the first hour, which, as the perceptive political observer Mario Missiroli once noted, took in the renegades of all the heretical movements of the time.

This diversity well served the fascist movement in both the short and long term. The Mussolinian old-guard, Margherita Sarfatti and Regina Terruzzi in particular, like the Duce himself, brought to the organization of the dictatorship important skills acquired in the socialist movement. The dazzling Sarfatti, born in 1883 to wealth, culture, and power, was the scion of a well-connected, conservative Jewish family of Venice. While still a socialist, she honed her skills as a political hostess in Anna Kuliscioff's salon, and she practiced her acerbic journalistic style in the columns of *Avanti!* and *La difesa delle lavoratrici*. These talents would both be put to good use first in Milan and then in Rome to manage relations among intellectuals, artists, and functionaries of the regime. The Milanese Terruzzi, born in 1862, was the most senior of the fascist women. A middle-school teacher of very modest social origins, she broke with the socialists to support the Italian intervention in World War I. Always an independent-minded character, she withdrew from active duty in the fascist movement in 1923, after having bravely condemned the violence of fascist gangs by raising funds for the orphans of Turinese communists slaughtered during the December 1922 "Bloody Christmas."[21] Not until a decade later, in 1933, would the Duce tap her rare and formidable skills as a teacher and organizer of working-class women to found the *massaie rurali* (rural housewives), much as he drew on male veterans of the left such as the former republican Armando Casalini, the ex–revolutionary syndicalist Edmondo Rossoni, and the onetime socialist Ottavio Dinale to build up the fascist unions and *dopolavoro* recreational clubs. With her rabble-rousing background, lower-class origins, and unpolitic dealings with fascist men, Terruzzi was obviously little suited to organize bourgeois women.

By contrast, Elisa Majer Rizzioli, the real founder of the women's *fasci*, was outstandingly suited to the task. Born in Venice in 1880, thus three years older than her compatriot Margherita Sarfatti, she was on her mother's side from the noble Marin family and on her father's from *La Serenissima's* wealthy assimilated Jewish bourgeoisie. With neither Sarfatti's intellectual flair nor her notorious physical seductiveness, Majer Rizzioli was nonetheless a capable journalist and editor, as well as an organizer who inspired strong personal loyalty from like-minded friends. At least two of them, Elisa Savoia, founder of the first *fascio* at Monza, and Olga Mezzomo Zannini, founder in 1924 of the National Association for the Families of Fallen Fascists, shared her talents as promoters of female patriotic formations. Married at twenty-four to a prosperous notary public, Niccolo Rizzioli, and childless, Majer Rizzioli had early been swept up by the patriotic fervor of the lands close to the territories "unredeemed" in the Risorgimento. A volunteer aboard Red Cross hospital ships during the Libyan war, she had also been much decorated for her three-year service on hospital trains in the Great War and had joined D'Annunzio's March on Ronchi in 1919. Her association with fascism dated from early 1920, when, in the wake of a personal meeting with Mussolini—whom she had approached at the *Popolo d'Italia's* offices for support on behalf of her latest initiative, the Association against Exaggerated Luxury among Women—she apparently overcame her prejudices against outright political action, about which she claimed to be both frightened and utterly ignorant.[22] Self-sacrificing and moralistic, and with a large stock of personal funds that she generously committed to the movement, she was ideally suited to dedicating herself to a thankless and ultimately futile task: to reconcile differences between profascist women in Rome and Milan and to placate liberal feminist hostility, while seeking official support from the Duce and the Fascist party.

The most controversial women of the movement were young activists engaged in street warfare against the left with the men-in-arms of the fascist squads. The most conspicuous was the Nationalist Ines Donati, a feisty little figure, whom her former comrade-in-arms Emilia Carreras remembered clad in the blue shirt, grey skirt, and felt cap of the Nationalists' girls group, the Explorers. Celebrated in the fascist and nationalist press for her *squadrista*-type escapades—the most notorious of which involved slapping the socialist deputy Della Seta at the Café Aragno in central Rome—she was also a gifted self-publicist: photographs of Donati working as a "civic volunteer" sweeping Roman streets during the May 1920 garbage strike are still among the most powerful visual representations of the "Bolshevik insanity" cured by the fascist takeover. Donati's original home was San Severino in the highlands of the Marches, "one of the small subversive centers of red madness" where her zealous nationalism earned her the nickname "la patriottica." At eighteen, she ran away to Rome, where she enrolled in the Nationalists' Explorers groups; sometime before participating in the March on Rome she joined the fascists. Thereafter she lived hand-to-mouth, her health failing, until November 3, 1924, when she died of tuberculosis, her last words allegedly being "I wanted to be too virile and forgot that I was but a frail woman." Understandably, fascist officialdom displayed little sympathy for this local Saint Joan's quasi-religious ecstasy, much less her ambiguous sexuality. Moralistic older women such as Majer Rizzioli feared that this unpredictable, if not uninhibited, behavior on the part of young women sullied the movement's good reputation. Not until the mid-1930s, as fascism reached out to female youth, was Donati's fanatical activism invoked with approbation: on March 23, 1933, her corpse was exhumed and reburied with pomp and circumstance in the chapel of the fascist fallen at Verano.[23]

Among these women, only Majer Rizzioli actually served in the *fasci femminili*, which were founded alongside, but with little support from, the men's *fasci di combattimento*. From the outset, the women's clubs led a precarious existence. The founders, including Amalia Besso, the well-known Triestine painter domiciled in Rome; Lucia Pagano, a secondary-school teacher; Countess Carmelita Casagrandi, a surgeon from Padua; along with Majer Rizzioli, were all well-connected and sophisticated women. But they were unversed in the cunning "transformism" of Italian corridor politics. Nor were they adept at the bully-boy tactics favored by the local *ras* as they jostled for position in the new regime. Not least of all, they were disoriented by Mussolini's feigned attention. Uncertain whether the fascist women represented potentially significant interests, Mussolini had much to gain in these first years from a pose that the women called "friendly and accessible."[24] Since Mussolini was the Duce, the women seemed to discount the antifeminist attitudes of PNF members who wanted women out of politics altogether, or, in any case, did not contemplate including their representatives in the PNF's national directory, as Majer Rizzioli wanted and as Mussolini apparently had promised.

Indeed, preliminary guidelines for the women's groups published on January 14, 1922, underscored the subaltern role women were to play in the Fascist Revolution. Thus women were to attend meetings and rallies and to support the movement by undertaking charitable work, promoting propaganda, assisting the sick and wounded, and serving as godmothers or *madrine* to the newly founded *fasci di combattimento*. But they were specifically barred from taking any political initiatives. The Milan contingent, which advocated a stronger political engagement than its Roman counterpart, tried to give this vocation for good works a more activist turn; at the 1925 congress, the members continued to equivocate over the relationship by affirming that the *fasci*'s "task was not precisely political, but social."

The fascist women's groups were conditioned for the worse by the momentous changes that the fascist movement underwent as Mussolini consolidated his power in the course of the 1920s. From the time the first small band of the "first hour" rallied at the Piazza San Sepolcro in Milan in March 1919, Italian fascism had been a chameleonlike movement, cuing its colors to potential allies and the rapidly shifting political terrain of the postwar years. Thus in 1919, as the movement looked for support from radicals and leftists disaffected with Italian socialism's snail-like reformism and its neutrality during the war, the fascists had embraced the positions of futurist intellectuals ready to flout conventional morality by supporting divorce and by suppressing the bourgeois family. In 1919 this opportunistically populist voice had also spoken out in favor of giving women the vote. By 1922, however, these positions were scrapped in the face of the antipathy of the veterans' movement toward women working and the reactionary outlook of the landed proprietors and small-town bourgeoisie who in 1920–21 backed the *squadristi*'s assaults on socialist leagues and cooperatives.

After 1923 fascism's antifeminism was reinforced by the hard-faced authoritarianism of Mussolini's new allies in the Nationalist party. They were the ones who held up the yardstick of the "state's interest" to which all "particularisms" were to be subordinated; their vision of a strong and expert state rallied criminal anthropologists, social hygienists, medical doctors, child-protection advocates, and other reformers long frustrated by liberal inaction, who hoped to breathe life into their projects for improving the Italian "stock." In 1929, following the Concordat with the Vatican, fascist misogyny combined with the antiemancipationist positions of the Church. The dictatorship's interventionist impulses were reinforced by Catholicism's claim to protect family and motherhood. That, finally, would be the political context in which a well-chastened "Latin feminism" was born and the so-called women's organizations of the PNF were promoted by the regime.

Bourgeois Feminism's Last Stand

In the wake of Mussolini's appointment as prime minister on October 30, 1922, Italian emancipationists' main energies turned toward the suffrage issue, thus reaffirming faith in what was basically a liberal notion of citizenship. Of course emancipated upper-class women were not the only ones to believe fascism could somehow be reconciled with a liberal political system. That old fox Giolitti, who should have known better, as well as many other prominent liberals, believed that they might still outwit Mussolini through parliamentary maneuvers. This belief was cherished until January 1925, when, in the wake of the Aventine secession in the course of which the opposition deputies abandoned the chamber to protest the assassination of the socialist deputy Giacomo Matteotti by fascist thugs, Mussolini closed down parliament, assumed full responsibility for the terroristic actions of his squads, and embarked on a widespread crackdown on the opposition.

In this context, the quest for the vote was a comprehensible, if doomed, strategy for women; there was no real alternative course of action. Through 1925, the suffrage issue alone still had enough appeal to rally women across partisan lines; socialist, liberal, and Catholic women, not to mention fascists and nationalist loyalists, all supported some kind of electoral reform. Moreover, a victory in this battle promised to offset the attacks on women's rights, manifest with both the Anile-Corbino bill of 1920 curbing women's right to work and the proposed school reform undertaken in 1923 by Giovanni Gentile, the minister of public instruction. These setbacks underscored the fact that women were not in a position to influence the new regime as it went about revising legal codes and revamping state institutions.

Mussolini himself had helped to focus women's hopes on the vote. On May 14, 1923, when he presided at the opening of the IX Congress of the International Alliance for Women's Suffrage in Rome, he stated that, despite the complexities involved, no party in Italy opposed giving women the vote. "So far as this government is concerned," he continued, "I am authorized to declare that, barring unforseen developments, the Fascist government pledges to grant the vote to several categories of women, beginning at the local level. . . . I do not believe that enfranchising women will have catastrophic consequences, as some misoneists argue, but in all probability it will have beneficial results because women will bring to the exercise of these new rights their fundamental virtues of balance, equilibrium, and prudence."[25]

Evidently, Mussolini was still of several minds on how women would fit into national reconstruction. First he promised women the vote. Then he allowed the suffrage to be narrowed to exclude most women. Subsequently, in 1925, he rallied his followers to push through a law giving some women suffrage in administrative elections. Finally, in 1926, he abolished elections altogether. To argue that these tergiversations constituted what historian Franca Pieroni Bortolotti called "reverse gradualism" suggests that the Duce regarded women as a substantial political force and thus as worthy contenders in fascist realpolitik. Clearly he did not. Still, the view that Mussolini treated fascist women basically the same as he did other interest groups (which is what some historians have implied) misses the different dynamic created by the femaleness of this lobby.[26] Benito Mussolini practiced a particularly merciless sexual politics: charm alternated with rudeness, seduction with total indifference, promises with deception. This conduct was exemplified when he turned on his promise to Majer Rizzioli to give the fascist women a voice in the PNF's national directory, bowing to the point made by the Duce's Nationalist counselor, Roberto Forges Davanzati, as parodied by the disappointed Elisa, that "women were good for an hour of pleasure, but not for an epoch of calm and balanced work."[27] Meanwhile the government's own plan, the so-called Acerbo project, put forward in 1922 as an alternative to the universal suffrage proposal advanced by the socialist deputy G. E. Modigliani, rendered the vote of interest to fewer and fewer women by limiting it to women decorated for special services to Italy, mothers and widows of war dead, women who were heads of families, and those who had a degree or who paid at least one hundred lira annually in local taxes and could read and write. All the same, the reactions of bourgeois women to political disappointment remained intensely personal and uncomprehending. When the Pro-suffragio's Roman leader Paola Benedettini Alferazzi heard there was yet another delay on the vote in early 1925, she decried it as an "unmerited offense." "It strikes me as an enormity that a President of the Council could promise something so securely and specifically, yet not carry through on it, that I am still awaiting his final word."[28]

This credulousness about fascism's good faith made the ultimate undoing of the suffrage law especially embittering. In the months after the Acerbo project was finally passed, local committees were launched to register women to vote. It was a difficult task, as the editor of the staid Roman monthly *La donna italiana*, Maria Magri Zopegni, recalled. Though her own feminism of Catholic stamp was wavering, she still wanted to defend the voter registration effort against onetime feminists who, after elections had been suppressed altogether, argued that women were unworthy of voting anyway. Several thousand women were registered in spite of the "innumerable and most bothersome steps [it took] to be identified officially." Most women lacked "an identification card or a photograph, or any other document suited to identifying them before the law." If they had been schooled by nuns, as Magri Zopegni had been, they lacked proper certification of their education. And the credentialing examinations set up by the state were of "some difficulty" for simple housewives and "extremely humiliating" for educated women. Worst of all, women registering to vote were subject to the "discomfort created . . . by the irony and jokes of the men at home, husbands, sons, brothers habituated by tradition and atavisms to divide women into two major categories: those good for their own needs; those necessary for their pleasure."[29] For women whose political identity had now come to hinge on the vote, it was crushing news to find that the laws passed on September 2, 1926, abolished local elections. Henceforth, the *podestà* (mayor) and town councilmen were appointed by the government in Rome, and although this dictatorial procedure did not specifically exclude women, in fact it did.

With the new laws, the emancipationist movement disintegrated. Before the suffrage became a dead issue, Cabrini Casartelli had been guardedly hopeful that within the women's movement proper there was "still no desire to revise old positions." Yet as early as 1924, she had already espied "a new tactic, filled with resignation and evangelical goodness." This she associated primarily with Paola Benedettini Alferazzi, editor of the *Giornale della donna* and head of the Pro-suffragio movement, who by 1930 would become a prominent voice in the fascist women's organization. Realism, as the Roman women grouped around Benedettini Alferazzi seemed to say, dictated the need "to look the situation straight on and without being discouraged, but without too many illusions, for the issue of the vote may drag on for many, many years."[30] Fascism, as the Pro-suffragio head subsequently was to console herself, at least "implicitly recognized" the right of women to vote. Now women had to focus on obtaining a voice in the new institutions. Some leading Nationalist women, who had long been alienated from liberal feminism, like the Sicilian-born journalist Ester Lombardo, signaled the arrival of a new era. In 1925–1926 this artful woman, who in addition to editing her own monthly, *Vita femminile*, was conniving to have it become the new organ of the women's fascist groups, replaced the politically unwelcome socialist Cabrini Casartelli as chronicler of the women's movement for the *Almanacco della donna italiana*. From that influential position, Lombardo heartily announced that the "feminist movement in Italy no longer exists." It had been "gobbled up by the Fascist Revolution." Perhaps there was a female

Duce in the making? Lombardo incited "energetic and strong-willed women" to rally the "Italian female world," to obtain a voice in the corporate state.[31]

The fascist women's groups were certainly in no position to advance such ambitious claims. Since their June 1924 congress, when the women's groups had demanded "full autonomy" without obtaining any satisfaction, they had fallen into an organizational limbo. Discouraged by the defeat of the suffrage issue, they were bereft of funding, except that which was provided by Majer Rizzioli, who personally subsidized their journal, *Rassegna femminile italiana,* which she had founded on January 25, 1925, and edited, subject to the pleasure of the PNF secretary. In early 1926 Roberto Farinacci suppressed her position as chief inspectress, and she was forced to resign. Why he did so is hard to say: Majer Rizzioli could not possibly have been considered a political threat in conventional terms— unlike the violence-prone hardliners around Farinacci himself—but she was annoyingly persistent in demanding autonomy for the women's *fasci,* and her middle age, evidently, made her not sufficiently malleable. To replace her, after Farinacci was ousted in March, his successor, Augusto Turati, appointed a fellow Brescian, Angiola Moretti. Young, single, and by all accounts very pretty, she had been a veteran Fiume legionnaire and a member of the PNF since November 1923. The ingratiating Ester Lombardo signaled the meaning of this changing of the guard: young women have "minds more open to new events and opportunities," whereas "old carcasses with very rare exceptions always constitute an obstacle."[32]

Turati still relied on Majer Rizzioli, however, to fund and publish the group's bulletin, the *Rassegna femminile italiana.* Called back to service in June 1922, Majer Rizzioli became the very embodiment of the self-abnegating "New Italian" her journal held up for emulation: "strong and decisive, well-aware of her mission's importance," she operated with "efficiency, collaboration, dignity, and strength of character" to resist the "doubts, troubles, and uncertainties" that would certainly have overwhelmed most any other woman.[33] Once again the PNF's utter ingratitude tested her stoicism, this time to the limits. In 1929 she moved back to Milan, apparently with the understanding that she would continue to edit the periodical. Only then did she find that Turati had decided to bypass the old-guard circles altogether by funding another publication. The new official journal of the women's groups was the polished *Giornale della donna,* founded in 1918 and the former voice of the bourgeois suffrage movement. By that time, Majer Rizzioli was fatally ill. As her husband, Niccolò, later wrote Mussolini, she was still hoping to get a "word of encouragement" from the Duce (with whom she hadn't had an audience in three years) when she died on June 2, 1930, at the age of fifty.[34] The leaders of the fascist women's auxiliaries in the next fifteen years were neither self-reflective enough nor sufficiently generous of spirit to record her contribution to their founding.

After 1925 organized women would never again be regarded as serious interlocutors of fascist politics. Socialist women were scattered with the suppression of the PSI in 1925–26, as were the militant young loyalists of the fledgling Italian Communist party. Because of their harsh experience of fascist rule, these women didn't countenance the ambivalence that women of other social groups felt toward the dictatorship. The dictatorship later recognized two women's "movements": the fascist organizations of women, which it boosted, and the Catholic groups, which it abided. As the former suffragist Valeria Benetti Brunelli pointed out in 1933, women from both groups made significant contributions to national society, "although knowing that they would receive neither honors nor economic compensation."[35] Which is to say, neither their demands nor their objections, neither their complaints nor their proposals, visibly promoted or hindered policies. This is not to say that women were not the objects of policy. By the 1930s, Italian women had become "important," in the sense that British feminist Winifred Holtby intended. They had become "exemplary wives and mothers," "angels of the hearth," "the mothers of pioneers and soldiers," "a civil militia in the service of the state." These were just a few of the honorific titles the dictatorship bestowed on them, in testimony of their duties under the dictatorship and the rights these allegedly carried with them. The transformations in their lives that these new duties and rights entailed are the subject of the chapters following.

3   Motherhood

A nation exists not only because it has a history and territory, but because human masses reproduce from generation to generation. The alternative is servitude or the end. Italian fascists: Hegel the philosopher of the State said: "He who is not a father is not a man."

Benito Mussolini (1928)

If men did the birthing, families would all have only two children.

Piedmontese farm woman, mother of nine

In fascist statecraft, the duty of women toward the nation lay first and foremost in making babies, though this was not a foregone conclusion, as we have seen. In the early 1920s Mussolini dallied with the idea of basing female citizenship on the vote, as indeed Italian feminists had long demanded. But by late 1925 the electoral system was being dismantled, making the vote for women a moot issue. Meanwhile, as the dictatorship spelled out a pronatalist population policy in the mid-1920s, women came to be identified as a vital national resource. In his notorious Ascension Day Speech on the twenty-sixth of May, 1927, Mussolini, "taking the Nation and placing it before its destiny," put strategies in "defense of the race" at the very heart of fascist domestic politics.[1] The following October, at Palazzo Venezia, the Duce for the first time received a jittery group of national delegates from the Fascist party's women's organization. On that occasion, he summed up their paramount task: "Go back home and tell the women I need births, many births."[2]

But why did Mussolini need "births"? For a nation as crowded as early-twentieth-century Italy was, a public policy in support of prolificity seems a puzzling course. Land hunger was endemic, and the terrible privations of large rural families were legendary. By the 1920s more and more Italian families—though not the poorest—sought to limit the number of children they had, and the fact that so many Italians were compelled to emigrate was considered a national shame. At the time, opponents of fascism dismissed Mussolini's much-bruited demographic "battles" as mere diversions. They supposedly distracted public attention from the jarring economic slump of 1926–27 and acted as a sop to the masses whose only respite from misery was "fornication and *figli*." Pronatalist propaganda also tried to put a good face on what was an awful predicament for the fascist government—Italy's population overflow. After its major outlets in the United States were closed off by the Immigration Quota Laws of 1921, the burgeoning population of the countryside threatened to spill over into urban unemployment and unrest. In the past, Italian governments had actively encouraged emigration abroad. Now the "New Italy" denounced emigration as an injurious loss of subjects and drew up restrictive measures to halt it.

The Normalization of Sexuality

The logic behind Mussolini's politics of prolificity is more comprehensible now that more is known about how population policy became subject to considerations of national-state power during the late nineteenth century in Europe. Under the slogan "force is numbers," the Duce ably translated the anxieties of anti-Malthusian ideologues into a concrete national goal: to expand Italy from a nation of 40 million people to one of 60 million by mid-century. To justify his actions, Mussolini referred to two distinct, if related, lines of reasoning. One might be described as pre-Malthusian or "mercantilist" in that it emphasized the desirability of sheer quantities of people as cheap labor. This argument seemed appropriate to a nation in the throes of early industrialization, in which high fertility rates still predominated. And such was indeed true for much of Italy's south and islands as well as for some of the more isolated parts of the rural center and north. In those areas, big population spurts promised to foster economic growth as they had done in eighteenth-century England or France. The other logic more typically belonged to a nation embarked on imperialist expansion. Italy's growing population provided fascism with a reason for demanding colonies. At the same time, it supplied the military manpower needed to conquer them. Demographic pressure had to kept up to justify Mussolini's claim that Italy would either expand or explode. If Italy failed to become an empire, the Duce obsessively repeated, it would certainly become a colony.[3]

In the short term, however, fascist pronatalist politics originated in Mussolini's determination to consolidate his dictatorship. The economic and political sides of what has sometimes been called "normalization" are familiar: stabilizing the currency at *Quota 90* in 1926; accommodating business elites, monarchy, and church; pushing through special laws to outlaw the opposition; harnessing organized labor in corporate institutions; and subordinating the Fascist party and its unruly squads to the central state bureaucuracy.[4] The social-sexual side to the dictatorship's consolidation after 1926 is less well known. Yet as early as January 1927, Mussolini referred to the demographic problem as "part of a more general endeavor to moralize Italian civil society." Consequently, local government authorities were advised to regard " 'moral order' among citizens as the premise and best guarantee of 'public order.' "[5] Pronatalist policies not just presumed the restoration of a gender order turned topsy-turvy during the Great War and by postwar social turmoil, but they also became the chief means to effect it.

Sexual normalization was built on solid pillars of hypocrisy. On the one hand, the Duce identified his own much-vaunted sexual prowess with the virility of the fascist system. Smirking at the impotence of antifascism, he identified its state-form as republicanism, and its main exemplar was his current worst enemy, namely, the demographically decrepit French Third Republic. Until the mid-1920s, the official iconography of the *squadrista* remained faithful to the image evoked by the futurist Mario Carli in 1919. With his "ardent-proud, guileless eyes" and "sensual-energetic mouth quick to kiss passionately, sing out sweetly, and command imperiously," the so-called fascist of the first hour was emphatically a free man; his "sober-virile elegance" left him ever ready "to run, fight, escape, dance, and arouse a crowd."[6] Young fascists continued to have their sexual coming out in the *case chiuse* of the new order, and the rank and file knew just enough about the Duce's peccadillos to admire his manliness. On the other hand, the Duce wanted his troops home. Henceforth real men would be family men—as Mussolini remarked elsewhere, "He who is not a father is not a man."[7] The Duce, who as a young socialist had been an avowed Malthusian and espoused the cause of free love for men, now lambasted those who failed to marry and propagate as middle-class egotists. In the New Italy, true men proved their virility not by beating up or purging with castor oil their "demo-liberal" or socialist enemies but by seeding numerous offspring. A punitive tax on male celibacy passed with royal decree-law number 2132, on December 19, 1926, was among Mussolini's very first pronatalist measures. In the penal code of 1931, homosexual acts among men were outlawed. Civil servants were repeatedly enjoined to marry, and after 1937 marriage and numbers of children became criteria of preferment for government careers; for some, such as town mayor, professor, and university dean—who were to be regarded as exemplars of civic leadership—fatherhood was declared a prerequisite. Thus, the trouble-making bachelor-*squadrista* was definitively demobilized, detached from the homoerotic possibilities of frontline camaraderie, and summoned home to the discipline of family life.[8]

For Italian women especially, the Ascension Day Speech, with its emphasis on increasing the birth rate, signaled a turning point in national sexual politics. Still-cherished illusions about the possibility of playing an activist role in the new order were dashed. As the Special Tribunals were mounted in 1927–28 to prosecute antifascists and the death penalty was mandated for the first time since the founding of the modern Italian state, there was no place for pleas for mercy or for the sentimentality that Mussolini characterized as typical of the "female element . . . whose sex often introduces into serious things its incorrigible mark of frivolity."[9] Above all, motherhood lost the special social meanings that almost all Italian feminists had invoked. Henceforth, maternity became tantamount to the physical act of making babies. Women's procreative role now potentially defined every aspect of their social being. Thus, Italian women not only confronted their exclusion from politics (in which their right to participate had at least been nominally recognized by the concession of the administrative vote in 1925), but they also risked exclusion from the entire public sphere: their rights in the workplace, their contributions to culture, and their service as volunteers were all called into question by the official message that their preeminent duty was to bear the nation's children. Worst of all, state authority now embarked on institutionalizing this narrowly cast vision of female roles.

The first step in this process was to remove illegitimate sexuality from public spaces. As early as 1923, at Mussolini's command, the police had ordered all prostitutes, including "isolated" practitioners, to carry a special passport with records of their vaginal examinations for venereal disease. By late 1926 local police forces, incited anew by the central government and armed with the rules on prostitution contained in articles 201, 204, and 213 of the new Public Security Laws, resolved to mop up delinquency and sexual turpitude. The first crackdown was accompanied by what the Florentine novelist Vasco Pratolini later called "the pogrom of the prostitutes." According to his chronicle of working-class life under fascism, *A Tale of Poor Lovers*, the vice squads roamed the city streets each night from ten to midnight with "the strategy of sportsmen lying in wait for larks in the shrubbery." Among the prostitutes residing at Ristori's hotel in Florence's plebeian Santa Croce district, one, Selvaggia, "managed to slip through the meshes of the police net, but Chiccona had been caught and released with a one-way ticket to Lucca, her home town. Ada was also caught, and the prison doctor certified her as having secondary syphilis." Rosetta, as a "veteran of the trade" and a recidivist, was shut up in the Santa Verdiana prison for six months. Others decided to go into the state-run brothels, though "this meant a loss of their former liberty as though they were in prison." In the closed houses, or *case chiuse*, the women were required to submit to obligatory medical checkups, police surveillance, and vexatious laws like that which imposed six-month prison terms for soliciting from the windows and a year for hosting dances or serving liquor. That was Olympia's fate.[10] So confined, the prostitutes serviced male sexual needs. Meanwhile, Italy no longer ran the danger—prophesied by Richard Korherr, the racist German population expert whose work was translated into Italian in 1927 with an introduction by Mussolini—that by tolerating unregulated prostitution, the state degraded motherhood. It was notorious that whores publicly mocked mothers as "slaves of husbands and children";[11] only by segregating illicit sex from public view and by drawing a sharp line between bad women and good ones might the state preserve the site and purpose of legitimate sex, namely, in marriage, at the initiative of the man, and for the purpose of procreation.

The next step was to establish a wide-ranging maternalist politics. Fascist Italy's involvement in reproductive politics, much like its initiatives in other areas of social policy, developed slowly. From a hortatory phase in the 1920s, it moved, hit or miss, to more and more concrete incentives in the mid-1930s. Alongside repressive steps such as the criminalization of abortion, the dictatorship initiated positive measures, including family allocations, maternity insurance, birth and marriage loans, career preferment for fathers of big families, and special institutions established for infant and family health and welfare. Although it can be shown that these policies did not appreciably stimulate birth rates, they had other important consequences. They laid the bases of the first modern public services related to the welfare of mothers and children in Italy. They also promoted a novel politics around maternity, which recognized women as new political subjects, yet granted them few real privileges and burdened them with many additional duties. Finally, these policies fostered new social perceptions of maternity.[12]

Italy's Two Fertility Regimes

At bottom, all of the regime's pronatalist measures were devised to contend with what publicists described as a national emergency. This was the tendency for Italians to control their fertility. Since the turn of the century, Italy, if more slowly and unevenly than northwestern European societies, had experienced the great shift toward limiting births. After a slight upward surge following the Great War, when the consummation of delayed marriages caused a small baby boom, Italian fertility trends swept downward. Once "most robust," birth rates dropped in the wake of what a contemporary demographer, Livio Livi, described as a "social tide" of neo-Malthusianism. Coming from France, this had already deluged most of Anglo-Saxon Europe. By the 1930s the Italian fertility rate was down

Table 1. Birth Rates, by Region, per 1,000 Inhabitants, 1921–1945

	Italy	Northern Italy	Central Italy	Southern Italy	Islands
1921–1925	29.9	26.6	28.2	36.3	31.0
1926–1930	27.1	23.5	24.7	33.8	29.9
1931–1935	24.0	20.3	21.5	30.8	27.2
1936–1940	23.4	19.8	21.2	29.7	27.2
1941–1945	19.9	16.6	17.5	25.3	24.2

Source: Associazione per lo sviluppo dell'industria nel Mezzogiorno (SVIMEZ), Un secolo di statistiche italiane Nord e Sud, 1861–1961 (Rome, 1961), p. 79, table 77.

from its 1880s high of 39 births per thousand persons, a figure typical of early industrializing regions, to 24 per thousand (see table 1). However, this decline had occurred unevenly. In the 1880s all regions had more or less the same fertility rates. By the mid-1930s at least twenty-five urbanized provinces of north and central Italy (out of a total of ninety-two provinces) had succumbed to what Livi called "demographic death"; that is, Italian adults were not producing enough offspring to replace themselves. Meanwhile, in the Italian south and islands, excepting several large towns and their hinterlands, population growth remained strong. In industrial Turin, birth rates were 14.6 per thousand; in impoverished rural Lucania, they were more than double at 33.7 per thousand. Among urban professionals, the median family size was 3.28 persons; among peasants, it was nearly twice that figure, 6.43 persons.[13] White-collar wives averaged just over two children each, whereas rural women averaged over four. Interwar Italy was thus characterized by two fertility regimes: one seemingly traditional, the other stigmatized as modern. This dualism affected every aspect of fascist policy, as well as people's attitudes toward it. (See chart 1.)

Indeed, the dictatorship's major worry was that the new reproductive habits of northern and central Italian townspeople prefigured national patterns. The great urban centers, with Milan in the lead, had become hotbeds of "denatalizing infection," a 1939 population study warned.[14] By 1928 in Bologna, the first city to be rebuked by Mussolini, there were "more coffins than cradles."[15] The situation in Milan, "fascism's birthplace," was especially deplorable. In the Lombard capital, "all classes were agreed on a violent politics of rationalizing offspring." The contaminating effect of urban customs seemed uncontainable. As soon as rural immigrants settled in, no matter where they had come from, they abandoned "the

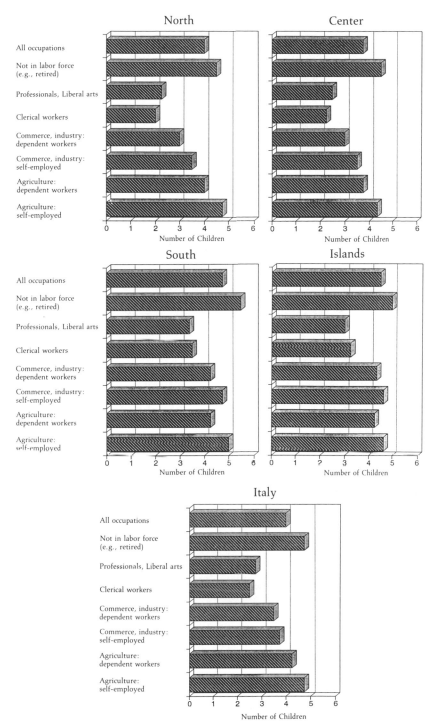

Chart 1. Differential fertility: number of children born, by father's occupation and place of residence, 1931 census. (Massimo Livi Bacci, *A History of Italian Fertility during the Last Two Centuries* [Princeton: Princeton University Press, 1972], p. 238).

proliferous habits of yore," and subscribed to local habits, having one child, or perhaps two, but rarely as many as three.[16] Everywhere that the new patterns took hold, it became common for Italians to defer having their firstborn, to space the intervals between births, and to limit the total number.

What more specifically motivated people to limit childbearing was an elusive problem for the regime. Like women everywhere, Italian women were not talkative about the subject with outsiders. Their reticence was all the greater after 1926, when birth control was officially proscribed and contraception and abortion were outlawed. Beginning in 1926 the regime sought to probe the causes of population decline with a plethora of national commissions and agencies, the first being the Commission to Investigate Malthusianism founded in 1926, the last, the Fascist Union of Big Families and the Ministry of the Interior's Demographic Office, both founded in 1937. Chief among these agencies was the Central Institute of Statistics. It was established in 1926 after several attempts to obtain an accurate population count failed because of suspicion of government and the habit of local officials to fiddle with census figures to curry favors from the central administration. Indeed, Mussolini commenced his population battles by denouncing "the crisis of Italian statistics," by which he meant the frauds and miscounts that had inflated the population count in the early 1920s.[17] In the next fifteen years, the Italian populace was subjected to surveys of all sorts as the field of population statistics rapidly developed in Italy.

Not uncommonly, these inquiries were contaminated by dire prophecies about racial exhaustion. Italy's leading statistician, Corrado Gini, head of the Central Institute of Statistics, indefatigably conjured up statistical surveys to ascertain the damage. His influence was matched only by that of the endocrinologist Nicola Pende who, in addition to achieving a certain celebrity as a society doctor—having been called in to treat Victor Emanuel III's daughter for anorexia—had built up his own little eugenicist barony in the *Istituto Biotipologico-ortogenetico* at Genoa before being called to occupy the chair of surgery and medicine at the University of Rome. Pende's influence was especially visible in the most comprehensive study of Italian population characteristics to that time; this survey was launched under Gini's aegis in preparation for the 1931 World Population Conference in Rome, and it purported to document the physiological factors which led people to have big families. To that end, the investigators poked into the lives of a goodly sample of the 1.5 million families in Italy which, according to a special census in June 1928, had seven or more live-born offspring. For nearly a year, with the aid of local officials, a score of young researchers assiduously ranked correlations between family size and morphological features such as pelvic size, body fat, height, hormonal secretions, and hirsute upper lips. Not surprisingly, their search for an ideal physiology for maternal—as well as paternal—types proved inconclusive. The best that could be determined regarding women was that "proliferous females" were shorter rather than taller, broader around the hips than narrower, and more slovenly than elegant. Though the researchers hadn't been looking for nonphysiological factors, some could not but notice the inescapably positive correlations between numerous children, family poverty, high infant mortality rates, illiteracy, and intensely crowded and squalid housing conditions.[18]

As population survey techniques became more refined in the late 1930s (and researchers more intent on penetrating the social psychology of their subjects), social scientists admitted that unfamiliarity with female motivation and insufficient contacts with midwives, nurses, or social workers were real handicaps. Breaking with the totalitarian and racialist presumptions of their mentors, a younger generation, including a small group of women such as Nora Federici, turned their attention to the socioeconomic milieu and the much belabored, yet still ill-explained, problem of accounting for sharp social differentials in birth rates.[19] Even so, practically the entire cohort of young researchers were inclined by considerations of career, if not ideological conviction, to treat female fertility decline as an aberrant (if remarkably widespread) tendency. In a less coercive society, some, judging from their research interests, might have become sex-reform advocates, following the example of Margaret Sanger and other pioneers in family planning. As it was, the only good that could be said of them was that their prejudices (by hindering research and biasing the results) deterred more accurate surveillance by the intrusive agencies of fascist panopticism. On the other hand, their findings were readily exploited by the self-promoting experts, propagandists, and outright cranks who largely shaped public discourse on matters relating to human fertility and reproduction.[20]

The motives that led Italians to manage their fertility were probably not much different from those of millions of other Europeans who in that era or even earlier had started to control their fertility.[21] As historians have reconstructed these motives, the first and more readily identifiable one might be characterized as socioeconomic; inspired by economic insecurity and worries about their children's future, family planning was usually a joint decision, involving both spouses. The second motive, far harder to probe, was attributed to women's emancipation. The casting off of religious fatalism as culture was secularized, exposure to new models of womanhood in the workplace and through the mass media, and a heightened sense of individuality emerging out of the political culture and social relations of turn-of-the-century liberalism interacted with the pressures of work and married life to enhance women's desire to control their bodies.[22]

The socioeconomic motives are the easiest to document, in part because men as well as women spoke about them. Moreover, they were the arguments that public authorities such as the town *podestà* or the local prefect could readily grasp when they were ordered to inform Rome about the family planning habits of their subjects.[23] And once articulated in public, such explanations became part of common wisdom. Resonating among the postwar generations and reaffirmed in ever wider social constituencies, economic calculations have come to be considered the most obvious and reasonable motives for family planning.

In interwar Italy, the widespread practice of fertility control as a socioeconomic precaution was identified primarily with the new middle classes: the families of salaried men, as the demographer Pier Paolo Luzzatto-Fegiz noted in 1937, had "long held first place for infertility." But during the interwar years, family planning became well-entrenched among urban skilled and even unskilled workers: like the salaried middle classes, they were "masters of [neither] their own nor their children's destiny."[24] The functionary's family sought thereby to maintain its social rank by guaranteeing the means to educate the children. Workers too worried about position: the physical prowess and restraint demonstrated in limiting family size, like the skill, foresight, and self-control they displayed in the exercise of their craft, set them apart from the profligate and ignorant urban subproletariat, rural people, and *meridionali*.

To generalize from the experience of an isolated agro-town of 11,000 in the hinterland of western Sicily, by the 1930s these considerations were operating not just in the big towns of the north and center or in advanced agricultural regions, but nationwide. In their reconstitution of family birth patterns at Villamaura, the anthropologists Jane and Peter Schneider found that local artisans, who had been badly buffeted during the interwar decades by economic distress, higher outlays for apprenticeship, and the cutoff of emigration outlets abroad, "seized control of the reproduction process," even while local rural laborers continued to produce large families. The artisans made assiduous use of coitus interruptus, dubbing it with affectionate irony "reverse gear" or "marcia indietro" in honor of the Sicilian debut of the great mechanical invention of the era. In this way, blacksmiths, stonemasons, shoemakers, and other craftsmen managed the transition to a controlled fertility that "was demanding of men as well as women, ideologically motivated, and thorough."[25] Indeed, as this and other evidence shows, the hardships of the interwar years, especially among the urban working class and artisans, on whom the heavy burden of the dictatorship's economic recovery measures fell, prompted people to limit family size.[26] The fact that demographic propaganda was so blatantly inconsistent with calculations of family interest perhaps even accentuated the tenacity with which people articulated this goal. "One child, professor, one child is all we want" ("Figlio unico, professore, figlio unico, noi vogliamo"), so scores of women of all ages, classes, and educational levels confided to a leading Turin pediatrician, Luigi Maccone, in the 1930s. Working-class women were especially vehement: "the government is not going to get anything from us. Let the fat-cat bourgeoisie and the rich beget children. Let the government go ahead and talk about the ever bigger need to make the country greater, with an ever higher birth rate, to keep the stock healthy——in my opinion, it's all yack."[27]

The desire of women for emancipation was a second force motivating the spread of family planning. Fascist propagandists made much of this, citing it along with women's work (itself sometimes attributed to female emancipation) as the major cause of lowered fertility rates. Under female emancipation they clumped together the joy-seeking of the young and privileged, female vanity, individualistic liberalism, a false sense of material needs, and godlessness. Yet it is hard to know what individual women thought of such intimate matters. Before becoming mothers, young women might well have regarded married life with children as a joyless business to be postponed as long as possible; that, at least, was the attitude articulated by Roman schoolgirls who in the late 1930s were surveyed about their feelings toward work and family life.[28] But once they had become mothers, whatever their own feelings about the physiologial or psychological toll of childbearing, they reasoned in terms of their family's status and their children's well-being. Dr. Maccone captured well the calculations of his lower-middle-class clients:

> You, professor, surely understand what it means to have a big family with our limited financial means! I certainly can't give birth in a public maternity ward . . . [or] accept a doctor chosen for us, no matter who he is, as if he were a butcher or a baker selected because he's nearby and convenient, [much less] pay to send the children to the seaside or mountains in colonies for the poor.[29]

Insofar as women were guided by emancipatory ideals in their effort to have fewer children, some obviously were freer than others to act accordingly. Upper-class women were more exposed to alternative models of maternity. They also had more chance to weigh the so-called opportunity costs of having children. Above all, they had readier access to contraceptive knowledge and techniques. But not even they exited from the "realm of necessity." True, there was ample help from family and servants; until World War II even the wives of middle-class professionals had recourse to wet nurses, provided their families still had ties to rural areas where the *balie* were recruited. However, child rearing was generally regarded as having become a more complicated, demanding, and prolonged affair, and the length of time women wanted to be absorbed in it was briefer. In Italy, vanity, self-interest, and the desire to be modern—when modern was defined as having few children—combined with a sense of the precariousness of bourgeois status to curb middle-class family size sharply.

For urban working-class women, the choice to limit births was more embattled and anguished. Notions of self-determination generated little sympathy in working-class environments, and poverty and prejudices limited the use of the only legally available contraceptive device, condoms. Consequently, the struggle to control one's own body exacted high personal costs: women fearful of unwanted pregnancies experienced sexual intercourse with nervous vigilance, warning their partners "fa tensiun!" (be careful!); in the worst cases, they turned to corrosive douches and makeshift abortion to interrupt pregnancy. Their determination to control their fertility was deliberate and conscious, even if it would perhaps be an overstatement to characterize it as a vindication of the individualist outlooks more common in the upper classes.[30] Drawing strength from a collective sentiment fostered by female camaraderie in the workplace and by informal community networks, younger women affirmed their notion of civility against both the rough sexuality of men and the frazzled existence of older female relatives, who, often of recent rural provenance, had undergone repeated pregnancies.

In 1930s Bari, according to the young sociologist Elena Saponaro, women were especially conscious that big families put them at a social disadvantage. Mothers tried to compensate by using intense cunning to keep up family appearances. Meanwhile, the older girls displayed an "audacity and determination" that set them apart from their male siblings; in an effort to distance themselves from the family environment, they entered the work force early and married young, though that course only led them, against their wishes, to repeat their mothers' fate.[31]

Eugenics, Italian Style

The complexity of human motives involved in family planning suggests how difficult it was for any government, much less a recently constituted one, to formulate effective policies. The difficulties were perhaps even more complicated than in northern Europe. Unlike, for example, Sweden or Great Britain, where fertility patterns were fairly uniform, Italy had to contend with not one, but two well-demarcated fertility cultures: that associated with the demographically modern north and central regions and that identified with the rural south. With the small family implicitly identified as modern and with so much of government rhetoric highlighting the desirability of modernity, pronatalist politics were built on a yawning credibility gap.

Moreover, for all his rhetoric, Mussolini was rather wary about the effectiveness of state intervention in population policy. A political realist, he was probably well-acquainted with the failure of the French state, for all its intrusions, to reverse France's demographic decline. Mussolini at least seemed to sense that the deep-seated causes of population decline defied simple solutions. He was also undecided whether initiative should come from individuals or from the state; in this his reasoning was not unlike that of spokesmen for America's Moral Majority and other neo-conservative movements. Should self-sacrificing heroism, perhaps fortified by religious fundamentalism, be invoked to counter the egotistical considerations which purportedly caused fertility decline? Or should the state encourage childbearing, as the Swedes and other proponents of strong welfare states had done, by guaranteeing the material well-being of large families? The fascist regime certainly never endorsed so-called negative measures, which distinguished it conspicuously from the Nazi dictatorship. Starting in 1933, Hitler's Third Reich enforced the sterilization of as many as 400,000 persons, half of whom were women, and it tolerated, if not compelled, abortions and other practices to limit births judged to be non-eugenic on social, ethnic, medical, or other grounds. Neither can fascist policy be compared to the drastic thrust of Nazi eugenicism, which was to purify the race. What Nazi racists theorized became practicable in the course of World War II as the Nazi state unleashed its genocidal race war against the Jews and other ethnic minorities.[32]

Indeed, behind Italian fascist policy, there was a very different conception of population engineering. This was in turn tied to a different conception of race and of the mechanisms of racial selection. Among Italian eugenicists, the French-Austrian Benedict Morel, with his emphasis on genetic mixing as a source of racial strength, was more popular than the "German" Mendel, who emphasized selection for pure strains. The reasons were as much ideological as scientific: Italy was a nation in which there was no ethnic minority problem to speak of, hence so-called admixtures were not feared. The belief that a biological free-for-all might not only invigorate the race but also renew the political elites, as Vilfredo

Pareto contended, prompted Italian liberals to be skeptical about the pseudoscientificity of Anglo-American biological selection measures and, later, of Nazi geneticism. Admonitions against "zootechnics applied to human species" were vigorously reiterated in Catholic doctrine. "The family is more sacred than the state, and mankind is born not for the earth or for time, but for heaven and all eternity," Pius XI eloquently declaimed in *Casti connubi.* "Public authorities have no direct power over the bodies of their subjects. . . . Where no crime has taken place and there is no cause present for grave punishment they can never, under any circumstance, damage or interfere with the integrity of the body, either for reason of eugenics or for any other reason."[33] The fascists, unlike eugenicists elsewhere, far from fearing "differential fertility," thus celebrated it. Fascism's revolution of youth would tap what the regime's chief statistician Corrado Gini called "the sole reservoir of vital energies," namely the countryside with "its low and prolific classes, on whose changing internal composition and mixing depend the revitalization of the nation." It was not until 1936, after Italy conquered Ethiopia and reinforced its ties with Nazi Germany, that eugenicists and political leaders started to regard the Italians as a "pure race" and to worry about "Israelitic contaminations" and the degenerative effects of mixing "Italian blood with the colonial half-breed."[34]

This peculiarly Italian vision of eugenics justified a social policy that was at once intrusive and laissez-faire, paternalistic and negligent. On the one hand, eugenicists recommended establishing strict norms of behavior for the female of the species, inasmuch as she was responsible for childbearing and nurture. Science had demonstrated that women were "ill-prepared for the sacred and difficult mission of maternity," Professor Pende pointed out. Women were "weak and imperfect in their generative apparatuses, intoxicated by voluptuary poisons and professional ambitions, their nervous and glandular systems in a state of imbalance because of emotional reasons and constitutional factors." Thus the entire purpose of "biological politics" must be to prevent these imperfect creatures from generating "abnormal" offspring. This meant "acting on the woman" not just in the last two or three months of gestation but from the very "preparatory phase" of maternity that lay in women's youth.[35]

Yet Italian eugenics also justified withholding aid. Since class inequalities were considered a cause of prolificity, reforms were not only unnecessary but potentially harmful. True, the middle-class standard of living should be protected, on the grounds that even small improvements might prompt a civil servant or small shopkeeper to have two children instead of one. But as a rule the poor needed to be preserved from the calculating mentality and excessive expectations that came with well-being. Suffice it to provide modest aid to reduce infant mortality. The unfit would die off anyway, and the "low classes" would make do in the conditions that caused their fertile nature to thrive.

At least until 1937, the dictator thus determined that the best policy was to give "a prod to mores" (*pungolo al costume*) sufficient to tip the balance in favor of more childbearing. This "prod" had three prongs. The first was repression, the second social-welfare programs, and the third propaganda. In theory all three were targeted to reach all Italian women and their families. And, of course, all women were touched in some way by policies that defined women's destiny as motherhood and measured successful maternity by the number of live births. But lower-class women were, in practice, the targets of specific fascist programs, the most reliant on their services and the most vulnerable to their overall impact.

Repression seemed the easiest way to stop birth control, and it was the method that the dictatorship found most congenial. The liberal state had already dallied with bans on information on birth control and laws punishing abortion. But fascism tightened them by making abortion and the dissemination of birth-control information crimes of state. The royal decree-law of November 6, 1926, number 1848, passed in the context of the notorious public safety laws, prohibited the display, sale, possession, distribution, manufacture, and importation of literature, engravings, lithographs, drawings, objects, and so on that offended public decency. This proscription was extended to apply to anything publicizing the means of preventing or interrupting pregnancy. These rules were confirmed in the new penal code approved on October 19, 1930, and put into effect on July 1, 1931, which contained an entire chapter (numbers 545–55) devoted to "crimes against the integrity and health of the race." Subsequent legislation also stipulated penalties against any person who publicly incited others to use means to prevent procreation or procure abortion, even indirectly or with scientific or therapeutic pretexts.[36]

Certainly, fascist Italy was not alone in obstructing contraceptive measures or banning abortion; liberal and authoritarian regimes alike had barred them by the mid-1930s. However, the dictatorship's policies stood out in several respects. First, the suppression of information on contraception was supported by the Laws on Public Safety; "impeding the fecundity of the Italian people" was a crime of state, and at times it was zealously prosecuted by the central government. Even fascist jurists underscored that the crime of inciting to use birth-control techniques had no precedents elsewhere. Second, the timing of government intervention made fascism's anti-Malthusian campaigns especially coercive. In Italy knowledge about birth control, suppressed since the Counter-reformation, had begun to be retrieved only two generations before, and then very unevenly. In rural areas, even in rural northwestern Italy, a secular ignorance still prevailed.[37] By the late 1920s, the few groups promoting neo-Malthusianism had been suppressed. Moreover, migratory flows to more sexually emancipated societies, in particular to the United States and France (from whence, for example, the Villamauran artisans claimed to have acquired their techniques) were curbed. Elsewhere, as in the United States and Great Britain, and in spite of official intolerance, birth-control clinics were founded and contraceptive information was widely disseminated, starting precisely in these years.[38] Even in Nazi Germany, pronatalist policies had to contend with the powerful sex reform movement of the Weimar era; though the policies were twisted to the ends of Nazi racialism, eugenicist principles kept family planning in public view.[39]

Finally, official sanctions were reinforced by canon law. Church teachings in the matter were updated by the publication on December 31, 1930, of the Pope's *Casti connubi*. In that encyclical, Pius XI underscored the Church's differences with respect to state policy by condemning eugenicist tendencies, defending the right of priests to celibacy, and affirming the preferability of Christian mutual aid and charity to state intervention in support of big families. Contemporary studies of fertility cast doubt on whether practicing Catholics were any less likely to use birth control than other Italians.[40] However, the encyclical itself, thick with 103 citations from the Old and New Testaments, was widely regarded as giving firm theological foundation to state policy. The Church's position, actively propagated by the clergy, the diocesan press, and the Catholic laity certainly contributed to the blackout on sex information.

But the ways to sexual knowledge are myriad: the dictatorship's noisy journalistic campaigns against the "horrible crime" may have had an unintended effect, as Gaetano Salvemini once remarked, of teaching "many innocent souls that one could enjoy oneself without paying the price."[41] Perhaps wily urban youths were adept at such sub-rosa readings of propaganda texts, and young men certainly suffered less from the sex blackout, if only because they did not risk becoming pregnant. Moreover, tradition had that, before marriage, boys were to acquire a sexual education from prostitutes or from frank talk with older men. But for most girls, repression seems to have compounded the private inhibitions of parents and tutors. At best, in the all-girl environments of boarding schools, as remembered by the Turinese novelist Lalla Romano, ignorance fed the romantic insouciance of well-protected girls. "What are they doing? Is he biting her chin?," she mimicked her friend Gangi's bemusement as she puzzled over the passionate kiss between a movie-star couple reproduced in close up on a tabloid cover.[42] But where premarital sex was both exceptionally tempting and threatening, ignorance made young women terribly vulnerable. For the inquisitive teenager of the 1930s, with aspirations to be modern, the effort to pierce the censorship surrounding sexuality could be endlessly frustrating. The experience of peasant women from the Piedmontese hill areas, recounted in Nuto Revelli's poignant oral histories, suggests a still more bitter legacy: Angela, born in 1918, reflected that "many marriages failed because we knew little or nothing." Everything was a sin, sex, dancing, "washing certain delicate parts of your body": "We grew up knowing nothing about sex or learning things the wrong way. It isn't true that we in the countryside understood because we were close to nature. Yes, we saw the animals [do it], but we didn't understand."[43] Like Angela, numerous other women recalled knowing nothing about menstruation until it came, hardly anything about male sexuality until the first night of their marriage, and little about birth itself, except for children's myths about finding babies under cabbages, until they actually delivered. Even among the self-consciously modern working class of Turin, there were women who recalled "almost with rancor" that nobody told them about the facts of life; they had been abandoned to themselves, ignorant, "like beasts," about their reproductive functions.[44]

Whether official bans on contraceptive information actually succeeded in promoting fertility among the sexually active is difficult to establish. According to an admittedly imperfect sample from 1930s Trieste, 40 percent of the sexually active practiced some check on fertility (more than in the United States at the time). In Turin a young inspector for the state maternity fund found that of the 68,000 working women he investigated the "near-totality" engaged in "neo-Malthusian practices."[45] Given the inaccessibility of contraceptive information, however, antifertility measures were taken haphazardly, and often after intercourse, if not after conception. Condoms provided the one sure method available (aside from abstinence). However, the single national factory producing them, Hatù, did so mainly for the armed forces, and by law advertising was limited to highlighting their prophylactic functions. Consequently, the product was associated with extramarital sex, prostitution, and venereal disease.[46]

Indeed, the main effect of the repression of information was to increase the acceptance of abortion. When abstinence or coitus interruptus failed, and douches and other postcoital home remedies proved futile, women resorted to abortifacients: emetics, irrigation with herbal infusions and chemical irritants, hair pins, knitting needles, scraping, and probes. They might range in cost from 400 lire for a douche or 600 lire for a probe from a so-called angelmaker to as much as 1,000 to 2,000 lire for a medical intervention—a huge sum considering that an average monthly wage for a *male* industrial worker was only 300 lire. Women, however, almost always paid for their abortions, either from their own wages or by scrimping on the household budget, pawning objects, or drawing on savings from small domestic industries. And whether carried out by the hack or the medical professional, all abortions were "backstreet." They thus carried extra risks of disabling infection, permanent health damage, and death. [47]

To check what officials surmised to be a major cause of fertility decline, the dictatorship sought to rally doctors, midwives, and socal welfare staff to prosecute abortion. The penal code of 1931 prescribed heavy penalties for illegal abortion, including jail terms of from two to five years for anyone procuring or abetting it and from one to four years for any woman performing an abortion by herself. During the 1930s, the regime considered more draconian measures, such as to require that all pregnancies be registered, though it was obvious that precisely those pregnancies most likely to be aborted would escape official notice. Administrative decrees issued in 1935 by the National Public Health Office *(Direzione generale della sanità pubblica)* ordered doctors to report cases of procured abortion; a few brave physicians denounced these rulings as clear violations of article 365 of the Criminal Codes, which honored the Hippocratic oath. [48] The many institutions managed by Church personnel may have complied. Many individuals apparently did not if, at the end of the decade, an Italian magistrate was correct to speak of a veritable "industrialization of abortion" in some northern cities. This was abetted not just by female companions and neighbors but by midwives, doctors, and provincial medical officials. In Turin it may even have had the complicity of magistrates: when chastised by central government officials for dismissing cases or handing down reduced penalties, local judges justified their lack of prosecutorial zeal on the grounds that firm evidence was difficult both to obtain and to corroborate. [49]

As abortion increased, society's perception of it seemed to change. In prewar Italy, it had been considered a bourgeois vice; the lower orders, meaning the city poor, were said to resort to infanticide or to abandoning their unwanted babies. Now it became a widespread urban working-class practice. Once a secretive act, concealed in the private spaces occupied by women, it now became clandestine and was defended against public scrutiny. Earlier it had been practiced as a necessity, conducted without much ideologizing around the act. Now, as the subject of official debate and penalized by Church and State, it became fraught with public meanings. To vindicate choice involved the violation of legal codes, official commands, and religious precepts. Thus, the decision to abort might become the occasion to protest oppressive official intrusions into private life: "Let the priest feed the kid, if he's so keen on making babies," "Mussolini's not the one who has to raise it," was how some women rationalized their conduct in the face of official proscriptions. Among the secularized working-class women of Turin, abortion came to be treated as a therapeutic physiological act, as if it were part of modern maternity practice: the women referred to it as a sort of induced menstruation or relief-giving hemorrhaging, in the face of which the objections of a spouse, the injunctions of religion, or the penalties of the state were irrelevant.[50] Whether it was immoral was also ambiguous. In Church doctrine, the place of abortion in the hierarchy of sinfulness was not easily calculated, given that any sexual act other than for procreation was ungodly—be it onanism, sodomy, or whatever. Given the bleak conditions in which most women chose to have abortions—and some had them repeatedly—guilt might be assuaged by a simple moral argument: in the face of dire necessity, God, too, preferred the well-being of the living to the existence of the unborn.

Modernizing Motherhood

There is an ugly, if common, paradox in the lives of twentieth-century women, namely, that state repression of birth control has often gone hand in hand with state efforts to modernize maternity practices. Women who lose by the former might gain from the latter, although in both instances, arguably, their capacity to control their own bodies has been violated. In fascist Italy, the dictatorship, despite itself, fostered illegal abortion—the most humanly wasteful form of antiprocreative measures. At the same time, it took many steps to reduce infant mortality and improve the health and welfare of pregnant and nursing mothers. The interwar years thus saw not only a proliferation of state-sponsored family welfare services— including the National Agency for Maternal and Infant Welfare and three party-run schools to train social workers—but also the professionalization of the practice of pediatrics (the order being refounded in 1932), obstetrics, midwifery, and even wet nursing.

In the process, Italian social welfare services acquired a peculiarly fascist cast. In liberal states, as the French sociologist of the family, Jacques Donzelot, points out, the growth of state responsibility for the social welfare of the family was tied to the extension of political rights.[51] In fascist Italy, by contrast, it went hand in hand with their suppression. Since there were only internal bureaucratic mechanisms for referring the requests or complaints of clients, or for monitoring the quality of service, and since the policymakers were almost exclusively male, the provision of welfare services was stamped with the arbitrariness of power. This power was exercised with a clear-cut ideological bias against women. In the interests of promoting the race, the welfare of the mother was subordinated to that of the infant. Thus while propaganda insisted that, by nature, women were fulfilled only in motherhood, government social services cast doubt on whether women were naturally the best nurturers, especially when the women were unwed, delinquent, or simply impoverished. And while propagandists idealized biological destiny, medical professionals and social workers silently undercut the control traditionally exercised by female kinship and community networks over childbirth and infant nurturing.

This pattern of relegating women to domestic duties, while diminishing their authority in the family, will come as no surprise to anybody familiar with how modern welfare states operate.[52] What distinguished fascist Italy is perhaps only that the state's claim to promote a modern maternity was so vigorous, while government services were so unevenly administered. The fascist family welfare services offered the allure of the modern, without its underpinnings. They set new standards, interfered with old customs, and stigmatized traditional practices. Yet they failed to provide the wherewithal for women to feel empowered by a modernized maternal craft—either as the providers or as the beneficiaries of new services. Italian mothers of all classes were thus made to feel inadequate, anxious, and dependent.

The institution pivotal to modernizing the maternal craft was the National Agency for Maternity and Infancy. Founded on December 10, 1925, with enthusiastic support from Catholics, nationalists, and liberals, ONMI's roots lay in prewar social reformism rather than fascist pronatalism. Since the turn of the century, socially conscious doctors such as the pediatrician Ernesto Cacace and the Roman obstetrician Tullio Rossi Doria, had urged the government to adopt measures to curb the very high rates of infant mortality. Much of the blame for infant mortality went to the age-old practice of abandoning unwanted, often illegitimate, infants on the public *ruota*. First consigned to the hodgepodge of Catholic charitable institutions, the infants, if they survived the crowding, wet-nursing, and dirt, were handed over to step-families, whom they eventually supplied with cheap labor. In 1907 the *ruota* was abolished and the orphanage system began to be reformed.[53] But not until World War I, when illegitimacy rates soared and the catastrophic frontline death tolls aggravated concerns about population replacement, did the government undertake to reform the infant-care system. Later, the commission, which had been established in June 1922 by the last liberal premier to formulate a plan for a national agency, was revived by Mussolini's cabinet. Using the internationally respected Belgian *Oeuvre* as a model, the new commission proposed a semipublic national agency dedicated not only to infant care (as in Belgium) but to the welfare of mothers as well. After a slow start, hampered by confusion about its aims, a plethoric committee structure, and untrained volunteers, ONMI was reorganized in 1933. Increasingly active thereafter, especially in the 1940s and 1950s, and continuing to 1975 when it was dismantled as a "useless agency," it operated with central government allocations and local funding. During the 1930s, it also relied on private donations and on the assistance of volunteer *patronesse*, medical and social service workers, and members of the fascist women's groups. Never did it seek to take over or compete with Catholic institutions as was certainly the intention of its liberal progenitors and perhaps its fascist proponents as well.[54]

The main focus of its services were women and children who fell outside the normal family structure. These were typically unwed mothers, impoverished widows, and married women whose husbands, because they were disabled, jailed, or otherwise absent, could not support them. It also proposed to look after the welfare of children up to age five whose parents were "unable to give them the care necessary for a rational upbringing" and to care for abandoned children up to age eighteen. In the words of the medical jurist Attilio Lo Monaco-Aprile, the State intended to act whenever "family action was inexistent, inadequate, or inappropriate."[55]

In a society such as interwar Italy's, in which local organizational traditions and social mores were so diverse, ONMI's goals were quite unrealizable, in part because the agency depended so much on voluntary initiatives. Indeed, it was often criticized for overextending itself and for passing from preventive to "therapeutic" measures. In the 1930s, these mainly took the form of distributing layettes, organizing soup kitchens, and setting up nurseries for desperately poor mothers and children.

ONMI's claims to innovation largely rested on its services for unwed mothers and infant care. The former was also its most controversial mandate. Italian illegitimacy rates were estimated at a quarter to a third of live births. While these seem quite high, they were at least partly caused by changing marriage customs. Until 1929 religious unions were not recognized under civil law. Consequently, in strongly Catholic regions like Julian Venetia, the offspring were regarded as illegitimate until they were legally recognized by their fathers. In other areas, such as anticlerical Emilia-Romagna, where about one-third of births were conceived out of wedlock, common-law marriages were normal, especially among the socialist and anarchist working classes.[56]

The marital history of Rachele Guidi, Mussolini's wife, had a familiar course. Their first child, Edda, was born at Forlì on September 1, 1910, after a year of cohabitation; since their union was not official, the baby was registered as his, a fact that subsequently led to gossip that Edda was the natural daughter of the Russian-born socialist Angelica Balabanoff, a companion of Mussolini during his socialist days. The couple married only on December 17, 1915, after Mussolini had been called up for war-time service and while he was convalescing from a bout of paratyphoid. Affection aside, the need to assign Rachele his service pay and, possibly, a survivor's pension must have been a consideration. Meanwhile, by a mistress, Ida Irene Dalser, he had a son, born in November 1915, whom he legally recognized on January 11, 1916. But it was not until a decade after his civil marriage, on December 29, 1925, that Donna Rachele and the Duce contracted a religious marriage. By then two more children had been born. Although personal reasons may have played some part in the decision—Rachele was bereaved by the recent death of her mother, who had lived with her, and Mussolini had just escaped the Zaniboni assassination attempt—the initiative was suspiciously opportunistic: the decision was entirely Mussolini's, it followed the moralizing conventions of the day, and it was treated as a gesture of goodwill toward the Catholic Church. Not until 1929, after the birth of his last child, Anna Maria, did the Duce's lawful wife and children move in with him at Villa Torlonia in Rome.[57]

However, in the many cases in which the mother was unwed, cut off from her family, and destitute, the infant risked being abandoned or neglected. Illegitimate children ran a significantly greater chance of dying of enteritis, bronchitis, and pneumonia in infancy than did legitimate children. These risks to infant welfare were notably increased as fascist laws made it harder to obtain abortions.[58] State intervention on behalf of illegitimate babies thus had a double scope: to promote population growth and well-being and to propagate the ideal of the conjugate family in which the father occupied the pivotal role. Indeed, ONMI's undertaking was closely related to efforts by reformers and women's rights advocates to revise the family codes to recognize "natural fatherhood," along with "natural maternity," by allowing paternity suits, equalizing inheritance rights, and otherwise ending all legal distinctions between legitimate and illegitimate offspring.

This was a highly charged campaign, for it called into question the powers of the state before the family and conventional notions of morality, not to mention children's rights. The ex-socialist Regina Terruzzi was a real gadfly on this issue. Her own son, Paolo, had been born out of wedlock in 1895, and this persistent and courageous woman had managed to have him legitimized by royal decree on August 23, 1913. To do so, she had cited articles 197 and 201 of the old civil codes, according to which the king himself, acting in loco parentis, could confer on a person all legal rights. As Terruzzi would remonstrate Mussolini in impassioned letters, books, and petitions, the existing laws were mean-spirited as well as unreasonable and costly. They caused illegitimate offspring to be abandoned to the care of the state. As government services on behalf of children grew, the law's effects became more inhumane. For a boy to have "child of unknown" stamped on his birth certificate—whence to be transferred to his school records, ONB or youth group registration, work passbooks, and military service cards—was a neverending cause of embarrassment and bias. If the laws were not soon going to change, Terruzzi reasoned, the state should at least show more respect for unwed mothers by substituting "natural" or "nubile" for the belittling term "girl-mother." Another way to mitigate the current law's effect, Terruzzi suggested, was to have town registrars record "John Doe" (Giovanni Fini) as the father or simply note "father dead." In sum, any subterfuge would do to avoid the dreaded words *figlio di ignoto*.[59] Other critics argued that to refuse to allow women to sue former companions for child support, for fear of embarrassing their legitimate families, was a legally absurd and openly discriminatory position: young women were compelled to recognize their offspring to obtain public assistance. The hard-nosed Teresa Labriola went even further by giving a eugenicist twist to the old belief that "love-children" were specially endowed: to improve Italy's racial stock, the state should free the family from "an excess of arbitrariness"and promote "new, more rational qualities". This meant that paternity searches had to be accepted.[60] In the end, however, neither eugenicist arguments nor sad accounts of personal humiliation and hardship succeeded before the Catholic Church's adamant defense of the integrity of the legitimate family. The new family codes allowed children who were born out of wedlock and recognized by their fathers equal claims on his inheritance. For the rest, the state intended to maintain "tutelage over abandoned infants . . . and encourage the formation of pseudo-family relationships based on ties of human solidarity."[61]

Given the law's irrationality, ONMI was thus charged with wide-ranging responsibilities toward unwed mothers and their offspring. The first step was to prevent unwed mothers from aborting or giving birth under clandestine conditions. In the three months before birth, the agency provided free checkups and modest financial support. In some cases, it kept young women in hospices. It also reimbursed clinics if, as the agency always urged, the births occurred there; this method of reimbursement was used to ensure that the clinic's quest for payment might not lead to scandals or reprisals disturbing family peace.[62] The next step was to get the young women to nurse their babies, the logic being that if they did so, they would not be as likely to give up the child. The third was to have the child recognized by the father, so as to obtain support for it, and if the father was unwed, to settle the couple in marriage. The feminist reformer Olga Modigliani, whose activities on behalf of unwed mothers long antedated the foundation of ONMI, explained this aspect of the agency's operations by citing the example of an unwed fifteen-year-old mother taken in by an ONMI hospice in Rome. Her affection for her child's father, who was a young city guardsman (guardia metropolitana), was reciprocated. But the couple was unable to marry without the company commander's permission, which was not forthcoming because the girl's family was not considered to be "moral." By acting in loco parentis and vouching for the girl's good conduct, the ONMI president obtained permission for the marriage to take place.[63]

Combining persuasion with monetary incentives and recourse to legal sanctions in the event the mothers proved recalcitrant or the fathers demonstrably irresponsible, ONMI carried out the Duce's command "to strengthen family ties to the greatest degree." Every year after 1927, it claimed to have prevented thousands of cases of infant abandonment by coaxing mothers to keep their offspring, findings jobs for the needy, pressing the parents to legalize their illegitimate unions, and filing paternity suits on the mothers' behalf. The agency's real success is harder to determine. At the very least it reinforced the tendency to legitimate irregular unions. By the early 1930s, about 77 percent of all illegitimate children were recognized, whereas on the eve of the Great War, the figure was estimated at 62 percent.[64] In any case, government social services fostered a more comprehending, if legalistic, attitude toward unwed mothers. In the name of social hygiene and the higher interests of the race, the regime defended itself against rancorous public criticism, fed by Church animosity, against policies that seemed both to distribute government largesse unequally and to reward wanton female behavior.[65]

ONMI cast an even wider net on behalf of infant care. By 1940, it oversaw a network of 9,617 institutions, including 167 specially built centers, or case della madre e del bambino. It also sponsored fifty-nine "traveling chairs of child-care" (cattedre ambulanti di puericultura), each of which visited about twenty towns weekly. Their services were available to all and in regions such as Tuscany and Julian Venetia as much as 15 percent of the population obtained assistance.[66] ONMI's influence on public attitudes was even more far-reaching, for its networks involved doctors, midwives, and pharmacists, as well as local officials, in publicizing new standards for prenatal and postpartum care, infant hygiene, and nutrition. In the name of a modern infant-care culture, it promoted breastfeeding. But it also boosted the use of infant formula, by distributing free samples of Nestlé's powdered-milk product Nestogen, as well as cleansers, medicines, and baby foods. These products were pushed not only by the booming growth of Italian companies but especially by giant British, Swiss, and American pharmaceutical and food packaging industries that deployed the most modern marketing strategems available. Pediatricians remonstrated against the "craze to innovate" and the tendency to replace "the simple with the complex, artificial, and manipulated," cautioning against the overuse of medicines.[67] Whether considered as incentives to or evidence of improved child care, these innovations were costly and freighted with new anxieties about their proper usage and potential benefits.

Infant welfare improved overall in the two decades between the wars. The death rates for the first year of life declined by about 20 percent: from the very high estimate of 128.2 deaths per thousand in 1922 (the first year calculations were made using improved statistical methods) to 102.71 deaths per thousand in 1940. But the latter figure suggests that Italian infant mortality rates were still about 25 percent higher than in contemporary France and Germany. Moreover, after a sharp decline in the 1920s, the thirties seemed only to continue a several-decades-old trend, which brought down infant mortality by about 1 percent per year, with no significant change in this pattern until the 1950s. The good work of ONMI may thus have been offset by the wretched living conditions of the urban and rural poor.[68]

ONMI was also pivotal in medicalizing childbirth. By the mid-1930s, there was already a visible increase in the presence of doctors at births and in recourse to clinics. But 93 percent of all births still took place at home, and 901 out of 1,000 were aided solely by midwives.[69] Even so, the practice of midwifery was changing, becoming more professionalized, more subordinated to male medical hierarchies, and more distant from the female patients and kinship networks with which the midwives had formerly collaborated. Mussolini's wife, Rachele Guidi, told how, against her will, a celebrated obstetrician had been called in to prepare for the birth of her fourth child, Romano, which occurred on September 26, 1927. The doctor determined that it was a "difficult birth," and then nearly drove her mad with his "nuovissimi metodi." These consisted of draping white sheets over everything and intrusive monitoring. After all, she *was* the "wife of the Duce." Immediately following the birth, a furious argument broke out between the doctor and the attending midwife over who should

Bourgeois maternity: a mother with her firstborn girl, circa 1939.
(Private collection.)

A peasant mother, her first three children, and elders in Emilia, 1930s.
(Reproduced by permission of Alinari.)

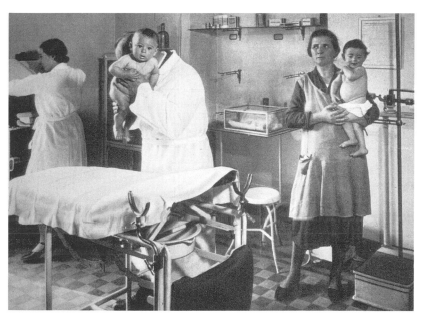

A working-class mother at an ONMI clinic in Rho, late 1920s. (Louise Diel, *Das
faschistische Italien und die Aufgaben der Frau im neuen Staat* [Berlin: Hobbing
Verlag, 1934]. Reprinted courtesy of the Butler Library, Columbia University).

be credited in the press release, the midwife claiming that her services, too, deserved some mention. The racket stopped only when Rachele interrupted: "Really, it was I who brought my son into the world" ("Mi sembra, di essere stata io, veramente, a mettere al mondo mio figlio").[70]

Similar struggles over control of the birthing process were being carried out in more humble abodes, as Nancy Triolo found in her finely wrought ethno-historical research on Sicily.[71] In the Islamicized society of the island's west, where women lived in cloistered domesticity exercising uncontested power over household matters through strong consanguineal networks, the midwife was an important figure. Not only did she attend at birth, aided exclusively by female relatives, she also introduced the baby into a public, male society, by carrying it in the baptismal procession. By the end of the Great War, as Pirandello's bitter-sweet short story told, the venerable Donna Mimma of the backwater villages, with her little blue headscarf and great fringed black shawl, her store of folk wisdom, and her firm hold on local affections was being displaced by the emancipated young "Piemontesa," who "seemed a boy in a skirt, with her hands stuffed in her pockets" (*pareva un maschiotto in gonnella, mani in tasca*) and was freshly licensed to practice obstetrical science.[72] However, under fascism, as the government sought to discipline errant practitioners and use them to promote its family policy, midwifery was more thoroughly professionalized. In 1926, when all professional groups were being organized in national syndicates, the newly founded Undersecretary of the Corporations ordained the establishment of the Fascist Midwives Union. This group was charged with representing the profession's interests and overseeing a national registry, enrollment in which was required to compete for public posts. From 1934 the corporation published *Lucina*. In 1937 it changed the old-fashioned sounding *levatrice* to the more scientific sounding *ostetrica*. Yet as it sought to legitimate its position in the male-dominated medical hierarchy, the profession's powers actually diminished. On the one hand, midwives were barred from carrying out treatments that doctors practiced increasingly commonly, namely, forceps deliveries, episiotomies, and the administration of drugs; on the other hand, they grew distant from their female patients, even while they appropriated decision-making powers formerly embedded in women's networks. In Sicily midwives brought the practices of male-dominated medical science into the household, at the same time as they were enjoined from partaking in the baptismal ceremonies. The end result was a constricting of female authority within the household—a phenomenon that was especially hurtful in Sicilian society, given the little visibility and power that women had outside the home.[73]

Fascist Fatherhood

In emphasizing that fascism redefined the social meaning of maternity, we should not forget that it also assigned new meanings to fatherhood. In Mussolini's world, children were proof of masculinity, much as in Sicily, blood on the nuptial sheets demonstrated the bride's virginity. This conviction was tied to the Duce's repudiation of the "onanist" D'Annunzio, Mussolini's old political rival who, until his death in 1937, was an ever-troubling figure for his powerful claims on the male as well as female imagination. There was a touch of Andrea Sperelli in all Italian men, the Duce suspected. Like the protagonist of the poet's celebrated *Piacere*—who stank of "sperm, of [female] thighs"—Italian men confounded heroism with eroticism, and were impotent before the call for real military or political action. Male sensuality, like female eroticism, had to be exorcised; it was unproductive, if not subversive. Having sex was another matter. In youth, the new fascist man displayed raw male energy in daredevil sports, including the conquest of the female animal; in maturity, he begat quantities of children and boasted of his near insatiable sexual desire. The regime thus joined the Church to denounce coitus interruptus as an abhorrent "fraud" against the laws of nature, God, and the state. Bologna's self-styled "demographic" mayor *(podestà)* A. Manaresi made explicit the Duce's "lofty admonition" to reproduce: "Screw and leave it in! Orders of the party." ("Dunque chiavate e lasciatelo dentro! Ordine del partito.")[74] By the 1930s, most of the fascist old guard had become family men. The Duce himself was the "solicitous and affectionate" father of five. For the youngsters of the "generation of the Littorial," who held aloft the heroic ideals of "fascism of the first hour," Mussolini "the father" likely had little appeal. But for the old guard, family came first, though this did not preclude well-publicized amorous dalliances on the side.

Despite all the talk about women being the pillars of household, the distribution of financial rewards for families presumed that it was the men who decided to start families, and it was they who determined the size. This belief underlay one of the earliest and the most loudly protested of the regime's pronatalist measures—the tax on bachelors. First enacted with the Royal Decree of December 19, 1926, and constantly revised thereafter, it taxed all eligible men from twenty-six to sixty-five, using a sliding scale to make the youngest and most eligible pay the most, in addition to deducting a flat rate of 25 percent from gross income. Priests, men certified as infirm, and servicemen on active duty were exempted. The tax was high—by 1936 a thirty-year-old bachelor had to pay double the normal income tax, plus 155 lire per year. The measure had a typically punitive and homophobic dimension. The Fascist party must act as "an irresistible moral force," as the churlish Carlo Scorza, the *ras* of Lucca put the issue: "Society today despises deserters, pimps, homosexuals, thieves. Those who can but do not perform their duty to the nation must be put in the same category. We must despise them. We must make the bachelors and those who desert the nuptial bed ashamed of their potential power to have children. It is necessary to make them bow their foreheads in the dust."[75]

The tax may have led couples to regularize common-low arrangements, and it might have offset the tendency to postpone nuptials out of fear of military call-ups in the mid-1930s and because of economic vicissitudes. But there was no rush to the altar. Non-marriage remained socially acceptable for men, not least of all because it testified to filial devotion to mothers as well as to mothers' dedication to their aging, if emotionally and materially dependent, sons. In 1936 8.3 percent of Italian men aged fifty or over were bachelors, and fairly late marriages remained the norm—the median age for marriage from 1936 to 1940 was 28.3 for men (compared to 24.9 for women), almost a year later than the median age in the early 1920s.

Not surprisingly, the tax met with approval from women. How could it not when all other laws were so biased in favor of men? As in Germany and France, marriageable women in Italy vastly outnumbered men, at least in the late 1920s, because of wartime losses. The tax also seemed reasonable to women because its returns allegedly went to pay for ONMI.[76] But in supporting the so-called tax on egotism, women failed to recognize that the arguments used to stigmatize male celibacy as deviant, parasitical, and antipatriotic behavior were similarly deployed against spinsterdom.

The fiscal and monetary incentives awarded to big families were also reinforcing of male power to determine family size. These took the form of tax breaks which, as stipulated by the law of June 14, 1928, phased out payments for families with six or more children, family allocations, marriage loans, and birth bonuses.[77] Insofar as such subsidies failed to compensate for the real expenses of having children, they certainly could not counteract the economic and social reasons for *not* having them. In Nazi Germany marriage bonuses and birth prizes apparently spurred couples both to marry and to have their first child, but those awards were more generous than the Italian allotments.[78] Moreover, in the late 1930s Germany had full employment, whereas Italy's unemployment was high, and inflation was rising. In addition, Italians faced an insecure future as the Duce ordered troop call-ups for the Ethiopian war in 1935, sent matériel and men to support Franco's rebels against the Spanish Republic in 1936–37, and launched the conquest of Albania in 1939.

Maternity in Service to the State

Unable to offset the costs of big families, the dictatorship sought to make childbearing seem as if it were a service to the state. Ultimately, the chief compensation offered was public recognition. Yet giving a general resonance to the intensely individual and private experience of procreation was not an uncomplicated process. Private feelings do not always have the desired public echo, especially when, as in Italy, opinion was clearly divided about the desirable family size. Against the few who were openly sympathetic to arguments on behalf of *quantities* of children, there were the many who were primarily concerned with the *quality* of their upbringing. These fundamentally different conceptions of maternity could not readily be reconciled within the regime's public cult of motherhood.

This groping for public meaning is nowhere more visible than in the dictatorship's celebration of Mother's Day. It was not until late 1933 that a special day was even set aside. By contrast, Catholics, at least in some cities, had already been celebrating Mother's Day for several years, on March 25, the Day of the Annunciation. The date the fascists contrived was December 24, Christmas Eve—a choice that exploited the Catholic cult of the Virgin Mary. The dictatorship thereby associated Italian motherhood not just with the Mother of God but with the Virgin's chastity, the joyous birth of Jesus, and the awful sacrifice of her only son. That no effort was made to establish Mother's Day as a commercial holiday is puzzling. Unlike either the American holiday or the recently founded German Mother's Day, the Italian celebration did not enlist support from florist lobbies or candy manufacturers.[79] Nor did it mobilize millions of school children to make small gift-tributes to their mothers. Was this simply because Italian society was poor, and gift giving a luxury? The more likely explanation is that the ceremonial was intended to honor mothers in a more indirect way, as the bearers and nurturers of children, as indeed the notion of a *Giornata della Madre e dell'Infanzia* made explicit. It was an occasion to ponder the ancient Italian cult of the Mater Matuta and the self-abnegating example of the Madonna. Not by chance, the main objects of celebration were not just any mothers, but *prolific* ones. The highpoint of the first year's ceremonial was the national rally in Rome, presided over by the Duce, in the course of which the most prolific mother from each of Italy's ninety provinces was passed in review like prize breeding stock. The role call trumpeted not her name, but the number of her live births: fourteen, sixteen, eighteen.[80]

This image of maternity was discomfitting to the *patronesse* who organized the holiday. For one thing, by discriminating against the majority of women who had fewer children, it complicated organizing the ceremonial. As early as 1934, local committees devised prizes to honor merit in "raising children": in 1934 some 17,910 such prizes were distributed, whereas 4,460 were granted on the merits of numbers alone.[81] Uneasiness about fascism's brood-mare image of motherhood was manifest in fascist iconography as well. The poster maker chosen by ONMI to advertise Mothers' and Infants' Day starting in 1936 was the Triestine master Marcello Dudovich, Italy's most renowned commercial artist. Yet the women familiar in his art nouveau concoctions for the Rinascente and other leading Italian commercial emporia had been bourgeois ladies out alone; bare-armed, with twirling umbrellas and sweeping hats, their lips parted and eyes glossy with consumer desire, they were the very antithesis of fascism's conventional rendering of prolific motherhood in the shape of a comely, nubile peasant girl. Dudovich, too, seemed embarrassed by the commission: his women were literally faceless, stylized like pillars of sand, backs to the observer; their individuality effaced, they looked to the nation's future, alone or firmly coupled, husband by side, with a single sturdy child (see pages 74–75).

Fascism's cult of fertility may not have successfully promoted having children, but it was a meaningful policy for those who actually had plenty of them. The Union of Big Families, founded on March 3, 1937, was part lobby, part propaganda organization. Fascist officials used it to inform eligible family heads of government benefits, and they, in turn, learned that they might obtain low-level government posts, preferment in promotions, and a fascist salute from a high-ranking official. In cases of extreme hardship, they might also turn to Mussolini's Personal Secretariat for a handout and perhaps even be brought to the Duce's personal attention. These favors may indeed have boosted the morale of parents, though the perception remained that in urban society big families were a social disadvantage. For those few who actually had children in pursuit of public honor and who, perhaps, even recorded the New Era on the occasion of their infants' baptism (naming the boys after Benito himself, or calling them, as he did his own, by the strong-sounding names of the Third Rome—Italico, Bruno, Vittorio, Romano, Imperia), there were the many who thought that this behavior was foolish. The photographs of big families juxtaposed against the imagery of modern life in the fascist press always bespoke something archaic, incongruous, and comic.

But fascist pronatalism is wholly misunderstood if its intentions and effects are measured only in terms of uplifting the condition of motherhood. From the start, anxiety about declining birth rates was bound up with concern about the threat of female emancipation; pronatalism was a bludgeon against those women whose elite class origins, liberal political inclinations, and emancipated mores identified them with feminism. Fascist propaganda manufactured two female images. One was the *donna-crisi:* she was cosmopolitan, urbane, skinny, hysterical, decadent, and sterile. The other was the *donna-madre:* she was national, rural, floridly robust, tranquil, and prolific. These contrasting figures, because they bore on class-based fertility differentials and social inequalities could not but resonate among women. Middle-class women saw numerous children as an embarrassment: they further confirmed the otherness and bestiality of the lower orders. Hence, stylish women's magazines like *Cordelia, Grazia,* or *Lei-Annabella* primly avoided the issue of demographic politics, except to highlight initiatives on behalf of child care and welfare. At the same time, women of the working class, though they desired to control their fertility, regarded large families as an element of their class's strength.[82] They may have been consoled by the regime's propaganda: exhausted, pampered elites had few, weak, and mainly female offspring, and the *donna-crisi* was the female counterpart of the effete bourgeois male that the Fascist Revolution had dispossessed. But the conclusions working people drew were not necessarily those encouraged by fascist propaganda. That the "rich" had few children and the poor many caused resentment not only against the wealthy but also against a regime that tolerated such inequalities of burdens and means.

Whether a state that in general demeaned women could hope to build respect for them as mothers is indeed questionable. Official propaganda exalted women as mythic figures—"the bearers of numerous children," "the mothers of soldiers," "the procreators of the race." At the same time, antifeminist ideologies provoked the petty despotic behaviors that in authoritarian regimes are commonly turned against society's most vulnerable members. Where both state and church, official publicist and priest confessor, united in upholding the cult of maternity, a woman whose husband's notion of virility was satisfied only when she repeatedly bore him children had no public recourse. Any woman whose dress or behavior violated the norm that confined sexuality to procreative marriage could be the target of moral zealotry. Phrases like "demographic battle," "denatality," and "defense of the race" licensed those small-time intellectuals wont to scribble on about the decay of Western civilization to climax their pamphlets with lurid allusions to "female corruption" and the "moral, financial, and economic havoc" it had wrought.[83] Men with or without employment felt justified in complaining about female

HONOR MOTHERHOOD: Posters for Mothers' and Infants' Day by Marcello Dudovich. (*Pubblicità d'Italia*, 1938, nos. 17–18: 49–53. Reprinted by permission of the National Library of Florence.)

Poster for ONMI of Milan: "Put your maternity and your offspring under ONMI's protection."

Poster for the national ONMI, 1935.

Poster for the national
ONMI, 1937.

Poster for the national
ONMI, 1939.

competition, for public discourse held that female employment was unnecessary, that it caused neurasthenia and sterility, and that it obstructed fulfilling family obligations. Women subjected to sexual abuse were treated as provocateurs rather than victims: if they had aroused sexual interest, that was evidence enough that their behavior was not sufficiently maternal.

Mussolini's own conduct could only have sanctioned such displays of masculinist irritability. He was well-known for heaving himself on foreign women journalists, and he regularly spewed out misogynist asides in interviews and speeches. His high-handed male chauvinism was manifest even in routine business, as when, in the course of reviewing the daily press, he chanced across an advertisement urging women to join a local air club. Immediately, he wired the prefect of Bologna to halt the director from taking female members: "In fascist Italy, the most fascist thing Italian women can do is pilot many children." Men should do the flying: "In Italy, at least for now, there are enough of them."[84]

But let us not leave the last word to the Duce. "Long distant is the time in which women were divided into two categories: luxury objects or machines of reproduction," wrote Alex, one of scores of publicists who, in style magazines, pamphlets, and mass recreational pastimes, urged that the modern Italian woman had a right to other aspirations.[85] Admittedly, state pressure, although not changing long-term trends toward controlling fertility, shaped important institutions, practices, public symbols, and perceptions bearing on maternity. In public discourse, Italian women rarely disputed that women *were* different from men, that motherhood was their paramount social role, and that their children's well-being and welfare justified all of the sacrifices of which they were capable. Public policy was a terrible handicap. Yet Italian women were not wholly disarmed in their battle against the propaganda images and policies that represented motherhood as unrelenting self-sacrifice and subordination. The condition of being a mother could still be compatible with myriad other female duties, vocations, and ambitions—as household managers and spouses, workers, patriots, and social activists, not to mention adolescent dreamers, lovers, and thinkers.

4   The Family Versus the State

> Since the community only gets its existence through its
> interference with the happiness of the family, and by
> dissolving individual self-consciousness into the universal,
> it creates for itself in what it suppresses and what is at the
> same time essential to it, an internal enemy—woman-
> kind in general.
>
> Georg Wilhelm Friedrich Hegel,
> *Phenomenology of the Spirit* (1807)

> A nation is worth only as much as the families that make it
> up; only as much as the woman who gives her particular
> imprint to the family.
>
> Eugenia Graziani Camillucci and
> Olga Lombroso, *Nel regno della donna:
> Manuale di economica domestica* (1935)

The perfect fascist woman was a remarkable new hybrid: she served her family's every need, yet was also zealously responsive to the state's interest. On the seventh of March, 1936, when the Duce extolled the "women of Italy" for having made "every Italian family a fortress of resistance" against the League of Nation's economic sanctions, this ideal creature seemed to have sprung to life and proliferated.[1] In the weeks after December 18, 1935, scores of thousands of Italian women had followed the lead of Queen Elena who, on that "fateful" day, standing before the Altar of the Nation in Rome, had offered up her wedding ring—her "dearest possession"—to the Ethiopian war cause. Later, Donna Rachele did the same, donating the *fede* Benito had given her. Subsequently, black-shrouded war widows and mothers of the Great War's fallen rallied at Fascist party headquarters, bearing the medals of the dead. Peasant wet nurses offered gold earrings, brooches, and rings, gifts bestowed by their charges' families when the babies cut their first teeth. The Church's "brides of Christ" contributed their scanty ornaments. The unwed too: one Roman woman, Giulia De Lorenzo, who could offer but a few silver trinkets after "an austere life of renunciation and sacrifice," threw in the marriage band and two gold rings belonging to her widowed eighty-seven-year-old mother. Prompted by these self-abnegating examples, public men added their emblems of service to the drive: awards of academic distinction, political decorations, war medals, episcopal regalia. In all, 2,262 kilos of gold were collected. As fascist women exulted over these "typically" female gestures of self-sacrifice, they acclaimed their female compatriots' entry as full-fledged citizens onto the stage of national history.[2]

This rallying to the cause did indeed appear to seal a new union between Italian women, their families, and the fascist state. As wives renounced their *fedi* to pledge faith to Mussolini and mothers sacrificed their household savings and intimate family mementos, female emotion was joined to *raison d'état*, household to nation, and peaceable domesticity to fascist militarism. Along with its symbolic charge, the ring ceremony had important practical ramifications. It sparked a nationwide scrap-metal drive and gave huge impetus to enlisting ordinary women in fascist institutions. By the end of 1936, over a half-million additional women had been enrolled, including nearly 250,000 rural housewives *(massaie rurali)*. Finally, the Day of Faith forged a direct link between household management and state policy. For nearly a decade propagandists had urged Italian consumers to "buy national," and reformers had long denounced household waste. With an overriding patriotic cause before them, bourgeois ladies were prompted to dim lights, monitor prodigal servants, and sip Italian brews—ATI or Carcadè—instead of English teas. Working-class women were urged to uproot the dahlias and geraniums in their window boxes and replace them with castor plants for cooking oil. Peasant housewives were motivated to cultivate small home industries.

Yet the ring ceremony also generated unorthodox messages about the relationship between women, their families, and the state. The very gesture of trading in gold bands for cheap tin substitutes cast uncertainty on whether a woman's first obligation was to the Duce, fascism, and the nation or to her spouse, children, and kin as decreed by custom, sacred church vows, and pronatalist sloganeering. There was a patent disproportion between the sacrifices asked of poverty-stricken, bereaved women and the scant profits thereby accrued to the state treasury. Moreover, appeals to familial interest and maternal instincts easily backfired. Rallying mothers by likening "besieged" Italy to a beleaguered family, the dictatorship made the nation appear more comprehensible. The nation was the family writ large; like the family, it had to be protected against "plutocratic" bullies and molesters. But suppose the state itself became an intrusive Moloch, immolating its own children, and the Duce turned out to be an abusive and bad provider? The same logic that justified altruism on behalf of the nation could just as easily condone what fascist ideologues denounced as the family's "sacred egoism."[3] It might just as readily justify defending the family "like a fortress" *against* the state.

The Family: Public Outpost or Private Haven?

The ambiguities inherent in fascism's ring ceremony reflected deeper conflicts in the dictatorship's policy toward the family. In keeping with the totalitarian idea of "all in the state, nothing outside the state," the family was regarded as the most distant outpost of government power. Accordingly, no conflict should exist between family obligations and patriotic duty. Fascism had to expunge the bourgeois "famigliuola," with its individualistic outlook, overbearing women, and self-seeking men. In its place, the revolution would forge a new public-minded "Fascist" family, one that was "never against the State or in opposition to the national collectivity."[4] Yet the family was also a private institution. Its strength, as well as its capacity to contribute to civic well-being, derived from its power to mediate between individual needs and the complex demands of modern society. Did not the Duce himself hold that in the family women's most important function, next to bearing children, was to shield anxiety-ridden modern men from the nerve-jangling impact of mechanical civilization?[5] In a Catholic society, in which even feminists boasted of their "familist orientation" *(orientamento familiare)*, many regarded the family as the "mother cell" *(cellula madre)* of society; the family, as opposed to the state, best guaranteed the continuity of race and religion through successive generations. If the state intervened at all, it should only be to support so-called natural familial functions, and ever mindful that excessive interference might severely undermine them.

These diverse visions of the family implied differing assessments of women's role within it. Diehard reactionaries who thought the crisis of the family could be solved by driving women back into private life and by bolstering the paterfamilias's authority over unquiet wives and insubordinate children were being unrealistic, the more farsighted insisted. Fascism required "the spiritual collaboration" of wives and mothers if it was to make families responsive to calls for efficient consumption and capable of educating a politically responsive citizenry.[6] Meanwhile, emancipated Italian women, in their quest for equal rights and the protection of minors, sought to overturn patriarchal laws and customs. In the end, fascism, having pressured women to identify with the "happiness" of the family, was caught in the dilemma Hegel had foreseen in 1807; short of convincing women that it guaranteed such "happiness," the state risked forging an implacable "internal enemy."

The competing claims that made the family at once pillar of social order and private haven were hardly peculiar to fascist Italy. The interwar years were a time of great change, as the extended "producer family" of preindustrial Europe became a more nuclear "consumer family." First the Great War, then the economic vicissitudes of inflation and depression, and finally rapid political shifts took a heavy toll on families that were increasingly smaller, more urbanized, and hence more dependent on the market and on government services.[7] In the name of a new welfare politics, governments designed programs to help the family reconcile private and public functions. "Family policy," as it came to be called, thus targeted not just the "needy," meaning the poor and problem families who had traditionally been the beneficiaries of public relief and private philanthropy, but the family more generally, treating it as a primary, significant institution of the modern state.[8]

In fascist Italy the conflicts between family obligations and national duties were especially fraught with tension, and the remedies prescribed to diminish them produced contradictory results. On the one hand, fascism exalted the family, and the Duce's government was the first in Italy to make family values central to the art of statecraft. Fascist ideologues linked the crisis of the family with sexual aberrations, social conflict, and national decline. Naturally, these disorders were at their worst where there was social revolution or unfettered capitalist growth. In the Soviet Union the family had purportedly been collectivized out of existence, whereas in the United States the corrosive force of commercialism had allegedly resulted in high divorce rates, alimony suits, and racial hybridism. Fascist leaders, like their counterparts in Nazi Germany, promised to rebuild social solidarities and to restore national power beginning *ab imis fundamentis*, that is, from that "primordial" or "natural" crucible of the race which in Italy was the Latin family. In the process, they intended to exploit family loyalties against class allegiances. The family—unconflictual, ordered according to a natural division of labor between the sexes, its authority structures defined by biological destiny—prefigured the corporate hierarchies of the nation.[9]

On the other hand, the fascist regime put family life under unusual pressure. In Italy, as early as 1927, a half-dozen years before Mussolini began to rearm, deflationary economic policies coming in the wake of farm crisis exacted heavy tribute from family resources. At the very moment Italian society was becoming more urbanized and the economy was shifting toward mass production, undercutting family solidarities based on rural and urban craft communities, the regime sought to exploit family networks to contain mass consumption and to reduce demand on public services. Its policies, as shown in the previous chapter, pressed people to have bigger families, whereas commonsense family strategies argued for smaller ones. Government propaganda maintained that men alone should be employed outside the home. In reality underemployment and low wages propelled entire families into the labor market to piece together a subsistence income. The state claimed that the family was sacrosanct and indivisible, yet, in the name of the nation, the dictatorship justified every kind of intrusion: from exacting different sorts of political involvement and degrees of loyalty from husbands and wives and from male and female children, to separating them physically in the name of military preparedness.

The dictatorship thus became trapped in a paradox of its own making. Propaganda insisted on the sexual puritanism, economic frugality, and austere leisure habits usually associated with early industrialism. Meanwhile, burgeoning consumer industries, often of foreign, especially American, provenance, publicized ready-made clothing, synthetic fibers, cosmetics, household items, and processed foods, as well as the commodified sexuality typical of a modern consumer economy. Government bureaus and an expanding educational system fostered a wider awareness of national standards of civic and cultural behavior. Yet impoverished family economies did not easily permit achieving them. Propaganda boasted about government help to rebuild family life in the interest of the state. Meanwhile, fascism's every policy seemed to teach Italians that they lived in a society where true concern for their welfare could be found only among their close kin.

In principle, fascism's expanding system of social insurance and family benefits calmed these insecurities. Under Mussolini, propaganda alleged, when a mother bent over to dote on and care for her offspring, the whole nation bent with her. By the late 1930s beleaguered families could turn to an alphabet soup of governmental and party agencies: INFPS, INA, CRI, INFAIL, GIL, and the already familiar ONMI, to name just a few. Yet fascist social bureaucracies, with their byzantine complexity, frequently aggravated uncertainty rather than allaying it. The system had been largely commanded into being by political expediency, and it was grafted onto a millennial legacy of private and semiprivate Catholic and municipal charities. Working on short budgets, uncoordinated in its many parts, it was heavily conditioned by political patronage and by the self-interested philanthropy of business employers. As a result, ordinary Italians met with *particularism* in their every dealing with government social and welfare services. Welfare provisions were supposed to be universal in scope, aimed, as the British theorist of the welfare state T. H. Marshall said, to give "equal care to similar cases."[10] Yet in Italy, citizens could obtain benefits only on the basis of the strings they could pull or the power they could invoke, or according to whom or what they represented. Only within the family, by virtue of ties of blood, did they acquire the respect to which family legislation claimed they were entitled as *padri* or *madri di famiglia*. And only by moving kin-linked patronage systems were they able to maneuver their way through the labyrinthine procedures for doling out benefits. Family relations thus provided a network of help, a focus for life strategies, and a vehicle of action not provided elsewhere in Italian society.

These same policies thrust women into new roles in the fascist state. In theory fascism put woman back into the home, where, as procreator and nurturer, she contributed to the good functioning of the private sphere. However, as fascism put more pressure on the family and proposed new models for its conduct, women were called on to perform new duties. The modern side of fascism's welfare system—unemployment payments, disability insurance, and family checks—was designed to guarantee that the male, through the wage system, was the family's main provider and the chief guardian of the family's well-being.[11] However, the fascist welfare state was a composite of old and new; both bourgeois philanthropy and party social work relied heavily on female volunteers to relieve poverty, and they designated women and children as their main beneficiaries. Upper-class women thus played an unexpectedly important role in defining new models of conduct, as well as in assisting lower-class women to achieve them. In the process, they acquainted petty bourgeois and working-class women with styles of household operation that presumed bourgeois ideals of respectability and rational household management. These could not be achieved without obsessive budgeting, fewer children, and self-absorbed calculations about how to use to the family's advantage schools, welfare services and political organizations. And the more families had to rely on government services, the more they became aware of conflicts between the family's interest and state policy. Ultimately, *fascist familism*—that is, an ideology of domesticity emphasizing family togetherness, paternal authority, and unswerving female dedication to family in the interest of the party and the nation-state—was turned against itself. In its place, there arose an *oppositional familism*, by which I mean an unresponsiveness, if not resistance, to appeals on behalf of the Fatherland.

The Family as Economic Resource

The contradictoriness of fascist policy toward the family stemmed in the first place from the dictatorship's unremitting pressure on wages and consumption. This in turn led it to exploit household economic resources deliberately and to an unusual degree for a country well-advanced on the path to industrialization. Evidence to support this contention is necessarily circumstantial: in fascist Italy, as elsewhere, much was written about the importance of family life, little about the significance of the family as an economic unit. Italy's leading economist, the staunchly liberal Luigi Einaudi, offered perhaps the most authoritative testimony of the family's weight, when, arguing against state intervention abroad (and in fascist Italy as well), he claimed that Italy's ability to ride out the depression was the result of the "many oases in which movements are not fettered by the regulations imposed by experts." "Going against international planning schemes, contrary to the advice of the experts," Einaudi noted, "deep-rooted Italian healthfulness has reacted, focusing itself in the infrangible family unit." Within the small family enterprise, "away from the curious eyes of statisticians," the family head was carrying out work below competitive costs, "helped by his children, in-laws, and close friends."[12]

Like the functionaries and propagandists who exalted the artisan or farm family when they spoke of skimming off small savings, launching anti-waste campaigns, or harboring resources in the name of autarchy, Einaudi's vision of the management of family enterprise was decidedly patriarchal. Women played no identifiable economic role, at least not until the Ethiopian war. In the wake of the sanctions, there was a surge of interest: suddenly women were pivotal to the household as consumers, as well as producers, of goods and services![13] But even thereafter, arguments on behalf of the efficiently managed family economy merely clinched the myriad political and moral arguments for returning women to the home.

Whether the dictatorship would have pressed forward with such exploitative policies without believing that Italian families could bear up under them is doubtful. Much can be made about the propagandistic brouhaha around the "crisis" of the family: its shrinking size, the alleged loss of authority by the father, the housewife's malaise. And it is true that many of Italy's 9.3 million families were undergoing the changes common elsewhere in Western societies, becoming more nuclear and more dependent on the state and the market to carry out protective, educative, and recreational functions they previously had not needed or had once fulfilled themselves. In Italy, an estimated 1.2 million people moved each year in the 1930s, and more and more families came to live in towns with over 100,000 inhabitants. Family units dropped in size from 4.7 to 4.3 members between the censuses of 1921 and 1936. In the cities, craft communities, in which places of work and residence overlapped, dissolved under the pressure of urban renewal, loosening ties with extended kin and old community networks. As their needs became more complex, Italian families developed greater dependence on the marketplace and the services of a fledging, often erratic "welfare state."[14] The urban working-class family (which made up about 20 percent of all families) "doesn't shine for cohesiveness" *(non brilla come coesione),* as the Roman party functionary Manlio Pompei blustered, opening a much-bruited "inquiry" into the state of the family in 1933. Nor did that of rural laborers (which accounted for 11 percent). The landed and rentier bourgeoisie were dilapidating their family fortunes, Pompei claimed, their members succumbing to decadence. But the white-collar family (about 7 percent of the total) was the most dispirited of all. "What the eye sees, the heart grieves over": its desires being incommensurate with its means, it mistook its excessive pretentions for real needs.[15]

Still, Italian family life had preserved many of its old virtues, even these worriers agreed, especially when compared to other countries. On average, family size was still relatively big; a special census in 1928 counted at least 1.5 million families with seven or more live-born children, and as late as 1936 one-quarter of all families had at least four. Divorce was virtually nonexistent, and marriage rates, though they dropped at the onset of the economic crisis in the late 1920s, were regarded as satisfactory.[16] The family unit still performed all kinds of services: in most urban families women sewed, and they prepared and conserved many foodstuffs (to which about two-thirds of the average working-class family budget was devoted); the old women and young girls looked after the small children. Most families still lived in small towns, and 38 percent of all drew a major part of their livelihoods from agriculture. Even in urban areas, workers sometimes still cultivated small orchards, while the bourgeoisie was kept supplied with sausages, oil, and wine from family properties in the nearby countryside. Auto-consumption—the sum of goods and services generated by family enterprise and not passing through the market—was high, estimated at 30 percent of the total national product.[17]

Best of all, more than three million households were still headed by artisans, small landowners, or sharecroppers. These were the pet families of the *strapeasani,* or ruralist ideologues. Among these, the best preferred were the 25 percent who were settled in *mezzadria,* or share-tenancy arrangements. The male *capoccia* or *reggitore* was the very image of the traditional *padre-padrone:* he headed multifamily groups in which the relations between generations and sexes were strictly regulated by custom and contract, and family size stretched and shrank according to the balance between land and labor. In 1931, share-cropper families consisted on average of 7.35 members.[18] Economically self-sufficient, conservative, and often religious, they also promised to produce stock of high quality, or so proponents alleged, citing the provenance of the great leaders of contemporary times—Mussolini, the small-town blacksmith's son; Kemal Ataturk, the former shepherd boy; and Josef Dzhugashvili (Stalin), offspring of a peasant turned shoe manufacturer.

Even if the family unit was not as resilient as it formerly had been, the dictatorship could tap a rich range of familist ideologies in this overwhelmingly Catholic and still largely rural society: from the patriarchal culture of the old rural household and the cloistered domesticity of Islamicized Sicily to the modern ideology of "separate spheres" typical of the northern Italian middle-classes. The words "scrimping" and "saving," *sacrifici* and *stenti*, were familiar to all.

In practice, the regime's exploitation of family resources was socially differentiated, hitting the peasantry and urban working class hardest. This was especially visible in two fascist policies, namely ruralization and the failure to implement the family wage. Important to the regime's economic calculations was reducing dependence on foreign food imports, especially wheat, and deterring the flood of peasants into the towns where they boosted unemployment and welfare rolls and aggravated social unrest. Mussolini's anti-city campaign was first introduced in his Ascension Day Speech, when he spoke of the sterilizing influence of urbanism and the need to return to a more rural way of life. Beginning in 1928 steps taken to deport the unemployed to their hometowns and to tighten internal migration were accompanied by government support for sharecropping contracts and projects to promote homesteading through long-term land-reclamation leases.[19] The net effect was to stretch the resources of the peasant household, forcing it to make do as best it could in zones of low consumption where it was devoid of social protections and often bereft of municipal and parish relief as well. Hence, ruralization exploited the safety net of kin solidarity. It both presumed and enforced family togetherness, the beleaguered head of family drawing on unpaid female and child labor in the home, the fields, and small rural industries.

Fascist action on the issue of the "living" or "family" wage evidenced a similarly exploitative attitude toward the working-class family unit. The idea that a man should be able to maintain a wife and dependents on his earnings alone was considered crucial to building a stable life for working-class families. Before Mussolini's March on Rome, bourgeois reformers had contended as much. Social Catholics likewise supported the notion, referring to Leo XIII's contention in *De Rerum Novarum* (1891) that social justice demanded that "the wage paid to the working man be sufficient for the support of himself and his family."[20] Although a similar position had been reiterated in Pius XI's *Casti Connubi*, the issue was not bandied about in government circles until March 1937, when the Fascist Grand Council seized on the concept to advance the Duce's demographic policies. Even so, in 1938, Giuseppe Bottai, the only high-placed fascist with the mind of a planner, argued that the regime had to settle for "a politics of the possible."[21] In Italy, Bottai seemed to be saying, the family wage was a luxury. To make it a goal of fascist policy would only encourage the captive unions to press for higher wages. Italian census data clearly showed what radical economic reforms would have been needed to achieve this end: in 1931 45 percent or 4,280,000 of Italy's 9,280,000 families depended on two or more wage earners. If census takers had bothered to enumerate those many other family members, usually female, who worked part-time, intermittently, and off the books, these figures would certainly have been higher.

From the mid-1930s, ostensibly to support its demographic policies, the dictatorship started to tinker with grants of family allowances. These allotments were to be paid by state agencies and private employers to heads of household according to how many dependents they had. The measures were passed in three phases. The first was the result of an accord signed between the Fascist Confederation of Industry and the National Fascist Corporation of Industrial Workers on October 11, 1934. This was designed to prevent further layoffs in industry by cutting the work week to forty hours with no increase in hourly pay. To compensate those on reduced time who had families to support, a fund was set up with monies from employers and from workers who still labored more than forty hours a week. In 1936, as more workers were put on short-time and as state functionaries recognized the existing plan's unfairness and impracticality, a second measure was passed. The August 21, 1936, decree granted family allowances to all industrial workers, regardless of how many hours they worked, and it called for the state to share the costs with employers and workers. The third phase started with the decree of July 21, 1937, which extended family allowances to the dependents of all employees in agricultural enterprises, as well as industry and commerce.

Far from being incentives to family growth, the family allowance system was thus tied to cutting wages to substandard levels. As Alva Myrdal pointed out at the time, such measures were usually associated with depressed industries like textiles and mining: "When the wage level is near the subsistence minimum, no other form of wages than that differentiated by increases per family will give the large families any chance to survive at all."[22] Fascist Italy was able to enact such measures because the unions lacked the means to block them. The family wage, Myrdal concluded, is "a bellystrap which is drawn as close to the spine as possible." By 1940, the family allowance system added from 4 to 15 percent to daily wages.[23] But its social costs were enormous: in addition to keeping the fascist unions in their humiliated place, preventing them from bargaining for wage increases based on output, they favored male heads of household over their working wives or other family members, who though working still lived at home.

By contrast, the dictatorship was conspicuously solicitous of the family situation of the approximately 700,000 state employees (including professors) and certain categories of private sector functionaries, mainly in insurance and banking, with similar educational backgrounds, professional skills, and social pretensions. At least one ideologue, recalling the glorious city-state patriciates of Italy's golden centuries, argued that the male offspring of the striving middle-classes would furnish the cadres of a new oligarchy.[24] Their outstanding quality presumably would have compensated for their skimpy quantity, the average family size of the salaried man being just 3.65 persons, about half that of the sharecropper. The main reason for making generous estimates of the salaried middle classes' family needs was purely political. They made up the regime's primary base of political support. To keep them in proper style meant enabling them to maintain a homebody wife (and perhaps both sets of parents), to support their one or two offspring through long years of study, and to keep up middle-class appearances in housing, dress, and recreation.

Provisions on behalf of this new middle class were made accordingly. The prewar differential between wages and salaries, cut down by inflation and hard union bargaining during the "red years" of 1919–1920, was not only restored, but greatly increased.[25] As early as 1928, the state committed itself to family allowances for state employees. These were granted for wives and for children up to age eighteen and sometimes for dependent parents as well. Workers received no allowances for their wives or dependent relatives, and their children ceased being eligible at age fourteen. Unlike wage earners, salaried personnel with incomes of over 800 lire a month had insurance and disability benefits organized through funds tied to their professions; by the mid-1930s, the *casse* provided excellent and comprehensive coverage. Moreover, state employees, like private-sector functionaries, were safeguarded with housing, special bonuses, premiums, family allocations, travel discounts, recreational facilities, and sick leave beyond that provided through the normal compensation systems. By contrast, the working poor and the destitute, as we will soon see, were subjected to systems of aid that combined the Dickensian rigors of nineteenth-century British poor laws, Bourbonic munificence, and the hard-faced calculation of modern welfare state politics.

The Birth of Fascist Family Policy

Overall, fascist family policy was as grandiose in its ambitions as it was flawed in its realization. Originally, family policy, as it came to be named in the mid-1930s, was born of the fear that economic uncertainty and social worries might cause further curtailments of birth rates, demoralization to the detriment of children's health and welfare, or the disintegration of the family itself. Typically, family policies included special social welfare bureaucracies, family allowances, and tax discounts for family dependents. In Italy, according to the not very rigorous definition of the head of the INFPS (National Fascist Social Insurance Institute), Professor Bruno Biagi, family policy could be said to include everything that "defends the family institution from the assaults that elsewhere weaken and degrade it . . . from the celebration of Mothers' and Children's Day to rigorous control over movie production."[26]

In reality, about the only thing Italian proponents of a new family policy could agree on after fascism acquired dictatorial powers in 1925 was that liberal "agnosticism" was to blame for a host of family ills, from declining birth rates and illegitimacy to infant mortality and juvenile delinquency, and that these were to be corrected by the appropriate state action. Until the early 1930s, however, everything seemed up for grabs. The liberal state's 1865 Pisanelli Codes had become totally obsolescent by 1930. First, the 1919 Sacchi Laws, by giving women equal access to public office and a right to salary, had curbed husbands' powers. Then article 34 of the 1929 Lateran Accords, by giving legal status to Church-blessed unions, challenged the existing definition of marriage. Finally, the new penal codes formulated between 1926 and 1931 under the guidance of the Nationalist jurist Alfredo Rocco, by legislating around issues of family morality and honor, inclined to treat the family as a public rather than private institution. In 1931, the reform of the family codes finally commenced, a draft came out in 1936, and the first book was published in 1939. The entire corpus became law in 1942, thereafter to weigh like a great albatross on the legal emancipation of women in postfascist society.

From the outset, the codifying of issues that liberal society had regarded as matters of personal judgment was a contentious process. Practically every subject, from deciding on whom to reward for child care to revising inheritance laws, threw open to question how the institution of the family was to be situated in modern Italian society.

The Catholic Church placed itself at one extreme. Catholic ideologues mostly advocated a "private" family, though some fundamentalist thinkers, out of eagerness to restore the so-called traditional family, sometimes advocated bold measures that challenged private property itself, such as confiscatory taxes on small families, the living wage for men, and the reimposition of primogeniture and entails to keep peasant properties intact from generation to generation. In the final analysis, Catholic jurists claimed that a privatized vision of the family had won out over fascist totalitarianism. In principle, the new family codes defined the family as a public institution: it was the "fundamental nucleus of national society," the "unity and moral and economic integrity of which guaranteed national power." On those grounds, the state claimed authority to "guarantee the moral integrity and sanctity of the succession of generations." In reality, this authority was exercised in only a few cases, to safeguard abandoned or neglected children, for example. Fascist law never proposed to meddle in family affairs to the same degree as, for example, France's 1939 *Code de la famille*, with its provisions for imposing entails on rural holdings to prevent their division and sale or, worse, Nazi legislation, which having declared the family a public institution, subjected it to the Third Reich's racialist doctrines. Indeed, out of deference to canonical and private juridical traditions, fascist family law codified Catholicism's idea that marriage was sacrosanct and upheld patriarchal notions of family honor.[27]

Women's rights advocates were at the other extreme, occupying a much weaker position to be sure, though they found allies among lay male reformers. Their effort to undercut patriarchal authority by improving the legal status of women and children was largely frustrated. As the conservative cast of the Family Codes began to be known, their main consolation was that real relations were changing much faster than the laws let on. Still, women jurists were relieved that the new codes upheld the limits on marital authority sanctioned by the 1919 Sacchi Laws, curbed fathers' rights to dispose of family property, and discouraged dowrying, which, though already on the wane, was still mandated for certain categories of state servants such as military officers. They also rejoiced that articles 570 and 591 of the penal codes promised to prosecute men "for violation of the obligation of family assistance."[28]

At the same time, the dictatorship sustained and sometimes even reinforced numerous legal measures that treated women as chattels of male and family honor. Men were more likely to run away or be unfaithful, as Italy's leading female jurist, the Neapolitan Maria Laetitia Riccio, pointed out. Yet women were still punished more harshly than men on the grounds that their immoral conduct was more damaging to the family's well-being. Hence, an adulteress, at the accusation of her spouse, could, if convicted, spend up to two years in jail. But her philandering husband would be sentenced to a maximum of just one year, and then only if he had behaved so flagrantly, such as by bringing his "concubine" into the family home, as to cause public insult to his wife. The infamous article 587 of the Rocco codes sanctioned "crimes of honor"; accordingly, "whoever causes the death of a daughter's or sister's spouse or lover at the moment in which he discovers illegitimate carnal relationship and in the state of rage determined by the offense to his or the family's honor" was punished with only three to seven years; all other homicides were punished by jail terms of at least twenty-one years. Rape, too, was prosecuted as a crime of honor, and men who seduced minors went unpunished, provided the malefactor either restored family honor (meaning the honor of the father or brothers) by marrying the girl or could demonstrate that the minor had already been "corrupted."[29]

The issue of how the family was to be situated in the state was fought over not only in the legal codes but also in projects to improve aid to needy families. Nowhere as much as in prefascist Italy had there been such bountiful numbers of confraternities, refuges, pawnshops *(monti di pietà)*, foundations, orphanages, and endowments. But their benefits—as befitting the corporate and municipal social hierarchies inherited from medieval times—were typically earmarked for inhabitants of particular districts or specific occupational groups, and their operation, being a main font of local patronage, were exceptionally costly. Endeavors to reform the provision of welfare and limit Catholic undertakings, like the 1862 law setting up municipal *congregazioni di carità,* had not significantly increased central government authority, at least not until 1890, when the prime minister, Francesco Crispi, passed legislation to enhance controls by state and municipal authorities. Even thereafter, patronage remained in the hands of local elites and Church groups.[30]

The preeminent goal of the pediatricians, social workers, and experts in social medicine who led the reform of the welfare system was to make it more responsive to both national planning and family interests. These reformers were originally grouped around a score or so of specialized periodicals. Several, such as *L'Italia sanitaria, L'igiene moderna, Medicina sociale,* or *Pediatra,* dated from the golden age of liberal reformism, about 1910; others, including *Difesa sociale* (later the journal of the INFPS), *Maternità ed infanzia* (ONMI's journal), *La difesa della stirpe,* and *La rivista dell'assistenza,* originated in the mid-1920s. Practically all of their editors and contributors had at one time or another argued for stronger government intervention, the professionalization of social services, and the overhaul of private, especially Catholic, charity organizations. Initially, most had liberal, if not social democratic sympathies. However,

ever fearful of clerical reaction and having lost sympathy for reformist socialism during the war and its aftermath, they came to welcome the dictatorship's seemingly bold measures on behalf of family and especially children's welfare and enthusiastically supported the professionalization of their craft under the aegis of the corporate order.[31]

In their quest for state intervention, Italian reformers found allies among women's rights advocates. In common with their male colleagues, they wanted to apply modern scientific practices to advance children's and mothers' welfare. Some were long-time leaders in social work, such as the politically prominent patrician Daisy di Robilant, who became ONMI's representative for Rome and was the founder and director, with Enrico and Olga Modigliani, of Rome's *Centro assistenza illegitimi*. Others were medical doctors: the founder of *Sua maestà, l'igiene* was Elena Fambri, a one-time feminist and well-known Roman pediatrician. The Piedmontese-born Maria Diez Gasca, too, was an exceptionally versatile doctor; her main field was social work but she also practiced in home economics and in the application of psychotechnics to women workers. There was at least one former socialist, Gina Giannini, a lawyer who founded the *Rivista d'assistenza* in 1927. Along with her husband, Cesare Alessandri, once a leading maximalist socialist, she wrote prolifically on family welfare issues. In 1932 she also advanced the idea of a Charter of Maternity. Like regime's Fascist Labor Charter of 1927, which laid out rights and responsibilities in the corporate state, this would have recognized "maternity as a national duty, supervised by the state inasmuch as the nation's fortunes hinge on its degree of development."[32] Teresa Labriola, true to her totalitarian conception of state power, was the most assertive advocate of the state's right to eradicate "anarcoid individualism," by which she intended male irresponsibility. In the interest of the "ethical" fascist state, laws needed to be enacted to punish the seduction of minors, regardless of whether the minor's "morality" was suspect, prevent fathers from abandoning children born out of wedlock, and protect against the dissipation of family goods by wastrel male heads of household.[33]

In their effort to build a comprehensive system of social services, these reformers, male and female alike, constantly had to contend with and were often frustrated by the fascist hierarchy. Under fascism, expertise won out only when it was politically opportune. The Swedes and the British followed the principle "Don't legislate before you investigate" before they embarked on family legislation in the 1930s. Standing parliamentary commissions and blue-ribbon citizens' committees reviewed poor laws and advised on population policy.[34] But Mussolini had no patience with complicated policy issues, especially if their resolution called for big budget outlays. Typically, measures regarding demographic policy were rushed through the Fascist Grand Council with little or no study except that required to avoid egregious legal inconsistencies. They then passed into the code books by decree-law, subject to further revisions and elaboration. Almost invariably when a service had been set up or significantly upgraded, its chief was duly praised for his service to the regime and shunted aside for a more tractable political appointee.

Moreover, the Duce wanted social policy on the cheap; in the 1930s especially, this resulted in improvised programs, geared to the moment, the political payoffs for which were easily calculable. Hence he favored demographic prizes, awarded in cash or goods, notwithstanding the timidly voiced opposition of persevering bureaucrats and family policy advocates. "The rhythm of demographic decadence has accelerated dramatically," he wired his prefects on January 25, 1933, after reviewing the latest census data. Denouncing once again "liberal agnosticism," he put in a plug for ONMI and announced a new watchword: "maximum of births—minimum of deaths" ("massimo di natalità—minimo di mortalità"). He also cited three examples for emulation: Novara's fascist *Federale* for granting a prize of 1,000 lire to each of the first fifty blackshirts married that year; Genoa's Institute of Popular Housing for having reduced rents for newlyweds; and the Rinascente department store's *dopolavoro* for offering its staff free honeymoon trips.[35]

Improvisation and personal patronage were similarly combined in the Duce's annual convocation of prolific couples to Palazzo Venezia. Every year after the first occasion, in 1933, eligibility rules were further redefined, as befitting the lotterylike cast of the event. By 1937 there were enough dos and don'ts to fill a small primer.[36] The basic criterion was a minimum of twelve living children. However, offspring who had died in war or for the national cause might be counted, but not under any circumstances would illegitimate offspring be included. State employees were ruled ineligible because they received prizes through a separate system. Couples married solely in civil ceremonies were excluded. Of course, all candidates had to be screened to determine their political loyalty. Meanwhile, the jackpot was greatly enriched. In 1933 ONMI's budget-minded chief administrator Fabbri urged Mussolini's staff to award no more than 2,000 lire: "You can't imagine how happy those good women will be." But Mussolini wanted 3,000. By 1935, the Duce was doling out 4,000 lire, in addition to a 1,000 lire insurance policy. These were quite extraordinary sums, well surpassing a skilled worker's entire annual income.[37] The winners were also encouraged to further their family's interests by availing themselves of government patronage. By the mid-1930s, many of the several scores of couples arriving in Rome carried petitions on behalf of immediate family members, relatives, or friends. Their requests—for housing, increased subsidies, licenses for wine or tobacco shops, and most commonly for jobs—almost always lay outside the purview of ONMI, which was in charge of the event. By passing on their requests to the proper authorities, the agency acted as the prolific mother's entry into the state patronage system.[38]

Italian Catholicism presented at least as formidable an obstacle to the lay reform tradition as did the Duce's noblesse oblige. From the outset of the dictatorship, Catholic ideologues were skeptical about enacting reforms to safeguard the family, fearing they would only abet impious calculations of "Caesar's" interest. The Lateran Accords calmed some worries, for they spelled out that the Italian state recognized the sacrosanct character of marriage, but the Pope still felt compelled to define the Church's position on welfare. In three encyclicals, "Christian Marriage in Our Day" *(Casti Connubi)*, December 31, 1930, "Restoring the Christian Social Order" *(Quadrigesimo Anno)*, May 15, 1931, and "Motion Picture Entertainments" *(Vigilanti Cura)*, June 29, 1936, Pius XI called for self-help and local and individual charitable undertakings as opposed to outright state interference. At most, state policy should aim to help the family help itself; society should always prefer private and religious philanthropy to public welfare programs. Under fascism, the Church renewed its exercise of influence through myriad religious charitable foundations and their staffs of tens of thousands of nuns, priests, and lay novitiates.

That the only truly totalitarian design for reconciling state and family interests in fascist Italy was put forward by a Catholic fundamentalist, namely, the arrogant, bright, young social scientist Ferdinando Enrico Loffredo, testifies to Catholicism's widespread influence. His often-cited, if much misunderstood, *Politica della famiglia* was a signally contentious, informed, and misogynist tract, published by the well-regarded Milanese firm Bompiani in 1938, with a flattering, if not uncritical, preface by Giuseppe Bottai. Loffredo himself, a graduate in Economic and Commercial Sciences from Milan's Catholic University, was a cultivated and well-traveled contributor to the pioneering journal of Italy's fledgling social sciences, the *Rivista internazionale di scienze sociali*, as well a member of the *Unione cattolica per gli studi sociali in Italia*, a loose grouping of young Catholic intellectuals likewise under the tutelage of Father Agostino Gemelli.[39] Fortified by Franco's crusade in Spain, willing to address the pros and cons of Nazi family policy—which by 1937 was in bad odor with the Vatican for its anti-Church and eugenicist tendencies—Loffredo purported to confront systematically the tensions between public and private interests and between state and family typical even of authoritarian states. He also intended to reconcile the Catholic position that procreation was a religious act, consecrated by marriage and pursued regardless of self-interest, with the eugenicist postulate that procreation was in the interest of the state and the *stirpe*.

The crux of Loffredo's 464-page summation of current thinking was his proposal to reconstruct what might be called a "neopatriarchal" family, the primary purpose of which was not to serve the state or a single regime but to perpetuate the race. To achieve this, the fascist state had to cease its "Manchesterian practices," forswearing all services and benefits catering to the individual. The worst offenses were the charity handouts, birth bonuses, and demographic prizes distributed in total disregard of the "family position of the individual." Loffredo also excoriated all of those fascist party initiatives, such as after-work clubs and fascist celebrations of the Epiphany *(befana fascista)*, which put politics before family life. The family unit had to internalize the goals of the state, rather than being incorporated into it. To this end, fascism had to devise a coherent "family policy," which would consist of a true family wage, taxation in proportion to family burdens, "the spiritual autarchy of the nation" to curb individualist ideologies of international provenance, and, finally, concerted pressure not only from the state but also from public opinion to drive women out of the work force and public arena. Loffredo's proposed "Family Charter," unlike Gina Giannini's Maternity Charter which promised to enhance motherhood through state aid, thus made the family unit the pivotal institution of the state, dominated by the father and organized around the mother's unremitting subordination in the household.[40]

The Arduous Quest for Aid

The outcome of these diverse and often conflicting conceptions of assistance was a peculiarly profiled family policy. Interventionist and highly bureaucratized, family welfare services had a privatistic aspect in that they relied locally on the good will of employers, Church personnel, and women volunteers. Services were universalistic insofar as the regime subscribed to the principle that all who labored were protected by the state. But they were patently unequal at the moment of their delivery. In intention services were strongly normative. In practice they operated in such an erratic and subjective way that they tolerated diversity. They were centralizing and authoritarian. Yet their operations strongly reflected the domestic ideologies of their women patrons, cadres, and clients.

More generally, family services had the Janus-faced character typical of the Italian social welfare system as a whole. There was its modern side:

this spoke the language of experts, was universalistic and accountable, as well as readily comparable, sometimes in fascism's favor, to contemporary developments in other Western states. ONMI, whatever its shortcomings, was its strongest feature, and its best profile was in the cities of north and north-central Italy, Milan in particular. Then, there was also the archaic face: its features recalled the bread and circus of Roman times, the handouts of Church princes, and the Bourbon provisioning boards set up to calm the *popolo minuto* in times of famine or political disorder and were formed out of the layers of noblesse oblige, Catholic magnanimity, and guild solidarity accreting from earlier historical epochs. Its modern aspects were best exemplified in the demographic prizes, the soup kitchens, or *ranci dei poveri*, and the allotting of a custodial job or other small sinecure; and its most congenial environment was the urban agglomerate of Italy's center and south: the rapidly growing capital city Rome, Bari, Palermo, and, especially, Naples. There, in particular, fascism abided by the rules which, as F. S. Nitti once remarked, had governed all successful parties since the nineteenth century: "The Party which wins is the Party that is at the head of the charitable institutions."[41]

Yet two characteristics were common to both the old system and the new. One was its unpredictability. All users were led to expect invidious and unequal treatment. Nor was it easy to see how patronage favored one class of recipients over another, though it surely did. Hence anybody with an unsure sense of class, or who, not being a convinced socialist or republican, did not presume that fascism was a capitalist dictatorship, discriminating as a matter of course in favor of the rich and powerful, was inclined to feel slighted and envious. The system seemed designed to discourage any sense of solidarity with others suffering from the same or similar biases. The other characteristic, as summed up in dispassionate jargon by a recent critic of the Italian social welfare system, was "fragmentation in the delivery of services" ("frazionamento dei centri di erogazione dei servizi").[42] The outcome of makeshift legislation, mediated by patronage networks and political expediency, the whole system was typified by erratic performance and lack of accountability.

The same word, "frazionamento," was used by an expert contemporary observer. Fanny Dessau was an admirer of the distinguished Weimar social worker Alice Salomon and was herself a pioneer in the field in Italy. Dessau was the first Italian to write family monographs in the tradition of the late-nineteenth-century French reformer Ferdinand Le Play. Rejecting the "hypothetical abstractions" of statistics for "flesh and bone" studies of family and individual lives. Dessau was perhaps the first Italian social worker able to comment with authority on the "interference, overlays, duplication, and uncertainty about one's own and others' authority" which "dragged on" welfare operations at the community level. In normal years in a single populous neighborhood of Rome, needy families might turn to the Dames of Saint Vincent de Paul for home care and food coupons for the destitute sick; they might also supplicate sanitary assistants who, though providing home care, were trained to inspect for faulty hygiene and tuberculosis. Meanwhile, the neighborhood *patronesse*, acting on the recommendations of the sanitary assistants, handed out clothing, food, and other necessities, while school surveillants *(vigilatrici scolastiche)* double-checked the work of local school medical officers. The patrons and patronesses of ONMI were on duty as well, together with the delegates in charge of social work from the local women's *fascio:* the latter's special charge was to ferret out children who were ineligible for the colonies of the Governorate of Rome, in order to bundle them off to the party's own summer camps. Not least of all, there were the fascist factory assistants who checked on workers in the area. During the gloomiest years of the depression, several of these outfits were crowded aside by or collapsed into the Fascist party's winter help organization or *Ente opere assistenziali* (EOA). No one was to refer clients for help until their records had been checked through the public security police or the Royal Carabineri.[43]

To obtain services from this notoriously complicated system called for persistence, cunning, and some sort of patronage. Some families were able to turn to special pressure groups such as the National Association of Families of War Dead *(Associazione nazionale famiglie caduti in guerra),* which, founded on February 7, 1924, by royal decree 230 and directed by Baroness Teresita Menzinger, widow of a distinguished World War I officer, had several hundred local sections set up to handle pension and other cases on behalf of parents, widows, and orphans of war dead. Until the death of its founder, Olga Mezzomo Zannini, in 1933, the Association among the Families of Fallen Fascists *(Associazione fra le famiglie dei caduti fascisti)* lobbied for special treatment for the survivors of the dead and for handicapped veterans of the Fascist Revolution. After 1937 the National Association of Big Families acted as a lobby as well. All other cases demanded concerted, unremitting individual effort: to locate the right office, fill out the correct form, deliver it to the appropriate functionary, and, if necessary, file suitable recourse.

In this quest, family women were the main movers. Under normal circumstances, if the male head of household fell ill, he needed the resources of his family for survival, because disability insurance covered only one-half of his wages and little in the way of medical bills. If he was unemployed—as at least a half-million men (and more women) were in the early 1930s—his power to be the chief household provider, established by the wage system, waned, and the woman became responsible for preventing the complete collapse of family resources.[44] In Italy the corporate order might thus be regarded as having perfected a new sexual division of labor: while men lined up at the employment offices, or fought work grievances before the labor courts, or hung out at the neighborhood circle, or caved in to dejected lethargy at home, women made the rounds of municipal offices, state bureaus, and private charities. For example, a mother whose child was suspected of being afflicted with tuberculosis—against which a concerted "battle" had been launched by the regime in 1927— would pass out of her neighborhood ambulatory into a long bureaucratic maze. Before 1929 she might then have been referred to a city office. After 1929 she would have found that the service had been moved to a provincial office to press the government's national campaign against TB. If her child had been born out of wedlock or if her mate had deserted her, she might seek help from ONMI or from the Governorate of Rome to send her offspring to the children's colonies for heliotherapy or a sun and air cure. Otherwise, depending on where her husband was employed, she could apply to his sick fund or to the National Fascist Institute of Social Insurance (INFPS).[45] By that time, she would easily have surpassed the five or six office visits that Fanny Dessau regarded as normal for any claim for assistance.

The working-class woman's best chance of getting help was to find a well-positioned sponsor; if she was a domestic worker, the mistress of the house might have performed this service. At very least, her employer might have commended her to the attention of the staff at the special offices set up by the women's *fasci* to assist thousands of semi-literate women through the intricacies of fascist bureaucracy. A Milanese servant's sickly eight-year-old, Rosanna, ended up in Piazza Belgioioso at the efficiently run *fasci femminili* headquarters established by Princess Trivulzio, brought there by her mother's *padrona*, Marisa Ferro. The moment the lady entered with her little charge, a graceful young attendant gently pushed aside the four or so other women who were pressing her with notes and prayers for assistance. Once acquainted with the child's needs, she wrote out the appropriate *raccomandazione* and sent them off to yet another—one hopes the proper—municipal office.[46]

Releasing aid was such an arduous process that contemporaries observed the very rapid development of a new subculture of dependency. In Agrigento, as a Sicilian landowner turned amateur social worker described the situation, women were becoming veritable "specialists in assistance";

they were so involved in making the rounds of public offices that they were rarely to be found in their shanty neighborhoods, and they neglected their households and children.[47] The worse effect, according to Dessau, was that needy people developed "all kinds of subterfuges" to survive, as well as to exploit, the chaos. Families lost "all sense of dignity and decorum" when visited by three or four social workers on the same case. By "the fourth or fifth visit," it was no wonder that "the needy person rehearses his little story, exhibits his little ills without any inhibitions." Dessau concluded by citing the British Fabians Sidney and Beatrice Webb's admonition: "Nothing, less than nothing, is given if material aid is procured at the price of moral degradation."[48]

Reforming the Home

Women were not just clients of the fascist welfare state. They also made up its main volunteer staff. This was particularly true during the depression as thousands of middle-class women were rallied to help the regime's campaign to "reach out to the people." As volunteers they were probably not especially efficient. Sileno Fabbri, ONMI's head, admitted as much (at the risk of offending the *nobildonne* and others who staffed the neighborhood committees): "The public might find voluntarism, passion, feeling at the *comitato di patronato*, but not always technical competence."[49] Given that male functionaries were frequently short-tempered, not to say abusive—and themselves ill-apprised of rule changes—this female presence made the quest for aid more humane. It may also have mitigated against the strict application of intrusive regulations practicable under more efficient systems.

That fascist family welfare services were by and large dispensed by women gave a broader scope to female domestic ideologies and visions of household reform than might be anticipated. As the first groups of women joined the *fasci di combattimento* in 1920–21, fascist leaders argued that the piazza was no place for women. Women belonged in the backlines, engaged in assistance. The male hierarchy clearly regarded even this service as subordinate and auxiliary. But female activists did not; they conceived their involvement in social work, much as they had before fascism came to power, as a means of modernizing female roles in the family and the society. In the course of their activity, they thus challenged certain prevailing notions of the family. First, they upended fascism's belief that the state came first; for women were the pillars of the family, so far as these volunteers were concerned, and the family was the pillar of the state. Second, they further exposed the class specificity of family conducts in the very process of trying to transcend it. The models of family behavior that they sought to impose, drawing on their own solidly bourgeois experiences, only highlighted awareness of the differences among women: that the salaried middle class was barely making do, the working class was experiencing severe distress, and the peasantry was patriarchal and backward with respect to urban mores.

This distinctively upper-class female ethos of reform was most visible in the practice of one form of aid, that associated with the household management movement, or *massaismo*. Unlike the state and party services organized on behalf of the family, the movement's origins lay in prefascist women's groups. Catholic associations had offered home economics courses in working-class neighborhoods since before the Great War, as had several bourgeois feminist groups.[50] In 1921, as thousands of women were pushed out of the labor force after the war, Augusta Reggiani Banfi, the head of the nationalistic Italian Woman's Association, founded APE, a mutual aid society to help middle-class women market home manufacture. The next year the republican Teresa Avila Peruzzi founded the Needle Federation. Later in the 1920s a group of Lombard women, in association with Regina Terruzzi, set up a rural housewives' organization, the main purpose of which was to prevent land flight by improving the living conditions of peasant women. Although these various groups appealed to different constituencies, they all foresaw the household adapting to changing times and regarded self-help through female networks as the best way to manage scarce household resources. Home economics, because it was organized by women for other women, was also the means by which upper class women without other political voice might legitimate the leadership of both their class and their sex over the lower orders of society.

Indeed, household reform held out a double promise for cultivated middle-class women: to exercise new leadership within their own households and to spread their "rational" managerial practices nationwide. The most prominent advocate of scientific management applied to the home was the Piedmontese Maria Diez Gasca. An industrialist's daughter trained as a doctor with a specialization in industrial medicine, she introduced this new "science" to Italy at the Fourth International Congress of Home Economics in Rome in 1927. Two of the leading speakers were the apostles of the American home economics movement, Christine Frederick and Lillian Moller Gilbreth. The latter was a particularly apt representative of its virtues. Gregarious and poised, Gilbreth seemed every bit as important as her husband Frank, the world-famed expert on scientific management, whose death in 1924 had left her in command of the family business. She was also the mother of twelve children, an enterprise that she and her spouse handled with humor and efficiency, to believe their children's charming memoir, *Cheaper by the Dozen*.[51] Like Gilbreth and Christine Frederick, whose 1913 work *Housekeeping with Efficiency* she translated, Diez Gasca had high hopes for applying rational methods to the home. This meant scheduling and timing tasks and using labor-saving devices whenever possible. In the United States the great "domestic appliance revolution" of the 1920s promised to eliminate the servant problem, at the same time as it emancipated women from household drudgery. It promised to raise standards of cleanliness and free up time for better quality child care. Not least of all, it promised to break down the socio-psychological and economic barriers between a private and inefficient realm of existence identified with women and a public and modern sphere identified with men. Consumption, Diez Gasca argued, was as important to economic growth as production; the homemaker who had grasped its "inner logic" could play as meaningful a role in retooling Italy's backward economy as her entrepreneur-husband. Not biological destiny but well-honed managerial skills inspired the modern homemaker's commitment to family and to household. In 1929, perhaps at the urging of Diez Gasca, ENIOS, the government office established the year before to promote scientific management in Italian business enterprises, founded a special monthly called *Casa e lavoro*. This was dedicated to its application in private homes. The magazine's editor, the indefatigable Diez Gasca, intended it for a middle-class public, including women whose households—like her own, one imagines—reflected a "comfortable, but not excessively luxurious existence."[52] The contributors were architects, business managers (Diez Gasca herself was married to a Turinese engineer), and industrialists, as well as women writers characterized as having "a modern outlook"—meaning egalitarian relationships with men and interests outside the home.

All told, American-style household reform models had little impact in fascist Italy. Though not at all surprising, this failure bears further comment, if only to highlight the many forces inhibiting the application of technology to domestic chores and obstructing the evolution of more emancipated family relationships. At bottom, the material conditions which made reformist initiatives at least plausible in interwar America (and Weimar Germany and Great Britain as well) were missing in Italy. On average, Italian families disposed of only about 5 percent of their income for sundries, including home furnishings (compared to 20 percent in the United States); very few were wealthy enough to purchase the battery of domestic appliances with which the modern American housewife dispatched her chores. In addition, with only a quarter of Italian families owning their own residences, investment in household plant was little worthwhile.[53] Finally, domestic labor was cheap and abundant, unlike in the United States or Great Britain, whereas gas, electricity, and labor-saving devices were costly. Significantly, Italy's consumption of electricity for the home barely increased by half in the 1930s (from 2.18 percent of the total national consumption to 3.34 percent), whereas even lower middle-class families came to employ domestic help. This may explain the lack of interest in household maintenance, which elsewhere concerned architects and reformers. In the so-called Architect's House of the 1928 Turin Triennial, which was conceived for a well-off, cultivated family of five—two parents, a girl, a boy, and the children's governess—the only indication that the household needed service were two miniscule cubicles in which the help was quartered. In the 1930 Triennial's "Electric House" which the Italian Edison Company sponsored to promote the electro-domestic revolution in Italy, there was indeed a sleek Hoover vacuum cleaner. But placed square in the center of the huge salon, it was a fetish of technological modernity and status consumption. In a society in which rags and water were basic cleaning tools, the Hoover in the living room was appropriately emblematic of most women's exclusion from an expanding social consumption.[54]

By the 1930s, that heroic pioneer of modern times, the homemaker–social engineer, had vanished from the pages of *Casa e lavoro*, and with her went the dream of making the fully modernized middle-class household central to a rationalized capitalist economy. Far from being the efficient vehicle of national development, the home was presented as a bulwark against brutalizing change. It was the proverbial haven in the storm where the neurasthenia of "today's man" was soothed away by "rest and serenity." At best, the forward-looking woman used the home to express her longing for the new: she championed a streamlined design aesthetic in reaction against the "decorative deleria" and "architechtonic absurdities" of *belle époque* interior decoration.[55] Most etiquette and home improvement manuals agreed that home economics, far from being a hard and fast science, constituted an art form practiced to keep up appearances, to present a "bella figura" in the face of the subtly shifting social lines within the bourgeoisie. As Eugenia Montinari noted in *Dea vesta*, the desire for home improvement arises out of "interior conviction, rather than instruction"; it demonstrates the many innovative ways in which women perform their tasks as "director of the household."[56]

Beneath a thin veneer of modernity, the bourgeois household operated by exploiting a hard-working servant class. The number of female domestics was calculated by government censuses to have increased from

381,100 in 1921 to 585,000 in 1936 as rural exodus and the scarcity of factory or clerical jobs produced a surfeit of young unemployed females. The mark of a *Signora* was to have a robust *tutto-fare* full-time; wealthier and more refined households distinguished cooks from maids, whereas at the lowest edge of the middle class, clerk's families hired women at hourly rates *(donne a ore)* for laundry day. The terms of employment were set pretty much at the discretion of employers, though sometimes they were made in arrangement with the girls' fathers. The mode of lodging was at the caprice of the *Signora*. If Irene Brin is to be believed here, young architects proposed "airy rooms for the service"; the *signore* "resisted, . . . arguing that collapsible beds, bunkbeds, wall beds, were ideal for maids."[57] Domestic work was so ill-reputed for its harshness, isolation, and humiliations that few went into service if they could find other work. Do-gooders tried to professionalize domestic work to make it more attractive and efficient by setting up courses for servants. But with scant results. Peasant girls seemed disinclined to train for their servitude.

The bourgeois household, far from being reformed, thus had its function as a separate sphere of social existence reconfirmed. Young couples, unlike their parents, may have enjoyed more companionate relationships, as we shall see below. But charity women still spoke of the household as their first and foremost duty, as if its position with respect to the state and society had undergone no changes whatsoever. There was one important difference, however: in the new era of fascism, once their own family duties were absolved, they codified their principles of household operation and set out to impart them to the lower classes.

Reaching Out to Housewives

Thus armed, upper-class women crossed the class divide to reform the households of the humble. This was a big step, for class divisions were perhaps nowhere as evident as in housing and household organization. In the interwar decades, the old intraclass neighborhoods of Italian city centers were becoming more segregated by class; urban *risanmento* broke up areas of artisan residence, and public housing projects concentrated salaried employees and workers, usually separately, in new, often isolated zones of settlement. Moreover, housing itself was planned with an ever keener eye to social and professional distinctions: the worker's house *(casa dell'operaio)*, the functionary's house *(casa dell'impiegato)*, the rural house *(casa rurale)*, not to mention the "architect's house," or the "engineer's house," were all conventions becoming inscribed in state and municipal planning projects at this time.[58] In addition, household plant itself was undergoing rapid change. As well-off entrepreneurs, professionals, and state functionaries acquired certain modern conveniences such as piped-in gas, electricity, running water in separate bathrooms, a telephone, and kitchen appliances such as gas stoves and refrigerators, the gap between rich and poor was accentuated. In the nineteenth century, Italians were said to be divided into two races, those who ate white bread, and those who ate black bread. In the 1930s the divide was between the 20 percent who had flush toilets and the 80 percent who did not.[59] Charity women might sympathize with the plight of working-class and peasant housewives. But sympathy went hand in hand with incomprehension of the causes of their degraded condition of existence, insufferance for their apparently shiftless husbands and disrespectful children, and rosy confidence that fascism's "rational system of social education" would win out.

In the prescriptive literature, the model family was that of the petty functionary. His was the most familiar to well-heeled bourgeois benefactors, who might meet the bank clerk or insurance agent on a daily basis. It was also regarded as suffering especially acutely from the disparity between the means available to it and the widespread publicity for new standards of living befitting a middle-class status. In her widely circulated 1933 manual on "living well in hard times," Fernanda Momigliano, a schoolteacher from a prosperous Turinese Jewish family, spoke to these issues in no-nonsense psychological and managerial terms. First, women had to stop "obsessing" about the cost of living; a panicky state of mind only risked aggravating the nation's economic situation. Next, they had to refrain from asking what caused the crisis and from bothering their husbands by whining and complaining. Above all, they had to learn how to budget. Momigliano then demonstrated how a hypothetical family of four, that of a Milanese insurance company clerk, could get by with "economy, not deprivation or waste," even after the government mandated a 10 percent pay cut in 1932. The numbers spoke clearly as Momigliano tallied up the outlays from the clerk's 1,300 lire net: the cut could be absorbed merely by eliminating the summer vacation. In sum, to live well, housewives need only subscribe to the watchword: "education, order, serenity."[60]

Momigliano's story, rather than soothing her petty bourgeois readers, may well have disturbed them. The more familiar people became with the new social norms, the more distress they experienced when they were unable to fulfill them. In fact, net earnings of 600 or 700 lire monthly were closer to the average than the 1,300 lire Momigliano had calculated. And the assumption that women exercised full decision-making powers over family budgeting, once the head of household had subtracted his pocket money, ignored that it was precisely in the face of straitened circumstances that stressful tugs-of war over money were likely to develop. The sense of injustice generated when women with disappointed expectations were confronted with new national norms was painfully evident in the plaintive letter that the wife of a Milanese man employed at the powerful Montecatini Corporation addressed to her "venerated" Duce on March 13, 1937, just nine days after the Grand Council passed its first ostensibly comprehensive package of family aid. Her plight, the woman alleged, was like that of many families in which the male breadwinner lacked a decent salary. She likely embellished the truth when she claimed to have married on October 28, 1922, with the idea of "giving [the Duce] a dozen children." In any case, ten months later she had given birth to a son. At the time, however, her husband earned only 350 lire a month, and he wanted her to work. She refused, wanting to wait until the little boy was three or four before putting him in a nursery, and the years passed "amidst fights, privations, and . . . hunger!" Having had to go back to work, she put off bearing other children. In 1937, her husband was thirty-eight years old, and he had attained the rank of bookkeeper (contabile di concetto). But his monthly net was still only 550 lire. With rent costing 250 lire, only 300 lire was left for everything else. None of them had enough to eat: "I especially deprive myself continually to leave more for the two of them." She was not alone in this situation:

> Ask everyone else why they don't have children (without forcing them to give their names), and you will see that 90 percent tell you what I've said. As for those scientists with their full bellies, get rid of them; we women know what family necessity means: the pain of not staying at home like our mothers did, and bouncing our children on our knees, without despairing.[61]

Two points bear particular comment. The first is that this woman had internalized not so much the idea of having more children, but of staying at home to care for her one child—as her mother and her friends' mothers had allegedly done. Whether true or not, the dictatorship said it had been so; hence not staying home became a deprivation. Further, the home, far from being the proverbial buffer against troubles, had become riddled by worries and disputes as husband and wife fretted over how to make ends meet. Second, the woman, notwithstanding her privations in the family, affirmed her loyalty to it and especially to her spouse. Observers of 1930s familial mores spoke of the triumph of coupledom in those years. The couple had become a new social figure, as Irene Brin described it, "with its sense of association, complicity, its bond of honor." Its fidelity celebrated in the face of lovers' seductions, its most meaningful event was not marriage, but the moment of first togetherness, the ever more fashionable honeymoon.[62] Our case here, however, suggests that coupledom was under terrible pressure, and being tested to the limit. Indeed, the very act of writing to the Duce, probably unbeknownst to her husband, constituted an infidelity of sorts. At the same time, this woman clearly stood by her spouse, blaming the employer, the state, and the scientists for the impossibility of living according to their desires. She took up her husband's brief: his position was respectable, but underpaid. She made no mention of her own position or income. In the interest of family solidarity, she sacrificed herself; in the interest of the family's right to thrive and multiply and of her right to stay home and nurture the family, she felt empowered to denounce bad policy.

Reaching out to working-class women was even more problematic, for often they were physically as well as socially distant from their putative benefactors. To reach them, social workers and bourgeois do-gooders had to pierce the tight-knit proletarian districts of the old city centers or travel long distances to tumbledown shacks and jerry-built *case popolari* at the city edges. The ideal project of reform integrated plans to uplift women with a general re-zoning of the working-class district. That goal lay behind the establishment of the *Casa dell'economia domestica*, which Adele Lancia, the wife of the motorcar manufacturer, inaugurated in 1936, in collaboration with other industrialist philanthropists, city planners, and fascist officials, to domesticate Turin's staunchly socialist San Paolo neighborhood.[63] In household economy courses on child nurture, home cleanliness, household decoration, and female crafts, charity women and social workers set standards of respectability not dissimilar to those promoted by reformers in liberal England and elsewhere. Italian charity women, too, distinguished the respectable working-class family from the unstable or troubled one. The proper kind of family had no lodgers, a few children well-taken care of, a father who was employed and exercised authority over his wife and any working children, and a mother dedicated to the home and capable of discharging all the myriad practical affairs of a well-run household.[64]

At best, household economics for these groups was a palliative; at worst, it was an irritant. To fulfill bourgeois ideals of respectability, working-class women were not to work, and though more and more women left regular employment upon having children, they often worked part-time and off the books. Not infrequently, women returned to work so that their sons could stay in school long enough to acquire a trade or profession, thereby improving the family fortunes. Decent housing, a prerequisite of orderliness, was ever more difficult to obtain in the 1930s because of rising rents, diminished private construction, and big urban population increases. Fascist antiurban campaigns notwithstanding, big city populations grew by two million from 1921 to 1936, mainly from internal migration, driving central city rents up, squeezing old family-based crafts and small businesses out, and pushing new arrivals to the periphery where costs were lower. A quarter of this increase occurred in Rome alone, causing the city to double in size and to surpass Milan (1,085,000 to 1,075,000). Each year Italy's population increased by 350,000 persons, whereas housing units grew by only 228,000. The dictatorship was not unmindful of the severity of the housing shortage. But the National Institute of Popular Housing, which was supposed to address it by constructing low-cost units, was just as corrupt as most other fascist agencies. Not infrequently, subsidized dwellings, embellished with balconies, marble foyers, and other refinements, would end up housing well-off state and party functionaries rather than the "popular classes" for whom they were supposedly destined. As a result, housing remained a grievous problem. In 1939 the city of Milan planned to build 4,255 units; the request list amounted to 40,000.[65]

The burden of making do, much less achieving higher standards of domestic upkeep and child care, fell on the women. In the best of times this was hard. Aurora, a Turinese woman interviewed by Luisa Passerini, although married and with a child, continued to "work, work, work," making bolts in the small machinery shop where she had started at age sixteen. Her wages were so low that she was forever in search of extra jobs: she worked as a charwoman in the afternoon, and on Saturday she assisted vendors at the open-air market who compensated her with fresh fruits and vegetables. On Sunday she cleaned and washed at home.[66] High male unemployment during the depression only aggravated the situation. In Rome, according to the shocked account of a young fascist volunteer, Maria Mayo Faina, wives of unemployed construction workers became the main providers, usually by doing cleaning. Home was a run-down apartment. There were four or five children underfoot, and the husband was in a "horrible temper." Families lived "under the threat of eviction" amidst continual scenes with the owners. Added to all the women's privations, there was the humiliation and the "fatigue of being assisted, the long waits, the incomprehension."[67]

Social workers dealt mainly with women, and though in public they spoke of the importance to a well-ordered household of having respect for the father, in private they may not have been so sympathetic. Most believed in a companionate style of marriage, or at the very least a complementary division of tasks, the man providing the income, the woman managing the household. Consequently, they poor-mouthed their clients' unemployed husbands who, they alleged, if out wandering about in search of work, took no interest in the household and, if at home, hung around complaining.

Whether state handouts further diminished paternal authority, as Loffredo and other Catholics argued, is harder to know. The elegant do-gooders with their charitable mien and models of orderliness must have presented a seductive picture to brow-beaten working-class wives. Still, historians of Turin's old socialist stronghold, Borgo San Paolo, and of other working class districts suggest that family solidarity was maintained in the face of the snooping *visitatrici fasciste*.[68] In the end, conjugal loyalty was indispensable to the solidarity of communities bound together by political as well as familial allegiances. Women may have suffered hurt pride from having to stoop to handouts. But their men suffered from outright political discrimination. Compelled by their families' needs to make the rounds of employment offices, they knew that if their work passes *(libretti di lavoro)* were checked and their socialist pasts were discovered, their efforts would be futile. Under these circumstances, working-class women were inclined to protect male authority in order to preserve the integrity of working-class family life and networks. Of course, that attitude didn't prevent working-class women from urging their husbands to forget the past, for the family's sake, or from complaining about the men's passivity in the face of hardships.

The most ambitious intervention on the part of upper-class women regarded rural women. The "budding bride of twenty," as well as the "wrinkly old housewife of seventy," may have been "ignorant," but she was also "quick, cunning, expert."[69] Among rural women, intervention was well-integrated with government strategies designed to halt rural land flight by reinforcing peasant family institutions. Social investigators professed faith that in the countryside "family sentiment is still solid and tenacious; marriages sustain the birth rates of the past."[70] Babies born out of wedlock were rare (but only perhaps because pregnant girls fled to the towns). War widows cast a small shadow on this idyllic picture; being reluctant to lose their survivors' pensions, they refused to legalize their new conjugal arrangements. Yet the lure of the city was ever-present as the spread of urban fashion demonstrated. The peasant women's laments about the lack of amenities such as decent housing, running water, and recreation were ominous signs of future land flight.

In the early 1930s fascist organizers, under the influence of Lombard *massaismo*, began to take stock of the huge female rural population. The 1931 census counted 4,716,000 rural families with altogether 23,970,000 people, including 11,300,000 female members of all ages. It classified about

6,325,000 as "housewives," meaning that they were principally engaged in household chores. Of the several million others listed as employed part- or full-time in agricultural work, only around 500,000 had been enrolled in the fascist trade unions. To sum up the concerns of the organizers, nine million women "escaped completely all organization."[71]

In response to these concerns, Luigi Razza, head of the Fascist Confederation of Agricultural Syndicates, asked the venerable fascist Regina Terruzzi to set up the *massaie rurali*. Having fallen out of favor because of her protests against the Special Tribunals in 1927 and because of her son's reputation as an antifascist, she had devoted herself full-time to her teaching at the Carlo Cattaneo Technical Institute of Milan. At her retirement in 1931, after forty-one years of service, she was sixty-nine and still obstreperous. But by 1933 the regime was under pressure to "reach out to the people" and was willing to overlook her sometimes disquieting views to exploit her talents as an organizer. Terruzzi started by putting her longtime acquaintance with Anita Cernezzi Moretti, president of the Housewives' Union of the Milanese Countryside, to good profit. That organization, founded in 1924 by wealthy land-owning women under the auspices of the Lombard Agrarian Society, became, if half-heartedly, the fulcrum of the new organization. Indeed, Terruzzi did such an effective job with her all-female staff that in 1934 the organization was removed from under trade union auspices and assigned to the *fasci femminili*. At that point, Terruzzi withdrew to private life with the diplomatic (and quite plausible) excuse that the 700 kilometer commute between Rome and Nice, where she lived with her banker son, wore her down. Thereafter the Rural Housewives' Organization continued to flourish; the Ethiopan war was a great stimulus, as were the inordinate needs of rural women. Ambitious plans prescribed "meeting rooms" in which women might find "not only moral and cultural aid, but all those accessories and utensils that are generally wanting in the rural house yet that every woman aspires to."[72] The real achievements were both more and less.

The major focus of the Rural Housewives' Organization was to promote petty household capitalism. Traditionally, chicken and rabbit raising, basket weaving and iris-root cleaning, silkworm cultivation, and small home gardens gave farm women some economic independence with respect both to the land proprietors and to their spouses. The *massaie rurali* strongly endorsed these endeavors to provide activities and more nutritious food during periods of seasonal slack and, above all, to promote national economic self-sufficiency or autarchy. Accordingly, it championed its members' interests in small-town markets, protesting the petty taxes and customs municipal councils imposed on every chicken, onion bunch, or egg brought to market; published price lists; and sought tax-free market stalls for members at farmers' markets. It also fostered rural industries, silk being the major one. By 1934 Italian silk production had dropped 45 percent from its pre–Great War high of 50 million kilos per year, largely as a result of competition from Asian silk and synthetic fibers; in the early 1920s farm women had received about 2,000 lire a kilo for silk cocoons, whereas in 1934 they received a tenth of that, and many had stopped production. The plan of the rural housewives' groups was to improve the quality of the silkworm eggs, instruct on the "rational" care of the larvae, and facilitate marketing the cocoons. On that basis and with the expectation of lower profits, peasant women might reenter the market; they were to anticipate earning from 300 to 400 lire a kilo rather than 2,000. Finally, the organization pressed to renegotiate those clauses of the early 1920s sharecropping contracts that barred farm women from raising livestock for market, and by 1938 this had been accomplished. Farm women were still unable to breed pigs or cows, or produce milk for market. But they could raise rabbits and chickens, subject to paying one-eighth of the produce to the landlord.[73]

Whether rural *massaismo* solidified the peasant household, as was its chief intention, is dubious. By promoting access to the market, it generated independent income, giving the wife and daughters of the *reggitore* greater autonomy. For the most part, these small sums went for urban goods—ribbons, new shoes, and especially the synthetic silk cloth with which young peasant women adorned themselves by the late 1930s. The organization may have fostered pride in rural costumes and folk festivities, but it also opened avenues of communication between urban and rural women that exposed the harshness of rural life. Thus paradoxically the ties that bound urban organizers and rural clients together caused a further unravelling of the fabric of rural society. Regina Terruzzi recognized as much in an editorial for the movement's news bulletin that she forwarded to Mussolini in 1934. Organizing peasant women, she wrote,

> [is] harder than uniting men. The former are used to community, to the inn, to the piazza, to the barracks. . . . Work obliges women to a collective existence in the factory, the fields, but this is temporary and in their youth. As soon as they marry, they stay at home. As soon as the harvest, the grape gathering, the threshing is finished, they go back to a solitary existence in the family. Spiritual life is fed by sermons, by the confessional, social life by chatter and neighborhood gossip.

Terruzzi recognized that the newness of modern organizations might at the same time "complicate their lives, even make them unhappy." Yet she concluded:

> To leave them alone, to leave them to adapt to contemporary custom by force of things, by natural process . . . would be blameworthy indifference on the part of all of us who live in the city, poisoned, it's true, by its dust, . . . defeated by its racket, but able to accept without violent shocks the daily transformation of existence, understand its necessity, follow its progress, and halt its excesses. To overcome as much as possible the distances that separate, that differentiate city life from country life, bringing them as close together as possible, fusing them together, is useful to those involved, hence to the nation, to the country, to the society.[74]

Monitoring the Children

The care the dictatorship displayed toward children is perhaps the most perplexing aspect of family policy and the most horrific in its contradictoriness. Fascism boasted of its love of little children, and its family codes spoke expressly of the state's legal duty to supervise their well-being. The regime supervised children's welfare through ONMI, as well as through the Balilla and other youth groups. Every year, it celebrated the *Befana fascista* and sent hundreds of thousands to summer camps. Not least of all, the Duce was advertised as a prolific and conscientious patriarch. At the same time, the dictatorship unabashedly characterized its measures as eugenicist, undertaken on behalf of the race and state, rather than in the interest of the individual or the family. As early as 1930, it set out to habituate mothers to the idea that their offspring belonged to the nation and that in case of war they had to be sacrificed to its well-being. The dictatorship thus combined paternalism in the familiar, humanitarian sense with a murderous, abstract claim on the lives of dependents; it obsessed about the privileged bond between mothers and children, and then brutally violated it.

Withal, state benefits to children constituted perhaps the most visible and influential change in family life. The dictatorship enforced wider attendance at schools, including preschool *(asilo)*, for which attendance doubled to reach 700,000 by the late 1930s. The fascist youth groups, or *Gioventù italiana del littorio* (GIL), organized recreational and social services, as well as premilitary training. By 1940 the party's mountain and seaside colonies hosted a million children annually. These were a particularly remarkable social experiment, insofar as parents who themselves had never traveled much beyond their town limits had to be convinced to yield up children as young as four years old for stays of as long as a month at seaside, hill, and mountain resorts. Doctors sometimes expressed misgivings as to whether the "brown color acquired by the skin under the sun's action" or obsessive checks on weight, height, and head size offered good indicators of healthiness. However, "aero-" and "heliotherapy," along with "marine cures," were widely regarded as being in the children's interest. To prevent the kinds of scandals long associated with Catholic asylums and orphanages, prefects and party officials propagandized their surveillance over all the colony and resort activities. In the end, the unanimous voices of employers, social workers, medical experts, and political cadres must have overwhelmed familial reluctance.[75]

That the colonies' purpose was eugenicist was never in doubt. Full-scale mobilization was perhaps a uniquely effective way to prise children away from their mothers—to fetch them out of slums, to check, inoculate, and, if necessary, quarantine them; neither summer amusement nor relief for mothers was ever mentioned as a purpose. The operations of the Duke of Catania camp inaugurated by the Fascist Federation of Catania in 1938 gives some sense of these attitudes. In its first year of operation, it hosted two thousand children aged four to twelve as day guests and another two hundred boarded for a month. In preparation for their stay, the children were "clipped, washed down, dressed, and shod." A medical check-up weeded out all those with contagious diseases, which included tuberculosis, trachoma, and hereditary syphilis, and all were vaccinated for typhus, diphtheria, and smallpox.[76] Well-run camps like that operated by the giant Fiat Motor Company at Marina di Massa boasted of sending the children home to Turin, not just clean, brownish, and indoctrinated with respect for their surveillants, the Duce, and the Church, but on average two to three pounds heavier.

Catholic critics were especially bothered by Mussolini's patriarchal gesturing on the occasion of the *Befana fascista,* or Epiphany of the Duce, a great public gift-giving on Twelfth Night that merged religious ceremony, the PNF's relief efforts, and, often, employer largesse. Typically, children's gifts constituted relief in kind, there were toys, but also underwear, shoes, and winter coats. The celebration ONMI hosted in 1932 at its soup kitchen refectory in Rome's Valle d'Inferno neighborhood close by the Milvian Bridge was typical. With Professor Cesare Michele of ONMI and Daisy di Robilant doing the honors, the patronesses handed out 500 pieces of clothing, including 200 coats; cloth for the latter had been donated, with the mothers themselves sewing the garments on machines provided for the pregnant and nursing women of the district. The political-symbolic functions were obvious; we leave the words to the sycophantic observer of one such occasion: "How fortunate for the children of Italy that every year their great friend remembers them, that every year, he increases the circle of his dear, faithful 'clients.' " The attending adults tweaked the kids' cheeks, asking " 'Now, who gave you so many nice things?' pointing out the tiny pants, woolen undershirts, little shoes, hats, illustrated books, toys, and sweets, . . . and each of the little lads piped up 'Il Duce.' "[77]

Whether fascist patriarchalism undercut paternal and more generally familial authority is hard to document. Fascist largesse was consistent with the exaggerated masculinism of a regime that taxed celibate men to pay for its children's welfare programs and then complained about "the decline in men of that robust virility which fascism with such love and constancy externalizes through other means."[78] It held up families to higher standards of child care. At the same time, it prevented many household heads from fulfilling these standards. Any legitimacy the dictatorship may have acquired from its humane treatment of children was undercut by Mussolini's brutally frank admissions that more soldiers was the main objective of his campaign for more babies. "You tell me, professor," a Turinese working-class woman confided to Luigi Maccone in 1935, "Is it just or humane that we women of the people should have many children, destined for war when they are adults? Oh, never! We love our children, we raise them as best we can given our measly means, for ourselves, for an ever better future for them, but not for the Fatherland."[79]

Oppositional Familism

Beginning in 1937, as fascist Italy moved closer to the Third Reich, and war making and colonization called for more citizens and more disciplined ones, the dictatorship sought to gear up its demographic policies. The first occasion was the several hour session of the Grand Council on March 4, 1937, at the conclusion of which the regime issued a seven-point program for increasing Italy's population. This put ever more emphasis on the authority of the father; in addition to providing priority in employment and promotion to fathers of large families and to increasing family allocations, it offered marriage loans to enable young men to marry. On June 3, 1937, by royal decree, the state also founded a new organization, the Fascist Union of Big Families. Funded with a huge grant of 500,000 lire annually from the Minister of the Interior, it was open, as its November 22 statutes indicated, to all families with no less than seven living children. Unlike the groups operating under the banner of *massaismo*, which worked through women, this organization was aimed at family heads, meaning by definition men. The entire governing board, headed by Prince

Gian Giacomo Borghese, was male. So were all the members of the provincial and municipal committees. Set up to funnel services to big families, it operated as an interest group, distinguishing its deserving constituents from those "morbidly egotistical" types who, by their refusal to contract marriage and father offspring, revealed "grave defects of character and arrested development."[80] Surviving the fall of fascism, the Union of Big Families became a leading lobby of the postwar era and, as a founding association of the Christian Democratic Party's Family Front *(Fronte della famiglia)* in the 1940s, a cornerstone of male-led conservative family politics under the Italian republic.

However, family interests were not easily tuned to the service of national politics in the late 1930s. Once family interests became legitimate grounds for demanding government action, they also became grounds to retreat from government impositions. Against a state that failed to safeguard family interests, family logic fed an antipolitics, if not an alternative, power. In bargaining with employers in the late 1930s, the usually docile fascist unions took up the workers' reasoning for not accepting the new wage package. The problem was not the workers, but their wives, who said the wages were not adequate to put bread on the table for the children. When protesting fascism's quotas on women workers in 1938, many women, as well as male family members, pleaded special family circumstances to exempt themselves from the law.[81] More commonly, individuals simply withdrew from public involvement, giving the excuse of family affairs.

Thus, fascism's cult of the family in the service of the state was undercut by antistatist attitudes that might be characterized as "oppositional familism." On the surface, these resembled the group ethos that Edward Banfield was later to characterize as "amoral familism" in his controversial 1958 study of Montegrano. The villagers of that rural southern Italian community were a factious lot, to believe the American sociologist's description; they resisted any association except that within their immediate families, they were incapable of working for the next generation's welfare, and they were generally self-serving in all political acts. To make their behavior intelligible, Banfield maintained that the people followed the rule: "Maximize the material, short-run advantage of the nuclear family; assume others will do likewise."[82] These and similar behaviors elsewhere are more plausibly explained as strategies of survival in the face of government hostility and economic scarcity, as others have argued. In *The House That Giacomo Built*, Donald Pitkin traced the peasant Tassoni family's widening circle of dependents over three generations, beginning with their move from Calabria to the land reclamation projects of the

Pontine Swamps in 1933. But he regarded the family's unswerving self-sacrifice on behalf of the next generation as an "affirmation of responsibility." In an environment in which economic relations were highly conflictual and government strikingly negligent or oppressive, kinship ties provided a "survival strategy" for the disadvantaged. Without these bonds, prospects were dim for building more complicated ties of solidarity through civic associations, labor unions, and political movements.[83]

Under fascism, doubtless, the taproots of such strategies of survival were varied: middle-class individualism—what one fascist intellectual called the "reactionary character" of the bourgeois family—was perhaps one; the residual feudalism of rural patronage systems and peasant clannishness another; urban working-class kin networks were a third. These family interests, turned against the regime, may not, generally, have fostered what Pitkin for a more recent period calls an "anti-hegemonic consciousness." On the basis of family interest alone, people were little likely to forswear political allegiances or perform acts of political resistance. Still, many did come to believe that the family existed apart from the society, as a refuge against political intrusions rather than as a pillar of the nation-state.

Above all, oppositional familism was bound up with the changing relationship between family and state and the new demands that this placed on female family members. As mothers, women ultimately had to square the circle: to nurture and educate with scarcer resources and in the face of rising standards; to find work even while discrimination against female employment aggravated conditions for unskilled, part-time, and unorganized female labor; to maneuver through labyrinthine social service bureaucracies, compelled to act as public persons, at the same time as official ideology pictured them as "angels of the hearth." As wives, they were supposed to offer a refuge for brow-beaten, dejected mates. As unwed sisters and daughters, they were supposed to perform maternal functions, with no social recognition whatsoever. So long as the state delivered butter and guns, women were supposed to put food on the table and prepare human cannon fodder.

No wonder that as the dictatorship mounted a more and more aggressive foreign policy in the late 1930s and the prospect of sacrificing children and spouses became more immediate, wives, mothers, sisters, and daughters fell back on kin and community networks, seeking other bonds of support in family ties, class subcultures, and religious associations. Brought into, yet never perfectly enmeshed in the burgeoning fascist welfare state, they learned to fall back on local resources. They were thus the best positioned to lead what might be described as a retreat of civil society before the state. This did not mean that women foreswore making appeals to the government on behalf of their families. Quite the contrary, these became shriller, more insistent, less appropriate. The underside of fascist totalitarianism, then, was patterned by the parochial, quotidian needs of family survival. Never articulated in an organized movement, the women's voices resonated at the public water pumps and in the courtyards of *case popolari*, in front of school gates and at outdoor market stalls, but became mute when the Duce demanded sacrifices on behalf of the Fatherland.

5   Growing Up

The Nation is served even by keeping the house swept.
Civic discipline commences with family discipline.
                    Decalogue of the Little Italian

Let me go where I will, let my name reach as high as my
dreams.
                    Ubalda, in Liala's *Tempesta sul lago*

"Would you want to marry one of those girls?" Louise Diel's question caught a middle-aged fascist official off guard. They were in a crowd of other black-shirted *gerarchi* at Rome's Mussolini Forum, the setting for one of the huge gymnastic rallies regularly held in the 1930s. The men's admiring attention had been aroused as phalanxes of succinctly dressed but stern-faced graduates of the elite female Orvieto Academy of Physical Education passed in review. "That is perhaps going too far," replied the *gerarca*. "But then I'm married." "And what is your wife like?" persisted the German journalist. "Believe me, my wife is the ideal woman," he replied with a self-satisfied smile, meaning, Diel thought, "she's dear, sweet, and lets me do just as I please."[1]

The fascist official's evasive reply captured a key dilemma in fascism's relationship with Italian women. Under the slogan, "Make way for youth," the fascist movement had mounted its struggle against the so-called passéism *(passatismo)* of "senescent" liberal democracy. As Mussolini consolidated power in the late 1920s, he reiterated fascism's faith in shaping a new generation of Italians. Male youths were, of course, foremost in his mind because they were to furnish the future elites and soldiers of the Third Rome. Hence, young men were to be molded through the militaristic discipline of youth groups to "believe, obey, and fight" in the name of fascism's revolution. For the same cause, young women were to be instructed to be prolific mates, dutiful mothers, and ardent patriots. The goals seemed clear-cut, yet by the late 1930s fascism had its own problems relating to youth. The big cohorts born just after World War I had swelled to 45 percent the proportion of Italy's population under the age of twenty-five, and their expectations of the Fascist Revolution were not being satisfied by the aging regime.[2]

116

The discontents of young women were not expressed with as much animosity as the frondist sentiments of young male intellectuals, whose antiauthoritarian exploits have often been recounted, most poignantly in Ruggero Zangrandi's memoir of his generation's "long voyage through fascism."[3] Nor were young women's complaints necessarily targeted at male officialdom. But there were manifest tensions between the ideals of self-abnegating motherhood invoked by the dictatorship and its endorsement of social activism, between the pressure to be docile homebodies and the challenge to be the fit companions of elites. Indeed, the exuberance and seeming emancipation of young women were, as Diel suggested, perhaps more discomfitting reminders of fascism's aging than the rebelliousness of young men. At best, the *gerarchi* could pretend, like their fifty-five-year-old Duce, to recapture their youthful vigor with infatuated lovers a generation or more their junior.

Make Way for the New Woman

Fascism's complex relationships with female youth, if conditioned by its contradictory expectations of women generally, essentially reflected a change in the way girls were growing up in Italy after World War I. The postwar generations enjoyed pleasures entirely different from those of their mothers as mass culture brought them into contact with more commercialized and seemingly freer sexual and social customs. Especially in the middle class, families were smaller, and more was demanded of girls. They stayed in school longer, with jobs scarce and marriage coming later, and their dependent status in the family was prolonged. Parents themselves were disoriented by changing customs; by the late 1920s, as the Bolognese writer Daria Banfi Malaguzzi noted, "there was utter confusion about how to raise girls."[4] The dictatorship only added to the confusion by making incompatible claims on young women, who were supposed to be at once responsive citizens and subordinate family members, both involved in the public life of the New Italy and submissive to paternal authority.

The rule of fascism largely coincided with the development in Italy of modern notions of "girlhood"—that period of time in which young women enjoy special freedoms, nurse common expectations, and develop shared attitudes toward family, sexuality, courtship, school, and work.[5] Under fascist rule, not one but two generations of *giovani italiane* were formed: the first came of age as the movement rose to power in the wake of the social earthquake of the Great War; the second reached maturity while the dictatorship was in its prime, under the influence of an emerging mass consumer culture. The former was composed of the roughly 3.5 million women born sometime between 1900 and 1910 and going through adolescence during or just after the war. The older girls were the female companions of the male Front Generation, and many of them had been as disenchanted with old liberal Italy as the youthful *fascisti* of the first hour. Disinhibited by the absence of men during wartime, their marriage prospects postponed and sometimes destroyed by war casualties, they had been thrust into the emancipatory atmosphere of postwar society, their image identified with the short skirts, bobbed hair, freer sexual behavior, and egalitarian demands common everywhere in Western societies in the 1920s. The Italian *maschietta* was in this respect the local counterpart of the American flapper, the British bachelor girl, and the Parisian *garçonne*.

The latter generation was the female counterpart of the so-called generation of the Littorial *fascio*. They comprised a far bigger cohort—counting the more than 4.5 million girls born just after the Great War and in the 1920s. Though they grew up knowing no regime but fascism, they were all touched in some measure by the cosmopolitan mass culture originating far off in Hollywood; its images and values were purveyed not just through the cinema, popular songs, pulp magazines, cheap novels, mass commodities, and fashions but even to some extent through the youth and leisure organizations of the dictatorship.

Though differences in age and outlook between these two generations were crucial in the lives of individuals, as our all too small stock of memoirs from those times shows,[6] Italian women growing up in the interwar decades had far more in common with one another than with their mothers' generations. In *belle époque* Italy, emancipated life-styles among the cultivated middle classes were identified not so much with being nubile as with being married. So long as they were unwed, girls were drearily cloistered at home under strict family supervision. Only outside their family of origin could young women flout the conventions of bourgeois domesticity.[7] However, in the wake of the Great War and especially by the late 1920s, girlhood began to be conceived of as a time of freedom, and marriage was regarded more ambivalently. At best, it offered to extend girlhood pleasures into young adulthood, improved by male companionship, yet with no immediate worries about childbearing. At worst, it foreboded curtailed freedoms, tedious domesticity, and difficult marital rapports. Moreover, the war itself, beyond fostering new modes of behavior, enhanced the perception of sharp differences between girlhood past and present. Increasingly thereafter the biological rhythms of girlhood were more clearly demarcated. The meaning of childhood, adolescence, and maturity was reinforced not only by social and cultural conventions—as schooling patterns dictated and as cultural industries singled out age groups for special appeals—but, as we shall examine further, by political conventions as well: the *leva fascista* marked the advance at fourteen from *piccole* to *giovani italiane*, at eighteen from *giovani italiane* to *giovani fasciste*, and at twenty-one, with special rites of passage, to the *fasci femminili* and full-fledged party membership. These had almost exact parallels in the Catholic formations for youth. Above all, the fascist regime fostered a sense of generational difference by condemning the older female generations' emancipationism as démodé and by exalting contemporary fascist youth as truly modern. But the "1900-style girl," or *ragazza '900*, was not easily digested. By the 1930s, her freer life-style, more myth than substance, led her to be vilified by the regime and aroused Catholic ire. She was also the butt of irritated denunciations by older women who put some of the blame for fascist antifeminism on the conceit, self-centeredness, and outlandish behavior of the young.

By the 1930s, there was a repertory of attitudes and behavior that advice columns, etiquette books, and novels, as well as the rare and not always objective social survey characterized as typical of modern girls. These qualities were revealed, for example, in the responses of 1,003 teenagers to a survey conducted in 1937 by Maria Diez Gasca, who though acting in her capacity as director of Rome's Service for Professional Orientation was primarily interested in discovering attitudes toward family and maternity.[8] The girls, who ranged in age from fourteen to eighteen, were typical of the capital's professional-school population: the daughters of striving petty functionaries, clerks, shopkeepers, and artisans. In Diez Gasca's stern but affectionate appraisal, they were "healthy, vivacious, garrulous, but not turbulent." Asked why they studied, most girls replied, in order to qualify for a job; they intended to work because their husbands could not be expected to support them. Their favorite pastime was moviegoing, "the most attractive of attractions," though gymnastics and sports were a close second. If they read, they preferred novels, historical romances, or adventure stories. They were mostly uninterested in traditional female handicrafts such as knitting and sewing, and they preferred dancing to singing, music, and painting. Housework was regarded as tedious, if not repulsive, and ideas about having families of their own were "extraordinarily vague." They strongly preferred the company of their peers, especially other girls, to that of young children, especially siblings; they regarded babies as burdensome, and thought births best limited to one or two, with a preference for daughters. Self-confidence rather than tractability was the virtue they prized most highly, and the

A modern young bourgeois woman in costume, Siena, circa 1923.
(Private collection.)

"desire to command, rather than to obey" was common. And this appeared to have been fostered by their own parents, who may have nagged
them about their studies and using makeup, but generally treated them
with what was characterized as "notable indulgence."

Withal, Italy's so-called *maschietta* was a more unevenly modern figure than her foreign counterparts. In the United States, the flapper was a
working girl or middle-class young woman in college. She lived alone or
with others of her sex, and her choice of dates, styles, and pastimes was
more or less her own, shaped by commercial cultural markets catering to
her cohorts' tastes. Differences of custom within the broadly spread middle
classes were increasingly slight, as were those between small towns and
the big cities.[9] In Italy notions of modern girlhood were just beginning to
penetrate many rural areas by the 1930s; in the plains, at least, and in
hill towns near urban centers, girls had begun to follow city fashion with
the same excitement as their brothers who were becoming empassioned
soccer and bicycling fans. In the prosperous Chianti valley of Tuscany,
for example, adolescent girls, having acquired all the latest embroidery
and crocheting stitches from sewing circles at nearby Greve, worked
away in the shade of the trees while tending the sheep or at night while
gathered around the winter fire. On Saturday they rushed to the market to sell their handiwork in order to buy "geegaws—wool and nylon

A modern young bourgeois woman in "costume," Siena, circa 1943.
(Private collection.)

stockings, ribbons, hairpins, combs and such, the likes of which they had never before even dreamed of."[10] All the same, in broad areas of the country the treatment of girls was still immune to the logic that led families to invest in the advancement of their male offspring. In hilltop villages and isolated farm homesteads on the plains, girls of three or four began tending younger siblings and were withdrawn from school after the third grade to do farm labor or domestic work. Sometimes they still sold their long hair to passing merchants. Short of being sent off to service in the towns, where they came in contact with urban ways, their life choices before and after marriage were determined entirely by their own family and then by their husband's.

Even in urban Italy, however, girlhood pivoted almost wholly around life in the family. Parental pressures, social conventions, and economic constraints—including a scarcity of suitable housing—foreclosed any significant stretch of independence in young adulthood. If attending high school or university, girls met female and male companions coming or going to school, after classes, and at occasional social events, political rallies, and Church activities. But any possibility of developing alternative life-styles was limited by geographic and social immobility, economic hardships, and the incessant attack on notions of individual rights by the Church and the State, as well as pressures from within the family. Victor Margueritte's 1922 best-seller, *La garçonne*, was translated into Italian in 1923. But there was no fictional, much less real, counterpart to Monica Lerbier, the bachelor-girl heroine. It was quite unimaginable that an emancipated Milanese *signorina* could act like her admittedly fictional Parisian sister. The latter, having fled her uncomprehending parents' luxurious Right Bank apartment to a Left Bank flat, not only thrived independently with the proceeds of a prospering art and antiquary shop but survived the shift from lesbian relationships to promiscuous heterosexual affairs before finally settling down in a properly companionate marriage.[11]

Moreover, the girl peer culture being forged in 1930s Italy under the influence of the mass press and commercial entertainments, although ultimately a powerful solvent of social distinctions, cleaved to the sharp class differences of Italian society. Indeed, the very failure of the market to standardize pastimes meant a proliferation of styles of modern young womanhood. Girlhood types thus ranged from the most emancipated, namely, the working girl of Milan who—like the Tippmamsell in *Bubikopf* of 1920s Berlin or the Parisian *midinette*—was a savvy consumer of fashion, fan magazine etiquette, and movie glamour, to the prim Catholic provincial who, in long braids and heavy socks, learned social responsibility and self-control in the female sodalities of the *Gioventù cattolica*. The most ostentatiously modern were the aristocratic and parvenue girls of the capital, with their *tè-danzante*, tango lessons at Pichetti's, and drives out to Ostia. The most timid consumers of mass culture were the scores of thousands of rural girls. Sent into service as early as age thirteen or fourteen, they glimpsed urban diversions while they hurried to run errands and do the marketing, or at odd hours off on Sunday when they attended the cheap movie matinees or public dances with soldier fiancés or hometown relatives and companions.

Generational Conflicts

Even so, no social group was impervious to the generational conflicts provoked by these developments. Among working-class families, in which girls had always started employment early, the changes were perhaps least dramatic. It was no surprise that parents' authority diminished once girls acquired some financial independence, socialized with other women in the workplace, and encountered male friends at work, in the neighborhood, or on tramways to and from home. The social bargain struck was that daughters lived at home abiding by their parents' rules until they set up households of their own. Parents, being unable to promise much help in outfitting them, except perhaps for bed linens and a sewing machine, afforded cheap hospitality until marriage.

Among the recently urbanized petty bourgeois, or in those families in which daughters had not previously worked, the conflicts between the ways of parents and children were doubtless sharper. Those arising in the family of a newly settled Milanese clerk's family were drawn with charming insight in the novel *Mary, Mariù, Maria*, serialized in the mass-circulation *Piccola* starting in November 1929. Its author, Murà, was one of the most prolific and popular novelists of the 1930s, her specialty being the romantic vicissitudes of that "heroine of modern existence," the young secretary. The protagonist Maria (who styled herself Mary at work and was nicknamed Mariù by the roué office manager) was fresh from the provinces, a few years behind fashion with her short skirts, bobbed hair, "gestures like Garbo, and glances à la Pola Negri."[17] On her first days at work Maria was accompanied by her father, and she was anxiously expected home for lunch as well as dinner. She turned her paycheck over to papà, and it was he who disbursed change for tram fare, magazines, an occasional book, and moviegoing. On her free day, Sunday, Maria attended mass, took a *passeggiata*, and perhaps went to a movie matinee, always in the company of her mother, her sister (who, being married to a traveling salesman, still lived at home), and her small nephew Boby. But soon, following the fashion, she wore longer skirts and curled her hair.

She also started wearing makeup, though to avoid her father's reproaches she never applied it at home. And counseled by a woman of experience, the thirty-year-old secretary Signorina Bini, Mary began to partake in urban pastimes—the predinner *aperitivo* in the Milan Galleria, a whirl round the city walls aboard the boss's auto, a day trip by Lambda to Lake Garda with office mates. Meanwhile, her parents, uncomprehending of her new milieu, were perplexed and irritated by her tardiness at meals and by her new acquaintances' inappropriate behavior, such as not securing the father's permission before asking Maria out for an excursion or not routing her get-well gifts through him. More and more, the mother was cast as an ineffectual, if affectionate, adviser, warning her girl against the seductions of newfangled courtship habits and urging on her the advantages of marrying for security, not passion.

Generational conflicts must have been at least as bothersome to the professional and property-owning groups, reflecting the worries they shared as a class in guaranteeing their offspring's bourgeois status during the interwar years. The uncertainty about their children's prospects was compounded in the case of girls by three concerns. The first was marriage, not just how, when, and whom they would marry, but if they would marry at all, given the much-publicized—and to some degree real—shortage of eligible men. The second concern was work: was it a necessity, a vocation, merely a fallback? Finally, there was schooling. The usual questions of how much to educate and for what purposes were greatly complicated by the regime's school reforms, as we shall see further on. These parental uncertainties were aggravated by changing attitudes among their offspring as they came into contact with new life-styles through the mass media, in school, and through fascist youth groups. At the same time that daughters were more financially and socially dependent on parents, they were more susceptible to pressures to act independently or at least to experiment with new habits. Bourgeois girls were attracted to new models of female conduct originating abroad or proposed by other classes, in particular the working class, whose girls were visibly more emancipated. Their parents tended to respond to uncertainty by proposing more conformist behaviors, which they justified as middle-class parents did elsewhere: these were intended to safeguard not merely family status but their daughter's "happiness." The middle-class family was thus trapped in a dilemma partly of its own making. By schooling its female children, encouraging a practical outlook on courtship, and, when necessary, urging girls to work, it fostered notions of independence. At the same time, it sought to preserve many old patterns of behavior.

This dilemma existed in every moment of a girl's life, starting with her earliest years. Prescriptive literature advised more liberal or "self-actualizing" child-rearing practices, the goal being to develop greater independence in the child and a stronger consensual bond between parent and offspring.[13] But little girls were still subject to what an Italian observer called "brood-hen" protectiveness. Indulged with a "warm, continuous, exuberant tenderness expressed by kisses, hugs, tributes to their beauty, and offerings of sweets," they were ill-prepared for the "real world."[14] Boys may have enjoyed more freedom: in keeping with official counsels about inculcating virile behavior in males, fathers were held to discourage mothers from over coddling them.

Outside the home no real middle-class children's culture existed; preschool nurseries *(asili infantili)* were practically unknown among the Italian middle classes. The pioneering work of Elena Agazzi, with her methods of "self-education" at Mompiano near Trieste, had been a major reference point for Italian educators since before the Great War. But her main concern was working-class children, who were also the subject of Maria Montessori's experimental *Casa dell'infanzia.* Initially popular among fascist school reformers, Montessori fell into political disgrace in the early 1930s and fled the country. Even before that, her progressive educational principles, for the children of the Italian poor, had given way to moralistic Catholic norms.[15]

Until age six, when they departed the "family cocoon" *(ovatta famigliare)* for elementary school, bourgeois children were entirely family-bound, meeting other children only in public gardens. Of course, family was extensive, including not just relatives but also servants and nurse-maids. The latter, usually of rural provenance, were fonts of peasant common sense. But they ministered to their charges with the fearful anxiety of country people used to high infant mortality rates and with practices culled from folk medicine. Bourgeois mothers still employed wet nurses, and in the public gardens of Milan it was not uncommon to see infants wrapped in swaddling, the nurses having overruled the advice of pediatricians and mothers. At the same time as a bourgeois child's mother, under the influence of the new-fangled commercial infant culture, was plumping up her little girl with Glaxo, an artificial milk, and fortifiers such as Ovomaltina, Mellin, and Proton, the *tata* might be applying garlic to her charge's chin as treatment for worms. But bourgeois mothers, too, displayed a deep mistrust of nature—at least as it might endanger their offspring—and the children were taught, as one woman plaintively recalled, "to be afraid of everything, sun, rain, and currents of air."[16]

The bourgeoisie's dilemma was even more acutely reflected in decisions about schooling their daughters. By the 1930s, most agreed that young women needed it, though for what purposes and by what means was much debated. As the future became less predictable, both girls and their families had to be more calculating. "Si sa come si nasce, ma non come si muore" ("One knows how one is born, not how one dies") was a saying dear to well-heeled northern bourgeoisie even before the war. This had justified entrusting the education of girls to the austere and practical approaches of old-style religious and exclusive public *educandati*.[17] In the interwar decades education was still regarded as a form of social insurance, in the event that the father died or the girl remained unmarried or was widowed. "Impara l'arte, mettila da parte" ("Learn the art, keep it as safeguard"), a common saying went. However, the men in young women's lives—fathers, fiancés, and husbands—now seemed more divided on the worth of this education. As the feminist pedagogue Maria Maggi observed, "the moment they meet the humblest standard of intelligence, the father wants his daughters to achieve a *posizione*, to conquer an official title. Fretful about their future, he wants them to become independent as soon as possible, not least of all to lift the load off a sometimes big family." In the process, he little heeds his daughters' "possibilities for families of their own," much less the opinions of "potential fiancés or future husbands who regard the issue rather differently than he does."[18] Perhaps the younger men realized better than the older ones that schooling left a legacy of emancipation if the young women subsequently worked and of frustration if they did not. That most parents did not see female education as a method of broadening choices or pursuing autonomy was evident in the little imagination bourgeois families brought to the problem of training their daughters. Their choices about schooling reinforced the biases of the labor market and conformist social attitudes that held that real work was a bourgeois woman's last resort. Only teaching or dispensing prescriptions were considered respectable female occupations.

Indeed, the talents of a gifted daughter seemed only to menace middle-class conformism. It was one thing for talent to be used to embellish conventional female roles. It was another for it to become a source of independence, much less celebrity, thereby threatening family obligations. Those parents willing (and never unambiguously) to foster such talents were rare: members of the cultivated Jewish middle class, or of foreign provenance, or perhaps from the eccentric patriciate. Even then, there was little enthusiasm for novel career paths. As the Nobel Prize winning scientist Rita Levi Montalcini recalled, her family's circle of well-off Turinese professionals believed in the Victorian John Ruskin's ideal of woman, educated to be "wise, not for self-development, but for self-renunciation." They steered their daughters toward a "future divided between family obligations and receptions." At twenty, when she told her mother of her decision to study medicine, she was urged to speak to her father: "I began in a roundabout way. . . . He listened, looking at me with that serious and penetrating gaze of his that caused me such trepidation, and asked whether I knew what I wanted to do. . . . He objected that it was a long and difficult course of study unsuitable for a woman." When Levi reassured her father once more that she was undaunted by the prospect, he replied, "If this is really what you want, . . . then I won't stand in your way, even if I'm very doubtful about your choice."[19]

The more common attitude was closer to that parodied by short-story writer Mario Massa in one of his fatuous little *novelle.* The story *An Obedient Girl* conjured up the battle waged by a stolid bourgeois, one Gualando Sgrignuoli, to domesticate the talents of a lovely, gifted teenage daughter.[20] The young woman had inherited the unquiet disposition, as well as the myriad talents, of her mother—once a free-spirited beauty who had renounced her wanderlust to keep house for her staid businessman spouse. Indeed, the daughter's talents seemed quite irrepressible. Informed by the principal of her lyceum that she had a brilliant future in medicine, Sgrignuoli stymied it by enrolling her in the National Academy of Music. Her gifts as a violinist threatened to make her a celebrity so he directed her to study singing, then draftsmanship, and, finally, astrology. Each time, she excelled. At last, he settled on a properly feminine pastime—fiction writing. Here, too, he was deluded. A renowned editor, hailing her first manuscript for having "broken with the banal sentimentalism typical of women's literature," predicted that she would launch a new genre. Despairing that she would be lost to family life, her father shut her up in her room to ponder the sign "Woman is guardian angel of the family," only to discover the day after that the girl had fled in the night. Yet a happy ending was in sight. A week later the daughter wrote home to confess that she had eloped. Although she had frustrated her father's incestuous desire to keep her forever his, she had at least obliged his sense of paternal duty in reproducing the social and sexual relations prefigured in her own mother's renunciation of freedom for marriage. In sum, the daughter had rebelled only to become "a woman according to your lights."

The ultimate stake was settling a daughter in marriage. This goal certainly appeared more complicated than it did before the war. The problems were part demographic, part psychological. War casualties combined with high male emigration had created hollow years. As one alarmist source indicated, in 1935 there were only 4,490,664 men between ages eighteen and sixty-four eligible for the 5,136,959 women between ages fifteen and forty-nine. The figures were more lopsided for women between the ages of thirty-five and fifty-four: 788,946 unmarried women for 496,552 unwed men.[21] Thus, for younger women, much of the worry was psychological. Marriages continued to be put off longer, partly because of the economic vicissitudes of the 1930s. The average age at which women married remained twenty-four to twenty-five, that of men rose slightly to twenty-eight. However, by age twenty-nine, only thirty-two out of one thousand men had decided to marry.[22] Heightening the sense of the competitiveness of the marriage market was wide-spread publicity about the problem of *caro-marito* (or husband shortage). In addition, daughters claimed to want to marry for love, making arranged marriages a more uncertain enterprise. Needless to say, if the family required the daughter's services, for example, to care for aging parents or incapacitated siblings, she might well remain unwed. But for the rest, there was no attractive local equivalent of the bachelor-girl, vaunting her independence past the age of marriage. The *signorina* approaching thirty was fast becoming a *zitella*, haunted by the spectre of spinsterdom, which in the public mind carried more than a social stigma. It denoted a moral and physical state, "an inability to inspire sentiments, because of physical defects, bad character, or lack of dowry." It signaled the arrival of an age in life when love was "no longer in season."[23] The status of being single was made worse under the dictatorship. Fascism publicly stigmatized women who were not wives and mothers. Moreover, in urban areas, low pay and the lack of decent housing made it impossible to live outside the family residence. In rural areas, as Ida Gosso, an old peasant woman, told Nuto Revelli, failing to marry meant "a life as spinsters, as maiden aunts, or as servants, which was more or less the same thing."[24] Short of joining a religious order—as thousands of young village women did in the 1930s—it took unusual singleness of mind, reinforced by the possession of a family house or an independent income, to live in comfort being unwed.

The Lure of Commercial Culture

The dilemmas usually attendant on growing up—which in Italy were no doubt greater because the family was such a stickily conservative institution—were certainly compounded by the conflicting messages emanating from forces outside the home. Not least, there were the institutions of the regime: An expanding school system opened its doors to more young women, yet made gender distinctions more explicit. Fascist as well as Catholic youth groups preached conventional roles, yet proffered openings into a wider world of social experience and political commitment. There was the market; it might not have offered sufficient jobs or decent wages to support any real measure of autonomy for women. But its all-pervasive messages questioned hallowed conventions, including the very notions of family honor and female virtue. Finally, there was the Catholic Church. To compete with state institutions and to counter market messages, it appealed to religious morality and Christian responsibility. It also invoked fears about the medical and social disorders that might ensue from violating its imperatives.

Which force was most influential? To answer involves weighing the respective influences of morals, values, and political loyalties on individual and collective action. No doubt, young people were exposed in very different degrees to the influences of fascism, Catholic religion, and the market. Their family background, their place of residence, their occupation, their religious beliefs, and their political involvement all mattered. Some generalizations are plausible, however. One is that working-class girls were less exposed to official culture. Since they left school at age nine or ten, if not earlier, they were little involved in the fascist youth groups organized around the schools. However, they were notoriously avid consumers of the new mass-circulation magazines and third-run movies. By contrast, middle-class children were more conditioned by fascist institutions, for their lives basically revolved around school and families who generally supported the dictatorship. Finally, young people involved in Catholic networks were perhaps the most buffered from the ideological appeals of fascism, at the same time experiencing mass culture through carefully filtered Church initiatives.

What bears emphasis nonetheless is that both the fascist regime and the Catholic Church followed the lead of commercial cultural enterprises in reaching out to a young female public. Before the war, the *Corriere dei piccoli*, which was founded in 1908, had been the only children's periodical with nationwide circulation. Moreover, youth organizations had been practically nonexistent, except for some local initiatives sponsored by socialist clubs and the *oratori* of Salesian and other Catholic orders. By the 1930s, by contrast, a whole panoply of organizations and publications catered to male and female youths, studied according to class, age group, as well as ideologicial tendency. Thus the regime itself sponsored a special review for girls, *Piccola italiana*, alongside of the *Balilla*, a periodical designed to compete with *Corriere dei piccoli*, as well as innumerable textbooks, pamphlets, and missives designed to educate school children according to grade and age. The dictatorship was also the architect of a whole run of youth organizations, as discussed below. At the same time, Catholic lay and Church-sponsored institutions devised a full run of newspapers, journals, and prescriptive literature for young women:[25] Catholic girls kept up with their youth movement by reading their weekly bulletin *Squilli di resurrezione* and its companion monthly, *Fiamma viva*; university youth read *Azione fucina*, directed by Professor Angela Gotelli, and, starting in 1937, the more cerebral *Studium*. The monthly *Matelda*, designed for "signorine," meaning girls of good family, was founded by Marianna Bettazzi Bondi in 1910 and after her death in 1933 it was edited by Luisa Santandrea. Small-town girls read the former feminist Camilla Bisi's *Ragazze* with its many correspondence columns, whereas *Alba*, a dreary illustrated weekly published by Angela Sorgato starting in 1922, was designed for, if not read by, somber working girls. A more stylish set of Lombard *signorine* read the illustrated monthly *La fiorita*, directed by Albertina Mistrali. In Rome a similar group, though with more intellectual pretensions, subscribed to Maria Rimoldi's cultural review *Il solco*. Movie fans could peruse film magazines such as *Primi piani* (founded in 1936) and *Rivista del cinematografo* (dating from 1927), though they might have been disappointed to find that the editors catered to censorious parish organizers rather than movie-avid female publics.

However, an unabashedly secular, cosmopolitan, commercial culture was the real pacesetter in forming the new girl peer culture. By the 1930s leading publishers had begun to break down female readership by age, class, and interests. Rizzoli publishers, founded in 1902, became in 1924 the first Italian firm to install American-style rotogravure presses. By the 1930s it was copying United States magazine formats as well. By the end of the decade it published ten mass-circulation journals, including the fan magazine *Cinema-illustrazione* (and briefly in 1929–30 Guglielmo Giannini's *Kines*), *Secolo XX* and *Il secolo illustrato* with short stories and news, *Novella*, wholly devoted to serializing popular romances, *Eva*, a weekly for women founded in 1933, and *Piccola*, for young women. In the 1930s, the Garzanti firm flourished, as did Sonzogno publishers, the latter building up a list of 6,000 books. These included the best-selling works of the so-called pornographers, Mario Mariani and Pitigrilli, called that for their erotic themes and salacious details, as well as dozens of novels by a new generation of women writers.[26]

The most popular of these writers, most of whom were born around the turn of the century and came from prosperous northern bourgeois families, were especially adept at capturing the contradictoriness of coming of age in those years. They laced their narratives of intense sentimental vicissitudes with moralisms and practical insights. Along with the prolific Milanese Milly Dandolo (b. 1895) and Giana Anguissola (b. 1906), well-known for *Il romanzo di molta gente* (1931) and *Pensione Flora* (1936), there was the Bolognese Murà, born Maria Nannipieri Volpi in 1892, whom we have already encountered. Murà published her first novel in 1917, several books in the 1920s, and two to three a year in the 1930s for a total of forty (all of the latter with Sonzogno) before she was killed in an airplane crash in 1940. Liana Cambiasi Negretti, born in 1897 to a high bourgeois family of the Comasco and rebaptized Liala by Gabriele D'Annunzio, became hugely successful in 1931 after publishing *Signorsì*, Italy's first "airplane" novel. By the end of the decade, she was celebrated as the Italian Vicki Baum. The Milanese Luciana Peverelli, who started writing in her mother's journal *Trionfo d'amore*, wrote dozens of short stories and novels, one of the most typical being *Trovar marito!* (1934). She was also a pioneer and doyenne among the advice columnists, editor of *Lidel*, *Excelsior*, *Stelle*, and *Bella* in the late 1930s and early 1940s, and founder in 1947 of the sensationalist *Stop*, Italy's *National Enquirer*. By the 1930s movie culture too had become increasingly sensitive to its young female audiences. Adolescent stars such as Lilia Silvi, Carla del Poggio, Alida Valli, and Valentina Cortese capitalized on the great popularity of young Hollywood stars, the vivacious Deanna Durbin, in particular. They were protagonists in a run of movies designed for adolescent audiences and set in school-girl settings, starting with Alessandrini's *Seconda B* (1934), starring Maria Denis, and including *Assenza ingiustificata* (1939), *Maddalena, zero in condotta* (1940), *Ore 9, lezione di chimica* (1941), and *Un garibaldino in convento* (1942).[27]

True, for young Italians to be modern was costly and a bit strenuous. Italy's intense city life may have favored the circulation of mass cultural fads and fashions. But national radio broadcasting systems and movie distribution networks developed haltingly and unevenly, at least partly because of widespread poverty. On the eve of World War II, Italy had about 1,200,000 radio subscribers (compared to Germany's 13,711,000 and Great Britain's 8,900,000) and the number of commercial movie theaters numbered just 2,700 (in contrast to Germany's 6,000 and Great Britain's 4,800), mainly located in northern and central regions.[28] Moreover, distributors were still loath to invest in the cheap third-run movie houses located in poor neighborhoods; the average movie ticket, costing over two lire, was expensive at a time when an average clerk's family disposed of perhaps forty lire a month for recreation. Likewise per capita expenditure on books and periodicals was relatively low; publications were costly, and working-class girls had to hoard their *centesimi* before buying their weekly *no-vellina*. In addition many people remained illiterate; as late as 1930, one out of five women, mainly in the rural south, were unable to read. As a result, cinema going, young people's favorite pastime, was less frequent than, say, in 1930s Great Britain, where young women went regularly, perhaps two or three times a week, and moving pictures were a major topic of conversation.[29] Even so, Diez Gasca found that half of the thousand Roman girls she surveyed in 1937 went at least once a week. Practically all the others, though wanting to go more frequently, were kept from doing so by family poverty.[30]

If Italian youth were less frequent consumers of mass culture than their counterparts in more advanced and evenly developed states, they were nonetheless intensely affected by it. The forms, the messages, the occasions were indeed highlighted by the overall traditionalism of manners and environment. Thus, Hollywood influence was strikingly visible on the main streets: the garish, action-filled, outsize movie posters crowded the advertising hustings, and an array of pulp magazines added dazzling color to neighborhood newspaper kiosks. Mass-circulation magazines featured the glossies distributed by American movie company publicists to illustrate not only their covers but also serialized *novelle*, special features, and advertising, and their editors mined American movie magazines for information about "modern" life.[31] Until 1937 more than 70 percent of the movies in circulation were made in the United States. Thereafter, the big Hollywood film companies withdrew from the Italian market to protest the dictatorship's attempts to restrict their operations. Fascist officials denounced American films as morally worthless, also asserting that they sapped the economy and hampered the takeoff of Italian movie-making. Yet American movies continued to circulate, along with dozens of domestically made facsimiles. Indubitably Hollywood films represented, if not a more explicit sexuality, one that was now the daily truck of commerce. They exposed young Italian spectators to customs seemingly more modern, more advanced, more desirable. They also supplied details on courtship and other social comportments such as fashion, makeup, and the art of the artistic embrace. "Quanto è bello il cinema / quante cose ci fa imparar," as a line from the popular 1930s song went, "How lovely the movies are, / how many things they teach us."

Mass culture, especially that consumed by women, has usually been treated as escapist, the assumption being that it diverts from social engagement and deadens critical thinking.[32] Yet a reading of 1930s Italian pulp suggests that it was an empowering force for young working-class and lower-middle-class women. Alienated from their families and isolated in the face of repressive Catholic and antifeminist ideologies, they turned to the stories, advice columns, illustrations, and jokes to comprehend and master the new sexual manners and social practices of their society. Much of the information these provided was of a practical sort, treating fashion, makeup, and etiquette. But contests, editorials, and quizzes also solicited young women's opinions, something certainly no other institutions did. Who would be a good mate for Garbo? The young respondents to *Piccola*'s query picked Fredric March. Has the cinema changed our ideas about beauty? Write in and tell us what is new in your community. Send in a snapshot and describe what you did on your holidays. Smudgy photos of young girls, their little brothers, and their pets set in vacation resorts and rural residences showed up in the monthly columns of *Kines*. Who is the most beautiful secretary in Italy? *Piccola* ran a series of photo entries in 1929 and awarded the winner 5,000 lire.

The most cogent advice regarded what was doubtless the most exciting, also the most perplexing, aspect of contemporary life, the relations between the sexes. Common wisdom held that in previous generations, marriages had been arranged; respect and affection, if not love, came later. At least until the Great War, and still long after, courtship was a matter of family honor and community interest. Marriage contracts were often initiated by the parents, and the engaged couples remained under strict supervision. In the countryside, it was not until 1919–20 that the obligation to ask the landowner's permission before marrying off a son or daughter was canceled from the sharecropper contracts. In fact, landowners continued to exercise some voice down to the 1940s.

Advice columns, by contrast, presumed a longer courting process and a more varied choice of partners. This was consistent with the new opportunities for young women to meet men in public places such as dance halls, public gardens, and tramways, not to mention in the fascist leisure clubs or *dopolavoro*. The various advisers, with their fanciful names— Doña Dolores de Panza, Knight of Hearts, *Super-revisore*, Aladin—saw their roles as equipping their young female audiences with entirely new stratagems to cope with such occasions. In a mix typical of modern commercial culture, their advice combined high romance with hard-nosed calculations about the costs and benefits of courtship. In prescriptive literature, romances, and the columns of mass-circulation magazines, instructors in the new etiquettes of love life advised on what was permissible and what illicit, what might be dared and what only dreamed about.

The most novel advice regarded the bargaining mentality that was to be brought into courtship. The new figure was the "flirt," or *civetta*; she strategically managed her sexual charms, deploying a whole repertory of self-conscious gambits about what to give and what not, the aim being to control the courtship process. When describing such behavior, one thinks of the term "repressed." And so it was, if we mean that flirting, Italian-style, reflected the impossibility on the part of young women and, for that matter, young men, to act in keeping with the commodified sexual mores purveyed through the mass media. Contrary to the media's often titillating advice, seductive images, and not-so-veiled allusions to affairs, common opinion put a high value on female innocence, on the presumption that young women had not engaged in sexual intercourse before marriage.

Indeed, in this period between the downfall of traditional notions of honor and the onset of so-called free love, the value of physical virginity soared. As families were less able to control courting habits, they shifted management on to the girls themselves: their dowry was an intact hymen, "a capital that must come to fruition and not be dissipated." In this context, as an astute observer of female mores, Anna Garafolo, recalled, "purity was no longer a state of mind or a moral imperative," *pace* the Catholic Church: it was "a physiological condition, one that might well have experienced every temptation, every intimacy, short of the only really dangerous one, namely, that which could be checked by a doctor or newly wedded spouse." Naturally, mothers worried, the middle and lower-middle classes especially exercising care lest a daughter "throw away a good if not necessarily happy match by having physical relations in a moment of generous abandon with somebody who either wasn't a good choice or was unable to marry her."[33]

Mass culture offered advice that mothers could not: about types of men, kinds of kisses, how to flirt. At base, it offered advice on how to negotiate with the opposite sex. Sex, like labor, should not be given away for free; indeed, its power came from scarcity. Consequently, it had to be withheld or disbursed in the appropriate quantities. According to this advice, the marriage market was as competitive and brutal as the labor market, and women, being naturally disadvantaged in the bargaining process, had to manage their resources. What was flirtation? As *Piccola*'s advice columnist Knight of Hearts answered "Dreamer": "It's an affair during which, by which, and without which, one should remain . . . exactly the same."[34] Even the "nicest and most honest girl" had to exploit "all that complicated weaponry which goes under the name of *civetteria* (coquettishness)." One effective strategy, it was advised, might be called "tug of war" or "Russian mountain": this consisted of a "charming smile, followed by complete indifference, utter attentiveness and then a disdaining attitude, moments of abandon while dancing and thereafter signs of ennui, a few minutes of intimacy then cut him off as if he were nothing." Admittedly, this was brutal treatment. But it was necessary. In the first place, being able to say "maybe" was "the only way for a young woman to be queen of the world, that is, of her love."[35] In the second place, contemporary values were anachronistic: given the man shortage, "women should be doing the chasing . . . but they aren't allowed to. . . . They have to act as if they were all rarities, with the risk that, by playing that game, they wreck the very few chances that come their way." Knowing that, the Knight of Hearts confided, "we should be more humane and indulgent in judging female coquettishness."[36]

Not inappropriately we might ask why such conflicts did not result in more sexually emancipated behavior. One thinks of the institution of "dating," which was perhaps the single most important innovation of America's 1920s sexual revolution. But in Italy, the *fidanzato* was practically always presumed to be the betrothed; there was no opportunity to pair off for couples who, though romantically interested in each other, were not necessarily or even likely to marry. The reasons for this casts some light on the constraints young Italians experienced on their freedom of action. In the first place, there was little physical space in which people could be intimate, homes being crowded and communities being so close. In the United States, to take the case where the sheer physical opportunities for young people to escape surveillance were much greater, on average there was a car for every four inhabitants, and roughly one cinema seat for every fifteen. In Italy there was one automobile for every ninety-nine persons and a cinema seat for every thirty.[37] Indeed, given the built-up urban neighborhoods and intensely crowded housing, the very notion of privacy was foreign to town life. Vasco Pratolini captured this well in his tales of young lovers in interwar Florence; his *quartiere* was so utterly under surveillance, criss-crossed by the intrusive gazes of neighbors, that the young *fidanzati* had to wander beyond the canals or up into the hills ringing the old city to consummate their relationships.

A second major obstacle to freer life-styles was the absence of information on sexuality and birth control. The mass media, though offering titillating advice on courtship, was silent about sexuality. This silence could only have made the issue more emotional and uncertain. "There was nothing circulating that helped me in any way to get the slightest idea," recalled one middle-class student.[38] In secondary school literature and philosophy courses, teachers discoursed upon Petrarch's chaste passion for Laura, Dante's inspirational Beatrice, or young Jacopo Ortis's pinings for Teresa. But there were no classes to teach sexuality, not even biology. Nor were sex manuals easy to come by. In the early 1930s, educated young people might have pondered the dense prose and complicated diagrams of G. Franceschini's *Vita sessuale*, published by Hoepli in 1933, which went through ten editions by 1945—if they had not already been frightened off by the author's two previous volumes, *Igiene sessuale* and *Malattie sessuali*. By the mid-1930s, demand for more practical information was being partly satisfied by foreign works in translation. The inspired prose of the American Reverend Sylvanus Stall, whose eight-volume work on sex education was an international best-seller, went through several reprints in Italy during the fascist period. *Married Love* by Marie Stopes, the British pioneer in birth control and sex education, was translated as *Amore e matrimonio* (Milan, 1937). Winifred Richmond's *Introduction to Sex Education*, published in a bowdlerized edition called *Enciclopedia sessuale*, with added attacks on birth control and divorce, went through twelve reprints between 1936 and 1943.[39]

Lack of information threw young people back on common wisdom that was little conducive to premarital sexual experimentation. True, public opinion did not deny female desire, unlike late-nineteenth-century positivist scientists. Quite the contrary, it was alleged that women were by constitution notoriously more sexually avid than men. This led to two positions. One held that female sexuality had to be repressed, though in young women this gave rise to flightiness and even hysterical reactions. Hence the current saying: "Quei nervi sono da maritar!" ("Those nerves need a husband!") The other argued that female sexuality needed to be managed. Ideally, this task was best undertaken by an older, experienced male, though this carried the eventual risk, much publicized in jokes about "horned" or cuckolded husbands, that the bride, awakened to pleasure, would seek more complete satisfaction with younger lovers. In either case, it was best to marry off the women early. Wise advice perhaps, but it flew in the face of middle-class custom. This would have had the young couple postpone their wedding day until the dowry was assembled, housing secured, and the young man, his *titolo di studio* in hand, was ready with at least a promise of employment.

Young women also came across other attitudes less supportive of sexual pleasure. The positions of positivist scientists merged with Catholic repressions and rural ignorance: the result was that the common Victorian fear that sexual deviation led to illness and to abnormality of the sexual organs was particularly exaggerated. Catholic moralists exploited the tendency to medicalize sexual transgression. Consequently, as Bruno Wanrooij wryly notes, "the sanctions ensuing from infractions of norms were ever less transcendental," ever more physical.[40] Hence, masturbation produced tuberculosis, impotence, and spinal maladies; birth control caused neurasthenia, urinary tract infections, and sometimes fatal cases of peritonitis. Lipstick led to lip cancer, and casual physical contacts, such as occurred in kissing, bred disease. Racial scientists and medical doctors, as well as worried parents, warned girls against physical overexertion, not to mention stressful intellectual pastimes, especially during the menstrual period. At very least the fatigue caused painful cramps, perhaps hemorrhaging, at worst irreparable damage to the reproductive organs. Such fears only compounded the insecurity about the ability to control one's body that resulted from the curbs on birth control information.

Female independence, especially sexual freedom, appeared so risky that marriage was the logical and inevitable culmination of the strategy of the flirt. Pressures to settle down were perhaps stronger than ever in the 1930s, or so it seemed to Irene Brin, who, coming of age in the same decade, heartily approved the propensity to postpone marriage. Yet she cattily remarked of her own cohort, "the 1930s girls, once superficially engaged in sports, fashion, Hungarian novels, concerts, interior decorating, and many other pastimes, were always ready to drop everything once their engagement rendered exterior embellishments unnecessary."[41] Elena Canino, who was of the same generation as Brin, forcefully rendered the conventional opinion that there was no real life outside of marriage: Clotilde, her autobiographical heroine, had seemed happily reconciled to the freedoms of a celibate existence, after having been affianced briefly at age twenty-six. But as the novel closes, Clotilde now in her late thirties, having refound an old love, is at last settled in marriage. The novel's last enigmatic words are: "men perhaps need space to live in peace, but a woman needs just four walls."[42]

This finale was entirely explicable in the light of the ideological pressures of the day. The 1929 Lateran Accords, by uniting church and state on the issue of marriage rites, together with Pius XI's *Casti Connubi*, gave new prominence to the institution of marriage. To promote its demographic policies and make state family codes uniform with canon law, the regime lowered the age of marriage for women from fifteen to fourteen and for men from eighteen to sixteen; the age of consent for the former dropped from twenty-one to eighteen and of the latter from twenty-five to twenty-one. To encourage marriage, the dictatorship, in addition to rewarding newlywed couples with loans and money for bridal suites, sponsored splendidly showy group wedding ceremonies. Above all, the dictatorship made marriage a fashionable event of state. The decade opened with the January wedding of Crown Prince Humbert to Maria José of Belgium, an event to which the Italian press devoted weeks of special spreads. On April 23, 1930, it was the turn of Mussolini's eldest and favorite child, Edda, to be married to the young Galeazzo Ciano. The following November, Victor Emmanuel's daughter, Johanna of Savoy, was married to King Boris of Bulgaria.

The union of the Duce's family line to that of Count Costanzo Ciano, chief of fascism's new aristocracy, was truly a marriage for its times. Although not actually arranged, the match was carefully weighed for its appropriateness. Its rapid consummation was also expedient since Edda, at nineteen, was an impulsive, headstrong, and bored young woman who had already thrown herself into several inappropriate love affairs. In her mother Rachele's forthright remarks to the groom's parents, Edda possessed a "loyal, but overbearing and lively" character, and she brought to marriage none of the traditional female arts and little vocation for maintaining a proper household.[43] The marriage ceremony itself was relatively simple, with none of the feudal pomp of the crown prince's. On that occasion, the royal couple reviewed a two-mile-long cortege, fascist dignitaries in the lead, followed by three hundred contingents of lavishly costumed peasants who laid down "gifts of the land." A conventionally grand bourgeois white wedding, the Ciano-Mussolini nuptials were celebrated with religious rites at the Church of San Giuseppe in Via Nomentana. Witnesses for the bride were Mussolini's patron Prince Torlonia, chief of Rome's "black" aristocracy, and Dino Grandi, the most respectable of the "fascists of the first hour," who, being foreign minister at the time, was also the twenty-five-year-old groom's employer. Following the reception, the couple left for a honeymoon on Capri.

Even the mass press, for all its emphasis on passion, taught young women that in the end they had to make their peace with the average man: this was the man of "middle intelligence," meaning the office accountant rather than the dashing boss, the engineer rather than the variety artist. As Murà advised impressionable young secretaries, they should expect a "love without surprises." For their suitors would propose "with a wholly bourgeois tact, the accounts in order, all obstacles overcome, the household budget already calculated, work divided up, and retirement plans laid out."[44] Nobody argued that marriage was not forever, and statistics on divorce and separation, practically nugatory by contemporary standards, bore this out. Yet even in marriage, it seemed, one could still sustain romance: childbearing was never mentioned as the end of married life, and women, like men, might still have affairs. Of course that called for what the stylish Daria Banfi Malaguzzi called "praticità amorosa," or skill in loving. The back street dalliance was not immoral nor to be feared as adulterous; honesty was better than virtue which spoke through hard, thin lips.[45] The problem that women faced was what to do when such affairs ended. The effects might be emotionally devastating. Unlike men, it was argued, women could not easily find consolation in family or work. The ideal woman for many moviegoers was Greta Garbo, who as Queen Christina knew how to love passionately yet triumph over the petty demands of men and states. La Garbo was her role model, one woman recalled, thinking back to her conventionally middle-class adolescence in the late 1930s, and "as for the idea of being born to procreate, that would have made her smile with refined disgust."[46]

To emphasize that commercial culture attuned courtship rituals to modern market logics is not to say that notions of family honor had been discarded either in law or custom. True, more enlightened families felt wounded dignity rather than dishonor in the case of affiancements gone wrong; they sought merely to salve family members' hurt feelings, especially their daughters'.[47] They had no intention of seeking recourse in the courts, much less resorting to murder, as occasionally still happened in the Italian south and in Sicily. However, the revised civil code still respected a patriarchal notion of honor by dealing indulgently with crimes committed in its name. More usually, dishonored girls rather than abusive or careless men felt the brunt of parental fury. Rural customs tolerated fathers who banished daughters pregnant out of wedlock, not only "because of offended honor, but because of the delusion inflicted on those who counted on a fruitful match."[48] Custom as well as law presumed the woman to be a consenting party to her seduction, if not actually the instigator. Efforts by women reformers to legislate changes to protect minors and guileless older women from seducers came to naught. Nor did they do much to change the widespread opinion that the lower-class girl who purportedly exploited her sexual desirability to seduce a young man of good family was more reprehensible than the man who preyed on a virgin, for the former could not make amends through marriage. In provincial centers, such cross-class courtships were misbegotten affairs, capable of producing all of the dramatic turmoil of nineteenth-century opera. Clara Calamai's story of growing up during the early 1930s in the Tuscan textile town of Prato anticipated the dramatic parts she played a decade later as Cinecittà's leading femme fatale. She fell in love with a school companion, but the affair was broken off by the boy's parents, wealthy bourgeois who disapproved of her lower-class status. Her father, a respectable municipal clerk, was ousted from his social club. Clara gave way to a nervous collapse and then left her native town forever.[49] In life, as in art, grand passion was defeated by class differences and the moralism of pettifogging provincials.

The Battle for Custody of Youth

As mass culture became a new contender for the loyalties of young people, it complicated the decades-long struggle between church and state for the "custody of youth."[50] The Catholic Church's interest dated back at least to the Counter-Reformation, but it was enhanced in the wake of Italian unification. Having withdrawn from the arena of electoral politics after the new Kingdom of Italy occupied Rome in 1870, the Church had become keenly sensitive to the need for alternative methods of influencing social tendencies. Since the first decade of the century, it had acquired formidable support in Catholic Action. Originally a loose coalition of societies and unions founded at various times by Catholic laity to re-Christianize Italian society, it had thrived after 1904 when Pius X lifted the *non-expedit* barring Catholics from political engagement. As early as 1908, Catholic Action had turned its attention to youth. That year, at the first general meeting of the National Council of Italian Women, Catholic Action's female adherents had broken with lay feminists in order to assert the Church's right to educate youth on religious matters in school. In 1916 Catholic Action founded its first national youth groups, the Catholic *Esploratori*, or Boy Scouts. In the next decade, they branched into more than a thousand locations, enrolling almost a hundred thousand youths. In 1918 Catholic Action backed the first groups for girls, the *Gioventù femminile cattolica italiana*. After the Milanese Archbishop Achille Ratti became Pius XI in 1922, a unified and strengthened Catholic Action came to consist of five main groups: the adult men's groups, the Union of Italian Catholic Women (UDCI) for adult females, the *Esploratori* for boys, the girls' *Gioventù femminile*, and the Italian Catholic University Federation (FUCI) for students. Organized and officiated by laymen and laywomen, with each local section advised by a chaplain nominated by Church authorities, Catholic Action's overall direction passed through a papally appointed central commission down to diocesan and parish councils. By 1929 some 250 diocesan committees supervised 4,000 sections for adult men and women, and 5,000 sections for university students and youth, including a couple thousand for girls. Just nine years later, as Catholic Action celebrated the twentieth anniversary of the foundation of the girls' groups, with a huge rally at St. Peter's, the leadership listed some remarkable accomplishments: along with the 15,000 local sections with their 300,000 members, 20 million lire had been collected for the church's overseas missions and 18 million for the Catholic University, while seventy-five young members had been blessed by apparitions of the Madonna.

Inevitably this flourishing Church organization competed with fascism's own growing ambition to educate Italian youth. In the early 1920's, fascism's efforts to mobilize youth had proceeded haphazardly under party auspices. But by 1926, convinced of the malleability of the younger generations (and of the incomprehension, if not outright hostility of the "intransigent" older ones), the regime began to organize more systematically, grouping old and new units under the *Opera nazionale balilla*, or ONB. Its earliest groups, which grew up alongside of the *fasci di combattimento*, were the Fascist University Groups *(Gruppi universitari fascisti)*, more familiarly known as GUF, which included men and, theoretically, women students as well. In the early 1920s, it also started to build up its most renowned formation. That was the *Balilla* for boys, named after the legendary Genoese street boy whose rock-throwing exploits against the city's Austrian occupiers in 1774 were often cited as an example of heroic protonationalism. Later, the PNF founded the *Avanguardisti* to prepare young males to join the party. Meanwhile, two girls' units, one for *piccole italiane* aged eight to twelve and the other for *giovani italiane* from thirteen to eighteen, grew up under the direct auspices of the women's *fasci*. However, in 1929, like all other school-aged children's groups, they would come under the control of the *Opera nazionale balilla*, which having been given a virtual monopoly over children's after-school activities was in turn placed under the supervision of the Ministry of National Education. By the early 1930s, the ONB's leader, the ex-*squadrista* Renato Ricci, had firmly grasped the signal importance of school plant and personnel in a backward society. The ONB, in addition to the semimilitary physical fitness drills it was originally intended to provide, supplied a whole gamut of instructional and social services not previously offered by the school system, from sports and gymnastics to schoolbooks and smocks. In 1937 in an effort to discipline this sprawling empire and rally teachers and pupils in its far-flung outposts, the ONB was reconsolidated under the Fascist party as the *Gioventù italiana del littorio*, or GIL.[51]

Conflict between the Church and the fascist state, practically inevitable given their competing goals, sharpened in the wake of the law of April 3, 1926, which established the ONB's monopoly over youth education. As a preliminary to the Lateran Accords of February 1929, the Vatican agreed to dissolve the Catholic boy scout troops. However, within months after the accords, on December 31, 1929, Pius XI published a major encyclical on youth called *Rappresentanti in Terra* (or sometimes called by its Latin title *Divini Illius Magistri*). Prompted by Pius's forceful claim that the Church alone properly educated youth, Catholic Action had stepped up its activities aimed at young men, especially at the growing numbers of working-class youth unemployed as a result of the depression. In reaction, during 1931, fascist gangs attacked Catholic Action outposts. Forced to back down, the Church hierarchy agreed to dissolve Catholic Action's politicized male youth groups and to desist from organizing sports and explicitly political activity. Consequently, over the next decade, Church personnel and Catholic laity worked assiduously through the social and cultural networks of civil society as they had in the past when debarred from political action. Some avenues were traditional: in 1940 there were thousands of children in Catholic orphanages and perhaps a half-million youngsters registered in burgeoning numbers of Catholic schools.[52] The ways of catechizing were myriad: papal encyclical went hand in hand with prescriptive literature, old-time religion with modern mass rituals, pilgrimages and devotional retreats with moviegoing and radio broadcasts. In the process, the Church developed positions on all of the cultural and educational issues of the day, but especially those of relevance to youth—including movies, modern courtship, and schooling. Ultimately, membership in Church-affiliated youth groups was never as high as that in the dictatorship's GIL. Enrollment having been practically obligatory for public school children, the GIL counted about five million members in 1939, or about 60 to 70 percent of the eligible age groups. By contrast, Catholic groups registered perhaps several hundred thousand members or about 15 percent of the age group from 16 to 25.[53] However, the quality of the Catholic appeal was such that it provided what was perhaps a more encompassing and enduring, if not more fulfilling, response to the disquieting effects of modernity than that which could be devised by a secular state. Unlike the fascist regime, which at bottom accepted them, the Church rejected the competitive values of commercial culture and defied the dichotomies of private and public, religion and politics, typical of modern national states.

Catholic Models of Girlhood

Italian Catholicism's capacity to compete with fascism for the hearts and minds of youth was especially evident in its treatment of female youth. Unlike the boys' groups, which were disbanded under pressure from the dictatorship, the *Gioventù cattolica* thrived. The groups were built on secure foundations: the first had been founded in 1917–18 backed by the archdiocese of Milan, which wanted to help local parishes resist socialist propaganda. For thirty years thereafter, the organization was led by the remarkable Armida Barelli. Born to a well-to-do Milanese family in 1882, Barelli had been seized by an awesome spiritual crisis after her father's death in 1906. In the course of resolving it, she dedicated herself to philanthropic work, took sacred vows, and then became a member of a lay spiritual group called the Tertiary Order of Franciscans. At the prompting of Father Agostino Gemelli—whose own background and religious experience were quite similar—Barelli refounded the Devotion to the Sacred Heart. She also became registrar for Italian Catholicism's leading intellectual center, Milan's Catholic University of the Sacred Heart, which her mentor founded in 1921. That same year Barelli established *Squilli di resurrezione*, the bulletin of the girls' movement. Geared to a cross-class public, it included special sections for female workers and peasants. With the young Perugian Maria Sticco, she also directed the refined monthly *Fiamma viva* for girls of good family. With its watchwords "organization, formation, action" and the militant Franciscan Saint Rose of Viterbo as its patron saint, the *Gioventù femminile* appeared to understand the limits of an explicit authoritarianism in addressing the problems of youth. Organizers thus had to understand their charges' concerns before deciding which to tolerate, which to exorcise, and which to discipline through ritualized outlets. Though the Church was interested in both male and female youth, the hierarchy was especially attentive to the latter.[54] This was not simply because the Church was barred from bestowing equivalent attention on male youth groups. Catholic missionary zeal was fundamentally egalitarian: contemporary life appeared to affect women in particularly pernicious ways, and special efforts had to be made toward saving them.

This concern is especially manifest in Catholic policy toward that "most attractive of attractions," the cinema. Since 1930 Pius XI had admired the American episcopacy's battles to enforce the internal censorship mechanisms devised by the United States film industry: the Hayes Code had stipulated that no picture shall be produced which will lower the moral standards of those who see it. Hence "the *sympathy* of the audience" shall never be "thrown on the side of crime, wrong-doing, evil, or sin."[55] Needless to say, these standards were difficult to uphold. When the pontiff issued his encyclical on the movies, *Vigilanti Cura*, on June 29, 1936, his main purpose was to lend support to the high-minded "holy crusade" undertaken by the Catholic Legion of Decency to pledge millions of Americans not to attend any motion picture condemned as "offensive to

Catholic moral principles or to the proper standard of living." With a solid commonsense appreciation of the cinema's power in "influencing the masses"—"it speaks by means of vivid and concrete imagery, which the mind takes in with enjoyment and without fatigue"—Pius decried "bad" motion pictures as occasioning sinfulness. "They seduce young people along the ways of evil by glorifying the passions; they show life under a false light; they cloud ideals; they destroy pure love, respect for marriage, and affection for the family." [56] Undaunted by this challenge, Pius put forward a detailed plan calling for a permanent national reviewing office to classify films and to oversee Church-affiliated movie circles (which in 1935 numbered about 1,600, or one-third of all outlets in Italy). [57]

Pius's encyclical thus gave at least tacit support to Father Carlo Canziani. The cofounder of a modestly successful Catholic movie-making firm called S. A. Lux Cristiana, he was also the youth movement organizer who in 1927, with Catholic Action's backing, had set up the *Consorzio utenti cinematografici educativi* (CUCE) to undertake a "new intense labor on behalf of honest cinema." [58] Naturally, Italian moralists could not hope to influence moviemakers as the American Legion of Decency did with the awesome threat of the box office boycott. However, Church censors, by means of diocesan channels and publications like Canziani's *Revista del cinematografo*, sought to guide priests and laity on how to distinguish good movies from socially useless or plainly immoral ones, and to instruct the faithful accordingly. Beyond simply rating and condemning films, Catholic censorship forged new community standards by teaching parishioners proper criteria of judgment: why "we Italians," "our Latin sensibilities," "our Christian morality" should be offended, say, by King Vidor's *The Champ*, which shows "so many lovely things, and such fine sentiments," yet is ruined by that "unfortunate divorce." [59] In the process, the censors shaped the public's awareness of new "sins"—including divorce, extramarital affairs, and nudity—as well as of new "values," in particular, anticommunism and patriotism. Moreover, unlike the state censorship board, Catholic moralists displayed a particular sensitivity to group psychology. Hence they evaluated material not so much according to the plots or intent, but according to its subjective effects. Women by nature were more easily aroused and swayed by film messages than men, and children acted like women, only worse. Consequently, censorship norms reflected churchmen's worries about the "agitated sleep" of housewives and the "disquiet" of adolescent girls.

In contrast, government censorship was ostensibly inspired by "reasons of state," in which moralism and politics combined in flimsily motivated judgments. One case might illustrate this. Church censors begrudgingly approved Charlie Chaplin's *Modern Times:* "Its social polemic which is lacking in true Christian inspiration is compensated by its overwhelming comicality." The state board passed over a scene in which Charlot accidently ingested cocaine while it deleted an episode in which he picked up the red warning flag that had dropped from a passing truck load and unwittingly led up a communist protest march. This scene, in the eyes of the state, justified subversion.[60]

Catholic prescriptive literature addressed itself to the modernization of mores as well as to traditional pieties. Catholic publishing houses such as Gemelli's Vita e Pensiero and the Turin-based Society of Saint Paul produced thousands of pamphlets, periodicals, and series that were then plied through religious bookstores, peddled door-to-door, or loaned through 3,750 parish libraries. *Gioventù femminile* also sponsored a special biographical series, devoted to female saints, including Elizabeth, Agnes, and Joan of Arc, as if through these exemplary lives young women might learn the path of righteousness. But the most widely circulated works highlighted the very issues that the mass press was addressing with secular messages: namely, contemporary manners. Marianna Bettazzi Bondi's *Verso le nozze* ("dedicated to the betrothed of Italy") was among the best-known primers for Catholic girls. For Zia Anna, as she was also known, was editor of *Matelda*, a well-regarded monthly for girls, and a stalwart of the UDCI. Moreover, her little book was the companion volume to *Il libro del fidanzato*. This had been authored by her husband, Rodolfo Bettazzi, also a leading member of Catholic Action, as well as the founder in 1912 of the League of Public Morality, and went through eight editions during the interwar years. In her work Bettazzi Bondi spoke to the problem of longer courtships and the new expectations of marriage. To make her points, she drew on the seasoned expertise of French social Catholicism (much in the way sex experts drew on United States and German manuals, and advice columnists turned to American fan magazines).[61] Her main message, like theirs, was that in equal measure both sexes should behave with sobriety and self-control. The longer courtships were good insofar as they allowed young couples to reflect on family duties and develop a sense of responsibility toward each other. But they were also worrisome insofar as they might lead to premarital sexual experimentation. To prevent this, girls were admonished not to arouse male desire by flirting. Boys were instructed not to lust after girls they had no intention of marrying nor to distinguish the good girls they might wed from the bad ones they might seduce.[62]

In a more reflective work, fittingly titled "Duty and Dreams," Maria Sticco collected her editorials from *Fiamma viva*. In the widely circulated volume, which went through ten editions in a decade, she addressed the main dilemma that confronted her young readers—spinsterhood and loneliness, or family life and self-abnegation. A common way for young Catholic women to answer such questions, at least in the early 1920s, was by idealizing their mothers' times. Women in those days, ostensibly, had not faced such harsh choices.[63] But Sticco urged them not to be nostalgic. Modern women no less than modern men had to confront the conflicting demands of contemporary existence by struggling against egoism and by nurturing their ideals. Her counsels on marriage reflected the experience of educated Catholic women. Some, like herself or Armida Barelli, were unwed yet had found personal as well as social and religious satisfaction within the Catholic movement. Others, like Bettazzi Bondi, Angela Gotelli, or Maria Guidi, were married, but to companions with shared interests in Catholic activism. To Dina, who was desperate to find a fiancé, Sticco replied:

> Between an unhappy marriage and unhappy singleness, I prefer the latter. Better to cry with two eyes, than four, six, or eight. Besides, singleness, if we want, can be productive, dignified, and serene. . . . What we can't do as wives or mothers, we can do, perhaps better, as sisters, aunts, teachers, or friends. Suffice it to have a heart heroic with sacrifice.[64]

In a similar vein, Catholic schooling emphasized the need to develop female individuality. This would enable young women to fend off the seductions of modern existence, without succumbing to individualistic forms of emancipation. In his 1929 encyclical on youth, Piux XI had denounced coeducation, which the fascist reform of schools upheld. The Pope argued that the differences between boys and girls which would eventually "complement each other in the family and society" ought to be "maintained and encouraged during their formative years."[65] His message reinforced the growth of parochial schools, a trend that had started as early as 1924 when the Gentile school reforms recognized the right of privately educated students to be licensed upon passing a uniform state examination. One suspects that the proliferation of nuns in teaching orders, as well as the opinion common in Catholic circles that girls' needs were not properly served in the public school system, encouraged this increase.[66] Most parochial schools were ruled in the rigid style commonly associated with Catholic schooling. However, some orders such as the Sisters of the Resurrection of Rome and the Ursulines undertook curricular reforms designed to "respect the student's personality." Discipline was to be effected without "constriction," by a process of "self-formation."[67] The nuns of the Roman Union of Ursulines were dedicated to a liberal education "in opposition to all standarization." To counter the "assembly-line assault on the spirit," they studied the "inclinations and resources of the individual" so as to develop a "correct conception of liberty": this meant not independence in any conventional liberal sense, but what they called "self-mastery."[68] Benefitting a small elite, this system produced well-educated and socially conscious young women. More generally, it evidenced the degree to which enlightened Catholic circles had meditated and acted upon the widespread perception that state institutions, the newly fascist as much as the old liberal ones, were unable to come up with a system of values or education suited to young women.

Educating Tomorrow's Women

Compared to Italian Catholicism, Italian fascism was riddled with contending attitudes about young women. Like the Church, the dictatorship was reacting against the emancipatory tendencies of interwar society. Yet unlike Catholicism, it exploited the desire to be modern as much as it curbed it. Thus at every level, fascist institutions sent out mixed messages. The youth group leaders harped on the virtues of domesticity. But by involving girls in activities outside of the home in the interest of the party, the Duce, and the nation, they undercut parental authority. Prescriptive literature preached subordination, yet praised displays of heroism. The reform of the school system, undertaken in 1923, was avowedly antifeminist, yet tolerated significant increases in the numbers of young women being schooled beyond the elementary level.

This Janus-faced outlook originated no doubt in fascism's dualistic vision of female roles. As "reproducers of the race," women were to embody traditional values, being stoic, silent, and fervid; as patriotic citizens, they were to be modern, that is combative, public and on call. Augusto Turati, the first PNF secretary to pay any attention to organizing female youth, tried to make the best of these inconsistencies when the party convened its first rally of *giovani italiane* at the Argentina Theater in central Rome in June 1930. He joked about the gaffe he had committed by convening the teenagers on their own. As it turned out, their protective mothers had not only accompanied them into the town center but insisted on coming into the theater. He urged the girls to be "modern," though not "Americanizing"; they were to be "neither falsely severe, nor stupidly frivolous." Like male youth, they had uniforms; but theirs really comprised a sports dress, a "pretty outfit," with "truly nothing militaristic or squadristic about it." To make his major point, Turati familiarly urged them to "look me in the eyes": "modesty and virtue certainly don't lie in lowered gazes!" Though he recognized their youthful strivings and dreams, in conclusion, he admonished them that their duty was to return to the "hearth."[69]

Surely behind this mixed ambition for youth lay conflicts in fascist leaders' own outlooks. At the same time as they were mistrustful of feminism and of emancipated women generally, they nursed the same ambivalent expectations of their daughters as other members of Italy's middle classes. They may have been inveterate womanizers, but they expected their female offspring, not to mention their wives, to be chaste and dutiful. They argued that women were incapable of the complicated intellectual synthesis which was the hallmark of true culture. But they wanted their daughters well-educated. These conflicted views were evident in Mussolini himself. His rural-rooted misogyny held that women were angels or devils, born "to keep house, bear children, and plant horns."[70] But he encouraged the tomboyishness of his unquiet daughter, Edda, whose escapades won her the nickname Sandokan from her family and a silver Carnegie medal from the government in 1925 for saving a drowning girl friend at the Cattolica beach. Educated in one of Italy's most exclusive finishing schools, Poggio Imperiale at Florence, she was one of the first young women in Italy to wear pants and drive a car. Yet her brothers, and even her feckless husband Galeazzo, were her father's true heirs. She lacked any power to control her own, much less her family's, fate; Edda's "greatest regret always," she told in her memoirs, "was not to have been a man."[71] Giuseppe Bottai too, although accorded much attention as the regime's most coherent modernizer, displayed the common ambivalence about educating women. As Minister of National Education, he was responsible for the School Charter of 1939, article 21 of which stipulated that women required a separate education suited to their primary mission as mothers and nurturers. Meanwhile, his own daughter was educated at Rome's Parioli Institute, a leading private school for girls. Moreover, in his preface to the Charter's passages on women, he admitted that none, if they truly wanted to go on, would be barred from pursuing higher courses of study.[72]

Fascist women who spoke as mothers of daughters expressed no less perplexity about their offspring's futures. In many ways, they welcomed the "new woman." For one contributor to the fascist women's press, "schools, gymnastic societies, and laws all agree on a new education such as will yield the woman citizen, as well as mother, capable of grasping all

the vast problems of contemporary existence, tempering love with strength."
But finding "balance in female education" was "difficult": for the young
women, lacking their mothers' "sentimentality," were capable of "dangerous exaggeration," and, according to Lucia Magrini Vinaccia, they fall
prey to "icy aridity, gigantic egotism, domination of all sentiment in favor of a monstrous ego, whose only desire is pleasure." Her major hope
was that "tomorrow's woman" might be at once "ardent and sweet, conscientious and charitable."[73]

Far less than we might anticipate, fascist women sought solutions in
their own version of mass culture. One of very few to try to come to
terms with the problem in a self-conscious way was Camilla Bisi, a one-
time feminist, editor at the Genoese newspaper *Il lavoro* and founder of
Ragazze. Furious at *Piccola*'s 1929 beauty contest for secretaries—which
as the first such event in Italy acquired a certain notoriety—she urged
that beauty contests be banned. Male editors manipulated poorly paid
girls, encouraged them in their silly passions, and then dumped them as
they aged. Yet Bisi was realistic enough to recognize that the flood of
American-style journals was not to be staunched. If this was the case, "let
them stay stupid, not dangerous." Instead of rewarding the "most beautiful of the beautiful," prizes should be given to the "most hardworking
of the hardworking," or the "most courageous of the courageous."[74] Fascist organizations did that in a manner of speaking; the hierarchies and
heroics they promoted were akin to the competitive values that the mass
press was accused of exploiting.

Sexual Bias in Schooling

The dictatorship's indecisive misogyny was especially manifest in its policies toward schooling young women. Arguably, the liberal state had no
explicit policy on the issue, in keeping with its record of inaction on such
questions. But Italy's founding law on education, the Casati Law of 1859,
had not prohibited coeducation and had failed to establish a separate post-
elementary system for females. Consequently, girls began to move up
through the system, and the first women graduated from the universities
in 1877. After the turn of the century, the school system as a whole
expanded under pressure from lower-middle and working-class families.
The former pressed for their children to go to the elite secondary schools
to gain access to university faculties, whereas the latter, backed by socialists and enlightened middle-class reformers, pressed for a strengthening
of the dismally underfunded elementary and technical schools. At the
elementary and secondary levels at least, enrollments for women rose

roughly at á pace equal to those for men. Meanwhile, in the wake of reforms, the need for lower-school instructors caused more and more teaching, or Normal, schools to be established. Their graduates, scantily educated, ill-paid, and overworked, were mainly female. By the eve of the Great War, women's presence in the Italian educational system as a whole thus had three salient characteristics. First, women had acquired a certain visibility at the university level, though they comprised but 6 percent of the total student body. Second, they overwhelmingly dominated teaching staffs in the elementary schools and outnumbered men by about two to one in the middle schools. Third, they were acquiring the same education as men. This made them, according to Maria Sticco—who was obviously no sympathizer to lay and coeducational schooling—"free thinkers, positivists, [and] disdainful of the maternal creed as pure childishness."[75]

Inevitably the position of women in the educational system came under fire as critics launched a broader attack against the schools. This assault dated from at least a decade before the war, and it had made allies of reforming pedagogues, nationalists, and cultural purists of various ilk. In the war's aftermath, criticism of the defects in public education had become so ferocious that the reform of the schools was among the very first issues on Mussolini's agenda after the seizure of power in 1922. The major complaint was that the school had become so democratized under pressures from petty bourgeois strivers and radical reformers that it no longer performed its chief function, to select the nation's elite. Instead of regulating the processes of upward mobility, the educational system accelerated them; rather than depressing expectations, it stimulated them. As a result, the system was turning out a "plethora of learned misfits." Workers and peasants had allegedly deserted the stable and workshop: "ignorant, clamorous, excitable," as they crowded into the elite schools, they were "supported by worthy relatives who yearn for their little dunces to advance at any cost to conquer the 'diploma' and then the 'position.' "[76] Worse, once in school, they came under the influence of female and dogooding instructors. With their positivistic precepts, pacifism, and sentimentality, they were incapable of producing the virile deportment, competitive zeal, and critical faculties needed to uphold Italy's nationhood. These accusations had become all the more caustic in the wake of the Great War, as the secondary schools threw a bigger and more feminized mass of *laureati* and *diplomati* onto the job market, nationalism and antifeminism became more virulent, and fascist and nationalist youth agitated in the universities.[77]

The main task of Giovanni Gentile, the revered Sicilian philosopher turned fascist ideologue who was Mussolini's Minister of Public Instruction from 1922 to 1924, was thus to remake this system. He had two goals: to inculcate Italian youth with the ideology of the fascist state and to select and promote only the elite so as not to overload the market for intellectual labor.[78] Predictably, the most significant innovations were introduced at the secondary level, first, by limiting enrollments in the *liceo-ginnasio* that alone gave access to university education and, second, by abolishing the so-called supplementary courses enabling students from other schools to attend university. The much-excoriated Normal schools, renamed *istituti magistrali*, or teaching institutes, were cut from 153 to 87 and a university-level (but decidedly second-string) *facoltà di magistero* was added for those specializing in teaching. At the same time, Gentile downgraded technical instruction by abolishing the technical schools and replacing them with the so-called complementary schools with no outlets to higher courses of study. At age ten or eleven, Italian children now faced even more restricted choices than under liberal rule. They might pursue the course of classical studies at the *liceo-ginnasio;* or they might prefer the new and not yet as prestigious scientific lyceum. Girls might also select the recently added *liceo femminile.* They might attend the *istituto magistrale* or the *istituto tecnico,* each of which was now divided into lower and upper secondary courses, or they might end up in a *scuola complementare.* As before, the *liceo* alone allowed entry into any university faculty; students attending technical institutes could only go on to faculties of economics, commerce, or statistics, and not, as before, to mathematics or physics.

The overriding aim of the reform was thus to cut the long school story short. By curbing the ambitions of the small bourgeoisie, the Gentile reforms intended to convert aspirants bent on social promotion and state employment into passably educated artisans, workers, and peasants.[79] Ultimately, this stringent policy was unsustainable. The dictatorship's own precious lower-middle-class adherents, seeing their sons and daughters closed out, protested until the upper schools opened up a bit. Technocrats too were aghast at the flippant disregard Gentile and other idealists displayed toward technical schooling, and in the 1930s the philosopher's successors would endeavor to correct that bias. Even so, the Gentile laws left a legacy of social discrimination, authoritarianism, and unresponsiveness to the needs of a developing industrial economy.

So much emphasis has been placed on the class biases of the Gentile reform that its discrimination on the basis of gender is easily missed. It is easy to interpret the greater number of women being schooled, the lower illiteracy rates for women, and the higher percentages of women in university faculties as signs that the system's elitism was gender-blind. In a fashion, that was true: the Nobel Prize winning biologist Rita Montalcini Levi was a product of the Italian public educational system of the 1930s, as was Natalia Ginzburg, Elsa Morante, and most other well-known Italian women of that generation. Yet the biases against women were numerous. Blatant and covert, they were the result of specific legislative measures, the idealist philosophy of education, and the complex interaction between family strategies and opportunities in the labor market.

To begin with, Gentile's brand of idealist philosophy was avowedly antifemale. Whereas nineteenth-century positivist thinkers like Cesare Lombroso put women lower down on the evolutionary scale than men, Gentile and his epigones put them on another and lesser planet. According to Gentilian precepts, the human spirit was the master of reality, provided that the individual, through critical reflection and without bending to vulgar reality, could grasp the life of the Spirit. Education was the process by which this occurred. Guided by educators, the student was led to apprehend the ethical nature of the civilization in which he lived and to partake creatively in its values. In pursuit of this higher truth, idealist philosophy was inevitably indifferent to, if not disdainful of, what were regarded as nontranscendent subjects—such as technical instruction, pedagogy, and most social sciences—not to mention concrete historical trends. It was also intolerant of other value systems, not least of all those identified with women. True to a system based on essentialist principles, Gentile viewed woman as "infinite nature," the "primordial principle," hence outside of history and with a subaltern relationship to the State and the Spirit. For woman to be "valued, respected, exalted," she had to "accept and not attempt to deny the nature of her difference."[80] Like a child's, her grasp of the ethical nature of being could only be approximate. She would thus benefit from the religious courses which Gentile, though not himself a practicing Catholic, had made obligatory in Italian schools to educate those subjects of a lesser nature and more limited abilities—females, youth, the lower orders—whose understanding of the Spirit was imperfect. Inevitably, Gentile's philosophy denied women any capacity as educators. The ability to educate could not be taught, for the true educator had to commune with his students, exercise his authority to illuminate higher truths, and act as *servitore* of the State, it being the universal expression of ethicalness and the means by which the individual might overcome the limits of his individuality. The "virile" educator was especially important in subjects regarded as formative of the elites: philosophy, history, literature, and languages.

This philosophy perhaps inspired and was certainly used to justify three specific measures. First, it offered a pedagogical rationale for defeminizing the teaching profession. In the wake of the sharp reduction of the Normal schools, women were barred from teaching in certain fields. Thus royal decree-law 2480 of December 9, 1926, excluded women from the *concorsi* for chairs of letters, Latin, Greek, history, and philosophy at classical and scientific *licei*. It also barred them from the competitions for posts in Italian and history at technical institutes. Another law in 1928 prevented females from being named directors of the middle schools. Yet another in 1940 stopped them from being *presidi* or principals of technical institutes. Second, Gentilian philosophy inspired the establishment of a new finishing school for girls. This was the aforementioned *liceo femminile*. Designed for daughters of good families who formerly might have attended Normal schools for cultural purposes alone, it offered a smattering of humanities, including Latin, as well as arts and crafts suited to *signorine*. When it was founded in 1924, Italian feminists denounced it. For the Bolognese Zora Becchi, it threatened to perpetuate "that insipid mannequin who is the woman (or, worse, the young miss) of our day."[81] Like the radical liberal Piero Gobetti who denounced the minister for creating "a school for masters and servants," Emilia Siracusa Cabrini condemned the *liceo* as signaling a return to "aristocratic-Catholic" ways of schooling. Whatever its limits, the liberal school system had been oriented to providing women with "a shared knowledge inspired by the need for concrete, modern know-how," whereas Gentile's system threatened "very real damage to the unity of thought of our class."[82] Long after feminist outrage had been stilled, fascist women would continue to express their utter perplexity at this "luxury school." For Lucia Pagano, the *preside* of the all-girl Maria Pia of Savoy Teaching Institute of Rome and a longtime fascist supporter (she was a founding member of Rome's first women's *fascio*), the school had been "conceived abstractly." Inevitably, it failed to "respond to the desires of a student body that pursued a practical end through studies with a cultural bent." Italian bourgeois families had reached the same conclusion long before; only 471 girls were ever enrolled in the small number of schools and in 1928 the whole enterprise was abandoned.[83]

Gentilian pedagogical precepts as applied to vocational training affected female students differently from men. In general, the reforms downgraded technical instruction, preventing motivated working-class youth from using vocational programs as stepping-stones to higher education. They thus hardened the educational system's caste-like character, as well as proving a great disservice to industrial employers. To remedy the latter problem, Giuseppe Belluzzo, the Minister of National Education and a prominent engineer, put through measures in 1932–34. These increased the number of complementary courses available to women to three: the basic course for *avviamento professionale*, a second for specialization called *preparazione professionale*, and a third called *formazione del personale insegnante e direttivo di laboratorio* to train shop teachers and supervisors. However, the spirit of Gentile's reform remained intact. Some schools were strictly vocational, offering no education to speak of. The majority did just the opposite, treating arts and crafts as "elements in the pupil's spiritual formation" rather than as skills needed for job placement. Consequently, schools that had once served mainly working-class girls drew more and more from a lower-middle-class and even middle-class constituency. These girls came from families with the means to sustain the costs of several years of schooling without the girls' necessarily having to find jobs; the concern was to acquire some cultural polish. Meanwhile, commercial schools, capitalizing on the growing demand for secretaries and translators, offered just enough practice in typing, stenography, and foreign languages to unload thousands of ill-trained graduates on a market already saturated with clerical workers. The schools did not try to make these wholly feminized occupations respectable or quasi-professional. The result was that no official messages contradicted the dazzling myths purveyed by *Novello-film* or *Piccola*: the secretary was the heroine of modern times, with a sexual rather than a professional identity, in youth the plaything of her boss, in old age the archetypal spinster.[84]

Though the dictatorship had no intention of opening up the school system, the sheer increase in population, parental pressures, and the bad job market of the 1930s led to an increase in female enrollments. At the elementary level, female enrollments stayed roughly equal as a percentage of the total, averaging annually from 47 to 48 percent, even as enrollments as a whole rose from 3,150,249 in 1907–1908 to 3,879,479 in 1928–29 and to 4,850,058 in 1937–38. The same pattern held true at the middle-school level; whereas in 1901 only about a quarter of the children aged ten to fourteen attended, in 1931 fully 60 percent did: in 1901 that broke down to 23 percent of the girls and 28 percent of the boys; in 1931 53 percent of the girls, but 65 percent of the boys. In the elite schools, the Gentile reforms initially slightly reduced the number of women candidates for the diploma. In 1920–21 30 percent of the 57,289 *ginnasi* or middle-preparatory school students were girls in contrast to 18 percent of the 16,444 students at the *liceo*. Similarly, in 1927–28 25 percent of the 38,373 *ginnasi* students and 19 percent of the 17,342 *liceo* students were girls. But by 1937–38, as the total numbers increased, the number of girls also increased to 32 percent of the 92,652 at the *ginnasi* and to 26 percent of the 33,899 students at the *liceo*.[85] At the university level, female enrollments had risen from 6 percent of the total student body in 1913–14 to 13 percent in 1927–28 and to 15 percent in 1935. In 1938 women received a fifth of all the higher degrees granted.[86]

Yet a closer look reveals the system's bias against girls. At every moment of passage, school teachers and parents made calculations that deterred girls from going on. Thus about 20 percent more boys than girls made it through to fifth grade. Although the new school laws made attendance obligatory through fifth grade, the last two grades were paid for by local municipalities: only about 45 percent of the elementary schools provided separate fourth-grade classrooms and only 24 percent provided fifth-grade classrooms. Moreover, child labor laws often went unenforced in rural areas, and for poor peasant families a child of ten was already a useful hand. For many rural children, girls especially, all schooling ended with third grade. One bright old peasant woman told Nuto Revelli how her *maestra* had begged her father to let her stay beyond third grade, arguing that if the girl were to become a school teacher, she could earn more than the whole family in a single year. (A similar argument was commonly used to send promising peasant boys to study at seminaries in bigger towns.) The old patriarch spurned this logic, and the ten-year-old was contracted out to herd cows in the mountains.[87] In urban areas, fifth grade signaled the great social divide. In June, as Anna Mellini recalls, "the various Nadias and company, the mob, in sum, abandoned school forever, some heading for the factories, others hiring out as domestics; the *liceo-ginnasio* took in the elite, whereas the technical and teaching institutes divided up the average achievers from the middle classes." Some of the latter, like Mellini herself, might go on to a teachers' college, for the reason cogently argued by Marzio Barbagli: with a diploma from the lower teaching schools, few young women could find work, whereas with a university degree, they might at least hope to find a secondary school position.[88]

Within the system, women pursued a straight and narrow course. In 1935 under one in four students at the *liceo-ginnasi* were women. There was only one out of seven at the scientific lyceum, one out of ten at the industrial schools, and one out of four in the commercial and artistic institutes. By contrast, three out of four of the students at teaching institutes were women. In 1938 nearly four-fifths of all women graduating from the university were crowded into letters and philosophy, the *magistero* or teachers' college, pharmacy, and to a lesser degree, mathematics and natural sciences—these last two being teaching subjects. In the first two, women degree holders far outstripped men: in 1938, 588 men graduated in letters compared to 788 women. By contrast, the faculties that prepared students for the liberal professions or to join the political elites, such as jurisprudence and political science, were unwelcoming, and most women regarded it as impractical to attend them. In 1938, to cite two figures, law graduated 2,806 men and 86 women, whereas political science, a newer faculty, granted degrees to 209 men and 11 women. The most obvious imbalance that year was in engineering, which graduated 890 men and 5 women. (See chart 2.) With the prospects for jobs so poor—two-thirds of all women with pharmacy degrees settled for being housewives—young women were easily discouraged from finishing. At every step they were "dogged . . . by an atmosphere of skepticism about the intrinsic value of instructing them." Not surprisingly, the dropout rate was high. On average, only about one-third of the female students entering university finished their courses of study.[89]

Young Italian women were thus in a persistently uncomfortable position. Urged on by parents who regarded education as a kind of dowry, they were discouraged by public opinion that held that higher studies damaged women's natural intellect. The school system's biases obstructed them, but the social system's biases allowed for a tiny elite of gifted, studious, and well-born young women to go to the top. Tracked into just a few curricula, educated women were ultimately confined to a small handful of already overcrowded professions. In the end, fascist schooling, to quote Enza Carrara, a fascist of the first hour, lyceum professor in philosophy at Naples, and *studiosa* of Rousseau and Pestalozzi, "could not but discontent everybody, because it tried to make everybody happy."[90]

These discontents were not easily corrected, however, not even after the much-touted School Charter of 1939 launched a new round of reforms to correct the Gentile laws. Article 21 set forth that "the destination and social mission of women, being distinct in fascist life, have at their foundation different and special institutions of instruction." To educate young women, the charter proposed new female "institutes"; these would "prepare them spiritually for running households and teaching in nursery schools." However, with an attention to national developments that was wanting in Gentile—an attention now more imperative than ever in view of mobilizing Italy for war—the plan's architect, Bottai, affirmed that it could only be implemented "as the corporative order defined the new direction of female labor." Pending such a time, women were in theory free to choose their course of study. As Bottai remarked with notable disingenuousness: "Nobody wants to block woman's access even to the highest studies. . . . [L]eave the way open to the woman, though guided toward her natural and best task, to find in life the situation most congenial to herself."[91]

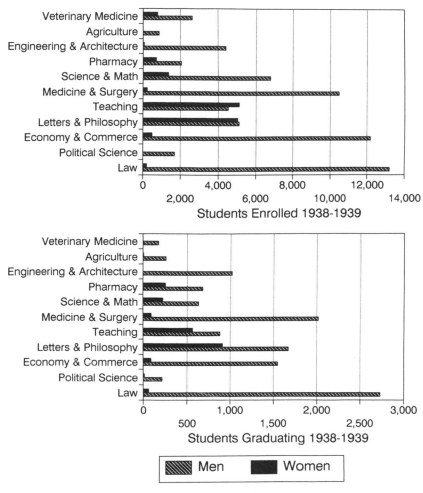

Chart 2. Distribution of female university students, 1938–39. (Istituto centrale di statistica del Regno d'Italia, *Compendio statistico*, 1940, p. 248).

Forming Little Fascists

For most children, especially for those from nonfascist households, the first impact with fascism went hand in hand with their first encounter with school. "Fascistization" through schooling proceeded slowly, however. Toward the end of the 1920s, the Minister of National Education, Belluzzo, mandated single textbooks for the elementary schools. In the course of the next decade, the old texts were purged and the new ones came out larded with examples culled from the life of the regime. By the middle of the 1930s, the "demo-masons" and the socialist-leaning school-marms had been forcibly retired; both the old and new teaching staffs were forced to swear allegiance to fascism. Toward the end of the decade, by order of the Ministry of Popular Culture, schools had begun to install loudspeakers in the classroom, the better to display the petty tyrannical powers of the principal, as well as to bombard students with static-ridden echoes of Mussolini's speeches before "oceanic" crowds in Rome.[92]

However, the one real moment of involvement in the mass politics of fascism, the first and for a majority of females the last as well, was through the after-school youth groups. The *piccole italiane* for girls between eight and thirteen, as well as the *giovani italiane* for teenagers fourteen to eighteen, had originally been promoted by the women's *fasci*, beginning in January 1925. They were assisted by the Milanese publicist, Angelo Tortoreto, who in addition to writing a widely used elementary school textbook called *Aquilotti d'Italia* founded two monthly bulletins for the party groups. However, in 1929, like other groups under party auspices, the girls' groups were put under the *Opera nazionale balilla*, which was in turn placed under the Ministry of National Education's supervision. Henceforth, their programs closely paralleled the boys', though the former received far less attention and fewer subsidies. Like the boys' groups, the girls' groups supplied after-school camaraderie, a common project, and occasions of sociability outside of school and away from family. Under their auspices, Italian youths experienced a new form of youth culture, one that paralleled the Anglo-American scouting experience and that, in the absence of scouting traditions for both sexes, had been missing in Italian life.

That the organization for girls was intended to reinforce the sexual division of social labor in fascist Italy is easy to document. Activities for boys emphasized competitive sports, military-type excursions, and in the 1930s exercises with mock-weaponry in keeping with the motto of the Balilla periodical, *Libro e moschetto*. By contrast, girls' activities emphasized first aid, rhythmic exercises, and charity, and courses included child care, flower arranging, and handicrafts. The Balilla platoons raised the flag while the girls stood at attention. The former practiced close-order drill while the latter danced around poles or played at an exercise called the "doll drill," parading in review with their dolls "in the correct manner of a mother holding a baby."[93] Nonetheless, girls seemed quite unaware that their treatment, though separate and different, was unequal to that of the boys. Like the boys, they called each other *camerata*. They responded to orders with the same disciplined *commandi e presente*. Eventually, when all of the groups were consolidated under the *Gioventù italiana del Littorio*, or GIL, in 1937, they took the same oath of allegiance to Mussolini: "In the name of God and Italy I swear that I will execute the orders of the DUCE and serve with all my strength and, if necessary, with my blood the Cause of the Fascist Revolution."[94]

Aside from the political faith in fascism such participation engendered, it also stimulated an aggressive self-confidence and competitiveness not necessarily encouraged by families in their female offspring. Iste Cagossi, who as Vampa would become a partisan leader in the Resistance, recalled that at age eleven, just around the time of the Ethiopian war, she was an enthusiastic and much-decorated *piccola italiana*.

> Passing through the street that brought me to and from school, I was anxious to keep my black cape open over my uniform, letting it fall back over my shoulders to show off the various awards fastened to my white blouse. I walked chest out, with a firm step, and every time I crossed somebody's path, I peeked at my reflection in the shop mirrors, to check the effect produced.

Moreover, her training fostered a spirit of *protagonismo* little in keeping with the subaltern deportments expected of women.

> At times, on my way, I imagined adventurous dreams of glory. Often, because of my quick response and diabolically clever intuition, I saved the beloved Duce from assassination attempts, accidents, drowning, and for every feat there was a solemn ceremony at which another shining metal cross was pinned on my white shirt, making me walk even more with my chest out and my stomach pulled in.[95]

For those who were shy, gauche, or athletically inept, as Iste's contemporary Anna Mellini admitted to being, or who could not belong because their parents were opposed, the girl fascists were an envied elite. They were successful in the world, it seemed, because they had broken not only from the apron strings of old-fashioned mothers but also from the stay-at-home habits of older sisters who at their younger sisters' age went out only when accompanied by mothers or aunts.[96] Some girls, like Anna Mellini's friend Lella, used the practice sessions and meetings as a pretext to escape the suffocating atmosphere of family life and the complaints of "backward" mothers, staying on after school or after the *Sabato fascista* to go out alone or with other girls. Like the slovenly homebody mother who in Ettore Scola's film *A Special Day* watches her adolescent daughter daub on lipstick before setting off for the great rally for Hitler, mothers could do little but chide their daughters. "You're going to a meeting, not a public dance."

However, the daughter who thought to mobilize an indifferent household on behalf of the new order did not get much except admiration for her snappy black-and-white uniform. Vampa, whose leadership abilities were evident at an early age, certainly met with little success. Her mother was apolitical, her father a depressed, brow-beaten ex-socialist. When she lined up female relatives to conduct drill practice in view of her promotion from *capo squadra* to *capo manipolo*, she became infuriated by their inability to follow elementary orders like forward march. She was particularly bothered by the "foolish smiles" and "malign comments" with which they greeted her rote recital "in strict chronological order of the founding dates of the many institutions of fascism," for they "reflected a total lack of faith in Mussolini and an obstinate desire to cast doubt on the 'radiant' future of peace, well-being, and liberty for our country."[97] To the degree that the girls believed uncritically, they, along with their male cohorts, parted company from their parents' generation.

The girls' groups did not necessarily aim to make drill sergeants of their members. The cult of maternity was pervasive. After-school groups produced a torrent of little trousseaux or *corredini* for the wives of emigrants repatriated with government and party help to give birth to their babies in Italy. Schools bombarded their female students with stories about the heroic mothers of Italia: Cornelia, the mother of the Gracchi; Adele Cairoli, mother of Risorgimento heroes; the two Rosas, Guitoni and Maltoni, *mamme*, respectively, of Garibaldi and of Mussolini. The ultimate sacrifice was that of Nazario Sauro's mother, who denied that he was her son in the vain attempt to save the World War I naval hero from the Austrian hangmen.

What ultimately unified the cult of nation and the cult of motherhood was the religious-sacrificial style, redolent of Mariolatry. Fascist youth ceremonials revolved around visits to cemeteries on All Saints' Day, wreath-laying rites, and pilgrimages of condolence to bereaved mothers of war dead and fascist martyrs. There was at least one attempt to invent a national cult around the figure of Carmela Borelli, a Calabrian peasant woman from Sersale, who was caught in a terrific snowstorm on the Sila mountains and died frozen, draping her poor rags over her two children. Locals strew flowers on the Altar of Sersale erected in 1928 to commemorate her deed, but she never came to be venerated at a national mother's day, as some promoters had intended. Evidently, the *protagonismo* of little Balilla who saved Genoa from the French or of the wild Sandokan was as congenial to young girls as it was to boys. It was certainly more appealing than the ghastly sacrifices of virgin martyrs and the ineffably sad tours of Great War burial grounds. The latter may have fed children's morbid fantasies, but little enhanced their vocation for self-denial.

A role model closer to home than the mythic male combatant or the self-immolating mother was that of the school teacher. Most were women, at least at the elementary and middle school level. Initially at least, most belonged to an older generation, not of fascism's making. Monarchists and stiff disciplinarians, they were often spinsters, or at least portrayed as such, dressed in dark ankle-length skirts, their hair pulled back in grey buns. For them, king, country, family, and religion came first; Mussolini was only a third or fourth founding father, a relative, as it were, of the king. By the 1930s, fascism was preparing a new generation of school teachers and sports instructors, "capable of reaching out to the people with a new mentality in diverse social arenas." Once a liberal institution, the School for Rural Teachers of Sant'Alessio was reorganized under the PNF, sending forth, as it had earlier, intrepid young women. Traveling to distant rural areas, usually accompanied hither by a male relative, they lived as boarders on miniscule salaries, braving the immense differences of sexual and social custom that separated urban and rural Italy, north and south. The model female instructors, those destined to staff the GIL, were trained at the Party Academy at Orvieto. Founded in January 1932, part convent boarding school, part military academy, it offered a two-year course, with a third to prepare for examination. The tuition, at 5,000 lire annually, in addition to 300 lire in school fees, was high, and the school recruited well-off middle-class girls who were promised secure jobs at high pay, starting at 9,500 lire and rising to 16,000 per year, in addition to various party-style emoluments of service.[98] The graduates brought a new style to teaching: "virile, but not masculine," they were fierce cocks of the walk at the annual Saggio Ginnico, celebrated May 24, proud to show off their charges' athletic prowess, before stepping up alongside of the prefect, PNF *federale*, priest, and school *preside* in the reviewing stand.

At the university level, the relationship of young women to fascist organizations was already visibly more fraught with contradictions. The tiny elite of women who overcame odds to go to university were on the whole a less politicized lot than their male companions. Those who sought to become involved in student politics by joining the renowned GUF received little encouragement. With no party support and no older women to help out, the young women eager to found all-female sections met with indifference, if not scorn. Though the all-male goliardic clubs had been banned, most university faculties were still male bastions. Antifemale pranks and jokes were rife: "Noi non vogliamo donne / all'università / ma le vogliamo nude / distese sul sofà" ("We don't want women at school / we want them naked, laid out on the couch")—one memorable line from a popular student song suggests the mood.[99] The politically correct male *camerate* of the GUF were perhaps the most egregious offenders, since they used fascist ideology to motivate their rejection of women. At worst, GUF women were unpolitical intriguers or insipid fools who understood nothing of corporativism or other serious issues. At best, they were companionable but inferior creatures. For Clara Valente, a political science major at Pavia as well as an intrepid but often frustrated national organizer of *gufine*, one classmate's obviously heartfelt analogy said it all: for him, woman complemented man "like the cork complements a bottle. In an uncorked bottle, the wine sours, likewise, woman conserves what is best in our intimate selves, without her we all sour," and when Valente argued with him, he maintained it was incontrovertibly "the Duce's concept." [100] Not surprisingly, there was no female GUF at all until 1931 and no journal ever, though for two or three years in the mid-1930s, fascist university women were allowed a special section of the fascist women's journal *Donna fascista*. There they vented their desire to be truly modern women, combining careers and social engagement with their maternal mission.

The most humiliating blow dealt this ambitious female elite was exclusion from the *Littoriali della cultura*. These were the highly publicized annual contests in sports and culture founded in 1934 to test the competitive mettle of the best and brightest university youth. Why precisely the PNF decided to limit the competitions to men is unclear, though its wish to cater to Church injunctions against female involvement in competitive sports probably played some role. In any case, the decision was infuriating and incomprehensible to young women. In an attempt to persuade the PNF secretary Achille Starace to reverse his decision, it was argued that "shut out of the organizations, [a woman would] end up being cut off from all avenues of work, and find herself excluded from competitions important and decisive for her profession and future." [101] But not until September 1938, following renewed protests, this time carried in *Il bò*, the journal of the University of Padua's rebellious GUF, did the PNF open the Littorial competitions to women. However, they were still separate from the men's, as well as scheduled on different dates. Moreover, when the spectacle finally took place the following April, the fascist press reacted with the condescending amazement usually reserved for performing animals. *Popolo d'Italia*'s editorialist marvelled at the "vivacity, brio, and enthusiasm" of girls gathered from a hundred Italian towns, adding praise for the "self-confidence and sureness with which they argued and defined their own ideas." [102] In 1941 the meets were held together at last. But by that time many male students had been called up for war service, so it looked as much a decision made in the name of boosting spectatorship as a gesture toward male-female equality.

The Long Voyage Out

Relative to their cohort in Paris, Berlin, or any big American city, the new Italian girls were provincials. Overall, there were fewer of them, given the still rural character of the nation, and their exposure to new leisure pastimes, work opportunities, or courtship habits was very restricted. To a degree unparalleled in any liberal democratic society, fascism sought to fill the public spaces outside the family. In this endeavor, it competed with only limited success against the Catholic Church. But fascism's own sexual and cultural politics were internally contradictory, demanding novelty yet beset by conflicting interpretations of what was new. The result was a thoroughly hybrid new woman: neither traditional nor coherently modern, she challenged fascist models and codes that said that women were either licentious or puritanical, dutiful or wanton, spinsterish intellectuals or devoted housewives. Still, fascism's new woman had no real sense of her power as a cohort. She was more self-confident and freer than her mother had been, yet as little or less emancipated.

Did young women, like many young men of the "generation of the Littorial," start their long voyage to antifascism before the final breakdown of the dictatorship in 1943? Memoirs stress their sense of malaise and disquiet. Laura Conti (b. 1921), the daughter of antifascists, who in 1939 was one of ten women medical students in a class of two hundred at the University of Milan, recalled that the middle classes subscribed formally to fascism's archaic ideas about women. Yet at the same time, they "incline[d] their offspring toward a change of roles, toward appropriating professional models that were new with respect to the past." In that context, girls like boys "saw the obstacles fascism caused to rise against their evolution."[103]

Yet for young women to translate disquiet into opposition, much less open resistance, was more complicated than it was for young men. For they had to struggle not just against a political regime, but against their own conflicted aspirations, parental expectations, and the widespread typing of female roles, not least of all among their own comrades. The complicated trajectories that brought about these breaks is illustrated in two stories; those of two very different girls, each born in 1925 and thus fifteen when Italy entered World War II. One was Iste Cagossi, later the partisan Vampa. She was from a working-class family, attended technical and then teaching schools, and was a self-described "enthusiastic" *piccola italiana* at the age of eleven. The other was Luce D'Eramo, a survivor of the German concentration camp system of 1944–45 and later a novelist. As the daughter of a well-placed northern Italian middle-class family, she attended *liceo-ginnasio*, and she was a self-described fanatical GUF member at age eighteen. Both broke with the regime, though with radically different motivations and trajectories.

Iste Cagossi would never forget the songs she learned as a *piccola italiana*, "Faccetta nera, sarai romana," "Duce tu sei la luce, fiamma tu sei dei cuori" ("Little black face, you'll be Roman," "Duce, you're the light, the flame in our hearts"). But by the late 1930s, she had graduated and was no longer active. Her older brother, serving in Ethiopia, had lost touch with the family and her mother was always in tears. Her father, a dejected former socialist, became more vocally antifascist. Iste sided with him when her mother tried to hush him up. By now, she was convinced that no matter how resourceful and honest he was, the family was not going to find the peace and tranquility sought after by her mother. After Genoa was bombed in 1940, the family fled back to Emilia, leaving Iste to return to the city alone to study in a Church-run teaching institute. By then, the use of slogans such as "Believe, Obey, Combat" to conjugate verbs, such as was required by Finocchiaro's textbook grammar drills, seemed puerile and inappropriate. In 1944 Iste joined the swelling ranks of resistance fighters in her home region.

Luce D'Eramo was born in Reims, France, the daughter of a strict French Catholic and a northern Italian. She was schooled in Rome where her father was one of the "new" men of the regime, a dapper womanizer, a specialist in propaganda and aviation; in 1943 he was either so loyal or so shortsighted that he accepted appointment as undersecretary in the Ministry of Propaganda in charge of aeronautics in the Republic of Salò. In 1943 Luce began to attend the University of Padua, a hotbed of fascist student activism. Her youthful idealism was doubtless related to the visions of a "third wave" of fascist revolution nursed by male students who wanted to rid Italy of the forces of monarchy, plutocracy, and religion to which Mussolini had allegedly capitulated. But Luce's cause was not revolution. Her beliefs were of radical and Catholic provenance: in international fellowship, peace, and a new world order. She was also convinced of the power of self-sacrifice. What finally swayed her to act was the news of Germany's abuse of Italians conscripted to work in Nazi labor camps. Her decision to investigate the camps firsthand led her to enroll as volunteer labor, destined for the Krupp works outside Dachau, a decision facilitated, if unwillingly, by her father's connections. Repatriated by the German authorities after being involved in plans for a work stoppage and escape, Luce allowed herself to be rounded up by SS troops at Verona and shipped back to Germany. This time she was sent to Dachau itself, in the environs of which, having escaped once more, she ended up in April 1945, her spine crushed by a falling wall in the war's final bombardments. Her story, as she later made clear, was both grotesque and confused; it combined political idealism with rebelliousness against uncomprehending parents, clearsighted action with half-conscious gestures.[104] Yet it testifies as well as any how complicated and wearing was the new woman's long voyage out of fascism.

6 Working

In the fascist era, work, in its infinite manifestations, becomes
the sole measure of the social and national utility of
individuals and groups.

> Benito Mussolini, in a speech to the
> National Assembly Corporation (1936)

It is a basic fact that work constitutes not a life goal for a
woman, but a stage in her life, one to be finished up as soon as
possible with her return to the home environment.

> First National Congress of Women
> Workers in Commerce (1940)

"Duce, do you want to increase the number of suicides, prostitutes,
expatriations?" Thereby, a distraught Turinese woman entreated her "beloved Duce" to mitigate the decree-law of September 5, 1938. The dictatorship had just ordered state and private offices to cut back female workers to 10 percent of their total staff, and she faced the loss of her job
despite twenty years of seniority. She was "anguished," comprehensibly
so, for Pierina B., as we shall call her, had never married and was the sole
support of aged parents. She also helped support two nephews whose own
mother and father were down in their fortunes. Without her job, the old
people would be shut away in a poor house, she said, and her beloved little
ones deprived of any chance for a decent future. Pierina's protest was
echoed by dozens of other women. How could the Duce expect forty-
year-old women to retrain as nurses, seamstresses, or social workers? Where
were the husbands whose livelihoods were supposed to maintain them?
What men would be satisfied to take over their miserably paid positions
anyway? The boldest, a group of Roman clerks, cried treachery: when the
Duce sought their sacrifices for the African war, Italian women had responded with "zeal." Today, the Nation "not only treated them as inferior, but even deprived them of their daily bread."[1]

Pierina B. and the others claimed to be writing on behalf of "hundreds"
of Italian women. In reality, hundreds of thousands shared their concerns. In the 1930s, over one-quarter of Italy's work force was female,
and one woman out of every four between the ages of fourteen and sixty-
five was economically active. In at least one and a half million Italian
households—16 percent of all in 1931—women were the main breadwinners. In several million others they supplemented the family income.[2]

Even if their jobs were not at stake, working women everywhere must have been jolted by the dictatorship's drastic ruling. Mussolini's vaunted corporative system had thrust them into a constitutional limbo: men's claims to citizenship were recognized insofar as they were producers and soldiers; women's only insofar as they reproduced the species. Unable to defend their right to work on grounds of sexual equality, working women adjusted their aspirations and claims. Hence they pleaded "family necessity" to justify their toils, or that work was simply a temporary expedient, or that the jobs they filled were too lowly or typically female to suit men anyway. What made the new legislation seem like such a sharp break with past policy was that even these defenses were now being denied them.

In reality the September 5 decree-law was the capstone of a multilayered politics of sexual discrimination. This emerged over a fifteen-year period as the fascist dictatorship addressed a basic policy dilemma. On the one hand, it tolerated high rates of male unemployment and condoned low wages, as was consistent with its alliance with big business and its strategies for building up the Italian economy. This strategy favored exploiting the cheapest source of labor, that of women and minors. On the other hand, the dictatorship wanted to secure positions for male heads of household. Otherwise, the self-esteem of jobless men was at risk, as was the cause of racial fitness and population growth. Accordingly, the dictatorship intervened at diverse levels. Building on long-standing sexual biases in the labor market, as well as the gender inequalities which arose as Italian workers were subjected to the corporate system, the regime passed protective laws, propagated discriminatory attitudes, and enacted statutory exclusions. State policy thus interacted with longer-term market forces to accentuate the biases women faced when they worked outside the home.

The scope of this chapter is thus twofold. At one level, we discuss how fascism's treatment of working women compared to that in other interwar societies. Under Mussolini's rule, the position of women in the sexual division of labor changed according to patterns common to industrial development elsewhere, though in Italy they occurred belatedly and then all at once. Thus, as agriculture's weight in the national economy declined with respect to that of industry, women fled from back-breaking rural enterprise. As the tertiary sector boomed in the twentieth century, office work became more and more feminized. As manufacture shifted from producer to consumer goods, women workers moved from the declining textiles and other light manufacture which had prospered in the first industrial revolution to the mechanized heavy and consumer-goods production typical of advanced industrialism.[3] In an effort to manage these trends, the regime intervened to make public sector employment a male preserve, with special privileges and good pay. It tolerated women working while young, then induced them to leave the official labor market when they married and had children. Finally, the fascist state promoted the formation of a largely female submerged economy of unprotected, underemployed, and ill-paid home workers. As a result, the several million Italian women who toiled outside the home during the interwar years experienced significant changes in occupational opportunities, work routines, and career patterns under especially disabling conditions.

The second object here is to understand how the social figure of the modern working woman was constructed in fascist Italy. Fascism came to power at a time when contemporary attitudes toward women's work were just being formed. Tapping into longtime prejudices against women working outside the home, propaganda and state policies sought to alter public perceptions about the worth of women's work—to women themselves, to the family, the firm, and the national collectivity. Above all, fascist policy fought against an especially dangerous notion, that work was a universal right—for women as well as for men—and that for women, it should also open the door to social emancipation. Of course work was indispensable to a man's identity, as propaganda often affirmed. But for women, as Mussolini put it, work "distracts from reproduction, if it does not directly impede it, and foments independence and the accompanying physical-moral styles contrary to birthing." By working, to quote the Duce's sententious remarks, "a woman might well save a family on the skids or even herself, but in the general scheme of things her work is a source of political and moral bitterness. The rescue of a few individuals is paid for with the blood of a multitude."[4] Short of driving women completely out of the labor force, the dictatorship tried to keep women from viewing work as a stepping stone to liberation. If they held jobs, it had to be out of family necessity or because no men would take them. Thus Mussolini's "civilization of labor" belittled women's professional abilities and vocational skills not only in the eyes of government, employers, and men but in the view of women themselves.

The Pre-fascist Politics of Female Employment

The contention of fascist propagandists that women's work was the fruit of desire as opposed to the bread of necessity flew in the face of an obvious reality, that Italian women had always toiled outside of the home. Indeed, in the very recent past, they had done so visibly and in huge numbers. Around 1900, with a third of all women aged from fourteen to sixty-five active in the economy, Italy ranked fourth among industrial nations for its use of female labor. Thereafter, as the country developed more rapidly, the number of women active outside the home decreased, as usually happens when a country reaches a more advanced level of industrialization. Even so, women still made up about a third of the country's total employed population on the eve of the Great War. Three out of the five million working women labored in agriculture, which still afforded livelihoods for a majority of Italians. Many were employed in rural-based cottage industries fabricating hemp, silk, straw, and food products or as day laborers recruited to harvest grapes and olives or commercial crops such as rice, tobacco, and sugar beets. In industry, women still accounted for 28 percent of the labor force, the majority being employed in cotton and wool textile firms and other light manufacture. In nonmanual occupations, teaching alone had any significant number of women, it being an underpaid and low-status occupation, and also a lonely one for those assigned to rural outposts. Italy's tertiary sector was still tiny before the Great War. But there, too, government and private employers were beginning to hire women, the former to fill posts as telegraphists and telephone operators, the latter to occupy various clerical posts and merchandising jobs.

That women's work outside the home was a fact of contemporary life had not prevented it from coming under attack in the prewar days. Some of the prejudices women faced under fascism originated well before the fascists came to power. In Sicily, for example, under the influence of centuries-old Muslim customs, only the poorest women worked in public, usually in field labor. As early as 1891 the Church had reaffirmed its opposition to women working outside the home; it violated female modesty, damaged the good upbringing of children, and disrupted family well-being, Leo XIII asserted in *De Rerum Novarum*. If women had to work, the Church wanted it to be within the confines of the domestic walls; cottage work, the Catholic hierarchy stipulated, unlike the factory wage system, promised to maintain preindustrial harmonies in the household as well in society as a whole. This Catholic-inspired cult of domesticity resonated with middle-class notions of respectability, encouraging their spread even among working-class families. By the turn of the century, social hygienists and reformers too began to denounce female wage work; their arguments were made on utilitarian grounds, specifically, that harsh exploitation damaged female reproductive capacities, threatening the health of the race. Finally, there was opposition from men who, in an economy in which male unemployment was chronic, feared female competition. The most vociferous came not from the ranks of working men, but from circles in the liberal professions, like law, which gave access to government patronage systems. As early as 1883 the Turinese lawyer Lydia

Poët, who practiced in her brother's office, petitioned to argue courtroom cases, only to be rebuffed by the Court of Cassation. Women continued to attend law faculties, and 124 had graduated by 1911. But repeated court appeals and the proposals merely to study a parliamentary reform advanced first in 1902 and then again in 1910 seemed only to harden opposition. In 1912 Teresa Labriola's attempt to be admitted to the bar was spurned. Not until 1919, in the wake of the Sacchi law, was she finally able to don the ceremonial hat and toga to plead courtroom cases.[5]

As elsewhere in Western societies, the Great War caused a sea change in patterns of female employment. In the short term, it portended vast new opportunities for women in all sectors of the economy. In the long term, it hardened discriminatory attitudes. In the wake of the war, the Sacchi law of July 1919, number 1176 opened access not only to the free professions but also to many civil service categories from which women had previously been excluded. From the outset, the law was hedged with some important exceptions—including posts that involved the performance of judicial duties, the military defense of the state, and the exercise of political power or executive authority in government—and feminists legitimately judged the measure as inadequate. Moreover, it came just as the ground swell of public opinion turned against women workers. The timing of this reaction could not have been worse, for patterns of hostility were set at the very moment that attitudes in Italy, given the country's relatively tardy development, needed to change in order to tolerate a more diverse female involvement in the economy.

Indeed, the politicization of the issue of women's work in the wake of the Armistice soon unleashed a veritable "war between the sexes over work."[6] As in other belligerent nations, women had seen opportunities to work as a liberation, and bore with what Donna Paola decried as the "ridicule, reproof, scandal-mongering, [and] disdain" heaped on those who through work sought "freedom from their economic, social, and mental misery." Moreover, salary differentials between men and women decreased, especially in the low-wage textile industries and agricultural labor, as militant socialist trade unions secured new contracts with cost-of-living increments and as minimum wages were increased.[7] Meanwhile, for demobilized veterans with dim prospects for employment, the so-called silk-stocking worker embodied everything that was topsy-turvy about postwar society: from the home front's ingratitude toward soldiers' sacrifices to changed work systems and the greater emancipation of women. The arguments made by veterans' leagues against employing women, although often specious, unfortunately made sense to many people. This was especially true once the press began carrying the woeful images that nationalist propagandists conjured up: it was simply outrageous for female postal workers to idle, smugly powdering their noses, while out on the streets maimed and destitute veterans waved their poor stumps to cadge a few lire from passersby!

Thus, the great growth of jobs that women filled while men were called up for war duty made it believable that the women had stolen them away from men. In reality, the positions women occupied in the low-skilled line jobs of recently nationalized industrial workshops, as secretaries in expanding bureaucracies or as shop helpers in stores, were often new. Likewise, allegations that women employees dragged down productivity or undercut the "organizational seriousness" of the firm because of their reproductive "disturbances," flightiness, or low intelligence were made to sound plausible. In reality, in three years of wartime hiring, employers realized that their fears about female shirking and absenteeism were largely unfounded. Indeed, by mechanizing machine and other enterprises that formerly depended on skilled men—who were also politically organized— they could operate with unskilled and for the most part nonunionized female workers. The feminization of the work force, though not as pronounced as in wartime Great Britain or Germany, carried much the same threat as it did elsewhere: it would eliminate the work rules, craft codes, and shop-floor solidarities to which male trade unionism, professional standing, and self-esteem had been tied. A final argument, that working women frittered away their wages in an orgy of cosmetics and sweets (not to mention silk-stockings), was as preposterous as it was widespread. The shop girl out to make a purchase or the *sartina* passing by the neighborhood newspaper kiosk catalyzed bourgeois fears of labor's advance in the immediate postwar years and their own class's economic decline. As inconsistent and contradictory as they were, such arguments added up to a compelling case for removing women from the work force. Those who maintained to the contrary that women worked out of necessity and that female heads of households, widows, orphans, or others who had been impoverished by the war deserved to work were denounced as if they were camp followers of the Bolsheviks.[8]

The push to eliminate women from the work force thus commenced before the fascist seizure of power. The Italian socialist movement, the one group that could be expected to spring to the defense of women's right to work, was unable to do so, being divided and under fascist attack. In the past, the PSI had often supported working women, on practical as much as doctrinal grounds. The Italian labor movement was never as strong as the British or German trade unions, who allied with reformers to pass protective legislation to eliminate low-paid female and child labor from the market. In Italy, however, since there was no reformist coalition to speak of and in the face of chronic unemployment, labor leaders were compelled to follow a different route: to treat marginal female workers as full-fledged workers, involving them as much as possible in the labor movement. This strategy was especially visible in the northern country-side, where beginning in the 1890s the Italian Socialist party backed the leagues of women farm workers. Indeed, from 1905 to 1925, the entire *Federterra* was headed by a woman, Argentina Altobelli. In the wake of the war, the Italian socialist trade unions, leagues, and chambers of labor, with their hundreds of thousands of female members, achieved the largest following of women of any labor movement in post–World War I Europe. Even so, as the fascist blackshirts launched their assault on the socialist redoubts in mid-1920, the Socialist party failed to grasp the specifically antifemale aspects of the reaction. Moreover, not a few socialist men shared the conviction, associated with the conservative mid-nineteenth-century French socialist Joseph Proudhon, that women belonged to the family. To return to more normal times—which everybody wanted—men had to be back at work, while women went back into the home.[9]

Bourgeois feminists, too, though for other reasons, were unable to grasp the dimensions of the problem. Their attention mainly focused on de-fending access to the professions and state employment. For example, the Rome-based National Association of Woman tried to correct bad press coverage. It also backed women teachers' protests against the veterans' campaign to hike men's ranking in national competitions and reintroduce sex-based pay differentials that had been eliminated more than fifteen years before. The trouble was that many feminists, out of patriotic spirit, accepted that war veterans with families deserved preference over women not in dire need of work. This put them in an awkward position, as the conduct of Adele Pertici Pontecorvo suggests. A leading Roman feminist, who in 1913 became Italy's first notary public after a precedent-setting court case, she scored highest in the nation on the first civil service ex-amination open to women in 1919. Assigned to the Foreign Ministry, she soon resigned her position in favor of a veteran with a family. Her pa-triotic gesture was much publicized, not least of all because her husband, Remo Pontecorvo, the so-called Cayman of the Piave, leader of the front-line *arditi nuotatori*, was a much decorated war hero.[10] Subsequently, Pertici Pontecorvo headed the Women's and Children's Bureau of the Ministry of Industry, Commerce, and Labor until it was disbanded with the ministry's reorganization in 1923. From that position, she, like Maria Zopegni Magri (who in 1922 founded the *Laboratorio Pro-disoccupate* in Rome) and other well-meaning equal rights advocates, worked prodigiously on behalf of self-help programs for newly unemployed middle-class women. These meant little to the thousands of female workers who were being laid off in the industrial sector in 1919–20, often without severance pay or unemployment benefits.

Female Labor in the Corporate System

The development of a characteristically fascist politics of bias went hand in hand with the dictatorship's restructuring of the economy in the second half of the twenties. As emigration abroad was blocked and agricultural prices plummeted after 1925, female as well as male workers glutted the market. At the same time, the demand for labor grew very slowly. Industrial restructuring encouraged employers to mechanize and introduce "rationalized" work systems, increasing output with smaller work forces.[11] For the moment, government offices slowed the pace of hiring in the name of austerity. Rather than resorting to costly employment-building programs, the regime devised other measures to reduce excess labor. One measure, under the guise of antiurbanization, was to ship the nonresident unemployed back to their places of origin. The other—with at least equal ideological appeal—was to curb female employment. "With women replaced by men, legions of men would raise their humiliated heads," Mussolini affirmed in a major speech in 1934, "and hundreds of new families would immediately become part of the nation's life. . . . [T]he very labor which in women causes loss of generative attributes, in men, brings out a powerful physical and moral virility."[12] First under the shadow of the revaluation crisis of 1927, then ever more zealously during the Great Depression, the regime promoted male at the expense of female labor. At first it did so more or less covertly, by passing measures that in the guise of protecting working mothers discriminated against working women. Then it did so overtly, by means of statutes and contractual agreements designed to expel women from the labor force.[13]

However, to focus too quickly on such patently discriminatory measures is to overlook that fascism's whole *inquadramento* or reorganization of Italian workers in the corporate system aggravated biases against women. In the process of smashing the left-wing unions in the early 1920s, devastating their headquarters, eliminating their leaders through jail and exile, expropriating their funds, and coercing their members to join fascist syndicates, the fascists hurt the interests of all workers, male and female alike. Thereafter, under pressure from its own unruly unions, the dictatorship established a new framework for collective bargaining. The Rocco Laws of 1926 provided for seating worker and employer representatives side by side in syndicates or corporative councils while at the same time outlawing strikes and lockouts. Not surprisingly, this arrangement prevented the fascist unions from being effective bargaining agents. The fulsome declaration of workers' rights in the Labor Charter of 1927, the system of recourse through the labor courts, and the monopoly over worker representation conceded to the fascist syndicalists were all for naught in the face of well-entrenched and politically favored business associations. The one advantage the fascist syndicalists had, namely, the great size of their organization, was lost when the National Fascist Confederation of Industrial Workers headed by the ex–revolutionary syndicalist Edmondo Rossoni was "unblocked" in 1928. Henceforth its individual units were forced to bargain one-on-one with the mighty industrial employers' organizations. The fascist syndicalists' power to negotiate contracts was further eroded when employers refused to recognize their shop-floor delegates or *fiduciari*. Moreover, hugely profitable firms like Fiat invested in company paternalism to seduce workers away from the hapless fascist unions. Not least of all, the unions' negotiating capacities were obstructed by the legalistic cast of the new bargaining system. Feisty ex-socialist or former revolutionary syndicalist organizers who had the temper to fight and knew something about shop-floor or rural working conditions were unfamiliar with corporatist legal jargon. By contrast, ambitious young labor bureaucrats, their doctorates in jurisprudence or political science attesting to their solid grounding in class-collaborationist cant, knew little about modern work systems, much less the temperament of their beleaguered constituents.[14]

Bad for all workers, fascist corporatism was especially detrimental to female ones. First, by enabling employers to slash men's wages, male pay became competitive with the even lower women's rates. All else being equal, there was thus little incentive to substitute women for men. The availability of cheap male labor also reduced incentives to mechanize firms, a process that elsewhere caused machine-tool enterprises and other light manufacture to increase the hiring of women. Second, the corporate organization of labor centralized and politicized the bargaining process. Unsuccessful in negotiating wage increases, the fascist unions settled for bargaining over benefits and special privileges. Hiring quotas in favor of men were one of several nonmonetary concessions fascist unions obtained to compensate them for their docility and to demonstrate to their constituents that they were still active—notwithstanding their obvious inability to defend wage levels or exercise control over work conditions. Moreover, national contracts codified sex-based differences. That women earned one-half of men's wages was nothing new; that skill levels and rate differentials were pegged to override local customs and market conditions perhaps more favorable to women was.[15] Finally, the corporate system prevented female workers from obtaining adequate representation. Unlike the socialist unions which sought to integrate the marginal into the labor market, the fascist unions favored the best-situated workers. Needless to say, the skilled and the senior workers, not to mention the employees in industrial or administrative sectors regarded as of strategic value to the dictatorship, were almost always male. If nothing else, the fact that few women graduated from law or political science faculties in the 1930s practically guaranteed that women would not represent women.

Corporatism, with its bewildering bureaucracy and intricate power plays, is a disarming system for any marginal or inchoate group, not least of all for women.[16] A few prominent fascist women, including Regina Terruzzi, foresaw as much, and as early as 1927, as the corporate system took shape, urged that female members be named to the Superior Council of Corporations. This did not happen. The only woman member ever was Vittoria Maria Luzzi, who was appointed by virtue of heading the all-female Midwives Corporation. Not until 1931 did Giuseppe Bottai, then undersecretary of the Ministry of Corporations, finally appoint the first (of a total of three) women counselors. That he chose Adele Pertici Pontecorvo, the already renowned labor law expert, suggests that the pool of women with the requisite familiarity with corporate law and the personal prestige needed to battle cases through the Roman bureaucracy was miniscule. Pertici Pontecorvo, who had earned her law degree in 1913 with a thesis on *La donna nel diritto pubblico* (and had a degree in letters as well), was a seasoned women's rights advocate: after winning her own suit against the king's solicitor general to become Italy's first female notary public, she founded the Rome-based Legal Consultation Office for the Defense of Woman's Work. Active in nationalist reform movements after the war, she drew on her experience in administrative affairs to help Mario Giani draw up legislation to establish the *Opera nazionale dopolavoro* in 1925. President of the Roman section of the National Fascist Association of Women Artists and Degree Holders, as well as holder of the chair in labor law at the venerable Regina Margherita Girls' Professional School, she was perhaps the most effective advocate of women's rights at work under the dictatorship. Nine times she brought cases of discrimination before Italy's *Consiglio di stato*, exploiting the legal loopholes offered by the 1919 Sacchi law.[17]

For the rest, working women were in the hands of male syndicalists whose attentions were ambiguous at best. Periodically, the trade union press denounced the phenomenon of "double earners." Occasionally, a hardliner put forward some farfetched scheme to favor men, one being to dictate to businesses that they hire to yield a ratio of three to four hundred dependents to every one hundred employees.[18] Yet trade unions could hardly afford to be as ideological as, say, the Catholic racist Fernando Loffredo, who rattled on about rallying public opinion to drive women back into the home. "The woman who is now fully entered into active life has to remain there," was the prudent opinion of Tullio Cianetti, the head of the National Fascist Confederation of Industrial Workers. "But every one in their place. Not women out of the work force, but women out of every job that can possibly be given to men."[19] In practice, this meant that fascist syndicalists defended women's interests, though only to the degree necessary to protect their own power. If women's wages went too low, employers would be tempted to hire women in the place of men. If women staged work stoppages, as happened in the hard-hit textile industries in 1927, fascist syndicalists rushed to the scene to offer their hand at negotiating, if only to uphold their own prestige. Under the circumstances, the best manner to prevent male-female competition was to advocate special treatment for women and to categorize labor by gender as well as by skill and occupation. Hence, the fascist unions welcomed the legislation passed in 1934 to exclude women from "all of those tasks recognized as damaging or dangerous,"[20] though it is not at all clear whether the unions had any say in the process of drawing it up. When not espousing the need to protect women workers and to prevent them from competing with men, the syndicalists pretty much ignored them. Unlike socialist organizers, at least some of whom dealt with locals composed wholly of women, syndicalists had no need to reach out. When they spoke of working-class recreational needs, the reform of technical instruction, or the improvement of proletarian culture, they referred to the wants of skilled males, such as type compositors, lathe operators, or bricklayers.[21]

In fact, to the degree that women were involved in the corporate system, they were recruited through a parallel network of organizations, one usually overlooked in studies of fascist corporatism. This network operated on the assumption that women worked out of necessity, but that their main activity was familial. And it fostered a different relationship on the part of its female constituents with respect to the labor market, nonworking women, and the state. The first of these institutions was the *massaie rurali,* which included peasant women of all classes and was promoted by the fascist agricultural unions before coming under the purview of the women's *fasci* in 1934. The second institution, called the Section for Factory and Home Workers, or SOLD, was similarly hybrid. Founded by the Fascist party on January 12, 1938, it operated under the leadership and with the staff of the women's *fasci.* However, its national bulletin,

Lavoro e famiglia, designed to "give simple explanations of the women's activities that most interest working-class families and home-workers," was directed from 1938 to 1943 by Tullio Cianetti, head of the Fascist Confederation of Industrial Workers.[22]

The operations of the SOLD testify to how fascism's organization of female wage earners differed fundamentally from that designed for males. In the first place, SOLD was open not just to factory and home workers but also to working-class wives and other female family members. Its foremost function was political education, which was intended to "improve on [women's] professional and homemaking capacities."[23] The organization also promised to assist job placement, inspect home-industry conditions, and disseminate knowledge of the welfare and insurance plans available to working women. Membership was a real bargain, as several thousand Turinese and Milanese working women appeared to have calculated in 1938 when they renounced their Fascist party cards for those of the SOLD.[24] It cost only two and a half lire, compared to ten for the party card. Moreover, the bright-colored triangular neck scarf purchased to wear at mass meetings carried far less ideological freight. With this low-key approach, the SOLD grew rapidly, from 309,945 members in 1938 to 501,415 in 1939. Swelling with the entry en masse of women into the war economy, it grew from 616,264 in 1940 and 761,927 in 1941 to 864,922 in 1942.[25] Far from empowering women in the collective bargaining process, the SOLD treated its constituents as welfare-state clients. Contractual haggling may have been appropriate for men; social work properly treated women. The female counterpart of the labor trustee (*fiduciario*) was the fascist home visitor (*visitatrice*). In the process of responding to working women's interests as mothers and family women, the SOLD thus contributed to effacing their social identity as workers.

As the corporate system was consolidated, protective legislation became but a second step toward defining female labor as substantially different from male labor. Enacted in final form in 1934, this legislation had two purposes: first, to safeguard underage males and female workers, and, second, to protect working mothers. The original legislation on safeguarding workers, which had only reaffirmed earlier bans on work at night and under unsafe conditions, was made more comprehensive on April 26, 1934. It prohibited night work for all women and for minor women aged fifteen to twenty and the use of youth under age fifteen for work judged dangerous or unhealthy. It also barred work for minors aged twelve and under. To police such legislation was not easy. The fascist unions agitated to stop the now illegal practice euphemistically called "de-aging" (*svecchiamento*), by which senior workers were fired and women and children were hired to replace them at the minimum wage. But on the whole, the laws contained enough loopholes and exceptions to accommodate all kinds of violations, especially when no trade union officials, labor inspectors, or fascist social workers were on site. At the same time, the fear that female employment involved undue obligations and costs, though perhaps unfounded, at times deterred the hiring of women.

The laws protecting working mothers were unquestionably the more path breaking. By 1931, 1,220,000 out of about 1,500,000 women employed in industry and commerce were insured under legislation passed in 1910 to establish maternity funds. The law of March 22, 1934, superseded all previous measures, expanding benefits and coverage. As a result, women became entitled to a two-month paid compulsory leave, one month before birth and one month after. If they took a longer unpaid leave, the job was kept open from the sixth month of pregnancy to six weeks after the birth and three months in the case of office workers; insurance might cover an extra month's leave in the event of a birth-related illness. The law also guaranteed time off on the job to breast-feed infants until they were a year old. It stipulated that factories with more than fifty women workers should install feeding rooms on the premises. And it provided a lump-sum payment for child birth. This comprised a birth bonus of 150 lire and unemployment benefits, the total amounting to about 400 lire, the equivalent of an average two-month wage. By 1938 the government extended these benefits to cover employees not only of commercial firms and industrial plants but also of agricultural enterprises.[26]

There was much to appreciate in legislation that treated pregnancy as "involuntary unemployment" rather than as a disability or illness and that provided for nursing breaks and infant day-care centers. That feminists abroad admired such measures is attested by the fact that in 1934 the International Congress of Women named the CNDI's president, Daisy di Robilant, to head its section on maternity and infancy.[27] However, given the dictatorship's prior commitment to male employment, its demographic campaigns, and its often reiterated antifeminism (as well as the timing to coincide with the first exclusions of women from the labor force), such measures might legitimately be regarded as "discriminatory protection," to use Robert Moeller's term, which is to say they discouraged employers from hiring women, while encouraging women to leave the work force in the years of childbearing.[28] If, subsequently, the women returned to work, the likely destination was the pullulating underground economy. There, they were wholly bereft of social protections.

In 1934, the same year that the dictatorship passed its major protective laws, it also drew up measures to expel women from the labor force.

Initially, fascist lawmakers, like their liberal predecessors, had formulated rules against hiring women on the grounds that women were unsuited to certain posts requiring a "virile" character. Thus, though the 1919 Sacchi law sanctioned the idea of equal opportunity, its article 7 had excluded women from "those positions that involve the exercise of public judicial authority, political rights or power, or the military defense of the state." Ordinance 37 of 1920 further stipulated that women could not be captains or owners of commercial vessels, officers of the courts, ranking civil servants, diplomats or consular attachés, or members of the armed forces. Moreover, in the course of reforming the school system, fascist legislators determined that women lacked the prerequisite "virile conception of life" necessary to direct upper-grade schools or to teach certain key subjects, including history, philosophy, Italian, Latin, and Greek. The royal decree-laws of May 6, 1923, and December 9, 1926, thus excluded women from competing in examinations for the fourth and fifth grades of technical institutes and the sixth and seventh grades of the lyceums, as well as advancing to the positions of middle-school director or lyceum principal.

By the late 1920s, specious reasoning about women's unsuitability for so-called virile posts ceased to offer an adequate rationale for labor-market policy. As high unemployment rates became a permanent feature of the Italian economy, more and more men risked becoming "devirilized." In 1928 the government advised all state offices that they should prefer male heads of households in hiring and career advancement, even if this meant passing over not just women but also unmarried war veterans. In the course of the Great Depression, as male unemployment rose, the government authorized public agencies to limit the numbers of women taking civil service tests. In some instances, they might exclude them altogether. In March 1934 the public administration limited to 5 percent the number of women in directive posts and to 20 percent those with lesser responsibilities. That same year accords in the private sector between employers and the National Fascist Confederation of Banking and Insurance promised to limit women employees to 12 percent in banks and 15 percent in insurance firms. Eventually, all such restrictions were superseded by the notorious decree-law of September 5, 1938, number 1514. This, as we noted, set a 10 percent quota on women in large and medium-sized public and private enterprises and proposed to exclude them entirely from offices or other business firms having less than ten employees.

Whether such exclusions worked is another issue. Evidence suggests that the myriad biases common to labor markets everywhere, aggravated by fascist economic policies and protective laws, had already gone far toward classifying jobs by sex. Consequently, women were well under quota in,

Table 2. Women in the Labor Force, by Economic Sector

	% of All Working Women Employed in			Women as % of Total Labor Force in		
	Agriculture	Industry	Other	Agriculture	Industry	Other
1911	58.8	24.2	17.0	43.2	43.9	39.5
1921	52.2	23.6	18.2	44.7	39.0	38.5
1931	53.3	24.1	22.6	40.5	34.4	40.0
1936	51.1	24.1	24.8	41.3	33.1	42.8
1951	41.4	28.0	30.6	32.6	28.0	42.7

Source: Rosa Anna Pernicone, *L'inserimento della donna nelle attività economiche in Italia,* Società italiana di economia demografia e statistica, Collana di studi e monografie, n.s., 1, 1972, pp. 35–36.

say, the upper-echelon central state administration and the professions. At the same time, many firms and services habitually used only or mostly women; in a market economy, employers had no intention of replacing them with men, state edicts notwithstanding. Not by chance, the list of exemptions of jobs characterized as "particularly suited to women" published by the royal decree of June 29, 1939, number 989, was a long one; not only did it include the custodial staffs of girls' schools, laundry and dry-cleaning establishments but also the secretarial pools of state ministries. To forestall further protest, the decree set a three-year grace period for phasing out women from other areas. However, the whole legislation was rescinded less than a year later. In April 1940, as the dictatorship sought to put the country on a wartime footing, the procedures for civil mobilization threw open the labor market to all minors aged fourteen to eighteen and to women, eighteen to forty-five.[29] By the summer of 1940, as women flooded the labor market, the fascist unions, social welfare services, and party organizations rallied with promises to help working women balance their triple burden: as mothers, homemakers, and laborers (see table 2).

To sum up, fascism oversaw a contradictory economic situation: It wanted a low-wage labor force, yet sought to secure the market for male heads of household. It wanted women out of the work force, yet in the interest of the race it hoped to protect those who worked. Its solution was to intervene at multiple levels, through protective laws, by *inquadramento*, and through statutes of exclusion. At one level, it sought to move women out of the work force once they married and had children, at another, to oversee them in the irregular, discontinuous labor typical of an economy that greatly relied on home work or putting out systems. Fascist policies toward working women thus seem less drastic than those of Nazi Germany, which in 1934 expelled women outright from state employment. Yet Italian female labor participation was lower at the start and occupied less qualified positions than in Germany. The combination of customary biases and new discriminations, operating in an economy where jobs were hard to find anyway and where the state picked up the slack by acting as employer of last resort, made fascist Italy a uniquely hostile environment for the employment of women.[30] This is especially visible if we look at various categories of working women and at how fascist patterns of discrimination interacted with biases in the labor market to condition the way female labor was valued.

Rural Women: Laborers or Housewives?

The contrast between fascist images of female labor and social reality was nowhere clearer than in propaganda about the Italian countryside. "Rurality makes woman queen of the home and family," trumpeted Mussolini.[31] Peasant women apparently thought otherwise. In the 1930s the greatest numbers of women active in the economy were still employed in agricultural work. Yet in the same period, rural exodus, undeterred by fascist efforts to staunch it, reached striking proportions, spurred by depressed farm prices and endemic rural overpopulation. In Italy women seemed to be hastening away from the farm even more rapidly than men: 326,000 women left the agricultural sector between 1921 and 1936, compared to 228,000 men. As a percentage of all economically active women, those in agriculture dropped from 59 to 45 percent. This decline was far greater than that in France, from 46 to 40 percent in same years, or in Germany, from 43 to 38 percent.[32]

The occupational distribution of the several million women who stayed behind was divided for census purposes into housewives or *massaie,* a new category added in 1931, laborers, helpers (*coadiuvanti* who assisted their spouses), and proprietors. Wage-earning farm women were clearly on the wane during the interwar decades, at least partly as a result of the fascist policy of "deproletarianization," which was supposed to settle landless (and radically inclined) peasants on small plots. But that did not necessarily improve the condition of farm women who, as helpers or housewives, were subject to the onerous labor duties their male kin contracted in order to maintain a small property, rental, or share-tenancy in an era of declining farm prices. The woman was the key to the "equilibrium between farm and family," as the agricultural expert Francesco Coletti remarked

in 1925, and the wise proprietor carefully calculated her skills before signing rental or share contracts.[33] He practically always stood to gain, for
contracts generally estimated women's labor as 60 percent that of able-
bodied men's following the accords formulated by the fascist state's foremost agricultural expert, Arrigo Serpieri, in 1926. This exploitation was
especially visible in share-cropping homesteads. On the basis of their studies
of some well-managed Tuscan farms in the early 1930s, investigators from
the National Institute of Agrarian Economy (INEA) estimated that the
hardworking patriarchs Giuseppe, Egisto, and Faustino worked, respectively, 2,926, 2,834, and 2,487 hours per year, whereas their wives, Lucia,
Virginia, and Maria, put in, respectively, 3,290, 3,001, and 3,655 hours.
Indeed, peasant women, no matter how they were classified by the census,
were at once artisans, domestic servants, tenders of animals, and seasonal
field hands as well; their labor in the home alone easily took up 1,500
hours a year. Household chores were a major undertaking given the lack
of electricity and indoor plumbing. To prepare meals meant first cleaning
out the hearth and drawing the fire, preceded by hauling water from the
well or spring and gathering kindling. Laundry was a twice-monthly days-
long enterprise by the time heavy linen sheets had been lugged to the
water source, ash applied several times, and the whole lot pressed with
stove-heated irons. In addition to laying away lentils, tomatoes, capers,
and other stores, caring for the chickens, and tending the orchard garden,
at harvest time the women served the men in the fields and often labored
there themselves. During their free time, they braided straw and mended
clothes. The conditions of labor were all the more burdensome as harsher
farm contracts and mounting debt put greater pressure on family units,
remittances from emigration dropped, and income from silk and other
cottage industries fell off. At the same time, the gap between urban and
rural living standards of housing, dress, education, and recreation was
widening visibly.[34]

Female field laborers, and especially the half-million migrant workers,
were a real sore spot for the regime, and when it couldn't conceal them
by fiddling with the census figures, it cloaked their existence with new
meanings. The figure most idealized by the corporate system was the
mondina, or rice worker, of the Po valley and delta. In late spring each
year about two hundred thousand women, at least a quarter of whom
were under twenty-one years of age, traveled by train, by truck, and on
foot to staging areas at Vercelli, Novara, and Cremona for the eight-week
rice "campaign." Starting in early May, when the misty dawns were still
freezing, and finishing in July, when suffocating heat settled over the
swampy fields, the women, in three reprises, waded waist-deep into the

muddy paddies to sow, weed, and harvest the crops. The fascists had much invested in the campaign's smooth operation. Rice, together with potatoes and corn flour, was to replace pasta in Italian diets, thereby cutting down on costly wheat imports; the 130,000 hectares planted annually with this "major source of national wealth," mainly in Lombardy and Piedmont, produced five million tons. The rice workers also tested fascism's capacity to manage labor. The *mondine* had been the mainstay of rural socialism. Though the red leagues had long been outlawed and fascist officials and prefects bullied the women with threats of long jail terms, the rice workers staged protests as late as 1932 as their wages were whittled down by the big capitalist farmers of the zone.[35]

Beyond that, the *mondina* was an affront to right-thinking public opinion, sensitized by fascist propaganda to the plight of working mothers. It was bad enough that mere girls worked knee-deep in the muddy waters, their skirts hoisted around their waists. Worse, working mothers dropped off nurslings and toddlers catch-as-catch-can in nearby villages or farm barracks. Moreover, the rice workers had the highest incidence of spontaneous abortion of any group, a fact doctors attributed to stooping water-soaked for long hours.[36] At the same time, the *mondina* was the agricultural equivalent of the "sexy salesgirl." Many were young and unmarried. Tough and uninhibited, they were notorious not only for their militant socialism but also for their bawdy sexuality.

This combination both intimidated and attracted potential patrons. When the head of the fascist union local of Pavia set out to organize rice workers in the spring of 1925, he entered into a courting contest with the rival, and practically defunct, "red" unions. Not only did he promise the young women "humane treatment" and "a stringent defense of your rights," he also offered to find winter work in the textile mills and to post wage rates and transportation costs. Moreover, he promised entertainment, for the *mondina*, as everybody knows, "her hard day's work done, sings, and if there's music, dances, and, if possible, she makes love."[37] The fascist trade unions' newsletter *Mondina* was at once lubricious and opportunistic: in Mammola's "Amore di Mondina" the heroine, Renata, who is being sexually harassed by Tonio, an arrogant revolutionary socialist, is saved by a "beautiful tall black-shirted fascist." He gives her a bunch of roses, protesting "we don't want to harm anyone," and she comes back singing the *squadristi*'s favorite song, "Giovinezza." "Love" also featured centrally in the "Mondina's Song," composed to the tune of "Giovinezza": "When the sun o'er the rice paddies / scorches the fields with heat / Joyous, fresh harvest ladies / sing their love songs so sweet." In mid-July, the syndicalists bid, "Farewell, lovely rice harvesters, farewell 'til next year."[38]

By the 1930s the syndicalists, who were never able to display what the *mondine* might truly have regarded as virility—standing up to drastic wage slashing—encountered less ardent, if more effective, rivals within the fascist movement. In 1930, apparently at the prompting of Angiola Moretti, head of the women's *fasci*, Augusto Turati founded the *Pro-assistenza mondariso*, coordinating the philanthropy of Lombard women with the services of the Rice Board *(Ente risi)* and other state, party, and trade union offices. When the *mondine* arrived that spring, they were welcomed at roadside canteens with sandwiches, soup, beverages, and canned and powdered milk for the children. The barracks were filled with camp beds. Last but not least, there were Sunday parties. The *Pro-assistenza* also arranged for parish priests to toll the church bells to signal work starts in order to prevent workers and overseers from the usual "sorry" squabbling over charges of lateness. After 1931, in the wake of renewed strikes and alleged communist infiltration, Starace himself took to touring Vercelli, Lomellina, and the lower delta, bringing Mussolini's personal greetings, along with sums of 40,000 to 50,000 lire to be disbursed in assistance. ONMI set up nurseries for toddlers, and the national government founded a special placement office for rice workers.[39] Finally, with the royal decree-law of August 7, 1936, maternity coverage was extended to agricultural workers, and on April 28, 1938, the General Directorate of Health forbade work in an advanced state of pregnancy, promising a check to cover lost wages. Whether such measures compensated for the loss of their own unions is another question: wages were cut 25 percent from 1925 to 1931, and they stagnated throughout the 1930s.[40]

Overall, the ruralist project fell on deaf ears, at least in the countryside, not least of all because the fiction of the regally becostumed *rurali* was so incongruous in the face of reality. By contrast, the virtues of going to the city were clear enough. In agriculture, women earned about 50 percent of the male wage, whereas in industry they could earn 60 to 70 percent of it and have social protections as well. In the countryside, the work year averaged 185 days, in industry around 300. In the cities, there was unemployment, but one could also collect unemployment insurance. At worst there was charity, the soup kitchens of the regime, and ONMI for illegitimate children. In the cities, women might toil nine to ten hours daily, six days a week in dark, dusty factories. But they had fun after work, and a wider pick of husbands. It was easier for women to find work in the cities than for men. At worst, they could hire out as maids. Familiar with these calculations, Maria Castellani, head of the National Association of Women Artists and Degree Holders and an expert on labor issues, nursed no illusions. On demographic grounds, to help the economy, and to pre-

vent competition between men and women, women's work in the countryside had to be "defended and strengthened." Yet the women departed
nonetheless, "at the cost of any sacrifice, whether to become servants,
workers, or teachers."[41] The regime's ruralizing campaigns only made
the move to urban life and labor immeasurably harder.

The Joys and Miseries of Factory Labor

The country girl's dream of finding factory work was usually disappointed. A generation earlier, young peasant women might easily have
found work in textile and clothing firms. But between 1927 and 1937, as
many as 120,000 jobs disappeared as firms mechanized or went out of
business during the depression. Altogether industrial jobs opened up at a
rate of less than 50,000 annually, so that by 1938, only 525,000 new
openings had been created. True, new consumer goods industries, including food processing, electrical manufacture, and shoe production hired
more women, as did machine and chemical firms. But overall, the increase
favored men.[42] That new forces were at play discriminating against women
is hard to document however. For in only one case, the booming synthetic
fiber industry, where past hiring practices had favored women, did men
displace them to any significant degree. Between 1931 and 1937, as Italy
became the world's leading exporter and its second biggest producer after
the United States, the female labor force declined, from 69 percent of the
work force to 45 percent. In this instance, one can imagine that hiring
accords, together with the application of protective laws (synthetics having the highest sickness and turnover rates of any industry), discriminated in favor of men.[43] More generally, as much because of the slow
growth of industrial employment as fascist biases, many women in search
of urban employment settled for intermittent and menial labor, putting-
out work, or domestic service.

Under fascism, urban wage-earning women might thus be classified
into two categories: those who held regular jobs and who therefore were
protected by fascist social and protective legislation, and those who labored outside the official labor market and who were not protected. Compared to the past, social coverage was relatively comprehensive by the late
1930s. Aside from pensions, sick leaves, unemployment insurance, and
family allowances (granted them if they were heads of household), mothers had paid time-off for the last month of pregnancy and up to six months
after birth, as well as brief rest periods at work for nursing. If they were
employed in textile firms, as about half of the female factory workers
were, they might also have benefited from employer paternalism. There
were long-standing traditions of company welfare work among Catholic

textile owners, whose managements were attuned to the special needs of their predominately female employees for room and board, child care, and firm tutelage. The fascist regime encouraged company largesse, in the form of housing, food plans, and recreation. These promised to compensate for wage cuts and to build labor-management harmony, as well as to mollify the fascist unions. They also kept workers healthier. "Better to aid the workers now than to underwrite tuberculosis clinics later," remarked the hard-nosed Luisa Spagnuoli, the clothing manufacturer and producer of Perugina Chocolates, as she steered a sympathetic journalist, Maria Guidi, around the company canteen. Most of her workers were adolescents and nursing mothers who walked twenty kilometers daily to and from work; they skipped meals, and ended up gnawing on old bread if not properly fed.[44]

To argue that women workers were protected is not to argue that they were well-off. To compete abroad, Italian cotton manufactures quintupled the use of mechanical looms from 1927 to 1933; trying to best the American record, at least one firm had its operatives handling forty-eight looms at once. Industrial doctors, with reforming spirit, recorded the high spontaneous abortion rates in synthetic fibers plants, as well as the numerous cases of dementia, lung lesions, and breathlessness brought on by the poisonous carbon disulfide employed in manufacturing processes.[45] Wages continued to be calculated as the equivalent of a second salary, and women, like men, were subject to pay cuts and reduced hours. In addition, collective contracts, by distinguishing men from women, and by calculating female skill grades as either semiskilled and unskilled—as compared to the five-category system for men—reversed the wartime and postwar trend toward reducing male-female pay differentials. In the declining textile sector, which employed mainly women, real wages—which had increased during the war and in its wake—dropped. In 1928 the average level of pay was 78 percent of the industry average, whereas in 1939 it was 74 percent.[46]

Italian working women thus faced a harsh dilemma. Low wages plus protective legislation along with pro-family propaganda encouraged married women, upon having children, to leave work. In theory, they could stay away from their posts for up to six months after their babies were born. But most women waited longer, until the infants were weaned, before economic necessity caused them to return. Increasing numbers apparently did return, fascist propaganda notwithstanding; in 1931 12 percent of married women worked whereas in 1936 20.7 percent worked. Indeed, according to one estimate, 40 percent of all Italian working women were married in the 1930s, a figure that was surpassed only in social

A demonstration of female handicrafts, early 1930s. Women spinners are dressed in early-fifteenth-century Lombard costumes. (Louise Diel, *Das faschistische Italien und die Aufgaben der Frau im neuen Staat* [Berlin: Hobbing Verlag, 1934]. Reprinted courtesy of the Butler Library, Columbia University.)

Sicilian women doing menial labor. (Diel, *Das faschistische Italien.* Reprinted courtesy of the Butler Library, Columbia University.)

Assembly-line workers at the ICO medical equipment factory in Bologna, laboring under the slogan "Build, and if necessary, struggle and win." (Reproduced by permission of Alinari.)

Migrant field laborers in Emilia, 1930s. (Reproduced by permission of Alinari.)

The secretarial pool at the Perugina Candy Works, 1928. (Reproduced by permission of Alinari.)

The company canteen at the Perugina Candy Works, 1928. (Reproduced by permission of Alinari.)

democratic Sweden where working women benefited from a wide range of social services.[47] Many Italian women who eventually returned to work did not go back to their previous jobs. They thus lost their pension rights and other protections. Perhaps the majority went into the underground economy where they found occupations more compatible with their myriad household duties.

The growth of this invisible female work force on the edge or outside of the official labor market has to be inferred, however. We know that Italian industry, before fascism as well as since, has always turned to "gray economy" putting-out systems whenever under pressure to cut costs. Under the dictatorship this practice was encouraged not just by the huge availability of women seeking employment and by fascist labor policies but also by the growing demand for services in an urbanizing economy. But how many women were involved and what exactly they did is hard to decipher. Technically, the women who went into the retailing sector, say, assisting at the family-run store or cleaning up after the outdoor markets, were counted. So were those who hired out as domestic help. But the true home worker fell between the cracks of the corporate system. A much idealized figure for fascist and Catholic ideologues (like the "rural housewife"), she might, at Turin, have found occupation painting luminescent dials for automobiles; in Rome or Naples, weaving straw mats and baskets; in Florence, crocheting doilies and trimming fancy clothes for the tourist trade. In theory she was protected by the Labor Charter of 1927, article 21 of which, in addition to affirming that "collective contracts extend their benefits and coverage to home workers as well," promised "special state-defined norms to guarantee the hygiene and cleanliness of their homes." But as much as labor experts decried the evils of the "Anglo-American style sweating-systems," and corporate laws ordered irregular laborers to obtain work passbooks (*libretti di lavoro*) clarifying whether they were artisans or dependents, few in fact were protected. In theory the women were covered by old-age and disability insurance, as well as against tuberculosis, a common ailment among home workers. But since they had to contribute five lire a month for five years before becoming eligible for claims, few joined the plans. By law they were excluded from maternity benefits, unemployment checks, and family allocations.[48]

The growing population of servants overlapped with the statistically invisible submerged economy of home workers. The census takers who counted their increase from 445,631 in 1921 to 534,973 in 1931 and to 660,725 in 1936 likely much underestimated their total.[49] But even these numbers put Italy on a different course from other Western nations in which declining middle-class wealth and new opportunities for employment in growing tertiary or consumer-oriented industries caused the servant population to decline in the interwar years. In Italy, by contrast, practically no middle-class families wanted for help; even the most strapped petty bourgeois households managed to hire washerwomen and call in seamstresses to replenish the family wardrobe. Many bourgeois families had several helpers: a chauffeur and a gardener as well as washerwomen, cooks, children's maids, and wet nurses, in addition to the hair stylist and skilled personnel called in for various household repairs. Unlike factory labor, private service involved ties of a personal, quasi-feudal nature. Families recruited their help from rural backlands, not infrequently from the villages where the *signori* had family estates or went on holiday. On their return home, Roman families brought back girls as young as eleven or twelve from the Ciociaria or Abbruzzi, Milanese families from the Veneto or the Lombard lake country. Wages, varying from thirty to sixty lire a month, were arranged with the girls' fathers or through the mediation of the village priest or local notable. For these paltry sums, together with occasional gifts of cast-offs, the girls worked interminably: up at 5:30 to wash and polish parquet or marble floors, they accompanied the cook to market at 8:00, burdened like porters; at 11:00 they prepared lunch and helped the chambermaid make the beds; at noon they served lunch, and from 1:00 to 2:00 washed up; at 2:00 had a half-hour lunch; washed clothes from 2:30 to 6:00, then were back in the kitchen to make and serve supper; washed up at 9:00; at 10:00 ate leftovers; at 11:00 retired in the alcove. If the relationship survived, it might endure a lifetime. The lady of the house would boast how "her" Maria starched shirt collars and mended to perfection; in turn the faithful Maria took the *Signora*'s side in arguments with rivals, was affianced but never married (only 11 percent of marriageable age were), and died clutching a family memento.[50]

The discontinuous nature of their work not only deprived women of using their skills but succeeded in effacing their identity as workers. In Rome during the depression years, the mates of unemployed construction workers, though they had been trained as seamstresses, took any odd job to support their families. Many worked as laundry women, barefooted in humid, cold underground springs, or hired out by the hour to the families of small functionaries and clerks too poor themselves to provide them with a meal. In terms of finding odd jobs, observers agreed that women were more resilient than men; the latter, their self-image being tied to the exercise of a trade or skill, refused base jobs to keep up their status and self-esteem. When social workers for the Mariuccia Charitable Society tracked down former inmates of its school for wayward girls in 1939, they found that few any longer exercised their hard-won skills as seamstresses, not least of all because of the demands of their families. The husband of Maria B., a shoemaker, hung around all day, waiting until he might obtain "capital to buy shoe leather." He refused day labor because he was an "artisan." The son-in-law of another woman was waiting for her to find him gainful employment. "What craft did I learn," lamented Ines F., when she was reminded of her long and successful apprenticeship as a seamstress. Once a bright-eyed girl, now a worn-out fifty-two-year-old with four children and five grandchildren, she had learned, she said, to be "the servant of her husband, first, then her children, and now her grandchildren; what do you expect? . . . in our homes, we are at once everything and nothing."[51]

No wonder then that the time of factory employment was recalled with fondness by those who had experienced it. The decade or so between fourteen or fifteen and their mid-twenties coincided with emancipation from the family and with youth. It was also associated with pride in skills and accomplishments identified as their own. "I liked work," "I was esteemed by my supervisor," "I had a perfect record," ("ero inattaccabile"), women recalled. So long as they worked, the girls nurtured a strong sense of collective identity as well. Some young workers, like the Turinese seamstresses who organized the annual Festival of the Caterinettes, carefully cultivated their public image. Their parade through the streets of central Turin, decked out in the high-fashion dresses they had sewn for themselves copying the patterns designed for their wealthy patrons, highlighted working-girl solidarity in the face of the bourgeois women who exploited them and the students who seduced but did not marry them.[52] The unskilled, too, clung to their occupations. At Turin, a young sick-fund inspector, Aldo Masciotta, was aghast at the "grave ills" affecting working girls aged fourteen to eighteen. Almost all suffered from chronic fatigue and at least half were afflicted with irregular menstrual cycles, varicose veins, and scoliosis or other skeletal deformities. But the average girl was willing "to sacrifice herself out of desire to win her independence." Work meant having "personalities of their own," and they were unwilling to marry if this meant losing the autonomy which was "the goal of their existence."[53]

The Sexy Office Girl

The most significant and rapid change in patterns of women's work took place in the area of nonmanual employment. In 1921 women amounted to 20.3 percent of the people occupied in what broadly might be called tertiary employment, including commerce, public administration, and private services; by 1936 the figure rose to 27.3 percent. The growing bureaucratization of public life and of industrial enterprises, together with the rapid development of larger-scale trade and retailing groups, created a rapidly increasing number of subordinate jobs for young women, as clerks, typists, stenographers, sales girls, and minor administrators. These jobs were eagerly sought after, for the work was clean and less strenuous than factory work, had higher social status, and was increasingly better paid. It was an Italian peculiarity that the state sector's rate of growth far outstripped the private sector's and that the latter's expansion was so concentrated in one area, occurring mainly in northern Italy, most visibly in Milan.

In other countries, the tertiary sector was rapidly feminized. In Italy, however, because of the slow growth of industrial jobs and the prestige attached to "brain work"—with a corresponding disdain for manual labor—this trend was powerfully contested. In no other sector were the men more "rigid and unreasonable," as Wanda Gorjux, a leading fascist woman, observed.[54] Because the public administration was the main employer of white-collar labor, with around 800,000 dependents in 1936, it strongly influenced public impressions about women working, if not actually affecting private-sector hiring practices. Starting in 1928, government put more and more obstacles in the way of women, beginning with the highest ranks of the administration and gradually extending prohibitions to bar women from ranks. By 1934 departments had been empowered to fix quotas for hiring at up to 5 percent of the higher ranking posts for which a university degree was required; at 15 percent for the intermediate ranks; and at 20 percent for subordinate positions. According to the 1936 census, women equalled 26 percent of the total staff, outside of the armed forces. Given these figures, the decree-law of September 5, 1938, by establishing a 10 percent quota, threatened to be devastating. In fact, the percentages of women were well below the quotas not only in the top-ranking A and B categories but in the subaltern rank C as well, at least once the secretarial pool was exempted.

Though it was meant to be a guideline for private commerce and local government administrations, state policy was followed only in insurance and banking. As early as 1934, contractual accords proposed to substitute men for women whenever possible, and these accords mandated that in banking firms with fewer than twenty staff members, women were not to exceed 12 percent of the total; in insurance firms, the limit was 16 percent. But this quota only reaffirmed the prevailing trend: according to the 1936 census, 88 percent of all such employees were indeed male, and the overriding majority of the women were unmarried. At the same time, where status was low and the pay poor, as in commercial establishments and local government offices, the number of women rose significantly. Withal, the overall totals increased very slowly indeed; in 1936, about 30 percent of office employees were women, as compared to 54 percent in the United States in 1940 and 40 percent in contemporary France. In the public service, the results of accumulated biases were especially striking. In Germany in 1933 25 percent of public employees were women, in France in 1936, 34 percent, whereas in Italy women tallied a mere 16 percent, and this percentage was declining in the late 1930s.[55]

This bias had significant social and cultural as well as economic effects. Elsewhere black-coated males were defrocked as office work was mechanized, and paper-pushing came to be stigmatized as unmanly. As office work was rationalized and automated, men were pushed toward more skilled occupations and executive posts, while the lower echelons were feminized.[56] In Italy, far from being feminized, bureaucratic work was virilized. The fascist regime built up male camaraderie by increasing pay differentials with respect to manual work, conceding special perquisites, and promoting military-like hierarchies, one goal being to allay fears that the work itself was indeed unmanly and parasitical as some reformers, including high-placed fascists, insisted. Over the long run, it inhibited mechanization and curbed efficiency, promoting the abusive treatment of the public and the low levels of productivity with which clients of Italian bureaucracy have long been familiar.

Whereas the male "brain worker's" image was exalted under fascism, the female's was debunked. True, mass-circulation magazines regarded the secretary as the "heroine of modern existence," and secretarial schools turned out masses of low-skilled aspirants. But office work was for the most part ill-paid drudgery, and the overly numerous, inexperienced young women were little able to defend their interests. Not until the fall of 1932 did secretaries acquire their first work contract: this called for a forty-five-hour week, limited overtime to two hours a day (twelve hours weekly) paid at time and a quarter, and guaranteed a month-long vacation in addition to the Christmas holiday. It also specified equal pay for men in the same work categories, though to what purpose is not clear, since there were practically no male takers.[57] The monthly pay of around 300 lire for typists and stenographers, as well as telephone operators and shop girls, was inadequate to live decently, no matter how economical they were. The only way to live was by pooling with the other family breadwinners. To make ends meet, as well as to enjoy small urban pleasures, some young women turned to the market of sexual favors. Public opinion alerted wives to the snares of the seductive secretary. But the secretary was more likely the person being entrapped. Luciana Peverelli's best-selling *Sogni in grembiule nero (Dreams in Black-Frock)*, published in 1940, rang true when Titti, a seasoned office girl, sought to disabuse the neophyte Loretta of her notions of professional integrity. Sexual favors were part of the job, explained Titti. The "same old story," it started with a little present, an increase in salary, a kiss, a request to stay overtime from six to eight, when "the studio is closed and the phone won't ring. I took the bait right away here because I had experience from before." "Really," asked Loretta, wide-eyed, "You mean they ask outright?" "Not with so many words," Titti started to laugh. "We all know where it ends up. And it practically happens to everybody, believe me. All of my friends are in the same situation."[58]

The Caste of Professional Women

Discriminatory legislation was most effective at blocking access to professions that depended on long years of study, intellectual commitment, and overcoming subtle peer discrimination. In fascist Italy, women never numbered more than 10 percent of the 108,293 free professionals. The number of female notary publics could be counted on one hand, the number of practicing lawyers was 60, there were 30 dentists, 13 architects, 297 doctors and surgeons, and 500 writers and journalists. Women outnumbered men only in librarianship, nursing, social work, and school teaching.[59]

The obstacles to professional women are at least partly explained by the nature of the Italian economy. So-called free professionals frequently depended on government patronage to build up their practices. Thus law school graduates staffed the corporate bureaucracies, architects performed as urban planners, obtaining commissions from government-sponsored agencies such as INCIS and INCP, and doctors consulted for public clinics. Under the best of circumstances, entry into patronage networks was complicated. Architecture offers a case in point. The faculties graduated very few women to begin with; a young woman would have had to be truly convinced of her vocation to continue her studies after the Duce, speaking to Emil Ludwig in a widely read interview, characterized the scant visibility of women in the field as a "symbol of her [subaltern] destiny": "Ask her to build you a mere hut, not even a temple, she cannot do it."[60] The mere dozen women with successful practices in the 1930s had to be at least as well-connected as their male counterparts. Elena Luzzatto's career was facilitated by the fact that her mother, Annarella Luzzatto Gabrielli, was a successful architect. Moreover, Elena's employment at the planning office of the Governorate of Rome put her close to sources of architectural patronage: the commission to build the elegant covered market of the Prince of Naples Place was awarded through her own office. Maria Casoni, a civil engineer with a degree in mathematics, with whom Luzzatto worked to design modernist seaside homes at Ostia, was a protégée of Bruno Biagi, head of the National Fascist Institute of Social Insurance; in addition to civil servant housing, she designed his villa at Bologna.[61]

Not by chance, journalism was the fastest-growing profession in the interwar years, for it responded to a market oriented to ever larger female readerships. Journalism was becoming a more cut-throat and lucrative profession under fascist patronage. Yet there was still a belletristic conception of the metier that made it seem a suitable female occupation. Whereas in 1921 7 percent of writers and journalists were women, in 1931 12 percent were. In reality, only a score or so of women journalists were truly *firme di successo,* making a living off their writings. These included Flavia Steno (Amelia Cottini Osta) of *Il lavoro* of Genoa; Haydée (Ida Finzi) of *Il piccolo* of Trieste; Willy Dias (Fortuna Morpurgo), Lucciola (Lucia Boccasini Tranquilli), and Margherita Cattaneo at the *Nuovo giornale* and *La nazione.* But the vast majority of the five hundred or so women who recorded their profession as writers scraped by with occasional pieces published in the women's press, living off other employment, their spouses' income, or family legacies.[62]

With the growth of a fascist warfare state in the 1930s, there was also a significant increase of women in the so-called helping professions, nursing and social work, in addition to the old standby, teaching. Once the province of nuns and aristocratic do-gooders—the latter working under the banner of the Italian Red Cross—nursing became a modern profession in 1925 as the government published statutes regulating the training of nurses and their status relative to other professions. Between 1921 and 1936 their numbers rose steadily from 27,264 to 39,646, without counting the Catholic nursing orders.[63] Social work too acquired a more professional guise in the course of the 1930s, though in the long run its development was inhibited by the government's reliance on religious personnel and Fascist party volunteers.

As before fascism, the main outlet for degree-holding women remained teaching. The dictatorship fully endorsed the common conviction that the "gentle sex" excelled where "there is need for love and refined learning: at children's schools, in family life, and on hospital floors." "Woman," as the slogan went, "is an educator insofar as she is or can be a mother."[64] At the same time, the dictatorship wanted male youth to be taught by men. But preferment to males in competitions, not to mention efforts at making teaching a more attractive profession with free housing, travel discounts, reduced hours to make moonlighting possible, free medicine after 1942, and retirement after twenty-five years of service, did not notably affect the sex composition of the lower schools. Women always made up at least 70 percent of the total.

Nevertheless, the regime did revamp teachers' relationship to their profession. The "schoolmarm in the red-plumed hat," the celibate teacher whose reforming zeal was celebrated by the novelist Edmondo De Amicis, had been retired by the late 1920s, to be replaced by younger and more submissive figures. In the fascist school system, men ruled the roost. Regulations barring women from directorial posts were reinforced by opinion that held that it was "better to be commanded by a mediocre man than an intellectual woman"; better routine male tyranny than the high-handedness of hysterical *prime donne*. This attitude was shared not only by men but, apparently, by women as well. Though far more women than men had higher degrees, men outnumbered women 1,362 to 480 as elementary and middle-school directors. Of 841 upper-school principals, 790 were men. Moreover, hierarchies of command became more rigid and school inspectors more intrusive. Teachers, in addition to joining the *Associazione fascista della scuola*, were obliged to volunteer to oversee the party youth troops, on pain of not being promoted. Fascist propaganda was added to the curriculum, only to render more authoritarian the rote teaching methods in use since the turn of the century. Increased school attendance caused increased class size and the doubling, sometimes the tripling, of sessions. Sixty-five children to a class was not uncommon. On the personal level, women teachers suffered more than ever from their ambiguous social position, which made it hard for them to find suitable husbands. Contemporaries spoke of the "tragedy" of the unwed teacher. Dispatched to a godforsaken rural outpost, she was then stuck there, for priority on transfers was given to the married, to enable couples to be near each other. However, the young woman was too educated to marry a worker, and her status was too low to make her a good match for the local pharmacist, notary public, doctor, or landowner. Short of staying single, her best chance was the town secretary or the tax collector, or even another teacher, though the men in the profession were generally of lower social rank and regarded as of inferior intelligence. Withal, none of these trials prevented women from being apostles of the idea that teaching was a preeminently female vocation, suited to express qualities innate to them.[65]

The fact that so few women were actually involved in the professions could not but condition the way their professional identity was formed. Everywhere during the interwar years, the modern professions organized themselves in pursuit of their interests. In Italy, as in other nations ruled by corporatist systems, government-sponsored chambers facilitated this process. The fact that the state sanctioned the exclusion of women from the professions and discriminated against their representation in the corporate bodies greatly complicated the construction of new models of female professionalism.[66]

This is not to say that professional women were unconscious of their collective interests. Women's professional groups, formed under the aegis of international women's associations, promoted a strong sense of corporate identity. For example, the Italian Federation of Women Jurists, presided over by the Neapolitan Maria Laetitia Riccio, belonged to the International Federation of Women Magistrates and Lawyers; its review of fascist legislation on women, drawn up in 1932 to celebrate the dicennial of the Fascist Revolution, suggested the considerable professional skills of the contributors (not to mention their dissatisfaction with several aspects of fascist legislation). The National Fascist Association of Women Doctors and Surgeons, founded in 1921 and headquartered at Salsomaggiore, had as many as 200 members in the late 1930s. Presided over by Myra Carcupino Ferrari and Giuseppina Pastori, it was affiliated with the National Fascist Corporation of Doctors (*Sindacato nazionale fascista dei medici*) and spoke out against discrimination against women in public competitions.

On the whole, Italian professional women reasoned as a privileged caste rather than as working women in quest of professional identities. Those prepared to argue that women had the same right as men to a career, and might be wholly fulfilled by it, were at best a handful. Maria Albini, a Milanese labor expert, stands out: an adviser to the *Alleanza muliebre*, she also founded the *Circolo sic* in 1933 to promote discussion on equal rights, the history of the suffrage movement, and the hostility of the press to women's work.[67] Maria Diez Gasca (who in the 1930s also acted as consultant to the Ministry of the Corporations) firmly believed in the need to train professional women, as did the fascist journalist and organizer Wanda Gorjux. But both these accomplished women believed that the new woman professional would operate in fields such as social work. They argued not just that these areas were especially suited to female talents and did not compete with established male occupations, but that they were indispensable and important to modernizing Italian society.[68] The majority, however, seemed to believe that theirs was not a career but a vocation, the practice of which reflected a special female refinement of intellect and aesthetic sensibility. Far from being professionals, they characterized themselves as "cultivated" women or female "intelligentsia" (*intellettualità*). These titles inspired an inner confidence in their superiority over men, but also convinced them of their capacity to transcend the vulgar dichotomy imposed by society: either motherhood or work. The mass of women had to make such a choice, perhaps, but not the elite. To justify their right to be exceptions, elite women thus affirmed that as a rule, work and motherhood *were* incompatible. When Mariella Tabellini published the first overview of the status of women in the free professions under fascism in 1942, she felt obliged to contend that "If a woman, to pursue a career, fails to fulfill her sacred duties . . . we would be decidedly against her exercise of professional activities. . . . [I]f instead [she] succeed[s] in finding harmonious means of carrying out [her] double duties, [she] will be worthy of the greatest admiration and respect." "A woman," she concluded, "may be useful in the hospitals, prisons, offices, law courts, and so on, but she must never forget that only at home is she indispensable."[69] That the professional elite, with their servants, education, and relatively emancipated life-styles, repeatedly made such arguments only rendered it more difficult for the mass of working women without such privileges to reconcile their duties to their family, their jobs, and themselves.

Class Conflict and Gender Solidarity

The effacement of women's identity as workers made it difficult for women to organize to protect their interests. But in spite of the fact that strikes were outlawed and striking workers risked being fired, if not arrested, for sedition, workers staged slowdowns and sometimes even walkouts to protest wage cuts and changes in work rules. On this score, women workers may have been at least as active as men. For they were occupied in declining industries, like textiles, which experienced considerable labor unrest in the late 1920s. In addition, the fact that women were excluded from the system of representation set up to mediate labor conflicts made them less prone to being gulled by the fascist trade union bureaucrats sent around to quiet them. Three of the major labor actions of the fascist period, the 1927 textile strikes in Valalona, the rice workers' strikes of 1930–31 in the Po Valley, and the great industrial strikes of March 1943 in the Turinese machine industries, were spearheaded by women or saw women as the major participants.

To achieve solidarity among women across class was a far more complicated issue. Working women organized around trade union issues, that is, they protested wage cuts, fought against longer hours, and defended against firings, whereas middle-class women mobilized around the right to gain access to state examinations and to earn respect for their professional status. The corporate system aggravated the divisions among the categories of the employed, dividing professional women, organized in ANFAL (the National Fascist Association of Women Artists and Degree-Holders), from commercial workers, who finally achieved an organization of their own in 1940, and from female factory and field workers. Under a regime that had forcibly isolated the working class, gender solidarity around labor issues was doubly difficult to achieve. Upper-class women displayed sympathy toward their working-class sisters only by means of charity. They did not empathize with them as workers who were also subject to sexual discrimination. Those like Maria Albini—collaborator of *Cultura muliebre* and sometime contributor on women's issues to *Problemi del lavoro*, the Genoese periodical founded by former socialists now loyal to fascism—who called for unity among women were like voices in the wilderness: "And when we realize that my problem is the same as that of all the other women . . . then we will truly be able to talk and listen, then we will be able to understand."[70]

It was only in the face of extreme measures of discrimination, as the September decree-law manifestly was, that working women were able to define their collective interests as women *and* workers. In the wake of the decree-law, commercial workers finally began to organize. In November 1939 provincial delegates gathered to prepare for the first national conference to "illustrate in detail" the legislation covering 250,000 female commercial workers. In the course of the meetings, convened in Rome on February 25–27, 1940, 130 women delegates presented their constituents' grievances.[71] These included long hours, low wages, and the widespread exploitation of untrained young women who were hired as apprentices and then fired. The litany was not surprising for a fledgling white-collar labor force. What was different with respect to the experience of women in other countries was the amount of time given to expounding the belief that women's work was just temporary and to itemizing the social welfare protections that would safeguard them and their families until they returned to their natural occupations as wives and mothers.

7   Going Out

When she parades her art of seductions through the public
ways, doesn't she consider the disturbance caused to mature
men who rightfully need tranquillity of spirit to take firmly in
hand affairs that determine the happiness of entire peoples?
  Don Paolo Ardali, *La politica demografica di Mussolini* (1929)

La donna e mobile . . . / She drives your car, / she's called the
frail sex / but she is stronger by far . . . / She's ever so
changeable: / supposedly true, / her memory is weak / her
thoughts not on you. / She's madly in love with sports . . .
  Popular song (circa 1940)

In 1930s Italy, café life still lay at the heart of urban conviviality. In Luigi
Preti's Padusa, Café Torino stood in front of the majestic clock tower just
off the most frequented artery of town, its ostentatiously Americanized
decor producing "an explosion of modernity" in the dour central plaza.
In the late afternoon, "all Padusa" gathered there for aperitifs. As big
landholders gossiped with merchants, well-heeled professionals, and public functionaries, the town's few intellectuals worked the tables like court
jesters, passing on smutty jokes about "that imbecile" Starace. By early
evening, the local *gerarchi* too gathered under the café awnings. Occupying the most forward seats, they were well-positioned to exchange limp
Roman salutes with other customers and to hear out postulants' whispers
without being distracted from their foremost pleasure—which was eying
the garrulous bands of girls of good family who in those hours crowded
through the central porticos.[1]

Café Torino, with its displays of all-male conviviality, may seem an
odd place from which to start to reconnoiter the leisure pastimes of women
under the dictatorship. Café get-togethers are usually associated with the
rise of modern bourgeois freedoms in the face of absolutist kingship and
with the new divisions between political life and privacy, public space and
domesticity, that accompanied their spread.[2] In mid-nineteenth-century
coffee houses, commoner patriots and moderate aristocrats bantered fra-
ternally about Italy's prospects for national unity. Later, avant-garde intellectuals met under the Milan Gallery, at Rome's Café Aragno, the
splendid Florian of Venice, or Florence's Giubbe Rosse to vituperate against
liberal Italy's defects. By the 1930s, the freedom of café sociability had
been curbed. Moreover, its easygoing pace seemed increasingly anachronistic in the face of the depersonalized cultural exchanges of mass com-

mercial pastimes. In all but the biggest cities, there was little turnover in the clientele. As always, it was predominately male. By contrast, the new world of mass cultural pastimes was quick-paced and exciting. It was also troubling as classes of people formerly distinct by rank and habits mixed cheek by jowl in public spaces. Not least of all, its main protagonists were women.

Still, Café Torino—or the Greco or Excelsior, as it might also have been called—is the right spot to start. The ongoing vitality of café society in the 1930s testified to the persistence of time-honored ways of thinking about how people occupied social space and how therefore the fascists themselves wielded power to control them. Café gatherings worked because the people involved knew exactly their place in society. Where status lines were especially sharply demarcated, as in Sicily, everybody recognized who belonged to the exclusive circle of the *capeddi* or *civili* and who to the workingmen's club. Class and status were as unmistakable as the difference between the bourgeois' hats and the craftsmen's caps. Legacies of ancien-régime distinctions in rank, these codes persisted in interwar society, manifesting themselves in dress, in the little gestures, in overall deportment. The police crackdown on public hostelries in 1927, which eventually caused thousands of working-class bars to disband, left the elites' circles largely intact. As in earlier moments of political transition, the daily gatherings they hosted offered occasions to show off rank, to exchange information, even to air a mild frondeur spirit. Not least of all, they presented fascist officialdom with two kinds of opportunities. One was to show off their movement's capacity to occupy all of the spaces originally associated with the construction of bourgeois sociability: from the public piazzas and their surrounding porticos to the theater, center-city street corners, and the salon. The other was to display their prowess as men—to other men, as well as to the girls as they passed by.

Recoding Public Space

From the vantage point of the café, male elites did indeed seem to dominate public space. The women's realm was elsewhere—at home with the household and kin as prescribed by tradition. Young women on their evening *passeggiata* might flaunt their new freedoms, and the most daring even braved bad reputations to join male friends at the tables. But this kind of female presence presented no real problem. Indeed, the parade seemed made for male consumption, the girls' fresh bodies being stylish ornaments attesting to fascism's modernity.

Yet more often than not, the young women thronging the central ways were heading elsewhere, toward places and pastimes in which the gender order and class hierarchies of bourgeois society were far less visible, and the state's reach was more tenuous. They might be going just around the corner to one of the big new department stores. By the late 1930s, Italy's five biggest cities all had their own Rinascente, the Italian equivalent of Paris's tasteful Galeries Lafayette, and at least forty major towns had one of the plainer *grandi magazzini* belonging to the Standa or Upim chains.[3] Young women might plan to stop by a dance hall to meet up with male friends, attracted by fashionably "foreignophile" names—Golden Gate, Blu-room, Pincio-Dancing Bar. Or they might simply be bent on window shopping, slowing down en route to chat with friends. The most likely venue, however, was the late afternoon movie matinee. No new recreational space was so strongly identified with these new female publics; no spots, as the modernist intellectual Giovanni Papini portrayed them, were as physically and sexually threatening to the old sites of male sociability as the movie houses:

> With their luminous petulance, their daily turnover of huge tricolor posters, the raucous wail of their phonographs, the tired invocations of their orchestras, the strident calls of their red-dressed boys, the cinematographs invade the central ways, drive out the cafés, set themselves up where once there were restaurant halls or billiard rooms, they consort with the bars, flash their impudent arch lights through the mysterious old squares, threaten little by little to dethrone the theaters.[4]

For a regime that treated rule over the piazza as a chief symbol of its public power, commercial culture presented a new order of problem. The power associated with modern leisure pastimes, like that of the mass market, was fundamentally decentered, to use the Foucauldian term. During the interwar years, the leading sites of invention lay abroad, whereas in Italy itself, at least until the early 1930s, the main points of production and dissemination were the chief northern cities, Turin and Milan, rather than the political capital, Rome. Moreover, the leisure pastimes of commercial culture were open, so to speak, for the price of a ticket. The dress styles, body movements, and beauty canons associated with them made women similar enough in outward appearance, so that, as snobby mothers opined, "you couldn't tell what sort she was until she opened her mouth." They fed new notions of collectivity, but also new perceptions of individuality. The new arenas of commercial culture thus challenged the symbolic order and territorial layout of nineteenth-century bourgeois society. But in equal measure, they defied those organizing principles of fascist mass politics which emphasized hierarchies of rank and function rather than of class and which abided by, if they did not reinforce, the traditional divisions between public or male space and a private or domestic female sphere.

In the last analysis, fascist policy toward organizing and representing women in public places was tied to fascism's capacity to respond to the semiotic confusion attendant on the rise of mass society. Like bourgeois societies elsewhere, Italy had experienced the breakdown of cultural "barriers and levels" demarcating class lines during the Great War and its aftermath.[5] In Italy, however, this had been accompanied not only by open class warfare but by the overthrow of the entire liberal order. One significant effect was widespread bewilderment about class position and sexual identity: Who was a man of order, and who a subversive? Who was a solid bourgeois, who a total parvenu? Was this attractive woman virtuous? Or was she "one of them"? Mussolini's own rapid changeover from left to right, his swift ascent from street-fighting bully *(teppista)* to prime minister, his relinquishing of the black shirt for a morning coat were themselves causes and symptoms of this confusion.

As it consolidated its power in the later 1920s, and especially as it became a mass regime in the 1930s, the dictatorship confronted this symbolic disorder. The era of *Staracismo*, culminating in 1938–39 with the so-called reform of custom must be counted as the most distinctive moment of the effort. During his eight years as PNF secretary, from 1931 to 1939, the indefatigably eclectic Achille Starace exhumed pagan ceremonials, borrowed from feudal-military traditions, appropriated Catholic liturgical forms, plagiarized from commercial culture, and raided communist agitprop to fashion a new repertory of social and cultural signals. Thereby, the new fascist regime sought to recode symbols of both class rank and gender identity to suit its new political order.

Fashioning a suitable public image for women was an especially problematic undertaking, particularly as social space became magnified and politicized. In its endeavor to represent women in the new "hierarchies of the nation," the regime was confronted with three vastly different models. At one extreme, there was the Catholic model, with its fundamentalist vision of female chastity and public decorum. At the other, there was the new American model: the "civilization of customs," as the writer Corrado Alvaro called it, had enabled the Italian middle classes to conquer a "new rights of man," meaning the "right to a comfortable existence," "to be young, elegant, well-dressed, and to aspire to be ever more so."[6] With their strong emphasis on outward appearance, American consumer models fed conformist behavior. Yet they were also egalitarian and nurtured new forms of individuality as well; alien, insofar as they originated abroad, they nonetheless offered the basis of a new national custom that transcended locality and rank. Somewhere in between the Catholic and the American models were the congeries of customs and conventions that might be called bourgeois good manners. Handshakes and nods of deference, habits of etiquette and titles of social distinction, physical appearance and dress styles were at least as important to bourgeois women as to upper-class men. Generally speaking, women's appearances, as evidenced by their consumption habits and the care of their bodies, signaled not just their own status but also that of their families and their consorts.[7] In fascist Italy, with its newly emerging national identity and parvenu political elites out to make a *bella figura,* this was particularly the case. When fascism launched its "reform of custom" in the late 1930s, to extirpate bourgeois conventions in the name of creating a truly "fascist civilization," the bourgeois "luxury creature," as propaganda liked to call her, was a far more conspicuous target than the bourgeois male "parasite."

Fascism's rapport with all of these models was ambivalent, but most of all with the Catholic one. In its public displays, fascism represented what the highest authorities of the Church denounced as "modern paganism." Mussolini was the first contemporary head of state to vaunt his sexuality: stripped to the waist to bring in the harvest or donning the sober black shirt of *condottiere* before Fiat workers, decked out as pilot, boat commander, or virtuoso violinist to show off his Renaissance skills, the Duce was as vain as any matinee idol pandering to his "female" publics. His chief minion, Starace, made it party policy to put the regime's virility on display: his own circus sideshow displays, diving bare-chested through blazing hoops, part lash-driven tiger, part daring trapeze artist, were notorious, as was his fondness for the starlets of Cinecittà and the Thespian Car. In its gatherings of female youth and party groups, the PNF showed off fit bodies. Thereby it demonstrated the health of the race; it also exercised a symbolic *droit de seigneur* over female youth.

These attitudes did not prevent fascism from rallying to the Church's cry of sexual danger. Interwar Italy was the natural home of papal "crusades for purity" and of Sunday hell and brimstone sermons about slackening public morality. The dictatorship's own moral restoration of the late 1920s encouraged the likes of Amadeo Balzari, the cranky fundamentalist from Verona, who at the head of the National Committee for Cleaning Up Fashion *(Comitato nazionale per la correttezza della moda)* that he founded in 1927, led a two-year "universal uprising" against the "horrid vice," the opprobrious "shameful wound" of "indecent and scandalous dress." With his denunciations of the "horrible reptile" of foreign fashion and appeals to "moralize" and "nationalize" Italian dress, Balzari won support from at least 150 Italian bishops and several cardinals, including Pietro Maffei, who urged that the "most brazen" females be subject to "public reproof and condemnation." Exhorted by Balzari's priest-followers, and with the tolerance if not support of local public authorities, several thousand small-town girl parishioners vowed to renounce cosmetics, wear sleeves to cover their elbows, and hem their skirts no more than ten centimeters from the anklebone.[8]

At the same time that the cinema-going public was getting its first glimpses of bare-breasted women and the PNF itself was marshaling cohorts of skimpily dressed girl athletes, the Catholic Church, with tacit support from fascism, propagated society-wide its strictures against female "nudity." By the late 1920s, major Italian churches had posted signs barring "immodest" dress. Conservative Catholics pressured local police authorities to enforce especially against women article 794 of the Rocco penal code. This prohibited the exposure of "shameful nudity in public places" or "acts against public decency," on the pain of a one-month jail sentence and fines ranging from 100 to 2,000 lire. The unwary foreign tourist, if she dallied along a river bank or by an ancient ruin, would soon find herself under surveillance by the morals police, were she not first put to flight by unwanted advances from male passersby. In public offices, the state authorities obliged conservatives scandalized by the promiscuous mixing of male and female staff by ordering all female employees to wear black cover-all aprons. At Alessandria, employers forbade factory *totine* to show up for work in short skirts. Small-town clerico-fascist intellectuals earned Church accolades for reviving male folk wisdom. The "modern street is more pernicious than a smutty book or dirty conversation," noted Professor Matteo Cuomo, prefacing the section of his proverbs collection dedicated to women going out. Some recalled old-time virtues: "A girl is like a pearl. / The less she's seen, the more her luster." Other sayings argued for new restraints: "Wives and sardines / keep fresh in sealed tins." Between church and state, there was a consensus that women out alone, their company unmediated by authority, were a public danger. A proverb alleged to be Swedish was cited to sum up these fears: "A woman alone crossing a stream keeps her shoes on. Two women hike their skirts to their knees. Three women cross it naked."[9]

In a society in which public hypocrisy had become an art of government, "going out" for women was never just that: for it implicated acts of the imagination along with physical movement, and it challenged the conventional divisions between private and public space, between male turf and female territory. To understand its significance under fascism requires that we follow a sometimes circuitous path. The first stop is to consider why political organizers, intellectuals, and technocrats regarded the "problem" of women's leisure differently from that of men's, and how this was expressed in debates over the "Americanization" of Italy. The next is to discuss fascist "body politics," meaning the competing discourses and policies developing around new canons of beauty, physical fitness, and fashion. Last, we have to pause to reflect on a paradox, that going out was also about returning home. Commercial culture, at the same time as creating greater self-consciousness about being in public, heightened self-awareness about the meaning of domesticity. The fascist regime, by intruding into what had conventionally been designated as female space, challenged the power traditionally attributed to women in the home; it rendered the personal nonpolitical, yet pierced it through with new ideological imperatives.

The Americanization of Female Leisure

When the fascist dictatorship boasted of having come up with an all-encompassing solution to the "problem" of leisure, it implicitly referred to men's leisure, not women's. For what men did in their free time, particularly working-class men, had been bound up with the "subversive" politics that fascism had vowed to eradicate in the name of national unity. The "wine circles" of rural districts, the small-town dives *(bettole)*, the neighborhood *bocce* court, the Republican mutual-aid society, and the imposing all-purpose *case del popolo* of the socialist labor movement had undergirded the working-class advance of the red years of 1919–20. By 1927 the dictatorship, having outlawed opposition parties and trade unions, wanted to eradicate these still powerful centers of local working-class subculture as well. In the *dopolavoro,* or after-work club, an invention of Americanizing reformers who rallied to fascism in the early 1920s, the fascist party planned the perfect mechanism with which to replace working-class voluntary associations. The fascist groups promised to counter the stress and anxiety of modern work routines with uplifting activities, to distract workers from degrading pastimes—including socialist politicking—and to offer discounts on group trips and small consumer items such as radios. All the while, they would purvey unobtrusive messages about the regime's benevolence. Promoted nationwide, in factories, city neighborhoods, and villages, the nearly 20,000 after-work circles founded by the late 1930s played host to the recreational pastimes of perhaps four million Italian working people.[10]

In principle, the after-work club was suited to women as well as to men. But the membership was nevertheless overwhelmingly male. Women's leisure, like women's work, differed from that of men. Employed men were more likely to work on a fixed schedule, to keep their paycheck, or at least part of it, and to be employed in the big firms and offices offering recreational services to their personnel. Most important, men were more or less free to dispose of their nonworking time. By contrast, women's leisure, especially that of married women, tended to be undifferentiated from work, being intertwined with the processes of household labor and relations of kinship. For younger working women, too, leisure time was not necessarily free time. Shorter work hours, coming in 1934, when the forty-hour work week and Saturday rest were adopted, together with new shopfloor and office cultures, certainly encouraged young women to think of leisure as a distinct realm, one to which they had a right. At the same time, domestic ideologies called on them to be dutiful helpers around the household, to hand over their pay envelopes to their fathers, and to stay in the neighborhood. Hence female leisure was not identified as a "problem," as men's was construed to be. Neither did it have a "solution" identified with a physical location, time slot, or institutional device.

Yet female leisure obviously *was* a problem, to the degree that the prevailing intellectual opinion identified mass culture with femaleness. In the process of defending the conventional distinctions between high and low and between traditional and modern commercial culture, Italian intellectuals, like their counterparts elsewhere in Europe, typically associated male with what they desired and female with what they deprecated. Accordingly, modernist and elite cultures were male, mass and low cultures female.[11] As Papini suggested, with his metaphoric allusions to the whorishness of the cinema, commercial culture, being venal, had the morals of a streetwalker; its transient images were as untrustworthy as a painted face; its spectators were as vulnerable as pliant customers; the drives it fostered as irrational as sexual desire. With its mercenary blandishments, mass culture induced passivity, and its standardized images fostered conformity. By contrast, its opposite, cultural modernism, was masculine. Male avant-gardes, whether identifying with futurism, the vigorous populism of *Strapaese,* or the urbane literary and artistic movement called *Novecento,* regarded themselves as active, incorruptible, and productive alternatives to the supine pleasures of mass entertainment.

In interwar Italy, this gendered discourse about mass culture resonated especially strongly in disquisitions about "Americanization." Beginning in the 1920s, the fantasy life of many Italian intellectuals was captured by America, much as was true elsewhere in Europe. This fascination testified to the prodigious strength of the United States economy in the wake of the Great War. It also testified to the unsettling power that American commercial culture exercised as it overturned conventional ideas about boundaries. Thus American culture challenged the old divisions between elite and popular and between avant-garde and mass. It also challenged state boundaries, confounding ideas about what was local and national, and what foreign and cosmopolitan. Not least, it challenged the boundaries between economy and culture. With the fox-trot, as one wag observed, the Americans had entered the European chicken coop.[12]

In Italy worries about United States cultural hegemony were especially disturbing. Domestic cultural production was unusually vulnerable to American competition, given Italy's relative economic backwardness. Moreover, fascism had vowed to defend national cultural traditions, but at the same time Italian intellectual elites were ambivalent about American culture: although they admired its iconoclasm, modernity, and freeness, the crassness of it disturbed them, and they feared it because it defied their control. These complicated feelings were played out in sexual metaphor: Sometimes the United States was feminine, a disturbing love object, as in the novelist Mario Soldati's *America, primo amore*.[13] More often, America was the dominating male, material civilization, as it were, bearing down on the supine female that decaying European culture had become. The effects of American "penetration" were at times interpreted quite literally: Hollywood images ostensibly devirilized Italian men, who, sapped of strength, lounged about with "dead-fish eyes à la Valentino, bow-legged like Slym, and flashing a Ramon Navarro smile." The close, dark theater spaces in which spectators ogled American love stories left couples debilitated; the onanistic play on screen aggravated the demographic crisis. Not least of all, Americanized leisure threatened to transform Italian girls, making them masculine and independent like their American counterparts. In America, as one scared visitor recounted, "the daughter, as soon as she can support herself, is a 'free girl,' and as such outside of paternal and maternal tutelage. The American girl, unlike our own, is a separate unit from man. Indeed, not having the burdens that weigh on men, she feels even freer, and for that reason a good span taller than men."[14]

At least part of the interest in deciphering the conduct of American girls came from intellectuals' desire to decode mass culture's impact on the home territory. Whether the American "new women" were desired or derided, their behavior promised to reveal much about the outcome of the contemporary sexual revolution. Italian observers disputed whether their propensity to divorce displayed licentious behavior or a new puritanism: likewise they debated whether American women were calculating fortune-hunters, accumulating bank vaults full of alimony, or moralists who insisted there be no sex without love and marriage. They also asked whether revealing dress, straightforward gazes, and strapping gaits denoted sexual availability, or a de-sexing diminution of male-female difference. Most observers, even those who, like the sharp-eyed engineer Pietro Lanino, saw the United States as the harbinger of industrial society, took pains to set American and Italian women at opposite poles; the former was ostensibly ruled by the market, the latter by love and tradition. As Lanino put the issue: "To ask an American girl her business is akin to asking one of our girls whom she is in love with."[15]

Such anxious responses to the freedoms of United States women suggested that they were not as distant as portrayed. The "new woman" abroad shared at least one trait in common with the girls back home: she was out and desirable, yet not available, at least not to all men. To the outsider, this exposure was perhaps particularly disturbing, forcing him to question whether it was his class, national identity, or lack of manliness that made him an unacceptable suitor. In his short piece *Amore a Brooklyn* (1935), the young Mario Soldati attributed unexpected female reticence to "fear of the masculine power incarnated in the physique of the Mediterranean man. . . . In their tall, blond men, they cling to the perverse innocence of childlike and consanguineal loves, whereas in the embraces of dark emigrants they fear and desire the virile force of the adult and foreigner."[16] By far the most common way to exorcise the problem of female sexuality was to dismiss unavailable women as "sterile" or "frigid," the cause variously thought to be Protestant culture, calculating minds, or standardized ways of living. "Puritan minds in pagan bodies" was the *Corriere della sera* correspondent Beniamino De Ritis's pat effort to put some distance on the matter.[17]

These accounts, though speaking to a well-traveled elite's attitudes toward foreign customs, suggest the attitudes of bewilderment, fear, and anger common in provincial Italy. The behavior of urban Italian women was at least as alien and indecipherable to rural and especially southern Italian men as the behavior of American women was to foreign visitors. In any case, the reactions were not much different: to exalt the figure of the "traditional women," to denigrate but secretly desire emancipated females, and to envy as well as malign the well-to-do and politically powerful males who possessed them, but who seemed unable to control them.

Fascist Body Politics

That fascist nationalism powerfully heightened awareness of the female body is not surprising. Mercantilist traditions held that the health of single bodies contributed to the health of the entire nation. When the Duce equated the health of individuals with the national health, he subscribed to a time-worn metaphor.[18] The fascist head of state's concern over the physical attributes of his female subjects was spurred by other factors as well. International rivalries had long been fed by social Darwinistic distinctions about racial fitness. During the interwar years, comparisons among national physiognomies multiplied. The Olympic Games, which began to include special women's events after the Great War, together with international sports tournaments for women, first at Amsterdam in 1928 and then at Prague in 1930, put female athleticism on show for the first time. The ever-wider and more intense circulation of images of beautiful women through the movies, photography, and advertising was likewise a stimulus to comparing female types. Commercial culture highlighted that birth was just one part of the female life cycle, not the beginning of irreversible physical decline. This culture of physicality was not only promoted by the circulation of new beauty and personal products but also by new medical specializations in sports and aesthetics. The fascist regime sought to manipulate this new awareness of female physicality in order to check the emancipatory impulses that stimulated and fed off of it, as well as to aggrandize itself by making female beauty, strength, and stylishness attributes of its exercise of national power.

Fascism's treatment of female bodies as an issue of state was first manifest in efforts to define canons of female beauty. Mussolini's own eye for women was well known: "Women today are pretty, prettier than they used to be. And fashion style is magnificent, it greatly suits them," the Duce asserted to one of at least a score of much-flattered foreign women correspondents who interviewed him.[19] This matter-of-fact statement revealed a rather more complicated set of attitudes, of course, attitudes the Duce shared with his own and successive generations of men in the face of the rapid turnover of female beauty canons. Since the turn of the century, stage and cinema actresses had transformed standards of female beauty. Around 1910 the Dannunzian heroine Eleonora Duse taught women to "duseggiare"; thereafter the silent cinema diva Lyda Borelli taught them to "borelleggiare"—languid poses, slow gestures, affected speech, dress of a classicizing and orientalizing taste. By the early 1920s, Paris fashion and American movies introduced the boyish gamine or *garçonne*. By the 1930s, Hollywood stars—blond, muscular, leggy, toothy, with big smiles and visibly made-up—had made the whole body, not merely the face, the vehicle of physical expression, influencing the way Italian women had of "sitting, getting up, walking, pausing, and turning."[20] "Have movies changed our idea of beauty?" inquired the fan magazine *Kines* in 1931. Emphatically yes, one girl replied: "If Leonardo came back and had to choose a model, he would certainly take Bébé Daniels over Mona Lisa."[21]

This turnover of physical types was, comprehensibly, a disturbing phenomenon. After all, to define female beauty or to judge who is beautiful or not is no small power. Not least of all, men could thereby exercise the influence that women exercised by manipulating their physical attractiveness. To be able to characterize a woman as pretty was also a way to relegate her to a subordinate role, as "an enchanting parenthesis in life," to use the Duce's expression. The Romagnuole *condottiere*, to believe Margherita Sarfatti's description, was a "typical male egotist," for whom woman was a "beautiful creature, her destiny to give pleasure." Persons so lovely and sensitive, as he confided to the French correspondent Paule Herfort, were unsuited to politics.[22]

To respond to the aesthetic mayhem unleashed by commercial culture, the fascist propaganda machine, with Mussolini's approbation, championed its own standards of female beauty: one ideal, the "crisis woman," was negative; the other, whom we might call "authentic woman," was positive. The former was a masculinized plaything, a false and alien creature, the product of Paris and Hollywood; the latter was homegrown— broodmare, mother, and mate. Fictions both, they were invented to de-eroticize females, so as not to risk sexual defeat.

The fascist state officially opened its campaign against the "donna crisi" in 1931 when Gaetano Polverelli, head of Mussolini's Press Office, ordered the press to eliminate "sketches of excessively thin and masculinized female figures who represent sterile female types."[23] An earlier source, however, lies in the ruralist "savages of Colle Val d'Elsa." Puerile and ribald, the Strapaese men publishing the Florentine cultural magazine *Il selvaggio* spoke from their carefully camouflaged homoerotic culture. "True" females, with their "homespun panties, perfumed with lavender," occasionally stimulated a line of poetry or an etching. But it was the denatured urban female who excited their best taunts. Some were blunt: "Woman without girth / for Strapaese has no worth." Others were playfully sexist: "In a narrow womb, / the chick is doomed. / In a rationalized coop, / no eggs are laid."[24] Mussolini, whose own rural-rooted prejudices were little different, championed the "battle for fat" (to use Salvemini's term) with more animus and to greater effect, mobilizing propaganda and censorship apparatuses and appealing to medical doctors to help to "correct the deformations of civilization," in particular, "the fashion of excessive thinning down."[25] By the mid-1930s, bits of doggerel, jokes, and songs suggest that fascism's attacks on the allegedly sexless, androgynous, socially useless "crisis women" had met their mark.

Yet to read Luciano Folgore's sonnet, the crisis woman was still a fearsome creature: "So ungracious and woeful she does appear / pallid and gaunt the crisis woman / that her sight stills every voice, / and not a soul wants to comfort her."[26] "Pale," "skeletal," "transparent," she eluded men and transgressed promulgated norms. Defying control by any single man, she also incited male rivalries. At the close of the student dance in Padusa, Luigi Preti had his characters rush a tall, thin woman, chanting a refrain from the popular song, "Donna crisi": "Go eat a sack of flour. / Don't cause me a sleepless hour, / and you'll see / the crisis it will pass." The youths' intent, aside from assaulting the woman, was to goad her fiancé into a fight.[27]

The florid woman of fascism's imagination was allegedly a more authentic figure. With her rosy lips, peasant costume, and rounded figure, she looked like maternity incarnate. In reality she had nothing to do with procreation. Nor was maternity ever associated with beauty, except perhaps in Mussolini's dictum "Maternity redounds to wifely beauty." As the much-cited fascist researcher Carlalberto Grillenzoni punctiliously recorded, on the basis of his research on fifteen hundred mothers, "elegance is manifestly unfavorable to fecundity." Indeed, "the artifices of exercise or cremes" caused women to lose "the gift of fertility."[28] Photographic evidence could only have confirmed that the relationship of motherhood to childbearing was at least problematic. The rare group photo of "prolific mothers" presents an aesthetically disturbing scene: the youngest women, at forty, look ancient, their faces worn, their baggy black-aproned dresses drooping over sagging bosoms. The comely peasant girls who denoted rural fecundity seemed like a different race of female altogether. Objects of desire to patriarchal power, they were no more future wives and mothers than was Manzoni's peasant-girl Lucia in the eyes of the lusting petty tyrant Don Rodrigo.

In the meantime, commercial culture went about producing far more influential images of female beauty. The earliest nationwide beauty contest was *Piccola*'s, in 1929, for the most beautiful secretary. The very first local competition dated back to 1911, the occasion being the universal exposition in honor of fifty years of Italian unity; that, however, was designed mainly for Roman consumption and drew costumed girls from the city's neighborhoods. The first American-style contest, using now familiar mass promotion techniques, was held in 1939 by Count Visconti di Modrone's GVM pharmaceutical company to launch a new toothpaste.

Under the slogan a "thousand lire for a smile," several dozen young women gathered at Salsomaggiore for the finals, looking much like their Hollywood progenitors, the Italian beauties being perhaps only a trifle less poised than their more seasoned American counterparts.

Around the same time, commercial culture was producing a more ambiguous figure, the *Grandi firme* cover girl. Its author was Gino Boccasile, the Bari-born commercial artist; its destination was Italy's first illustrated tabloid for men. Cesare Zavattini's invention, *Grandi firme* was directed by the self-styled "pornographer" Pittigrilli; it appeared monthly from April 1937 until September 1938 when Mussolini, who was alleged to have picked up and perused a copy in the train en route to the Munich conference, had it suppressed. Boccasile's invention was a big-bosomed, whittle-waisted creature. Far and away her most extraordinary feature was her huge long legs, around which her whole body pivoted and from which, Boccasile claimed, he always started his sketch.[29] Indeed, planted on these two priapic appendages, the Boccasile girl was as dominant and emancipated as a man was; she not only wore the pants, she represented them. *Grandi firme* suppressed, Boccasile moved on to design propaganda posters and the covers of fascist tabloids. In the war years, Boccasile redrew the very same figures as Nazi soldier-heros and Italian prisoners-of-war; so transformed, they seemed to castigate the feckless female homefront.

How such conflicts over female aesthetic standards conditioned Italian women's entry into the "age of self-consciousness" is harder to say. No sign exists that women subscribed to fascist canons, not in any strict sense. But overweening public attention to female physicality gave an especially narcissistic turn to these great changes in aesthetic conventions. The young journalist Maria Coppola spoke for her generation in the venerable *Cordelia* yearbook when she highlighted the "1900 girl's" preoccupation with appearance:

> More beautiful than our grandmothers, for her more intense activity has made her healthier and stronger, she doesn't conceal her eagerness to be admired; everything is a pretext and an aid. She's at the typewriter and knows her nails are shining; she's out driving and she knows that her attentive expression elicits glances; she caresses her children and she knows full well how sweet her gesture appears; she smokes a cigarette, her lovely lips pouting. At the most important moments of the day, thoughts about how she looks, worries about her appearance, never leave her.

This self-concentration, far from being debilitating, made contemporary women more resilient, at least so Coppola argued. "The problems of

An American-style beauty: "Will he come by, or won't he? It's time." (*Eva* 2, no. 1 [Jan. 4, 1934]. Reprinted by courtesy of the National Library of Florence.)

Fecundity incarnate: rural beauty holding rooster. (*Gente nostra* 1, no. 28 [Sept. 8, 1929]. Reprinted courtesy of the National Library of Florence.)

"Virile, but feminine": academicians of Orvieto on parade. (Louise Diel, *Das fa-schistische Italien und die Aufgaben der Frau im neuen Staat* [Berlin: Hobbing Verlag, 1934]. Reprinted courtesy of the Butler Library, Columbia University.)

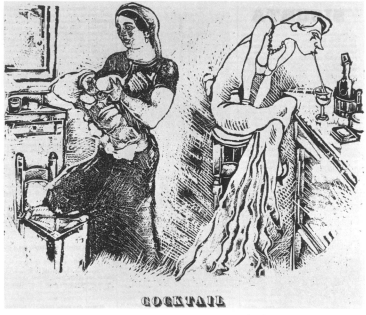

Strapaese's nemesis: the crisis woman. (*Il selvaggio* [1931].
Reprinted by permission of the National Library of Florence.)

Gino Boccasile's priapic " '900 girl." (Gino Boccasile, *La signorina Grandi firme* [Milan: Longanesi, 1981]. Reprinted by permission of the National Library of Florence.)

"Maternity redounds to wifely beauty": prizewinning mothers with a total of 180 living children, Cuneo, 1933. (*Maternità ed infanzia* 9, no. 2 [Feb. 1934]. Reprinted courtesy of the National Library of Florence.)

aestheticism," she concluded, "help make her brain more elastic."[30] Perhaps for middle-class women, in the absence of significant other ways to exercise influence, this preening served as a sort of mental work. Certainly, to determine one's own individuality in the face of state-proclaimed aesthetic standards represented no small act of self-confidence.

The Great Sports Debate

Fascism's manipulation of female physicality was equally manifest in sports policy. Initially, fascist sports promoters were enthusiastic about female participation; modernity meant sports for women as well as for men. Sports policy thus contemplated women's involvement in the fascist recreational clubs and youth groups. By 1930, however, faced on the one hand with Church protests and on the other hand with the threat that women would treat sports as a step toward emancipation, the regime backed off. In the 1930s, it promoted instead a highly regulated, medicalized model of physical culture for women.

The regime had a wide-open field in which to operate. Italian feminism had invested little in the arena of physical culture.[31] There was no feminist sports movement along the lines of British feminism's 150,000-member Women's League of Health and Beauty or the Scandinavian or German gymnastics societies, and there was no Italian affiliate of the *Fédération sportive féminine internationale* that the French feminist Alice Miliat founded in 1921. The Italian socialist movement had never been especially sports-minded either. Its local people's houses and outing societies included women along with the men in family-style entertainments. By the mid-1920s, Catholic modernizers, Father Gemelli in the lead, endorsed promoting "a Catholic gymnastics," and in 1923, under the leadership of Professor Teresa Costa, the *Gioventù femminile* began forming "Strength and Grace" sections. But this "feminine" version, as Gemelli specified, meant "no shorts, no athleticism, and above all no competition with men's sports." Its ultimate purpose was to form "good, Christian mothers who were physically and morally healthy, hence capable of creating a generation of equally good and healthy Italians."[32] This development was cut short, however, when on April 9, 1928, the fascist government banned all nonfascist sport groups. Shortly thereafter, Pius XI, alarmed at the rapid growth of the fascist sports movement after 1926 and outraged at public parades of girl athletes in the Holy City, condemned fascism's moral sensibility as "weaker" than that of pagan Rome and, possibly, of "the even more corrupt" towns of ancient Greece.[33]

Pius's fulminations worked, but perhaps only because fascist officials themselves suspected that women's sports lowered birth rates and fostered promiscuous behavior. On October 16, 1930, the fascist Grand Council undertook a much-bruited reassessment of sports politics. The stated purpose was not to rule against female gymnastics and physical education, which it claimed to accept, but to scrutinize female "athleticism," meaning competitive sports. Out of the desire to avoid public polemics, the Grand Council in effect medicalized the problem by ordering the head of the Italian National Olympic Committee (CONI), in consultation with the National Federation of Sports Doctors, to determine activities appropriate for women. The main principle to guide them was that "nothing distract woman from her fundamental mission: MATERNITY."[34] Leandro Arpinati, the free-thinking Bolognese who headed CONI at the time, took the mandate seriously enough; that is, he set up a foundation, under the direction of Professor Pinti, to group together studies of sports, gynecology, and female physiology. But Arpinati too argued that sports medicine had to factor in moral considerations:

> There being no sexual mixing as there is in America such as to habituate the sexes to shared habits from early childhood . . . we cannot distance ourselves from traditions and customs that are our strength and safeguard. Therefore we must subscribe to a norm that offers women the most decorous and broadest sports opportunities, yet preserves them from all deviations. . . . In short, physical health cannot be to the detriment of moral health.[35]

The rules governing women's sports were thus part positivist physiology, part Catholic prudery, the whole well-dosed with fascist opportunism. Females, current medical opinion insisted, were starkly different from males of the species. From their brains to their bones, they were products and prisoners of their reproductive systems, which were the basis of their social roles and the source of their most common ailments. Physical recreation, if properly administered, ensured the gracefulness that made women attractive, perhaps increased their longevity, and helped, or at least did not hinder, their reproductive performance. Ultimately, childbirth was the best exercise, of course, and all physical culture was to facilitate that purpose.

By the mid-1930s, a host of rules, injunctions, and customs distinguished women's sports from men's "in all circumstances and at every event." As the ONB head Renato Ricci specified, this meant "separate itineraries, events, hours, days, and personnel, which should only be female." Budgets too were separate, he might have added. Women traveled to meets second-class, while male athletes and their trainers went first-class. So-called male games, in particular soccer, were discouraged; with trepidation, Arpinati acquiesced to the formation of a single "woman's soccer group" at Milan, on the condition that it never play in public. Lest girl athletes cause public scandal, the Italian Field and Track Association ordered that female members "never for any reason go outside the sports field without putting on long pants and keeping them on until their event began. Athletic trunks are not to be excessively short and shirts are required to have half-sleeves." Not the least of the sports trainers' duties was to stand guard lest the female friendships encouraged in the name of team camaraderie degenerate into lesbian relationships.[36]

The effects of this fascist-promoted female sports culture were far-reaching. Far more young women practiced sports of some kind than ever before. On fascist Saturdays in the 1930s, school groups massed for calisthenics and parade routines. For the first time, there were regional and national competitive meets in track and field, basketball, and swimming. After staying out in 1932, Italian women began to be trained for Olympic competitions. Indeed, at Berlin in 1936, Ondina Valle won Italy's only gold medal in the 80 meter hurdles, and Italian women placed fourth both in that event and the 100 meter relay race. Women's journals followed international and local sporting events, treating the feats of Amelia Earhart and other women as accomplishments on behalf of their sex.[37] In a way they were: Ondina Valle wryly recorded that Pius XI, who had excoriated female athleticism, made a special point of meeting her at a papal audience.

Yet the overall meaning was little liberatory. Feminists had regarded physical recreation as a means of self-expression. For the emancipationist Amalia Musso, who had been instructor at the Royal Normal Superior School of Gymnastics of Turin before she was forced to retire in 1927, gymnastics was "a wholly individual way of externalizing ideas and sentiments by expressive poses and free movement of the various parts of the body."[38] By contrast, fascist physical culture instructors regarded it as discipline in the name of the party and race. Its purpose, wrote Professor Carlo Alberto Ragazzi, summing up the advice of Rosa Maria Miedico, the physical therapist advising Milan's ONB, was "to assure woman a high degree of muscular validity without forgetting the qualities and ends specific to female nature."[39] Above all, female athleticism was closely bound up with being soignée and chic. Pastimes such as skiing, tennis, swimming, horseback riding, or sailing were like piano playing for nineteenth-century bourgeois young women; they enhanced social grace, offered occasions to meet eligible young men, and were part of a common modern upper-class style of life, one shared by the royal young women of the House of Savoy as well as by the new fascist bourgeoisie—Mussolini's firstborn, the lively Edda Ciano, being the most visible among them. As for the mass of young women in gymnastics courses, their bodies belonged to the medical doctors who certified their fitness, the Academy of Orvieto graduates who drilled them for competitions, the fascist officials who passed them in review, and the foreign observers who, extolling their grace and beauty, attributed these qualities to the discipline and healthiness brought by the fascist order.

Nationalizing Fashion

Fascism's third aesthetic "battle," after beauty and sports, focused on national dress codes. In Italy, as elsewhere, the fifteen-year period from roughly the Great War to 1930 was characterized by a great transformation in fashion styles. During the *belle époque*, Italians still "dressed according to social as well as moral categories."[40] Fashion itself changed only every five to ten years and then at a deliberate and predictable pace. Most clothing was made by artisans, designed to be handed down. Aristocrats and the wealthiest bourgeois women followed fashion whereas the middle and petty bourgeois adjusted to changing styles. Peasants and working-class women wore a uniform of sorts, dark-colored aprons, pulled-back hair, shawls, boots, and heavy stockings. By the 1930s, fashion turned over at least twice a year, spurred by movies, advertising plates, and at least forty fashion magazines. Style transcended class lines; everybody could aspire upward, and outward as well, to emulate mass-disseminated models from Paris and Hollywood. Village girls wore the same bright colors, "autarchic" silks, hiked-up skirts, and shorter hairstyles as urban working girls. The latter on their days off were virtually indistinguishable from the lower middle classes.

The battle over fashion was partly dictated by economics. Fascist industrial policy, by revaluing the lira, favored heavy industry and raw material imports, aggravating the already weak competitive position of export-oriented Italian cotton, wool, and silk firms. Meanwhile, industrial retooling and innovations in marketing and retailing favored the growth of standardized wear to the detriment of artisan cloth and clothing production. In response, the government promised to build up home markets. This aim fit nicely with its efforts to staunch trade deficits. The fact that several billion lire annually were expended on luxury imports spurred campaigns to "buy Italian." Propaganda berated the upper classes for their "foreignophilia." Fashionable women bought Parisian dresses and perfumes, newly marketed American personal products such as Palmolive and Lux soaps and Elizabeth Arden cosmetics. Even plaids and cashmere, it was complained, though manufactured at Alessandria or Biella, sold better with British labels. In keeping with its policies of national autarchy, the regime thus promoted the fashion industry by backing special state and private oversight committees on cotton, silk, wool, and autarchic fabrics, by sponsoring craft shows, and, in 1933, by founding the National Fashion Agency *(Ente nazionale della moda)* at Turin.

However, the battle over fashion was also about social rank. Fashion, as Georg Simmel observed, signals the cohesiveness of those belonging to the same social circles, at the same time as it closes off these circles to those of inferior social rank.[41] There was no more visible sign of parvenu, often ill-gotten, wealth accumulated in the war and its aftermath than the so-called luxury display of bourgeois female dress. At the theater, to recall Corrado Alvaro's description, wartime profits on guns and boot leather were transmuted into bedazzling jewels and furs: "The women of the old aristocracy, dressed less luxuriously than the women of the new, served as ornaments for them, with some laughter about it, but also some envy."[42] This display of luxury put upper-class women in a delicate position. On the one hand, they believed in luxury dress; to the degree that it expressed the supremacy of the elite, it bound together the new aristocracy of fascism and distinguished them from the mass of women. On the other hand, they wanted to assert control over luxury expenditure to prevent attacks that damaged their standing as a sex. In both cases, there was an interest in "nationalizing" fashion, not least of all to signal the elite's patriotism. However, short of Italianness becoming a mark of quality and social distinction such as to compete with Paris labels, status-conscious Italian women would never convert to domestic products.

The cause of national fashion thus brought together the oddest imaginable group: there was Elisa Majer Rizzioli, the austere head of the women's *fasci*, but also Lydia De Liquoro, the star-struck, self-made Milanese publicist who in 1923 founded *Lidel*, the most luxurious of all Italian fashion magazines. There was the bigot Amadeo Balzari reviling fashion as a "seductive serpent" (or "diabolical magic wand"), but also the pioneering journalist Umberto Notari. The futurist Marinetti's former comrade-in-arms, Notari was founder of the Milanese sports tabloid, *L'ambrosiano*, and the husband of Delia, editor of *La cucina italiana*, as well as a longtime promoter of Italy's New Woman.

Their purposes, however, were very different, as the diverging positions of the two women, Majer Rizzioli and De Liquoro, make very clear. Just after the Great War, both were active in the Action Committee against the Exaggerated Luxury of Women, founded by patriotic Milanese women close to fascism of the first hour. The little we know about this group suggests it was of two minds: one, to curb conspicuous displays of parvenue wealth in the name of female solidarity, moderation, and patriotism; the other, to promote dress codes that in their rigor and simplicity defeminized women enough to let them safely enter male public space. But from the start De Liquoro saw that in an era of excess, simplicity was stylish. She thus endorsed the futurists' designs for a "standard dress-type" *(un tipo unico di vestito)*, like the tailored suit. The "tuta" or jump-suit designed by the avant-garde painter De Michelis for the Florentine Baroness Rucellai's famous dress ball was decreed a fashion event.[43] By the mid-1920s, however, these simplifying impulses had been stifled, together with emancipationist stances on fashion. Subsequently, the prudish Majer Rizzioli and the exuberant De Liquoro went their separate ways, the former to head up the prim Italian Women's Consortium for the Valorization of Italian Products *(Consorzio femminile italiano per la valorizzazione di prodotti nazionali)*, the latter to become the main promoter of luxury style. Eager to affirm "female expertise" and leadership in the fashion industry, De Liquoro's elegant magazine *Lidel* spearheaded a veritable movement of the parvenu: staging balls, charity fetes, and fashion shows at chic, central meeting places such as Rome's Grand Hotel, the Excelsior, and the Rose Casino of the Borghese Gardens, it selected and excluded. Each of *Lidel*'s events, to quote De Liquoro, showed society life "at its most stylish, but also its most elegant, aristocratic, and exclusive." They were open enough to accommodate the consorts and daughters of war profiteers, the fast-rising *gerarchi*, and the lawyers and notaries milking government prebends, yet sufficiently closed to attract wealthy dowagers and the scions of Rome's "black aristocracy." De Liquoro's success seemed to testify that new and old appreciated meeting "not in a promiscuous environment, as happens elsewhere, but among persons of the same rank, in an atmosphere of cordial sympathy."[44] As social involvement became fashionable in the late 1920s, De Liquoro, with her legions of "zelantissime" patriots, pretended that luxury was an economic and cultural necessity, hence a contribution to the good of society. Far from being irrelevant, fashionable women testified to the dictatorship's vitality and to the harmonious social mixing of new and old wealth under its leadership. The crowning moment of De Liquoro's battle to make fashion central to the representation of the new epoch occurred in April 1933 when, under the presidency of Virginia Agnelli Bourbon del Monte, party functionaries, state officials, industrialists, and scores of elegant women gathered at Turin in the presence of Queen Elena to inaugurate the first Permanent National Fashion Exposition.

However, the moment state policy shifted to a more autarchic and populist position, so-called luxury women became vulnerable together with women generally insofar as their sex was identified with conspicuous display. Propagandists could plausibly demonstrate that fashionable upper-class women were ever-ready to short-circuit autarchy: indifferent to patriotic appeals, they bought what they thought they looked good in, whether it came from Paris or from Turin or Milan. That was no less true of the Duce's much-photographed daughter Edda than of other wealthy, fashion-conscious women. The old dictum "Men make the laws, women the customs," once used to exalt women's importance to society (while justifying their political exclusion), was now cited to highlight female resistance to the regime's struggle to revolutionize consumer mores. The "luxury female's" chief critic was none other than Umberto Notari, whose once-appreciative eye for the foibles of the so-called woman of the third type ("neither courtesan nor wife-mother") had apparently dimmed with age and his wife Delia's premature death in late 1935. "Sentiment" had to triumph over "truck" *(bottega)*; women, as custodians of the moral economy, must espouse a fascistic "national sensibility" in place of liberal "love of country." The ever-more peevish Umberto's particular targets were the million or so women he estimated spent 8,000 lire a year on dress (a sum more than double the average annual skilled working-class wage and more than fifty times the 150 lire per year that working-class women spent on clothes).[45] Of course fascist women were not loath to do battle against the appearance of class difference, as long as that only meant denouncing foreignness. In the wake of the sanctions, however, the attack on "xenolatry" slipped out of women's hands altogether, to become part of PNF secretary Starace's misogynist "reform of custom."

As Starace launched his "reform of custom" in 1938 to extirpate bourgeois civilization, the disparity between the leveling and uniformity the PNF was able to exact of men, using military models, and the vaunted individuality of bourgeois females became more manifest. The militarization of society accelerated with the start of the Ethiopian war—by causing many more women to be involved in party groups—furthered the application of military styles of organization to fascism's female subjects. Hitherto, fascist women had rarely worn uniforms. Down to World War II, even fascist women inspectors wore the uniforms of the upper classes, that is, well-styled gabardine suits, graceful walking shoes, and perhaps an inconspicuous fur stole. The only respectable uniform, if we exclude the peasant regional costumes resuscitated for public events, was that of the Red Cross, not least because even the CRI's national patrons, the princesses of the House of Savoy, wore it. During the Ethiopian campaign, the PNF had ordered its *visitatrici* to wear uniforms on duty, and the Fontana sisters designed flattering dress uniforms of blue gabardine with white piqué blouses for the Orvieto academicians. But for the majority of loyalists, it sufficed to "dress Italianly": one fashion maven suggested a black monkey-fur jacket, a broad-brimmed, veiled felt hat, or perhaps a "political wrap," decorated with Mussolini's March 9, 1936, Declaration of the Empire. Starace, though he tried to persuade women to dress in the Sardinian rough-wool uniforms *(orbace)* he recommended for men, earned nothing but ridicule for his efforts, as he complained to Mussolini. He was especially offended by the joke-epitaph in circulation: "Here lies Starace, the fool, dressed in rough wool, may he rest in Hell."[46]

By 1939, the last year of peacetime, fascist military aesthetics and female fashion consciousness had achieved a reconciliation of sorts. Only then was the PNF finally able to mount a national spectacle around women, in which conventional signs of class distinction and social rank were effaced. The "monumental gathering of the female forces" of fascism, rallying 70,000 women in Rome on May 28, 1939, was, in the words of the official Stefani News Agency release, "the most total and thrilling demonstration ever of the party's efforts toward forming a full-blown fascist and imperial consciousness . . . among its female forces."[47] Organized by the PNF's women's auxiliaries, 15,000 uniformed women filed out of the Circus Maximus. They then paraded through the Via dell'Impero passing in front of the Duce's car before marching by the reviewing stand where representatives of mothers and widows of war dead, princesses of royal blood, male political authorities, fascist *gerarchesse,* and Nazi youth delegations were seated. With an incongruous mix of fashion coverage prose and military jargon, the Stefani release instructed the Italian press on the phrases to employ to represent this extraordinary event:

> The antigas cohort passes and with it the first aid troops, gas masks around their necks and packs flung over their shoulders. Rural housewives, all in costume. And from everywhere. Scarves and shawls; wide skirts cinched to display the grace of young bodies and robustness of maternal flanks; jackets and corsets and belts. The severe softness of Sardinia; the clamor of Basilicata, the explosion of colors of Emilia and Tuscany (red and sky blue predominate), flowered aprons and lace from Venetia; and clogs, sandals, kerchiefs. Harmonious and discordant colors; altogether in lock step. . . . In their wake . . . the women workers' sections pass—in azure jumpsuits, walnut color, the outfits of the textile, artisan, and tobacco workers cohort. The leisure-time troops pick up the motifs of the sports groups. Then, the handsome ranks of the women professionals and artists, and, last, after a brief pause to allow for the faster pace, the speed cohorts: the young fascist bicyclists and motorists.

> . . . Then the Red Cross nurses of the great wars for Africa and
> Spain pass, on tanks and ambulances, severe in dress and demeanor,
> their faces turned toward the Duce, then straight ahead, their blue
> veils lifting from their white headbands. . . . The whole parade
> drawn up superbly by the young fascists on horseback.

In the variety of organizations represented and the range of functions
and female types on display, the rally suggested women's total involvement in the hierarchies of the regime. Yet the failure of the rally—or
better of the rally's description—to distinguish what was particularly female about this participation was equally striking. The overlap of two
such incongruous jargons—the fashion show and the military review—
only highlighted the nonuniformity of the women, as well as the uncertainty of how to characterize their appearance in public. Were they feminine fashion ornaments, or displays of masculine military prowess? The
reporter evidently sensed the greater symbolic power inherent in the
homoerotic bonding among male troops: at the parade's culminating moment, as the female cohorts passed by with a "jaunty, quick masculine
step," the Duce's "face lit up with virile, satisfied pleasure."[48]

The New Domesticity

Modern commercial culture, at the same time as it creates new public
occasions of consumption, creates new private ones as well. The other side
of the expanding consumer and service economy that brought more women
into the work force and into familiarity with new leisure habits during
the interwar years was the exposure of the household to mass consumer
culture and of women, and men too, to a new culture of domesticity. By
the end of the 1930s, 424,000 Italian households had telephones, compared to around 150,000 in 1925; and over a million households had radios, whereas only 20,000 had them a decade earlier.[49] The telephone
obviously was still a luxury, and only 13 percent of Italian households
were radio subscribers. But the radio had become such a popular acquisition among urban working people and broadcast hours so much longer
that a cacophony of Viennese waltzes, home economics conferences, and
sports news signaled "the end of absolute solitude and of absolute sociability."[50] At the same time as modern amenities pierced through what
were once hermetic walls, the physical act of going out, of being involved
in modern consumer-culture pastimes, brought a fresh perspective on home
life. The woman of tomorrow, for Maria Coppola, "bursting out of her
little sparrow uniform . . . robust, active, and frank . . . with her mind
open to the fundamental issues of existence . . . will return to her life-
course, to home and family life."[51]

The growing permeability of the household was not in principle incompatible with a growing sense of intimacy. It was with greater confidence, perhaps, knowing that the home was not cut off from but indeed in the mainstream of commercial culture, that women could idealize the "nest" or dream of their own "dear little home" *(casetta)*. With the help of myriad publications and etiquette books, the house became an extension of the self, a place from which to gaze out into the public world, a site from which to launch oneself into society. Home furnishing became an important affective as well as social investment. Hence to stay at home was a form of social engagement. This dream was not unique to young women; if contemporary novels are to be believed, young men too shared the dream. The "casetta moderna" was like an adolescent's clubhouse "where friends might come at all hours of the day; a house with a radio, a record player, and the little woman in her at-home outfit."[52] It was as indispensable to a young man's rite of passage to adulthood as it was to a young woman's. The foundation of the new generation's companionate relationships, it distanced him from his own father's power, as well as offering protection against the nerve-jarring tempos of modern existence.

But fascism was of two minds about the cult of domesticity. At one level it indulged it; at another it despised it. The intransigent "reformers of custom," who railed against foreign names, who insisted that the strong-sounding Italian *voi* replace the obsequious Spanish *lei*, and who wanted the virile Roman salute to do away with the effeminate handshake, treated the "alcova"—boudoir or home, as it were—with disdain. This led to some fanciful inventions on what might be the alternative. The aging futurists were in the forefront of the "antialcove struggle," their first assaults dating from before the Great War. Certainly the most memorable episode, in view of Italy's attachment to pasta, occurred on November 15, 1930, when at a banquet at the restaurant Penna d'Oca in Milan the famous futurist Marinetti launched his crusade against *pastasciutta* and the pettifogging homebody culture that had foisted it on the Italian people. No doubt Italian diets were changing. Or better, various forces wanted them to. Commercial culture appealed to the modern woman to toss together canned asparagus and salmon to make an elegant meal for the spouse who brought his office mates home, while state propaganda urged the *massaia* to consume home-grown polenta flour and rice in place of imported wheat. Marinetti's message was altogether another: "Spaghetti is no food for fighters. In the conflict to come the victory will be to the swift: pastasciutta is antivirile. . . . A weighty and encumbered stomach cannot be favorable to physical enthusiasm toward women." To "drastically modify our race's feeding habits," Marinetti intended to transform food making into an art. This implied purging food culture of female influence altogether. To revive the old café culture the futurists invented preposterous new dishes, and they renamed foreign concoctions. A bar thus became *quisibeve* (here-one-drinks) and the cocktail a *polibibita* (multidrink). At their first full meal in the new style, the antipasto was a female-shaped concoction, *la passione delle bionde,* consumed in a thrice by the celebrating anthropophagi, Marinetti, Giulio Onesti, Enrico Prampolini, and Fillìa.[53]

The Decline of the Salon

As the public aspects of social life were magnified and bureaucratized and private space redefined, the salons in which cultivated women once exercised personal power over major political events declined in social importance. In nineteenth-century Italy, the salon had played an unusually important role in orienting political life because political parties were little cohesive and the elites of the single Italian states personally unknown to one another. Clara Maffei's mid-nineteenth-century "salotto italico" had demonstrated the importance of "the art of receiving well, of being the center of an order of civic and liberal ideas, without making a show of it." Before Italian unification, her salon had been a gathering place for patriots, including her cherished friend Giuseppe Verdi; after 1860, it became the "antechamber for ministerial portfolios."[54] Down to World War I, the *salotto* was central to Italian socialist strategizing as well. The PSI was a great mass party by 1910, with its farflung press, trade unions, and local sections. Nonetheless, at Anna Kuliscioff's sprawling flat beneath the porticos of the Duomo Square in Milan, the Russian-born socialist brought intellectual rigor to the soft reformism of her companion Filippo Turati, the PSI's head, and to the left-wing intelligentsia, reformers, and socialist politicians who gathered there under his leadership.

Salon life was uncongenial to mass society, however, and in the wake of the war, the heyday of the salon was over. Perhaps Raffaello Barbiera, Countess Maffei's admirer, was right when he recalled her words to the effect that "the art of receiving is the art of self-sacrifice."[55] Contemporary women had their own agendas, and those who were socially engaged had both more interests outside of the home and more occasions to pursue them in public. Moreover, social life was becoming more commercialized and more specialized. Unlike Clara Maffei's salon, which was nearly always open when she was in Milan and which welcomed a liberal elite transcending profession and nationality, interwar salons catered to distinct groups and met at fixed, well-publicized times. Futurists knew when to gather at Delia Notari's in Milan; Rome's *jeunesse dorée* passed by

Countess Elena Morozzo della Rocca's on Tuesday afternoons; on Mondays, intellectual friends met with the painter Amalia Besso in via del Babuino. If, at first, salon life was encouraged by the establishment of the dictatorship, insofar as it offered occasions of meeting for new and old elites, in the long run it was dampened by the bureaucratization of political life. The salon, like the café, was the legacy of an artistocratic notion of rank; like the café, its centrality to social life waned as fascism refashioned ties between public and private space in the 1930s.

This is nowhere so evident as in Margherita Sarfatti's career as cultural promoter under fascism. Arts patron, intellectual, former lover and longtime companion of Mussolini, Sarfatti wielded immense personal power through her capacity to bring together intellectuals, artists, and the political personnel of the regime. Of Jewish origin, baptized Catholic, the young Margherita Grassini's self-described "vocation" as a "celebrity collector" had come naturally and early. Partly it was her character, that of an exuberant, handsome, and self-disciplined woman. She was endowed with "a sort of impassioned instinct," which "compelled her toward people of genius, even unknown or misunderstood ones."[56] Partly it was her upbringing and education in the refined middle-European culture of her wealthy Triestine-Venetian family, whose friends included the novelist Antonio Fogazzaro, Pius X, and the young Guglielmo Marconi. From her youth, Margherita was in the mainstream of ideas. Converted to socialism very young and married to Cesare Sarfatti, a well-established if never wealthy or notably successful lawyer, she eventually settled in Milan in 1909. There, at age twenty-eight, she was introduced to the circle of Anna Kuliscioff. The aging but still fascinating Kuliscioff's exercise of her "female attractiveness," her withering epigrams and her unremitting political passion, left an indelible impression on Sarfatti. In turn, Sarfatti herself was a merciless observer of socialist sexual politics; the aging Kuliscioff may still have been the "only man in the Italian socialist party," as the saying went, but she was unable to prevent Turati from distracting dalliances with younger women or to use her formidable personal influence to reconcile the differences between reformers and maximalists that signaled the crisis of socialist strategy on the eve of the war.

Sarfatti's own career as promoter of fascist cultural politics, though wholly self-interested, was not without parallels. She stayed on in Milan after the March on Rome, opening her home to the young artists of the *Novecento* movement, including Anselmo Bucci, Marino Marini, Ubaldo Oppi, and her favorites, Achille Funi and, especially, Arturo Tosi. In 1922 she promoted their first collective show at the Pesaro Gallery, and in 1926, their first major public exhibition. In 1926, as fascism consolidated itself, and in the wake of her husband Cesare's death in 1924, she moved to Rome, where, in the next decade, she manipulated the regime's burgeoning artistic patronage networks to promote the *Novecento* as a "national school," or a movement of "revolutionaries in the name of a modern restoration." Ever close to Mussolini, who had continued to meet her on his visits to Milan, she helped him found in 1922 the monthly *Gerarchia*, the main font of fascist orthodoxy, which she directed after 1924. Her immense power as an image-maker (the *artefice del Duce*, propagandists called her) was first displayed in his authorized biography, *Dux*. For a decade thereafter, she reigned, doyenne of official intellectual life. Her Tuesday receptions in her home at number 18 via dei Villini were "like a great market, with people of every sort." The cars—backed up into the nearby streets—let off generals' daughters and women of wealth and beauty, well-cared-for regime intellectuals and the highest-ranking party functionaries, not to mention scrounging young artists. To the fury of her numerous enemies, especially the bullying Roberto Farinacci, who in art opted for an insipid realism and was jealous of her close relationship to the Duce, Sarfatti worked the patronage mills on her friends' behalf. All in all, she was the most powerful woman of the regime.

But Sarfatti's was inevitably a tenuous power, and by 1934 it was clearly on the wane. That Mussolini had fallen out of love and was then smitten by the proverbial younger woman, twenty-year-old Claretta Petacci, was not a minor cause. But the nature of the regime, too, undercut Sarfatti's power. *Staracismo*, with its bureaucratic dispensation of art-world patronage, its hierarchies of political privilege, and its highly formalized displays of public power, was inimical to the informal and personal exercise of persuasion that a woman of Sarfatti's sharp intelligence so successfully practiced through salon life. Mussolini himself was more and more like the image created by Sarfatti in *Dux* (though she obviously had regarded herself as unaffected by it). That is, he was a man alone, with no need for women or children. When the Duce peremptorily stopped receiving her at Palazzo Venezia and when she was removed as editor of *Gerarchia* in 1934, the sycophants slipped away, the toadying police informers became more impudent, and her avowed enemies grew shriller. Her own aging, with her loud dress and ostentatious style in public events, were used as weapons to feed personal attacks on her. She was perhaps the more vulnerable, not just because her power had indeed depended on her seductive stratagems, but because she herself remained so wholly convinced that these typically female arms were the most important she commanded.[57]

Sarfatti, defeated politically, came to terms with her discomfort in a

Margherita Sarfatti. (*Der Querschnitt* 10 [Nov. 1930]. Reprinted courtesy of the Butler Library, Columbia University.)

manner not unlike that of other emancipated women of means. She traveled abroad frequently, to Paris, to London, and to the United States as well. She made several trips there after 1934, and she was always well-received, primarily because she was regarded as Mussolini's personal emissary. The last stay, in 1937, was recalled in a travel memoir entitled *America, or the Pursuit of Happiness* in which she ruminated about the meaning of female emancipation. American women, she wrote, had "conquered the right to happiness." This might not have seemed like much. But as an Italian woman, she knew that it was an "enormous heresy, given the European and Latin conception of femaleness; indeed it was subversive of the unimpeachable and unwritten laws of custom."[58] The fascist racial laws of 1938 were the final blow. By 1940, she had moved abroad with her family, finally settling in Argentina. Even in exile Sarfatti, cosmopolitan, emancipated, and of independent means, put an optimistic face on the constraints of tradition. In public, at least, she never reassessed her relationship to feminism, to fascism, or to the Duce. The events of her youth and middle age, to quote the title of her autobiography, were "water under the bridge."

It fell to more ordinary women to articulate the perception that their flights of fantasy as well as physical freedoms were curbed by the fact of being women. This was best conveyed by the young cosmopolitan Alba De Cespedes's first successful novel *Nessuno torna indietro*, published in 1938. Its setting is the Pensione Grimaldi in central Rome, a boarding house run by nuns for women students; part prison, part haven in the storm, it is a microcosm of urban life "with its own laws and tribunals." Once inside, as the spinsterish Sardinian Augusta, a covert novel writer, says, speaking for all, "You can't go home again. . . . Those who stayed behind, who went from their mothers' arms to those of their husbands, will never forgive us for having seen new things, new faces, for having had the key to our own room, for having been able to come and go as we wanted."[59] Free to go out and be on their own, the young women are unfree in spirit. Augusta is so incorrigibly self-conscious about her femaleness that she can only turn out sentimental claptrap. Xenia, driven by her "desire to make it," escapes to Milan, but only to end up living the trite fantasy life of the shop girl, first her boss's and then his rival's lover. Emanuela, who seemed on the verge of consummating a humdrum companionate relationship, her hidden past discovered, is precipitated into an international travel scene, only to consort with faceless cosmopolitans. The hardworking Silvia, the only one to defend her thesis and with the highest distinction, is doomed to a schoolmarmish existence at Spoleto.

Women were at greater liberty to go out than ever before. The dictatorship could not bar their access to mass culture. But fascism conditioned how freely they could use it. It was one thing for women to exercise their powers of fascination in the boudoir, another in the salon, in public social gatherings, or in the streets. Though mass culture put more power in the hands of women to carve out and rule domestic niches, the regime nevertheless sought to check the individualist impulses that nurtured and thrived on these new domestic cultures. In sum, under fascism, women's freedom to go out could be compared to the freedom reigning at Pensione Grimaldi, a halfway house with fixed hours, closely watched group routines, and the strictures of newly internalized conventions.

8   Women's Politics in a New Key

Woman must obey. . . . My idea of her role in the State is in opposition to all feminism. Naturally she shouldn't be a slave, but if I conceded her the vote, I'd be laughed at. In our State, she must not count.
    Benito Mussolini, in Emil Ludwig, *Talks with Mussolini* (1931)

Does there exist a political function for women in Italy? Can woman under fascism and on behalf of fascism think and act for specific ends with ideas and abilities of her own? We firmly believe so!
    Giornale della donna (1928)

When emancipated Italian women returned home from abroad in the 1930s, Italy's repressive provincialism oftentimes weighed on them. This was especially true if they had encountered women from more emancipated environments. So it was a surprise of sorts that Italy's delegates to the International Conference of Woman, coming back to Rome after their July 1–2, 1934, meeting at the Palais Royal in Paris, expressed no envy in the face of the liberties of their foreign "sister friends." Indeed, one of the group, Olga Modigliani, noted that she and her companions had basked in the "interest and comments" excited by fascism's dedication to the welfare of mothers and children. Modigliani's own "profound sense of elation and gratitude" was heightened as she recalled her embarrassment a dozen years before when, with just two other women, she had gone to Paris for the Third International Home Economics Congress. At the time, Italy had seemed "at the very rear of civilized nations" in terms of social legislation; to think, the only trace of Italian influence outside the congress halls had been Cappiello's dazzling poster advertisements for Cinzano! A restrained person, Modigliani groped for the appropriate rhetoric to convey her own awakened patriotic pride. She settled on a version of Massimo d'Azeglio's old adage: "The greatest thing that Mussolini has done is not to remake Italy, but to remake the Italians."[1]

The political beliefs of Olga Modigliani (née Flaschel) would be little understood were her opinions, or those of women like her, merely shrugged off as "fascist." An Italian of Jewish ancestry who had long been involved in reformist causes, Modigliani had once been an exponent of the "practical feminism" of the early-twentieth-century emancipationist movement. Like her friends in the National Association of Woman, Modigliani had advanced her claim to citizenship by volunteering her time, skills, and financial resources to build up a network of good works on behalf of mothers and children. This service was undertaken with the particular zeal of a Jewish woman intent on assimilation.[2] Her special cause was the *Opera di assistenza materna* for unwed mothers and abandoned infants, which she had founded in 1918 with her husband, Enrico Modigliani, a highly regarded pediatrician, and their patron, the rich and pugnacious nationalist countess Daisy di Robilant. In 1923, perhaps at the recommendation of the well-connected di Robilant, Olga was named as the only woman to the committee advising Mussolini's first cabinet in matters regarding maternal and child welfare. Its recommendations were later incorporated into the 1925 decree founding ONMI. In the late 1920s, Modigliani withdrew from public life; like others she was disappointed at fascism's failure to give women the vote, for which she had campaigned in the ranks of Rome's *Pro-suffragio* group. Just a few years later, after her husband's premature death in 1931 and with her children grown, she again became active. Unburdened of her family obligations, which had included employing her fluency in English and French to promote Enrico's scientific work, she attended conferences, managed the center, and helped train young fascist social workers.

By the mid-1930s, Modigliani was, like many educated bourgeois women, personally freer and more socially engaged than a decade earlier. Whether she still regarded herself as a feminist is another question. The emancipatory and reformist impulses which once inspired her work on behalf of maternal and child welfare had faded. Now when she spoke of Italian women's accomplishments in the field of social work—as she did in early 1935 while lecturing in courses to teach young Roman women to become *visitatrici fasciste*— she presented service as a self-abnegating duty rather than as an empowering act. Service was to be performed with the same selfless zeal that Italian mothers allegedly displayed as they carried out household and family tasks; it was practiced not for purposes of professional fulfillment nor to render social justice, but to demonstrate Italian women's capacity to fulfill their assigned functions within the fascist state. Confident of their record of accomplishment, Modigliani was able to reassure her young listeners that Italian women could proudly reply as she had done to "those foreign women who at international conferences regard us with compassion because we are neither deputesses nor senatoresses":

> Be it in the family, be it in the state, we Italian women are always
> ready to sacrifice petty personal vanity and outward appearances to
> collaborate effectively with work and advice toward spiritual unity,
> toward real uplift, with absolute dedication of our persons to the
> Chief to whom we have vowed our faith and our love.[3]

Latin Feminism

In her prideful, if labored, defense of Italian women's worth in the fascist state, her renunciation of liberal definitions of citizenship, and her own self-effacing devotion to service, Olga Modigliani well represented the new political synthesis which in 1930s Italy went under the name of "Latin," "national," or "pure" feminism. These were the terms adopted by women who themselves were once active in the emancipationist movement as they sought to reconcile fascism with feminism. Their feminism was "pure," in that it was unsullied by the intemperate leveling of socialist reformism or by the strident individualism of the Anglo-American equal-rights movement. It was "Latin" because it championed attitudes they regarded as peculiar to Italian womanhood, namely, devotion to family, love of tradition, and respect for the race. It was "national," insofar as it recognized the need to subordinate female aspirations to the higher interests of the Italian state and people.

What was *feminist* about Latin feminism was rather more problematic. Having reluctantly renounced their belief in an independent women's organization in order to accommodate government restrictions and party interference, these women still struggled to preserve an autonomous female voice and to safeguard and build opportunities for companionship in all-female organizations. They may no longer have championed equal rights in a strict sense, but they had by no means renounced improving the situation of women in Italian society. Only now they thought this could best be achieved by what the voluble conférencière Marziola Pignatari called "a happy equilibrium between the new needs of the times and a return to those traditions which make the family institution one of the most important factors behind national greatness."[4] Latin feminists thus repudiated political engagement as conventionally understood; women, they concluded, could best exercise their powers of suasion by means of cultural uplift or through philanthropy. Their "politics of culture" strived to create a nationwide female culture more authentically expressive of

Italian womanhood, or better of the New Italy's female elite. Their "politics of the social" endeavored to support fascism's avowed goal of "reaching out to people," at the same time as it demonstrated the readiness of privileged women to sacrifice on behalf of the national good.

At bottom, what we have characterized as the Latin feminist synthesis was the endeavor to reconcile two wholly antagonistic political traditions: one was the emancipationist legacy of the early-twentieth-century Italian women's movement, the other, fascist mass politics. The former was egalitarian, individualistic, and pacifist; its organizations were locally promoted, voluntary, and all-female. The latter was hierarchical and militaristic; its institutions centralized, male-dominated, and coercive. Arguably, each accommodated the other, if in greatly unequal measure. Bourgeois feminists, including Olga Modigliani, were unprepared to resist a regime that promised Italy national greatness yet left their family patrimonies intact, all the while trumpeting its commitment to "higher social justice" for Italy's humble poor. With the hope that fascism would enable their own charitable enterprises to survive and perhaps prosper, they redefined the purposes of their networks with respect to the state, to their clients, and to one another. They distanced themselves from the international women's movement to which they had been tied by bonds of affection, intellectual curiosity, and political solidarity. Finally, they rewrote their own history, condemning the "old" feminism for its shrillness and alleged incomprehension of the true nature of Italian womanhood, family, nation, and race.

In turn, the dictatorship, in the endeavor to broaden its base of support, was compelled to recognize the historical trends that since the turn of the century had brought women out of the home and led hundreds of thousands of them to advance demands for equal rights, civic recognition, and social reform. In effect, the foundation of mass organizations for women under the aegis of the Fascist party acknowledged that, in some form or another, the modern state had to satisfy women's desire for social engagement. Before its own organizations for women were finally launched in 1935–36, the dictatorship, in order to legitimate its positions on women, exploited the press and the networks of self-help and philanthropy founded by bourgeois feminists. It also capitalized on the personal prestige of former leaders such as Teresa Labriola, Ella Goss, and Paola Benedettini Alferazzi. Through the mid-1930s, the vocabulary and concerns of the old feminism thus suffused the rhetoric of fascism's own leading women functionaries. Not until after 1936, with the militarization of the regime, the formation of a new generation of cadres and followers with no recall of historical feminism, and, finally, the outlawing of the surviving bourgeois feminist groups in 1938 was the emancipationist tradition finally obliterated.

Throughout its course, however, the relationship between Latin feminism and fascism was unendingly equivocal. The most fundamental issue over which they equivocated was what sexual difference implied for women's capacity to be citizens of the fascist state. Latin feminists saw difference as meaning complementarity and collaboration between men and women, whereas fascist men understood it to mean sexual hierarchy and female subordination. The women clung to their single-sex solidarity networks to promote what they regarded as the best virtues of Italian womanhood. Meanwhile, fascist hierarchs sought to mobilize these bonds to deny all individual or group freedoms. Women such as Olga Modigliani, Marziola Pignatari, or Giulia Boni—to name just a few of the most articulate—sought to uphold traditions of service to the state, treating their volunteer work as acts of social duty. In turn, the Fascist party regarded such voluntary efforts as acts of subordination to the regime. For many women, the "New Italy" was a source of patriotic pride; their belief in the need to defend it against foreign aggressors justified their deference to the collective cause. The dictatorship exploited this emotional identification with the nation-state, converting it into a self-righteous and militaristic chauvinism that could legitimate any sacrifice—of women as a sex and of family and kin. In this sense, Latin feminism was the discourse and practice of the politically subaltern, questing to speak about their changed relations with one another, with their clients, and with the dominant political system.

The Disremembering of Historic Feminism

The complicated story of Italian feminism's accommodation to fascism is not unrelated to what Nancy Cott, in a compelling generalization from the experience of American feminists after the Great War, has identified as a "more widespread 'disremembering' process by which Feminism was selectively absorbed and repressed."[5] Like American feminists and their counterparts elsewhere, Italian feminists were confronted with a wholly new political, economic, and cultural setting in the course of the twenties. First, they had to reorient their goals, having hitherto concentrated primarily on obtaining suffrage. In Italy this reorientation was even more difficult because, unlike in England or the United States, women's bid for the vote had been frustrated. Next, they had to come to terms with mass culture, as well as the "life-style feminism" of younger women; for family-oriented persons like Modigliani, the free ways of younger women seemed misguided, if women's causes were to be taken seriously. Finally, with the rise of the welfare state, women everywhere had to relate their philanthropic endeavors, which had been rooted in flexible, local networks, to the professionalized social work practices managed by central bureaucracies. In Italy male advocates of welfare reform declared philanthropy outmoded, along with liberal freedoms, and sought to organize social work in the light of a totalizing social security system.

For the broad front of women who had been active in the emancipationist movement of the early 1920s, the years after 1925 were thus a bleak time. One huge segment was crushed as the socialist and communist movements were suppressed and the left was forced underground. The hope that moderate, not to mention fascist, women leaders might be represented in the newly formed corporate bureaucracies was deluded; at ONMI only two women were appointed to serve on the twenty-two-person board, both of whom were stylish Roman noblewomen, Countess Bice Brusati and Donna Isabella Borghese. The fact that a third woman, the "intelligentissima" Baronessa Maria Blanc, assisted the head of the board, her husband, Dr. Gian Alberto, was small comfort. At the corporations, there was only one woman, Maria Vittoria Luzzi, the head of the Midwives' Union. Unlike during the Giolittian era or in wartime, the economy promised no automatic progress through new professional opportunities. Aside from laws restricting women's work and educational prospects, the PNF made it very clear that women were to contribute to what in a 1930 speech the party secretary Turati called "healthy parsimony."[6] In no uncertain terms, this meant sacrificing as they had done during the home-front battles of the Great War. Finally, the reform of the penal and family codes, started in 1926 by the nationalist Minister of Justice Rocco, betrayed hopes of ameliorating women's legal status.

There was some protest against this inexorably antifeminist drift. The Marchesa Maria Spinelli Monticelli, secretary of Milan's *fascio femminile*, disbanded it in August 1926 to protest against the abolition of local elections, only to be expelled from the PNF for "unworthiness and indiscipline."[7] And several groups petitioned that rulings against women's right to work be overturned. But on the whole, the regime's actions were so overwhelming, striking at so many levels, that women were shamed into believing that Italian womanhood itself was somehow blameworthy for its own repression. Embarrassed by Violet Gibson's attempt to assassinate Mussolini on April 7, 1926, as the Duce exited from Palazzo dei Conservatori on the Campidoglio, former feminists rushed to disavow the act, lest the sixty-two-year-old Irish woman's demented gesture implicate all women. Demoralized, once-emancipated women rewrote the history of those postwar years of exhilaration and hope: "Never before were women as disoriented as in that period," averred the journalist Margherita Armani, Margherita Sarfatti's bosom friend, who in 1928 wrote an overview of the situation of women in "fascist civilization" at Turati's behest. The war had "upset the intimate psychology of many of them." Hence, "the first major social task was to restore their composure and settle them back in the family order." Like the infantile workers brought to perdition by their Bolshevik leaders, women had lost their way: they needed, nay, they desired, fascism's firmly "antihedonistic" grip to exercise "a serene check on all forms of individual egoism endangering the nation."[8]

The renunciation of activism always carries high personal costs: "The turns from the private to the public life and back again are marked by wildly exaggerated expectations, by total infatuation, and by sudden revulsions," Albert Hirschman observed in *Shifting Involvements*.[9] Such changes of prospect are all the more disturbing when alternative compensations are slight, as was most certainly true in late-twenties Italy both on the professional plane and in personal life. The thought of once more becoming marginal, when, as Michela De Giorgio delicately phrased it, "their relationship to politics was so recent and fresh," caused anguishing moments for the protagonists of postwar Italian feminism. These feelings were complicated by the fact that their often precarious livelihoods as journalists or poorly paid staff members of female associations were in jeopardy unless they quickly realigned their political loyalties.[10] Now entering their mid-thirties or forties, life choices seemed more urgent. At the same time as they were being disabused of the idea that fascism and feminism would prove "sister forces," they were confronted with younger women whose life-styles seemed freer yet were unconflicted by emancipationist urges. Tempted to resolve their social frustrations by turning to private life, they met with the great dearth of eligible male partners. By the end of the decade, as Irene Brin wrote, echoing the ironic self-commentary of women's fiction of the late 1920s, "the heroines of the postwar suddenly disappeared; they married, or committed suicide, or simply aged. The survivors can be recognized by a certain bitterness, by the angry way they stub out their cigarettes in the ashtray, by their sighs of disgust." It seems no coincidence that the years 1924, 1927, and 1928 registered the highest number of female suicides in modern Italy.[11]

In the decade following, those women who returned to public life within the fascist groups would sometimes cite their own chastening experience as an object lesson for the younger generation, as if to protect it from similar disappointment. When the Roman writer Ada Felici Ottaviani sought to reassure irate university students that fascism's decision to exclude women from the Littorial events must have been made in good faith, she recalled her own generation's experience: "It is difficult to live through this period of transition with balance and moderation, especially for those women who were obliged by the necessity of the war and of the postwar era to take up personal and individual activity."[12] Whether younger women heard that message is another question, as we noted earlier. The only message they seemed to have picked up from their elders was that feminism was the obsolescent ideology of "old carcasses," as forgettable as all other relics of the liberal past.

Under the shadow of the dictatorship, the fading bourgeois women's groups, like the archetypical spinster, scraped along ever industrious and unappreciated, rather than succumbing outright in solitude. In keeping with its practice of being "selectively totalitarian," the dictatorship countenanced the persistence of bourgeois associations until the late 1930s—provided they did not compete with the Fascist party for middle-class loyalties—as the Masonry had until it was outlawed in 1925. Accordingly, upper-class women's networks—along with the Rotary clubs, cultural academies, and sporting fellowships of bourgeois and artistocratic men—were spared the dragnets, closings, and confiscations that befell thousands of working-class reading circles, cooperatives, and trade union halls as the prefects, police, and local party officials cited them in violation of the dictatorship's public safety laws. It may have been that the PNF's own women's groups, their rivals, curbed their animosity toward these fellow associations of women. But just as likely they lacked enough influence with higher authorities to denounce them as a public disturbance.

However, to survive for long under fascism demanded ostentatious servility or keeping a very low profile. The early 1930s thus saw members of the organizations of historic feminism tinker with their statutes, rewrite their professed aims, and adjust the composition of their boards. At the death of the independent-minded Countess Gabriella Spalletti Rasponi in 1931, the National Council of Italian Women (CNDI) displayed unerringly good political sense by selecting Daisy di Robilant as her successor. The credentials of this "intrepid amazon" of old Piedmontese stock were already well-appreciated in aristocratic and high bureaucratic circles; a formidable horsewoman as well as indefatigable backer of philanthropic causes, de Robilant was founder of the patriotic group *Italia redenta*, vice-president of Rome's ONMI, and director of the *Centro illegitimi* (formerly Olga Modigliani's *Assistenza materna*). The PNF approved the choice wholeheartedly. Her first order of business was to "adapt" the CNDI to the corporate system. This meant packing its committee structure with professional women knowledgeable about the fascist administration. To revive the CNDI's flagging prestige, di Robilant opened the council's library in Rome to a series of debates on urgent legislative matters. One of the first meetings generated a petition that would have barred landlords and tax collectors from seizing sewing machines belonging to mothers of families in order to satisfy debts. The countess herself presented the petition to Mussolino who, magnanimously, gave it his full and immediate approbation.[13]

Other women's associations adapted less successfully to the new times. FILDIS, the organization of Italian women degree-holders, could never shake its strong ties to the international women's movement nor to the independent-minded Jewish, lesbian, and other intellectual women who socialized around its *case della laureata* in Milan and Rome. Its protests against the discriminatory rulings on women in the professions during 1927–29, though directed to Mussolini's attention, seemed to have been disregarded. Ultimately, its nemesis was the rival fascist ANFAL. That group, headed by the attractive and ingratiating Maria Castellani, insisted that the International Federation of University Women withdraw its recognition of FILDIS so that ANFAL could be named the sole representative of Italian professional women. In May 1935, as Italian relations with England deteriorated and with the London-based IFUW showing no signs of cooperating, the public authorities invited FILDIS to "dissolve itself spontaneously." It was impossible not to comply.[14]

Likewise, the *Pro-suffragio*, with its emphasis on equal rights, had trouble accommodating to the dictatorship. Its name changed in 1928 to *Federazione per il suffragio e i diritti civili e politici*, it added to its advisory board Augusta Reggiani Banfi and other nationalist women who were well-placed in "official good society." Moreover, its new aims were all pragmatic modesty, that is, to "group, maintain, and enhance those forces which have tended to disband out of the mistaken notion that women's suffrage should no longer be discussed, when indeed it can still be exercised indirectly in Italy by means of the syndicates and consultative bodies."[15] However, the new head, Ada Sacchi Simonetta, a medical doctor from Monza, displayed none of the political tact of her pliant predecessor, Benedettini Alferazzi. In advance of the 1932 Geneva talks on disarmament, she called Mussolini's boast of being a man of peace by circulating a petition asking women to support universal disarmament; Sacchi Simonetta was convinced that women would endorse the petition with enthusiasm, "since the nature of woman is inspired by maternity, that is to say by the essential function of caring for life." How many responded we do not know. What is sure is that the police did, ordering her to desist and opening a dossier on the group. Subsequent steps to sever ties with its emancipationist past were apparently half-hearted, though in 1934 the organization did disassociate itself from the international suffrage movement by renaming itself FIDD, or Italian Federation for Women's Rights. Its membership much diminished, it was finally disbanded on December 14, 1938.[16] At Milan, the venerable *Unione femminile*, after disputing its far-flung territory with the invasive ONMI and PNF bureaucracies, retrenched, to focus mainly on charity. Its depleted personnel was at least partly replenished by Jewish and Catholic women who felt uncomfortable in the fascist party formations. It too survived until late 1938, when, together with the long-compromised CNDI and the Rotary and other male bourgeois clubs with international ties, it was forced to disband under accusation of being antinational and harboring Jewish members.

The Catholic Counterreformation

In the new times, historical feminism was quickly overawed by two new movements: the Catholic on the one hand, and the fascist on the other. In some respects, the great growth of the former was the more surprising. Once regarded by anticlerical emancipationists as the religion of aristocratic bigots and backward peasants, Catholicism, starting in the 1920s, successfully exploited the reaction against liberalism and modernity to appeal to ever-wider circles of urban middle- and working-class women. At its first postwar conference in 1919, presided over by Pope Benedict XV—who saw no conflict between advocating suffrage for women and restoring them to the home—the main Catholic women's movement had changed its name to *Unione femminile cattolica italiana* (UFCI). Led by women of exceptional intelligence, boldness, and unwavering dedication, including Maria Sticco, Fanny Dalmazzo, and Armida Barelli, the Catholic women's movement grew unabated in the 1920s; the talents of these women, unlike those of the more modestly gifted fascist women, were nurtured, not frittered away, by their movement. How, more specifically, fascist associations related to the Catholic groups, is unclear for now. When Mussolini first met with the national delegates of his *fasci femminili* in 1927, he purportedly told them to "keep an eye on the sacristy. I distrust the bigots, but I respect the true believers."[17] But the dictatorship never seemed to bother the "bigots" either. If there was rivalry between Catholic and fascist groups, as one suspects, the fascist women's press tactfully never alluded to it. In any event, Catholic women's groups thrived during the next decade, presenting a clear-cut alternative to the women's *fasci* and exercising enormous influence over female political culture as a whole.[18]

Italian Catholicism, being unequivocally determined to confront modernity by finding new ways of relating private anxieties and values to public concerns, played a winning hand with respect to fascist female politics. Since before the war, Church leaders had mounted watch against the complex of dangers unleashed by industrialization—identifying these in freemasonic skepticism, socialist radicalism, and the psychological disorders caused by mass culture.[19] By the 1920s, Catholic associations were thus well-armed to launch a veritable counterreformation. To re-Christianize urban Italy, they employed all the paraphernalia of modern mass movements—radio, cinema, and a flourishing press—as well as the techniques of modern behavioral psychology. With relatively little invested in the suffrage issue (though they had readied themselves to make use of the vote if granted), the Catholic women's groups were free to focus on reforming customs and culture. Whereas the fascist women were hobbled by male hierarchy and (at least initially) by disputes over how much to invest in politics proper, the Catholic women never lifted their eyes from civil society. Hence they occupied the vanguard of battles against indecent fashion, luxury, and dance, launched in the name of national morality in the 1920s. Whereas the fascist women lacked youth groups of their own— the *piccole italiane* having been assigned to the Ministry of National Education in 1929, when it also took control over the *balilla* and Catholic boy scouts—Catholic women managed a full complement of cohorts: they started in 1920 with the *effettive* for ages sixteen to thirty-five, and the aspirants, for ages twelve to sixteen; they added the *beniamine* for ages six to twelve in 1923, set up groups of *piccolissime* aged four to six in 1933, and founded the *angiolette* from birth to age four in 1937. Behind the fascist models for organizing women, there lay the militaristic hierarchies of the PNF and the positivistic breeding schemes of provincial sociobiologists. Behind the Catholic models, it is true, there were unimpeachable male ecclesiastical hierarchies. But there were also the optimistic behavioral studies of cosmopolitan educators around the Catholic University of Milan; their faith in human self-motivation argued for the capacity of the female personality to cope with the malaise of contemporary existence by severe self-analysis. Not least of all, there was the discipline of closely watched all-female sodalities.

Indeed Catholicism's success in the interwar decades lay at least partly in the bonds of solidarity it fostered among women. Building on a far-flung parish network and small-group sodalities and basing their appeal at once on allegiance to the faith, the Church hierarchy, and the female community, Catholic women's organizations achieved a genuinely cross-class composition, including housewives, working-class women, and middle-class professionals. Antiemancipationist, insofar as they rejected bourgeois notions of individualism, they nevertheless underscored the virtue of acquiring strong personal identities as the foundation of good works and religious solidarity. On these bases, the Catholic organization was both immense and intense: In 1925 the Union reported 3,162 groups and another 541 in formation, with 160,000 members—the same year the women's *fasci* had perhaps a thousand sections and 40,000 members. In 1931 the UDCI counted 6,000 groups and more than 250,000 enrolled, whereas the women's *fasci* numbered 5,570 groups with 150,000 members.

The catholicization of Italian civic culture manifest in this great growth of women's groups—like the vitality of Catholic youth culture to which we referred in Chapter 5—signaled the reversal of a decades-long secularizing trend and the habits of the mind, and the heart, connected with it. In towns, Catholicism was no longer regarded as a leftover from the preindustrial past; and Catholics no longer experienced an uncomfortable conflict between their religion and modern society. The union between Church and State brought about by the Lateran Accords meant that a socially engaged woman such as Maria Magri Zopegni, editor of *La donna italiana*, who once characterized herself as "fervidly Catholic and fervidly patriotic," was no longer wracked by the "struggle between faith and fatherland."[20] By the early 1930s, leaders of the local women's *fasci*, who were also staunch Catholics, reportedly prayed to God at Mass to help them do Caesar's work, "to illuminate their mission and to make them worthy of helping their brothers and serving in humility."[21]

With Catholicism confirmed as religion of state and liberal credos of philanthropy in disrepute, neo-Thomistic arguments on behalf of charity enjoyed a new popularity. Better the gospel of Christian good works than the cold "reason of state" of fascist totalitarianism, one-time lay emancipationists seemed to argue.[22] Even the *Unione femminile*, long regarded by the Archdiocese of Milan as the long arm of freemasonic culture, softened its anticlericalism. Its great hospice for wayward girls, the Asilo Mariuccia, had since its founding in 1902 sought to rehabilitate its charges according to sternly moralistic but lay precepts. In 1924, to stay true to this tradition, its founder, Lisilia Majno Bronzini, petitioned the Ministry of Public Instruction to exonerate the girls who attended the nearby public schools from the obligatory religious instruction mandated under the Gentile reform. Just three years later, the hospice's board reversed its position. Whether or not this was to appease the girls' requests, the fact remains that their new-found religiosity was no longer discouraged by the staff as it had been in the past. Indeed, skilled lay personnel being in short supply, the Asilo recruited religious women whose spiritual vocation evidently made them willing to shoulder the difficult and ill-remunerated positions.

Agnese Pietra, the woman hired in 1927 on the Bishop of Pavia's recommendation to manage the supply warehouse, was a member of the Tertiary Order of the Franciscans. In 1930 she was appointed the hospice's general director, a position she held for the next decade.[23]

To say that Catholic networks offered a real alternative to fascist organizations is not to argue that Church organizations did not support the regime in an immediate political sense. Nor is it to contend that conservative Catholic views on the role of women in family and society did not reinforce fascism's own. Throughout most of the dictatorship, Catholic organization was not oppositional; to the degree that its very impetus was in reaction to the same emancipatory trends to which the regime was opposed, Catholic and fascist associational life shared a common goal. Still, friction between Church and party associations was almost inevitable as the dictatorship pressed its organizational drives in the late 1930s. Ultimately, the fascist women's groups may have been far more visible. But the Catholic identity formed around the Church's groups was the more enduring, being integral to what one historian cogently characterized as the "latent hegemony" undergirding Italian Christian Democratic power after the war.[24]

Fascist Mass Organization of Women

By contrast, fascism's female politics was a new invention. Not unlike fascist trade unionism, which developed haltingly to avoid the errors of socialism and lest it arouse the animosity of capitalists, the organization of a fascist women's movement advanced slowly amidst male diffidence and female defeatism. Not until 1932–33 did the women's *fasci* acquire any real organizational momentum; not until 1935–36, in the wake of the mobilization of women on behalf of the Ethiopian campaign, did the PNF regard its operations as mature. Before that, the movement's growth largely reflected the activism of female party loyalists, not to mention the interest in obtaining a fascist party card on the part of thousands of bourgeois women eager to attest their allegiance to a regime that, after 1925, was clearly there to stay.

But the PNF hierarchy too finally swung behind its women's groups in the late 1920s. Eager to put order in all of the party auxiliaries, from the youth groups to the *dopolavoro*, PNF secretaries overcame their ignorance of and distaste for women's issues, at least enough to identify the rank of the *fasci femminili* in the fascist hierarchy. This process had started in 1926, when Roberto Farinacci forced the resignation of old-guard leaders like Elisa Majer Rizzioli; it was not completed until May 26, 1931, when a later PNF secretary, Giovanni Giuriati, ordered the women's groups to obey party directive number 2137, issued on December 20, 1929. This order, in addition to commanding total subordination to all PNF directives, stipulated that the party's provincial *federali* needed the PNF secretary's approval on all local personnel nominations. Henceforth, the appointment of the women's group *fiduciarie* too had to pass through Rome.[25] They could no longer be selected catch-as-catch-¢an, according to the patriarchal whims of the local party boss, with an eye to the well-titled *nobildonna*, her retainers, and friends.

However, the first significant step toward turning the women's *fasci* into a mass organization—and an obviously belated step for a party whose good fortune in the past had been tied to Mussolini's deft political journalism—occurred in 1929. In October of that year Augusto Turati chose Paola Benedettini Alferazzi's *Giornale della donna*, founded in 1918 to promote "female social education," to become the official organ of the *fasci femminili*. Starting in July 1930, the PNF also undertook to subsidize its bimonthly publication. This was a shrewd choice, for Benedettini Alferazzi was a competent journalist as well as having a certain personal prestige, as a onetime leader of the moderate women's suffrage movement. Best of all, she had no apparent political agenda of her own, unlike her major rival, Ester Lombardo, the Sicilian-born journalist and former National Association women's group activist. Lombardo, who was then just thirty-four years old, had been plotting in 1926 to have her stylish, two-colored tabloid *Vita femminile* selected to represent the new women of the regime. However her pushy manner and clever wit, not to mention her schemes for "a syndicalism along sex as well as craft lines," made her too much for PNF men to handle, and her unsisterly manner of pitting women against one another alienated some leading fascist feminists as well.[26]

As the cautious Benedettini Alferazzi brought her newspaper around to the party line, she secured the collaboration of old timers such as Teresa Labriola and picked up Camilla Bisi, Bice Basile, and Willy Dias from the recently defunct Genoese publication *La chiosa*. She also promoted young writers from the ranks of the student GUF, such as Clara Valente, Clelia Lugaresi, and Maria Guidi, as well as her own daughter, Silvia. From 1930 to 1934, Benedettini Alferazzi was as much of a national leader as the *fasci femminili* had, given that, after the ouster of Turati in 1930, the PNF statutes provided it with no chief. Ostensibly the Fascist party secretary himself was in charge; in fact Giuriati delegated the *fasci*'s day-to-day organizational business to a male flunky, one Gabriele Parolari. This distance, or lack of interest, as it were, allowed the newspaper to remain a surprisingly strong promoter of women's interests at least until 1934.

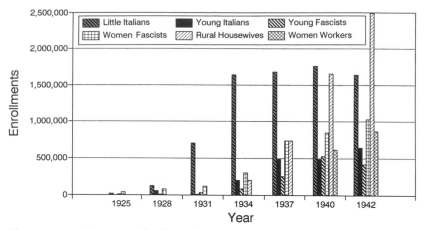

Chart 3. Enrollments in the fascist female youth and women's organizations, 1925–42. (Archivio centrale dello Stato, segreteria particolare del Duce, carteggio ordinario, f. 509.006c, Relazione dello Ispettorato dei fasci femminili, 1925; Istituto centrale di statistica del Regno d'Italia, *Compendio statistico*, 1938, p. 16; ibid., 1942, p. 14.)

That year Benedettini Alferazzi was removed as editor, and the following year the *Giornale della donna*, renamed *Donna fascista* and now edited by a male party appointee, took to running numbingly dull party directives, celebratory paeans, and American-style publicity.

The same year Turati promoted Benedettini Alferazzi, he also set up the *giovani fasciste* for young women from eighteen to twenty-two to replenish the *fasci*'s aging cohorts. On the basis of these organizational innovations, membership tallies mounted: from 106,756 in 1930 to 121,087 in 1931 to 145,199 in 1932, they accelerated to 217,206 in 1933 in the wake of orders to found a women's *fascio* in every place that there was a men's group. Thereafter, the tallies continued to increase: to 304,313 in 1934 and to 398,923 the following year.[27] (See chart 3.)

The question of what political function women might finally exercise under fascism was by no means resolved by this momentum. Nor was this issue worked out on the doctrinal level. This lack of definition troubled men who disapproved of female activism, even in the form of the innocuous pastimes that the *fasci femminili* were sponsoring. It also bothered women activists who wanted to reason about the significance of their actions in the larger scheme of things. The goals of their militancy being unclear, they were regarded by some as "too advanced" and by others as "retrograde." This made them feel even more vulnerable to the "diffidence," "ill-concealed hostility," "condescending airs," and "ironic smiles" of male kin and PNF *camerate*.[28] True, Turati, composer of a new theme song for the women's groups called "Mamma" and the best-advised of the PNF secretaries on women's issues, had put forward a mandate of sorts: that fascist women strive "to distinguish the qualities innate in Italian womanhood from those of other nationalities."[29] Yet in the early 1930s, the virtues of the New Italian were still being defined in the negative: as being antithetical to Anglo-American flapperism, French cosmopolitanism, or German pedantry.

Ultimately, Teresa Labriola alone regarded herself as having the courage and erudition to give doctrinal coherence to Latin feminism. With her self-assured familiarity with contemporary doctrinal disputes and uncommon power to recapture with some cogent and quotable insight the reader lost in the meanders of her grandiloquently abstruse prose, this pertinacious figure—prolific journalist, omnipresent board woman, and successful litigator—acted as Latin feminism's major theorist. Admittedly, there were few other contenders for this exalted position; Labriola's age made her senior to the regime's leading ideologues (Gentile, born in 1875, was two years her junior), and her "virile" intellectual commitment (as female contemporaries described it) surpassed that of most. Until late 1939, when she ceased writing, beset by personal and business troubles (she died alone on February 6, 1941), she spewed forth her views in a half-dozen leading women's publications. Male intellectuals and ideologues seemed wholly to disregard her. However, Labriola had a considerable following among educated women. Perhaps they took courage from Labriola's undaunted confidence that in the New Italy, "virile, but not masculine" women could overcome the hiatus common to modern societies between "individual and commonality, liberty and limit." And she must have cheered them with her disparaging treatment of the "Germanic" antifeminism of unnamed male fascists whom she patronizingly dismissed as "second order" thinkers. At the same time, her factious denunciation of egotistical females who forsook the right of "future generations" for an "individualist right that is wholly momentary and transient" made her discomfittingly ideological.[30] Few women now wanted to engage in tedious and divisive cavils; that was something the old feminism was accused of having encouraged. Hence, they foreswore debate and settled for a blander mix. For the unrigorous majority, Latin feminism was a potpourri of the behaviors and outlooks that, propagandists alleged, made Italian women special and indispensable. Such were "cooperativeness, education of the woman and mother, desire for peace, honesty, and the social-moral elevation of womankind." Fascism being the "strengthening" rather than the "negation" of values, it oriented women to pastimes and services more congenial to their "national gifts" and "inclinations."

Even Labriola vaguely conceded that the path of high theorizing was too torturous, the signposts too contradictory, and the outcome too prob-

lematic for there to be any solid doctrinal foundation for women's participation in the fascist state. Latin feminism, as she concluded in one of her
flashes of brilliant common sense, was best understood by its practices.
Since the 1920s, Italian women had become involved in two sorts of "experimentations"; each was "as distant from the abstractions of international feminism as from the naturalistic antifeminism of the men of
our country." These practices had arisen more or less spontaneously, in
reaction to the old feminism's debacle. They responded "to what we Italian women are and also . . . to what we are in the process of becoming."[31]
One endeavor was in the realm of culture, the other in the field of assistance.

The Politics of Culture

That women should have used cultural politics to claim citizenship is not
such a surprising development, given the character of the fascist state and
the submissive behavior of Italian intellectuals toward power in the past.
Modern nation-states have typically contended that the basis of sovereignty is an all-inclusive culture, transcending gender divisions as well as
class and ethnic lines. And just as typically, feminists have questioned
how their sex is to relate to the prevailing definitions of national culture,
indeed to culture *tout court*. Fascist intellectuals envisaged their movement as performing a special cultural mission: to fulfill the Risorgimento
idea of unity by using state authority to create an all-inclusive national
culture. On the face of it, this goal represented no problem to patriotic
women. Quite the contrary. For if it was true that they played a special
role in educating children, and if—as nationalists such as Labriola had
long maintained—women were uniquely sensitive to the problem of the
race and specially connected to the legacy of tradition, Italian womanhood
was destined to occupy a key role in forming the culture of the new era.

In practice, fascism's own cultural politics was far more masculinist
than that of any preceding regime. At least since the first decade of the
century, under the influence of Giovanni Papini and other men around
the Florentine literary review *La voce*, young Italian intellectuals had been
formulating projects to renew national culture that put militant male cultural activists in the vanguard. Many fascist intellectuals saw themselves
in that role. Indeed, following the precepts of the major philosopher of
the regime, Giovanni Gentile, they envisaged the reform of culture as a
two-step process: first, to renew elite culture as the means to a dynamic
new synthesis between the national heritage and fascist ideology; second,
this accomplished, to use the state as a positive educational force to impart
values to a citizenry that had hitherto perceived the state as a mere name

or as an external coercive force. Included in this "citizenry," aside from the working classes, were those groups who were immature according to both idealist precepts and positivist canons, in short, children and women. Women might exercise a role as educators of children, but it was obvious, given idealist premises, that in the hierarchy of cultural institutions they occupied a wholly subaltern position. This justified their exclusion from the academies, university institutes, and other centers where high culture was ostensibly being created.[32] Thus from the very pinnacle of cultural power in the Academy of Italy—from which Grazia Deledda, winner of the 1926 Nobel Prize in literature, was excluded—down to the pullulating magazines of the student GUF, the presence of women was tacitly barred. The "illustrious" Margherita Sarfatti was of course the exception to the rule.

This antifemale bias was propounded not just by cultural prejudices but also by the prevailing system of cultural patronage. The dictatorship visibly cultivated intellectuals, for in this highly urbanized society, in which middle-class interests were as yet poorly organized, the writer, artist, or professor who rounded out his income by journalistic writing played a uniquely important role in forming public opinion. Consequently, Mussolini's regime promoted a whole new hierarchy of cultural institutions— from the high-brow Academy of Italy and the middle-tone National Fascist Institutes of Culture down to the plebeian *dopolavoro* circles. It also backed the publication of Italy's first national encyclopedia, the Treccani, and sponsored art, architecture, and film expositions. Compliant intellectuals were doled out huge amounts in prizes, subsidies, and favors. But this patronage mill served very few women. It paid a monthly pension to the onetime feminist and socialist sympathizer, Sibilla Aleramo (only after she was forced to beg abjectly for it). It accorded more ample recognition to another former socialist, the poetess Ada Negri. In 1930 the pretentious Academy of Italy, Margherita Sarfatti's invention, awarded Negri the Mussolini Prize. But not until 1940 did this all-male bastion elevate her to membership. After that, Negri too had the right to be called "Your Excellency," receive a monthly stipend, travel first class on a pass, carry a sword, and wear a plumed hat. In 1938 the commission of the annual Poets of the Epoch of Mussolini Contest conceded its first prize to the journalist Fanny Dini, a fascist of the first hour and in 1937 the first woman journalist to visit Italy's newest African acquisition; her winning entry was the lachrymose "Mother and Son" *(La madre e il figlio)*, celebrating an Italian mother's fortitude in the face of her son's death in Ethiopia. In spite of this accolade and her unceasing work as a journalist, Dini, who was unmarried, still earned only a thousand lire a month in

1941, with which she supported six persons.[33] In 1937 the exceptionally talented composer Barbara Giuranna won the first prize of the National Fascist Syndicate of Musicians for her symphonic poem *Decima legio*. Recently widowed and with a family to support, Giuranna was still thwarted in her attempts to win a conservatory professorship. This was in spite of the fact that her prizewinning composition had been performed sixteen times, counting its Milanese premiere at La Scala (which was ruined for her when a man in the audience shouted out, "Get a husband!").[34]

The virtual exclusion of women from the regime's highly visible patronage system seemed only to enhance the belief shared by cultured women that they were bound together by a separate and equal, if not superior, culture. This predisposition is not incomprehensible; being excluded from politics, intellectual women sought consolatory refuge in cultural pursuits. Beyond that, political powerlessness made them keenly sensitive to the exercise of female influence outside of the political system proper, for example, through the thriving female reading public of the interwar years. Since before the war, male attacks against what critic Ferdinando Zuccoli decried as the "periocolo roseo" or "rose menace," by which he meant the feminization of publishing, had accompanied the growing output of women's fiction and periodicals. Under the dictatorship, however, women writers and critics probed the meaning of this new fame. They were assisted by the well-documented columns on women writers in the *Almanacco della donna italiana* and other women's magazines with literary pretensions, not to mention Mario Gastaldi's accounts of the accomplishments of five hundred contemporary women writers, *Donne, luce d'Italia* (1930), and the volume *Poetesse e scrittrici* that Maria Bandini Buti compiled on behalf of the Academy of Italy's national biography project.[35] By 1938 Daria Banfi Malaguzzi, whose own literary successes had confirmed her belief in the power of publishing, concluded with relief (and not a little animus toward male literati) that "the position that women's literature has won in Italy is by now so vast and so rich as to impress even the most obstinately misogynist spirits. . . . The troops are now becoming ever more numerous, ever bolder."[36]

This victory was attributed, not incorrectly, to a socially constructed female sensibility that caused women writers to be "more modern." Male literati, as Banfi Malaguzzi pointed out, had social standing and a vested interest in tradition that bound them to the precious and provincial hermeticism prevailing in contemporary prose and poetic canons. By contrast, women writers, prompted by the need to maintain a rapport with their readers, observed daily life and spoke to issues such as love, maternity, social class, and race, which contemporary publics wanted to read about. In fact forerunners of neorealism under fascism, the writers Romano Bilenchi, Elio Vittorini, and Vasco Pratolini, made much the same point when pressing for a new populist literary canon. It was common in the 1930s especially for young male writers to look abroad for realist experimentations: the Americans Faulkner, Steinbeck, Sinclair Lewis, and James Cain were special favorites.[37] Italian female writers did. Their models were the Hungarian Jolán Földes, the American Helen Carlisle, and the British short-story writer Katherine Mansfield.[38] Daria Banfi Malaguzzi, who from the observation point of her Milanese salon (alongside her husband Antonio, the philosopher) was as acute and widely read a critic as one could imagine in fascist Italy, was ready to claim that women writers such as Bianca De Maj, Giana Anguissola, and Ada Negri were closer to the "new sensibility" of their female counterparts abroad than any major men writers were to Huxley, Mauriac, or Dos Passos.[39]

Whether this was true or not, novel writing had clearly become the single most important manifestation of the new female cultural politics by the second half of the twenties. Women publishing new works included the seasoned favorites Grazia Deledda, Matilde Serao, and Annie Vivanti, not to mention the famed Sibilla Aleramo. Unfortunately, the latter's quavery epistolary novel *Amo dunque sono* (1927) and self-pitying *Frustino* (1932) once more deluded the expectations to which twenty years earlier her feminist heart-cry *Una donna (A Woman)* had given rise. But politically engaged women too began to turn out fiction. In 1929 Margherita Sarfatti published her only novel, *Il palazzone*. In 1930, the year she died and one year after her forced retirement from political life, Elisa Majer Rizzioli finished *Quasi un romanzo*. And the numbers of so-called scribblers also multiplied: the standard sort was a fortyish bourgeois woman who, as a female critic unkindly mimicked, had always felt an "overwhelming, excruciating" vocation to write. But only now that family demands had become less pressing was she able, as the critic put it, to "dedicate myself a bit to me, to tell everything I feel inside."[40]

In the late 1920s, the subject matter and tone of female fiction changed with respect to the first years of the decade. The postwar "exhibitionism" of self had given way before a melancholy "involution." The femmes fatales with their Dannunzian sensuality were transmogrified; sad moralists, they were torn between passion and duty, "between enticing follies and the call of family, with the commendable triumph of the latter."[41] Ester Lombardo, always quick to size up and seize commercial advantage from mood shifts, changed tone in a thrice. In her titillating and hugely successful *Lettere d'Amore* (1925), her protagonists were the hard-nosed, demanding heroines of the postwar years. The countess Adela was typical. She wrote to her jilted lover, the musician Ermanno Lollini, "I betrayed you" because "I want a man who doesn't become enthralled in philosophical issues while making love to his woman nor become alarmed if he thinks about her when she's not with him."[42] In *La donna senza cuore*, published in 1928, Lombardo's protagonist was the embattled Anna Santi, a young woman who, after the death of her lover, forges ahead in the world as a banker. Comforted by the small boy she has adopted, betrayed by a man whom she loved and trusted, she has to make her own way in the end, "hardened against the snares of men; . . . covered like the winter landscape with an icy crown, but life, sentiments, illusions are not killed off. They nurture us like the earth, and will not die."[43]

Was this flight into fiction mere escapism? There was something so deliberate about the phenomenon that one observant contemporary characterized it as "a movement of sentiment," likening it to an outright political act. Images of self-denial, abject renunciations of love and happiness, were not political acts, of course. Yet sometimes fantasies of subordination enable people to avenge themselves on the world, while they appear fatalistic about their lot. Masochism, it has been observed, is a "form of adaption to an unsatisfactory and circumscribed life." It is one of the strategies people use to convince themselves that constraints are really opportunities.[44] By the late 1920s, female novels in Italy were peopled with sad heroines: loving women jilted by caddish men, aspiring artists forced to choose between career and family, hapless orphans seduced and abandoned. That otherwise emancipated Italian women should now have resorted to such subterfuges, stooping to claim a monopoly over self-sacrifice and morality in order to assert themselves, not unnaturally bothered staunch feminists. Maria Maggi, the morose young pedagogue who edited the National Fascist Teachers' Association's weekly *Cultura fascista*, mocked this affected complaisance: the protagonist of the new fiction "hurriedly retreated into the secrecy of her home, barred the doors and windows, relit the spent hearth, gave without asking, waited patiently, became mother, wife, heroine, and taught morality to one and all."[45] Yet Maggi too subscribed to these painful canons and perhaps to their subversive spirit as well. Her own protaganists—particularly the painter, Enrica Maspero, and the impoverished clerk, Ada, of her 1927 novel *Circolo della vita*—lived utterly joyless lives, deluded on every occasion they aspired to achieve independence and happiness.

Teresa Labriola also thought that this passionate female complicity with restored morality might be a means to garner power. She made the point in a fleeting comparison between Sibilla Aleramo's famed *A Woman* (1907) and *Le catene* (1930), the acclaimed novel of the gifted Molisan writer Lina Pietravalle. In *A Woman*, Labriola identified a powerful spirit of "resistance"; in *Le catene*, "an effort at finding peace . . . but without consensus from the 'depth' of the female spirit." The latter attitude was at least as disquieting a critique of the gender order as the former.[46] Aleramo's lightly fictionalized autobiography told of the emancipationist striving of an unnamed northern woman. The eldest daughter of a Milanese businessman, she had been thrust into the Italian south when her father transferred jobs. There she had been raped by an employee and forced to marry him and bear his child. Ultimately she deserted him for freedom, but at the cost of renouncing her son. Labriola, like Aleramo herself, interpreted this escape in the name of emancipation as causing an irrevocable loss; the woman gained freedom, but at the cost of peace of mind, and the anxieties augmented as the years passed, her female spirit diminished rather than enhanced by the suffering. Pietravalle, by contrast, gloried in the entangling patriarchy of the Italian south. Her protagonist, Felicia, was the unquiet scion of the aristocratic Caldoro, a family whose psychic and physical deformities, rendered with Faulknerian grotesquery, reflected "the clashes and contrasts of an opulent, perfidious race, rich in the fatalism imperative to obey laws of immemorial sway, commanded by God and time." Felicia, separated from her scapegrace of a husband, her stern father having been murdered by a crazed communist peasant, her daughter Giuliva entrusted to a Neapolitan convent-school, sought to throw off the patriarchal chains in quest of amorous pleasures in northern Italy. But the death of a beloved nephew and the need to defend the family honor besmirched by her inept spouse's arrest for bank fraud once more brought her home to the manor. Yet this was no return to conventional domestic roles; passion was not being subordinated to morality. Felicia returns as the first female head of the Caldoro, her powers are those once assigned to the patriarch, namely, to restore wounded honor, repair the family fortunes, and ready her own daughter for duty. Giuliva, brought home in the final scene, consoles her mother with a rending love song, *La ritornata*:

> I come to revere you, beflowered one.
> Let my refrain make you welcome.
> Every moment, I sought after you,
> Tear you from my mind I could not,
> Every moment, captive to my pains,
> And now I am back once more in chains.

Ti vengo a riverire, ingarofanata
La ritornata mia ti consaluta,
Ora per ora aio domandato,
Dismenticare a voi non ho potuto,
Or per ora un carcere di pene,
E ritornato sono alle catene.[47]

Acquiescing to her destiny, Felicia acquires power but not fulfillment: she accepts the restored order, but without "consent from the depth" of her spirit.

That the clever Margherita Sarfatti should have used her own 1929 foray into novel writing to legitimate the fascist restoration—not just in the social order but also in the domain of sexual politics—suggests that she had a good understanding of, if no sympathy for, her contemporaries' fictional subterfuges. Already known to a mass public for her bestselling *Dux* (1926), Mussolini's first authorized biography, and with a sizeable following among intellectual men for her cultural criticism, Sarfatti had no particular affection for a "female republic of letters." She did not, however, share the views of her male colleagues when they spluttered against "female literature consisting of chlorotic women, latter-day Bovarys, the misunderstood, the confused . . . a terribly antidomestic literature . . . our poor socks, poor sauce, poor wash."[48] Yet her novel, *Il palazzone*, in its grasp of the prevailing formulas and its determination not to accede to them, suggested nothing so much as the enlightened male fascist's view of love and struggle in the new order. Sarfatti's story told of the fortunes of the spirited young Fiorella Maggi. The orphan of a wealthy and industrious Milanese family (the father of which, an engineer, had perished in a mining disaster because of the "disobedience of some workers"), Fiorella had been welcomed into the home of the noble family Valdeschi of Brianza: the old count was a troubling, melancholic figure; the older son, Manlio, a bull-like fellow with "enormous and prolongued strength of tolerance"; the feline young Sergio, outgoing and selfish. A conventional love story, Sarfatti's novel was self-evidently a parable about the new Italy: the vivacious Fiorella, who at first contact with the chivalric world of the Palazzone "never talked so much about herself, her sentiments and concerns," soon discovers that the old regime is riven with incomprehensibly perverse passions that culminate in the old count's suicide. She marries Sergio, abandoning herself in a jealous love that ends only when the young war hero, an *ardito*, is killed after volunteering for an assault mission in the war's final battle. At last, with Manlio, a powerful and patiently constructive figure, she finds a new relationship. This is consummated in a world that is right-ing itself after the vicissitudes of the Great War and the "red years." In this new world in the making, a woman once more becomes "woman, woman, woman, unremittingly woman!" and a man with "imperious sureness of tone" is once more capable of commanding "Say that you're mine. Say it, that you love me. Answer!" before leading his troops off at dawn to punish the effrontery of the plebs by assaulting a nearby *casa del popolo*.[49]

Sarfatti's story of companionate happiness in a restored social order was too contrived as well as too overtly political to garner much success. If it tells of her effort to reach out to women, the truth remains that the world in which she sought success was largely male. Margherita's intellectual vivacity was hard for most women to deal with (not unlike the "virile genius" of Teresa Labriola). She "wants to know everything, that is her constant attitude. . . . She argues over everything, not a problem escapes her."[50] And as powerful as she was, Sarfatti was diffident and jealous of other women. When she would later visit the United States, one of the features of women's lives that would most surprise her was the "affectionate expansiveness toward one another," "the immediate and cordial solidarity," unlike in the old world, where women looked at other women "with diffidence, if not preconceived antipathy," until their rivalries were reconciled.[51] Not that Sarfatti did anything to allay the distrust of other women. As promoter of the *Novecento* art movement, she never demonstrated any particular attention to women, except to determine whether they threatened her power. On one occasion as a member of a prize jury, she opposed awarding the prize to a woman, Fanny Dini, whom she accused of plagiarizing her work.[52] Nor would Sarfatti have admitted of any special female sensibility in art or culture. Not the least of the evidence for this is that in the decade she headed *Gerarchia*, she published but three articles by other women, and the only political commentary on women's issues (other than her own dismissive treatment of the 1925 election reform) was an innocuous bit, dedicated to the women's *fasci*, by an old family acquaintance, the aged Venetian pedagogue Maria Pezzè Pascolato.

The more practical struggle to articulate a new woman's culture was meanwhile going on in the far-flung network of clubs and circles which hosted expositions, talks, libraries, and concerts and in which Italy's refined "female intellectuality" met weekly in the late afternoons and evenings to hear poetry readings, talks, and debates. Some associations were in the old style. For the "cultivated genteel ladies and worthy professional women" of Florence, there was the venerable old Lyceum, whose "numerous, choice public" was presided over by the Princess of Piedmont; it was the oldest of a national circuit of sister institutions, with other seats in Rome, Genoa, Catania, and Milan. At Turin, the seventeen to eighteen hundred women members of the *Società pro cultura femminile* embraced a broader social spectrum—from the most refined aristocrat to the modest clerk. The circle, founded in 1912 and headed by Lea Mei in the 1920s, was particularly proud of its 16,000-volume library and its special section of works in braille.

The two most recently founded organizations were especially attuned to women's widespread demand for cultural pastimes. On October 21, 1930, Luigia Pirovano, an intrepid thirty-five-year-old school teacher from Genoa, launched an entirely new national network called the Italian Female Cultural Alliance *(Alleanza muliebre culturale italiana)*. In the next two years, it expanded to twenty sections with a considerable following. Of course Pirovano made it plain that this was no feminist outfit; she intended to avoid creating "useless adversaries" in the process of inculcating a "spirit of sacrifice, rigorous morality, and intellectual and cultural seriousness" among her followers. Still, she distanced herself from "feminine antifeminism," and the group circulated petitions protesting discrimination against women workers.[53] Moreover, her ambition to build a support network for women of working-class and small bourgeois backgrounds—who had been kept from higher studies by family poverty or bias and were thus frustrated both by limited career choices and by scarce cultural opportunities—was implicitly critical not just of the old FILDIS but also of the regime's own recently founded, yet already haughtily patronizing National Fascist Association of Women Artists and Degree Holders.

The latter organization, ANFAL, was by the mid-1930s, in terms of following and political visibility, the most important female cultural grouping under the dictatorship. Founded in 1929 by Roman women, including Adelina Pertici Pontecorvo (who hosted its inaugural meeting at her salon in Palazzo Altieri), it was led through most of the next decade by its main promoter and president, Maria Castellani. The very model of the modern fascist professional woman, Castellani, who was then in her early thirties, had been trained in mathematics, and she had numerous contacts abroad, especially in the United States, where she had studied, and in Geneva, where she had headed the League of Nations' accounting office. Her decision to found the organization was stimulated by the visit of the American representative of the International Professional Women's Organization to Italy in 1927. The inauguration of both the Rome and Milanese sections in 1929 was made to coincide with receptions in honor of Alice Garrett, wife of the new United States ambassador to Italy and a member of the parent organization. An excellent propagandist for the regime who possessed a "vivacious and enthusiastic temperament," Castellani earned the full confidence of Giuseppe Bottai, then Undersecretary of the Corporations. In February 1930 he charged her group with representing professional women in the National Fascist Syndicate of Professionals and Artists. With already eighty sections in 1934, ANFAL promoted a nationwide network of "cultivated women," reaching out into smaller centers, to bring together women who previously—and perhaps still—felt that flight to the big towns alone would liberate them from the torpid provincialism of small-town life. Crafts fairs, painting expositions, and conferences thus created "a healthy atmosphere of female engagement and collaboration with the mighty fascist cultural activity." Thereby, such gatherings promoted greater self-awareness about the meaning of being "Italian women."[54]

Those were indeed years of many "firsts" for bourgeois women's culture: there was the first exposition entirely devoted to women's work at Milan, the Women's Show of the Pure, Decorative, and Craft Arts organized by Elisa Majer Rizzioli in 1929. There were the first regional and provincial shows for women painters and sculptresses sponsored by ANFAL. There was the great Show of Summer Colonies and Children's Welfare on June 20, 1937; its opening events, according to the Duce, who inaugurated it before 60,000 fascist women, "had no precedents in the history of the world . . . for the style, immensity, above all, for the ardor [of the public]."[55]

There were also the first volumes of national biography devoted to women, edited under the auspices of the Academy of Italy. One, edited by Maria Bandini Buti, was devoted to women writers; the other was dedicated to "Heroines, Inspirers, and Exceptional Women." This was directed by the fascist academician Francesco Orestano, who had the good grace to thank his female researchers for this "first—and hence laborious—effort at a roundup of Italian women." There was something disingenuous about Orestano's prefatory remarks, to the effect that conventional history, by focusing exclusively on the founders of states and religions, military *condottieri*, rulers, and pioneers in various fields of endeavor, had "made no place for woman except to the degree to which she fit into one or the other male category"; he also recognized the difficulty of undertaking research since "chroniclers and historians rarely stopped as long as necessary to illustrate the female moment in history." Or worse, they remembered the "sad notoriety" of the likes of Lucrezia Borgia. In the end, the twenty-five hundred or so entries were composed with conservative good faith, to highlight the "exemplary conduct," the "silent suffering," the "heroic sacrifices without histrionics," and the "efficient purpose" of the majority.[56] "Illustrious mothers" were of course well-represented in the volume. But readers might also refer to the entry on Cristina di Belgioioso, founder of Italian women's emancipation, or to the business pioneer Giulia Buitoni (1781–1877), founder of the famous Borgo San Sepolcro pasta firm. There were the great female saints, Santa Scolastica, Santa Chiara, and Santa Caterina of Siena, the last presented as mediator between the Republic of Florence and Gregory XI. And there were the heroines and martyrs of the Risorgimento, Luisa di San Felice, Eleanora Fonseca Pimental, and Teresa Confalonieri. For those familiar with monumental public histories, there was nothing extraordinary about this cultural operation. However, in fascist Italy, it signaled that the history of the Italian woman was being integrated into the history of the race and nation; she had been present, from the beginning, since the putative founding of the Italian *stirpe* in the distant Roman past.

To argue that the female cultural politics that lay behind such initiatives was conservative or oppositional would be to miss the complexity and ambiguity of subcultures generally and their significance in defining citizenship, especially under authoritarian regimes.[57] At one level, female cultural politics was surely protective and nurturing; it offered a means to restore self-esteem, to safeguard autonomy, and to articulate new female identities across generations and among women in Italy's very diverse regions. By supporting contacts abroad, albeit under official aegis, it fed an unquenchable female cosmopolitanism in the face of fascist nationalism. It seemed to nurture an inner confidence that girded cultivated, middle-class women against the regnant antifeminism. In general, there was a tacit policy not to dignify antifeminist sloganeering with a response, unless it had particular political resonance, like Manlio Pompei's refrain "three, five, ten times mother," which a leading fascist functionary, the journalist Wanda Gorjux, blasted not just because it was given prominence in Bottai's reform-minded *Critica fascista* but because it circulated in Roman salons.[58] In a society in which public discourse had become so debased, one can imagine older women saying soothingly, "words are meaningless, what counts is influence." There is something to be said for this stoic posture, though whether it betokened self-confidence or resignation is not easy to tell.

At another level, the world of "cultured women" was smug, snobbish, and insular. Its very existence depended on a certain kind of self-selectivity; as Daria Banfi Malaguzzi once appreciated, "the typical element is the modern woman with a small family or better yet free of family engagements."[59] The newer organizations, it is true, tended to promote a greater self-consciousness about, if not a more inclusive definition of, who was cultured. Thus Castellani's constituency, which embraced women professionals and artists, was wider than that, say, of FILDIS. The latter was limited to degree holders, and would thus have excluded the genteel *artista*, whose talents had been honed in a convent school or by the family governess. But neither organization welcomed the young seamstress or the unemployed technical school graduate, whose cultural strivings were at least as strong. Still, under the dictatorship, the identification of female culture with the humanistic pursuits of women of the aristocracy or rentier classes gave way to a more encompassing and activist notion—one nurtured by professionals, party and social welfare functionaries, and middle-class women with *lauree* but with no prospects or intention to work; their interests included painting but also handicrafts and musical soirées, not to mention conferences on the state of the empire and on women's and children's welfare in the era of Mussolini. Accordingly, female cultural activism purported to enhance women as individuals and citizens; it was neither a futile pastime nor a reflection of the old-time female vocation to safeguard humanistic culture from the debased utilitarianism of contemporary life.

The Politics of Social Work

When in December 1930 PNF secretary Giuriati decreed the regime's intention to found new cadres of social workers, called *visitatrici fasciste*, fascist women were plainly pleased. Labriola had never been one to see charity as the main object of female political activity. However, as plans became more concrete in the following months—to culminate on May 26, 1931, when the PNF ordered the women's groups to take charge of "assistance"—she labeled the measure "healthy fascism and healthy feminism." It was "healthy fascism" insofar as it offered "recognition of the existence of the diverse types making up the whole of our complex and articulated society." The winter Labriola spoke that phrase, the first sad lines of the jobless were forming at soup kitchens and employment offices; we must suppose that Labriola was alluding to the fact that fascist women were discovering that Mussolini's corporate society still contained rich and poor. Giuriati's move was "healthy feminism" in that it testified to "a female destination beyond the domestic conflixes." [60]

That Labriola and many other emancipated women still felt obliged to insist that it was woman's right and duty to do social work is rather a surprise. At least since 1925, the fascist hard line seemed to have won out, that is, fascist women were supposed to eschew politics to dedicate themselves exclusively to volunteer work. However, the issue was not so simply resolved. As the PNF became the governing party, it discovered that well-directed relief work offered an expedient means to pay back political debts and undercut political rivals. Barely had fascist women been assigned the cause of charity in 1925, when they were rankled to discover that the party was doling out monies to favorites and assigning newly released funds to state agencies over which women had no say, such as ONMI or the National Fascist Institute for Social Insurance.[61] Moreover, fascist women themselves were tempted to treat volunteer work not as a gesture of selflessness, but as an act of social politics, the end being, like that of practical feminism, to widen women's influence and win them citizenship rights. By the 1930s, such activist interpretations of the purposes of social work had run up against a new reality: the changing nature of philanthropy with the rise of the welfare state. As Mussolini's corporatist order boasted the triumph of the brave new world of totalitarian "social reclamation" *(bonifica sociale)* over the piecemeal handouts of the old "benefaction," bourgeois women whose very notions of volunteer work had been formed in another era had to come to terms with new definitions of social protection, impersonal administrative hierarchies, and complex and vast regulatory minutiae.

As the frontline figure in fascism's war against poverty, the *visitatrice fascista* was pivotal in the shift from one system to another. In her early 1930s incarnation, she was basically an upper-class do-gooder. To ladle out soup at the people's messes *(ranci del popolo)*, greet clients, and lend a hand at party headquarters or municipal day camps, she needed no training; it sufficed to choose her from among "those ladies who, for intelligence, tact, or familiarity with the people and its needs, are best suited to perform this lofty task effectively."[62] These women served staunchly, according to Maria Pezzè Pascolato, the Venetian educator and children's book writer who headed the province's women's groups until her death in 1933: in spite of having "a beautiful, comfortable, and well-heated home, [they] spend hours and hours each day in a squalid little room, dressed in their overcoats (they don't wear furs to the office out of embarrassment in the face of such poor rags . . .), listening to trials and tribulations until late in the day . . . and [they] return home dead tired . . . sometimes to find awaiting them requests for statistical data from the *fiduciario* or party *federale.*" Although their sacrifices were ill-appreciated by party men, not to mention their male family members, volunteer work evidently offered them great personal satisfaction.[63]

By the late 1930s, however, the *visitatrice* was a full-fledged party social worker. The cadres had graduated from training programs devised in cooperation with the Italian Red Cross, wore uniforms, and were salaried. Much of the responsibility for professionalizing the service lay with the noblewoman Itta Stelluti Scala Frascara, a professional nurse, who had studied pediatrics in London, knew four languages, and showed an idiosyncratic, if not audacious, streak by frequently writing on social work topics under a male pseudonym, Elio Silvestri. She had been a member of the PNF since 1927. In 1933 she was appointed fiduciary of the Roman women's groups. In 1937, along with Clara Franceschini, she was named the first national inspectress of the *fasci;* her special assignment was to act as liaison between party-run charities and the royal patronesses of the Italian Red Cross.[64] In 1937, as party winter-help programs were turned over to local municipalities, the *visitatrici* were charged with running town clinics and day-care programs. By the end of the decade, a few thousand young women had studied Wanda Scimone's 400-page tome *Nozioni per visitatrici* and had graduated from training courses. The model graduate, as Angiola Moretti, head of the party social work schools, described her when presenting the most recent class to Queen Elena in May 1940, combined "the noblest traditions" with a sense of the "modernity of the present"; she was a "bundle of active forces, yet rich with ulterior energy to fill her home with poetry," "a creature of virile courage, yet of rare femininity."[65] Once graduated, the young women ran soup kitchens, sewing circles, craft shops, summer colonies, and job placement offices for women, as well as snooping into the private lives of families whose economic misery, moral failings, or bad health singled them out for home visits.

This transformation in women's voluntarism was of course tied to the broader changes that the very concept of social obligations underwent during the dictatorship. For women raised in the tradition of philanthropic feminism, benefaction involved moral, as opposed to legal, obligations. Its conduct was by nature voluntary, personally involving, and intermittent. That *beneficenza* was necessary at all reflected badly on the nature of the society. All the same, the opportunity to do good forged bonds of social human solidarity as well as female networks. To the inexpert eye *assistenza sociale,* or social work, may have looked as if it offered the same, if not greater, opportunities for doing good; only it was more systematic and had a wider outreach. In fact, it made a very different argument about the nature of society: poverty was the fault neither of the bosses nor the workers; and social insurance was the only rational way of coping with the inevitable risks of modern society.[66] Moreover, once *assistenza sociale* was harnessed to the ends of an all-encompassing *previdenza sociale,* it would be guided by the science of experts operating through well-defined bureaucratic channels. Inevitably, its advocates had little patience with the sentimental do-gooding and unscientific maternalist ethos behind female philanthropy.

What bourgeois women hoped to achieve from service was thus inevitably complicated. They could not but cheer the dictatorship for its measures—fascist propaganda ensured that nobody ever questioned that the liberal state was wholly neglectful of its citizenry whereas Mussolini's corporate order safeguarded people's rights. Yet this massive state intervention was interpreted differently, according to whether women were staunch party loyalists or were from social Catholic or liberal philanthropic traditions. The former emphasized a military-like discipline: "To be truly present, you need to stay in rank—become a soldier—albeit without a knapsack or gun, your march step never failing, as strong at seventy as at twenty," was Marquess Irene Giunti di Targiani's stern message to her students. They had to throw off their "society dress" for the "uniform of discipline." "Private initiatives," this authoritarian Piedmontese admonished, "have value only if coordinated, if subordinated to discipline, faith; otherwise they run the risk of feeding individual egoism."[67] By contrast, one-time practitioners of liberal feminism, though they welcomed the modern and indispensable social practice that social work had become, were suspicious of becoming cogs in the wheel of a vast overweening bureaucracy. Whereas male theorists such as Ugo Manunta regarded social work as a transitory phase on the path toward perfecting the system of claims and dispensations of the welfare state, Olga Modigliani argued that women volunteers remained indispensable, for they alone could identify "deficiencies where they exist and study improvements in social work."[68] Likewise, Dr. Giulia Boni lectured Pisan women that female voluntarism complemented state action: "True, the state has to intervene in many cases because it alone can prescribe the norms, but private initiative is indispensable . . . to fill the inevitable lacunae in state provisions and to . . . go beyond the limits set by state action." Like Modigliani, Boni insisted that women alone were equipped for this purpose, for "the woman is more and better able than a man to penetrate the secrets of others' hearts and to comprehend their real emotions, much as a mother's vigilant eye and tender heart intuits both the needs of her baby and the hidden passions and afflictions of her fully grown son."[69]

No matter what their political provenance, all women involved in volunteer work insisted that women had both the right and the obligation to serve outside the home. "It's a false preconception," Boni insisted, that women involved in social work "neglect their families and lose their femininity." Women's "contribution to civic life and well-being" was accomplished by ministering as wife and mother, but also by caring for the afflicted. Indeed, a woman who because of "apathy" or "egotism" *only* did housework, using her leisure to hang about knitting, failed to fulfill her social duties. The modern woman had to act outside of the "narrow domestic walls," provided of course she didn't "waste time and energies in vain feminism or masculinize herself by usurping the functions of the man, whose competitor she was not, but faithful collaborator, following and comforting him in the bitter circumstances of life."[70] In sum, circuitously, with repeated protestations of political faith, always insisting that their primary obligations to family and spouse were being fulfilled and with no illusions that their contributions entitled them to special privileges, Latin feminists claimed that service was their way to be political.

By 1937 the Duce himself recognized that women wielded a new public power. On June 20 he welcomed the sixty thousand fascist women who had congregated at the Circus Maximus to inaugurate the Show on Fascist Welfare and Colonies as "protagonists of a political event." True, they were first and foremost "custodians of the hearth." But fascism counted on them for something more: "for its action of national and social assistance to reach from the cities to the countryside." Rehearsing his well-worn rhetoric of participation on the female crowd, the Duce boomed out: "Can the regime always rely on you for the work of the future, which we hope will be peaceable? (The multitude shouts, 'Yes! Yes!') On your discipline? ('Yes! Yes!') On your faith? (The fascist women shout out an enthusiastic, super-vibrant 'Yes!') Then I say to you that there will be no obstacles to the triumphal march of the Italian people."[71]

How to reward this service was another issue. In 1938 Mussolini was tempted to propose that women be represented in the much ballyhooed Chamber of Fasces and Corporations, but King Victor Emmanuel vetoed the idea. Also in 1938, an inspectress, the stalwart Clara Franceschini, was named to serve in the Party Directory, but that too failed to come about.[72] Indeed, the growth of female activism must have troubled the fascist old guard. It was but another instance of the bread and circus politics of the much despised Starace. A political party whose reason for being was relief and entertainment was not only a depoliticized movement but an emasculated one as well. To restore tone to the PNF's flaccid bureaucracy, the diehards wanted Starace ousted, an event which finally occurred in November 1939, and the PNF to be reinvigorated along the lines of Hitler's all-powerful NSDAP.

Paradoxes of Fascist Female Politics

By the outbreak of World War II, the so-called women's organization of the Fascist party counted approximately 3,180,000 members: 750,000 mostly middle-class women were in the *fasci femminili;* there were 1,480,000 rural housewives; a half-million working-class women were in the SOLD; and 450,000 in the *giovani fasciste.* This was equal to a quarter of the female population aged twenty and over. In large measure, the drive to incorporate women in party organizations paralleled the dictatorship's ef-

Angiola Moretti (left) and Wanda Gorjux address fascist women. (*Giornale della donna* 12, nos. 12–13 [July 1930]. Reprinted courtesy of the National Library of Florence.)

fort to organize the entire society. Uneven during the 1920s, quickening after 1932, especially during the 1935–36 mobilization against the League of Nation's sanctions, the pace of recruiting women picked up dramatically after January 1937, when the PNF, with order of the day 696, commanded that "the maximum impulse [be given] to fascism among Italian women." (See chart 3, p. 248.) But women's relation to the fascist order was fundamentally different from that of other groups. For women had been identified above all with the social realm, with private life, with the family. To rally them called for the dictatorship to exact claims on women's time, resources, and sentiments, the effects of which ran counter to its deeply held antifeminist impulses, as well as the conviction that women's "custody of the hearth" was indispensable to national welfare.

This fundamental paradox was reflected in how the Fascist party organized women. Like other fascist organizations, such as the after-work clubs or the student GUF, the women's auxiliaries were ruled by hierarchical chains of command. Yet women leaders never acquired the power that the male leaders accrued. One thinks of Renato Ricci, head of the ONB, Tullio Cianetti at the National Fascist Industrial Workers' Syndicates, or even Enrico Beretta, director of the OND. Nor was there any lady *Führer über Alles* of the likes of Gertrud Scholtz Klink, head of the Nazi's Women's

Left: Countess Daisy di Robilant. (*Bulletin of the International Council of Women* 2 [March 7, 1933]. Reprinted courtesy of the Butler Library, Columbia University.) *Right:* Maria Castellani, head of ANFAL. (*Almanacco della donna italiana, 1931.* Reprinted courtesy of the Barnard College Library.)

Left: Anna Maria Giusti Dalla Rosa, fascist national inspectress, 1941. *Right:* Olga Medici del Vascello, fascist national inspectress, 1941. (*Frauentreffen in Berlin vom 7. bis 11. Oktober, 1941* [Munich: Obpacher, n.d.]. Both reprinted courtesy of the Butler Library, Columbia University.)

Bureau, who, although low on the NSDAP organizational chart, boasted of regular conversations with Hitler. Except for Angiola Moretti, whose brief stay as secretary of the women's *fasci* ended with Turati's ouster as party secretary in 1930, the women's organization never had a true national leader. Indeed, it did not even have a national oversight committee until January 1937 when the PNF appointed the first two party inspectresses, Clara Franceschini and Itta Stelluti Scala Frascara, to supervise the provincial fiduciaries and their *colluboratrici*. In 1938 Starace appointed four more: Wanda Bruschi Gorjux, a prominent journalist and cultural organizer, long active in Apulia, Laura Marani Argnani, the former fiduciary of Reggio Emilia, Olga Medici del Vascello of Genoa, and Teresita Menzinger Ruata, the head of the National Association of Families of War Dead and Wounded.[73] Like lesser party functionaries, women leaders had to master the art of writing ingratiating letters and passing ahead in the antecamera; those inspectresses with noble titles were sure to emblazon them, along with their party functions and professional rank, on their calling cards. No doubt, women leaders, by living in the close-knit, gossipy world of the capital, were well-connected to official channels through their spouses or shared social circles and were thus informed of the twists and turns of party policy-making. But the big decisions were handed down by the men on top. There is no evidence that the advice of female leaders was ever sought on any major issue regarding women: not in 1929, when the *piccole* and *giovani italiane* were handed over to Renato Ricci's ONB, nor in 1930, when the women's *dopolavoro* was detached from the men's and its 100,000 members were given to the OND; not in 1933, when it was decided to found the *massaie rurali*, nor in 1938, when the PNF launched the special Sections for Factory and Household Workers (SOLD). The men in charge, first and foremost Starace, dictated the little details as well: from the fabric to be used for uniforms to the stitches designing the banner and flame on the SOLD's neckerchiefs.

Fascism's traditionalism in the domain of female politics was equally manifest in how it chose women leaders. Since the early 1920s, fascists seemed to feel especially at home around titled women. The various *principesse*, *contessine*, and *marchese* selected to head local committees added lustre to provincial events. Their presence also signaled that the old elites had compromised themselves with the parvenu regime. High-born women must also have been reassuringly delicate when advancing what occasionally looked like excessively feminist demands. As late as 1935, the social provenance of the ninety provincial fiduciaries was a cut above that of the PNF *federali*: 20 percent were titled and another 30 percent were doctors, lawyers, or professors. Half of the first six inspectresses were nobles (though

Teresita Menzinger's baronetcy was allegedly usurped from her dead husband's family). Angiola Moretti, who in 1940 was appointed inspectress, married the fascist notable Count Nestore Carosi-Martinozzi in 1938, adding his title to her own as middle-school teacher and inspectress. Of the five others added from 1938 to 1940, three, Anna Maria Giusti Dalla Rosa of Cremona, Ignazia Cavalli d'Olivola, and Sofia Bertaina Chiesa di Cervignasco, were aristocrats.[74]

The propensity to treat women leaders as partners in patriarchy rather than as professional organizers perpetuated women's exclusion from bureaucratic power and perquisites. Male party functionaries were well-paid and could be expected to pick up a second or third salary, not to mention whatever could be accrued from plain corruption. But women's stipends were pieced together. This represented no problem for rich aristocrats such as Olga Medici del Vascello, wife of Giacomo, Mussolini's chief of cabinet, or Itta Stelluti Scala Frascara, who had real estate in Rome in addition to big landholdings in the Abbruzzi region. But the stipends of many others were paid by virtue of their onetime employment by the Ministry of National Education, at least until the war. This posed a certain problem, since the school system discriminated against promoting women to higher ranks and salary levels, as the case of the inspectress Rachele Ferrari del Latte demonstrated. She was the widow of a prominent fascist of the first hour, and at her father's death in 1933 she became the sole support of her family. In 1939, to obtain the rank of school inspector, from which she would have been routinely excluded because of her sex, she had to plead with Mussolini's personal secretary Sebastiani to intercede in her favor.[75]

Ultimately, fascism's suspicion of female politics could not but inhibit the cohesiveness of the women's groups. Having wreaked havoc on the networks of friendship and interest that underlay the first *fasci*, the PNF belatedly rebuilt them as a national mass organization. Thus, it was not until May 27, 1935, with PNF directive number 408, that Starace highlighted the *fasci's* national character by ordering prominent women leaders to give speeches before women in other provinces. Not until December 1937 did the party directory provide its fiduciaries with automobiles, the Fiat 1100, without which it was nearly impossible for them to tour outlying rural centers.[76]

In the end, fascism's organization of women as political citizens rested on a fundamental paradox, one that can be traced back to fascism's own contradictory definitions of female citizenship. Women's duty was maternity; their primary vocation was to procreate, nurture, and manage familial functions in the interest of the state. Yet to perform this duty, they needed to be responsive to the public weal; they needed to be conscious of societal expectations and the effects of their essentially individual acts on the collectivity. This need required that women be engaged outside of the household. Moreover, the PNF, mobilizing ever larger crowds to demonstrate public support, became obsessed with numbers. Women, though excluded from consultation in the plebiscites of 1929 and 1936, could be tallied up to display totalitarianism's organizational might. Consequently, the very women who had been consigned to and declared protagonists of the social domain were fetched out of it, to be fashioned into a fresh, apparently malleable constituency. As members of mass organizations were they beholden to the Duce-patriarch? or to their own organizational hierarchies? subordinate to male superiors in the PNF or to their female leaders? wholly self-effacing in sacrificing for national causes or serving their own self-interests to promote organizational solidarity? The mass organizations of women ultimately reflected unresolved tensions within the dictatorship over how to define women in the Italian state. These reflected in an acute form the dilemma of modern states generally insofar as they assign females to the private and social for procreative purposes, yet pretend participation in the public interest in part to achieve those very ends.

As a result of the dictatorship's ambivalence, the organization of women was a tenuous effort. Subcultures and networks that rose up to protect women as individuals and groups escaped governmental control, undermining the logic of a totalizing national politics. Only when the militarization of Italian society collapsed the distinctions between private duty and public service, and between personal self-abnegation and social sacrifice, was fascism able to reconcile modernity and tradition. Under the Duce, the path out of the household led not to emancipation but to new duties toward family and state, not to autonomy but to obedience to new masters.

On the eve of World War II, historic feminism had been obliterated, even in memory, and fascist female politics was ever more cravenly subaltern. In November 1938 the last surviving organizations that had sought to reconcile fascism and feminism were disbanded and their Jewish members banished from public service by the racial laws. Among the latter was Olga Modigliani, soon to flee into exile. In the name of the Duce, the nation, and a spurious class solidarity, the *fasci femminili* renounced any pretense of sisterhood among women. In December of 1938, Rachele Ferrari del Latte offered her cadres' "expert competence, their limpid honesty, their serious conduct" to address a pressing national issue: to place all of the servants who had been compelled to leave Jewish homes under the terms of the racial laws. Her organization embarked on this mission with zeal, out of the conviction that "in the near future, our servants will personally come to understand their great good fortune at having been able to free themselves from the influence, the insidiousness, the domination of the avid Jewish race to develop as Italians and Christians in homes where they think, believe, work, and live with an Italian spirit."[77]

9 There Will Come a Day

The home front is the family front . . . that our women rule
with age-old understanding and European balance. . . .
[T]hrough their voices, needs, sacrifices, and faith in the future
are translated into the simple language of everyday life.

Critica fascista (January 1, 1941)

I never said, "I'm doing it for myself, for my future. . . . At
best I said . . . "Let me save this one, he's a mother's son just
like mine," my hope being that somebody would treat my
own with the same care.

Amelia Maccarnelli, Resistance worker

Ada De Morvi, a forty-seven-year-old Milanese, to add weight to her protest against the anti-Semitic Manifesto of the Race, began her letter to "His Excellency" Mussolini by detailing who she was. An Italian woman belonging to the Roman Catholic apostolic faith, she was the mother of several children, knew the satisfactions of work well done, and was an ardent patriot as well. In 1914 she had backed Italy's intervention in the Great War to save "invaded" France and "heroic" Belgium from impudent "bullies." In 1919 she had draped the tricolor from the window to shame "the reds with their ignorant bluster." She had long admired Mussolini, and she "still admired his social provisions and the audacity with which he conquered the Empire." Yet the "oppression of the individual" had always horrified her. Consequently, she "couldn't understand" him since the previous July when the regime unleashed its campaign against Italian Jews. Castigating Mussolini for failing to stop the "hypocritical incitement to hatred"—which set 41,960,000 Italians against 40,000 of their own kind—De Morvi recalled the awful fate of Manzoni's despotic Don Rodrigo. She envisaged Mussolini alone in his huge study at Palazzo Venezia, and before him, Brother Christopher. The saintly man pleaded with the Duce to stop the "dreadful persecution," and when ignored, he burst out, "There will come a day," his fierce words foretelling the tyrant's downfall.[1]

The Women's Resistance

In its boldness, De Morvi's protest could hardly be regarded as a typical manifestation of public sentiment. True enough, the anti-Semitic measures with their resemblance to the Nazi Nuremberg Laws seemed outlandish to many people. Even before they were passed, starting in November of 1938, local party leaders and policies spies, as well as the underground opponents of fascism had begun to pick up on the myriad expressions of disaffection as the regime's popularity crested in the wake of the Ethiopian war.[2] But few people acted with De Morvi's startling sense of impunity. Mainly they muttered, fearful that police informers would overhear them and that they would be summoned to party headquarters, reprimanded, and, if they were men, shoved around, beaten up, and maybe jailed as well.

Yet De Morvi's protest combined two qualities that made it emblematic of the resistance of Italian women under the dictatorship. One was her reference to modern notions of citizenship; the other was her appeal to old-fashioned family and religious values. From the outset, this severe Catholic woman justified her right to speak out on the grounds that she had fulfilled her duties to family and nation. She specified that she was a mother. But she gave equal weight to being a patriotic and hard-working citizen. Furthermore, she believed what the dictatorship itself had repeatedly affirmed and never so loudly as during the war against Ethiopia: that all Italians whose loyalty had been proven by taking part in the "major events of national history"—from the Great War to the Anti-Sanctions Campaign—shared exactly the same rights.

At the same time, there was an archaic quality to De Morvi's decision to send a letter of protest to Mussolini. She bypassed political channels and was apparently uninterested in connecting up to any broader movement of opposition. In addressing the head of government *tu a tu*, as if the nation were one great family and "His Excellency" its chief patriarch, her language was simple: that of a chastizing mother or an authoritarian schoolmarm castigating an unruly child. Government was supposed to protect, not bully; the Jews whom she knew were no better or worse than anybody else. Her vision, that Mussolini, like Don Rodrigo, would be struck down by plague, was familiar to any literate Italian. It must have resonated especially strongly among the conservative Lombard middle classes of which De Morvi was a part. In sum, De Morvi's protest was hardly unambiguous. It was certainly naive. Yet one feels certain that her opinions, multiplied several thousand-fold, and conveyed with like passion to children, shopkeepers, neighbors, and friends, played a significant role in undermining consent to fascism. Eventually, such attitudes legitimated the determination of many others, if not De Morvi herself, to hide draft dodgers, assist persecuted Jews, and protect the partisan forces.

The sheer presence of Italian women in the Resistance would seem to confirm this. The movement sprang up from Naples northward in the late summer of 1943 after the Fascist Grand Council with the complicity of the king ousted Mussolini in a palace coup on July 25. It then spread through the north-central regions when Marshall Badoglio's cowardly caretaker government, after signing an armistice with the Allies, fled the country on September 8, abandoning it to the occupation of the German Army and the SS. By early 1945, the Resistance had around 250,000 activists; 70,000 women were in the Women's Defense Groups and 35,000 women were troops in the field. In addition, thousands of other women hid and cared for Resistance fighters and disbanded foreign soldiers, assisted Jews on the run from the Nazi-fascist police, and protected Italian men from being conscripted for forced labor service. Forty-six hundred women were arrested, tortured, and tried, 2,750 were deported to German concentration camps, and 623 were executed or killed in battle. Working-class and peasant women, most of whom were close to the communist resistance, made up the majority. But there was also a Catholic women's resistance, and thousands of middle-class women were affiliated with the Socialist party and the newly founded Action party.[3]

Still, interpreting the resistance of women to fascist tyranny is a more vexed issue than these facts suggest, and is tied up with the problem of writing the history of the anti-fascist Resistance as a whole. Italian feminists, responding to the underestimation of women's role, have argued that this contribution is not reducible to numbers alone. Women were uniquely intolerant of tyrannical rule, they argue, motivated by the altruistic and caring values that were special to them as mothers and providers, and uncounted numbers staffed the rear echelons that were indispensable to conducting a partisan war. At the same time, conventional images of the struggle against fascism have been challenged by new left social historians. To clinch their arguments that the communist and socialist party leaders of the old left betrayed the radical hopes of resistance workers, they have turned from the clandestine networks, underground operations, and military-style formations to study the more informal kinds of protest such as the demographic strike, the work-place slowdown, or the seditious joke. These quotidian or "everyday life practices," to refer to the term used by Detlev Peukert and others in the context of Nazi Germany, though perhaps unconnected to any broader political design, affirmed the self-worth of individuals, sustained a sense of alternatives, and preserved civic values in the face of totalitarian pressures. Women figured prominently in these informal practices, by virtue of their marginal social position as much as any innate intolerance of arbitrary rule.[4] Feminist practitioners of textual criticism have moved even further in this direction. By studying the "discursive systems" of films and novels, in the course of documenting how acts of thought "transgress" even the most impermeable codes of meaning, they implicitly question whether it is right to differentiate among degrees of oppression and to favor those acts of opposition which are most overtly political.[5] The issue of resistance as traditionally conceived thus becomes moot, for "decoding" does not entail distinguishing the effects of transgression on the larger system. Indeed, it is at least as likely to be applied to the study of the melancholy prose of bourgeois women writers (who to all appearances collaborated with fascism) as to the protests staged by Lomellina rice workers, whose sitdown strikes and communist sympathies jeopardized their livelihood and freedom.

In the course of this work, we have indeed come across numerous and varied expressions of dissent. One may recall Pierina B., who protested being fired; she justified her need to work for her old parents' and nephews' sake and because at age forty, she was too old either to find a husband to support her or to retrain for proper women's work. Or consider Dr. Maccone's tough Turinese patients who affirmed their right to control their bodies: "one child," and none for the Duce's wars; children were to be taken care of to the best of their family's ability, with the state helping out. Or take the Neapolitan jurist Maria Laetitia Riccio's celebration of fascist legislation on the family on the occasion of the Dicennial; reading between the lines, there is a scathing commentary on its antifemale bias. What links these women's briefs together is not, however, some shared female sensibility, so much as the fact that all were responding to a common system of rule.

Indeed the system itself was the source of and gave focus to their grievances. For over two decades, the fascist dictatorship articulated new notions of rights and duties for women, yet frustrated their achievement. Thus, from the outset, fascism resolved to treat women as a single entity, harnessing their common biological destiny as "mothers of the race" to the end result of national state power. However, the fascist state, by aggravating differences of wealth and privilege, divided women by caste and function. Laws, social services, and propaganda affirmed the paramount importance of motherhood. But poverty, a stingy welfare system, and, finally, war making made mothering an exceptionally arduous undertaking. Fascism spoke of the family as the pillar of the state, but family survival strategies in the face of terrible economic want accentuated the antistatist tendencies of Italian civil society. Mass politics dictated that women participate in political life. But family demands, social customs, and the fascist leaders' own ambivalence about involving females in the public sphere prevented women from being fully integrated into the ritualized enthusiasms of fascist mass politics. Nonetheless, even if fascist policy toward women was inherently contradictory, even if it ultimately

A fascist women's luncheon under the banner of the House of Savoy, Pavia, early 1930s. (Louise Diel, *Das faschistische Italien und die Aufgaben der Frau im neuen Staat* [Berlin: Hobbing Verlag, 1934]. Reprinted courtesy of the Butler Library, Columbia University.)

The ring ceremony: mothers of fallen soldiers with PNF secretary Starace and Church prelates, 1935. (*Gente nostra* [1935]. Reprinted by permission of the National Library of Florence.)

A soup kitchen for mothers at Turin, staffed by fascist patronesses, early 1930s. (Diel, *Das faschistische Italien*. Reprinted courtesy of the Butler Library, Columbia University.)

First gathering of rural housewives in Enna, Sicily, 1935. (*L'azione delle massaie rurali* 3, no. 6 [June 1935]. Reprinted by permission of the National Library of Florence.)

failed to increase births, drive women out of the work force, or subordinate women to men in the family, it still conditioned the way women— and men too—conceived of their destinies, couched their grievances, and saw the consequences of their protests.

The point here, then, is not to argue that the armed resistance of 1943– 45, with its conscious political design and emphasis on toppling fascism, was the most legitimate or useful form of opposition, nor that the oppositional practices or transgressive behaviors that women may have displayed before then prepared them to support it. However, the Resistance did offer Italian women, along with Italian men, the first occasion to act more or less freely after two decades of coerced inaction. The re-formation of political groups was the occasion to set forth grievances, to repudiate the dictatorship's institutional and ideological legacy, and to constitute a new social-moral as well as political order. All the same, women were constrained to articulate their demands in terms of the roles in which they had been cast under fascist rule, as mothers, nurturers, and providers. When, as a result of their decisions to become involved, they upset conventional gender roles, they elicited little sympathy from their male comrades. When the time came to celebrate the victories of the Resistance, the contribution of women was by and large "silenced." The new Republic, though admitting formal equality and significant gains such as the vote, maintained laws and conventions that had been codified under fascist rule and that treated women as subordinate.

The Militarization of Society

The war and the German occupation were the occasions in which disquiet developed into widespread discontent and outright rebellion. The Italians were at war longer than any other people in the West, considering that Mussolini's aggression started with the Italian attack on Ethiopia in October of 1935. And by 1941 the conditions on the home front were far worse than in any other belligerent nation. Typically, war accelerates change and, though the opening of hostilities may temporarily stifle internal conflicts, these soon flare up more strongly than ever. This was especially true of fascist Italy. For the dictatorship had set itself on a war course largely to shore itself up politically, and the country's economic structures were too stressed to sustain prolonged mobilization.

That said, we must remember that fascist militarization was not something external to Italian society. True, during the Duce's first decade of power, he had acted with conservative good sense to put distance on the catastrophe of the Great War. In Italy, as the fascists well knew, total war had heightened tensions between social classes faster than it recreated new social alliances. It destroyed old notions of manliness more radically than it was able to recreate new ones. Not least of all, it put women into new public roles that in peacetime were not easily redomesticated. By the mid-1930s, however, the dictator had reversed his priorities in domestic and foreign politics. Rather than a radical reformation of Italian society at home paving the way for conquest abroad, war itself would consolidate the fascist revolution within Italy. Militarization was thus envisaged as a process of internal as well as foreign conquest.[6]

Accordingly, militarization presented a double face with respect to women. On the one hand, it offered the occasion of participation and social assertion. Militarization joined together household and nation; it submerged the individual in the collective, it treated soldiering and mothering as complementary and equally meritorious operations of society. Fertility redeemed death; reproduction compensated for destruction. In the late 1930s, Mussolini multiplied his appearances before female audiences, and the fascist organizations for women swelled in the wake of membership drives. Female leaders spoke out with new authority, and hundreds of young cadres rose in the ranks. On the other hand, militarization accentuated the polarization of gender relations, frustrating the efforts of women to identify with the fascist hierarchy and national collectivity. With the September 5, 1938, decree-law, the fascist state passed its most comprehensive act to expel women from the labor force. By the late fall, it had outlawed the last surviving autonomous feminist groups. In 1939, with the publication of the Fascist School Charter, the regime backed a sweeping plan of sex segregation in schooling. The PNF, as part of its "reform of custom" and campaigns on behalf of racial purity, vituperated against female emancipation as epitomizing bourgeois and individualist resistances to the demands of a totalitarian collectivity.[7]

At least initially, militarization was successful in garnering women's support, as De Morvi's own tribute to the "audacity" of the African war suggests. War fever seems even to have penetrated the northern working-class communities, though their pacifist sentiments, cultivated by the socialists and dating to before the Great War, had seemed well-rooted until then. The Ethiopian campaign was the perfect war for mass consumption. Fought for what seemed a just cause, on foreign soil, and with relatively light Italian casualties, the seven-month conflict had a clearcut outcome: the foundation of the Italian Empire in May, followed in July by the lifting of the sanctions. It had a worthy final goal as well, colonization. When the League of Nations established the embargo on war-related matériel on October 5, 1935, the cause against the Negus was brought home. Women cadres rallied to conduct "capillary, assiduous, daily" propaganda, exploiting "the faculty of persuasion, the strength of sentiment that we women know so well how to make work when we want to impose our passion and our faith."[8] For the first time, the white nations had forsaken the "principle of solidarity in the face of the colored races," to cite the impassioned phrases of Olga Medici del Vascello. Arrogant plutocrats sought to "outlaw a people guilty only of having wanted to civilize where today barbarism reigns."[9] In the tradition of imperialist social motherhood, female propagandists spoke of Italian women's civilizing mission: of the Catholic religious orders proselytizing Africans, of the colonial governors' wives and daughters whose lives had been dedicated to the cause, and, not least of all, of the new burdens white women must bear as Italians settled in East Africa. The chief and most delicate one was of course the "rigorous defense of the race" needed to prevent their men from "succumbing to blandishments that would inevitably lead to damaging and dolorous combinations."[10] No voice was raised in protest of the ban on miscegenation in the African colonies, decreed before the birth of the Axis, which demonstrated that Italian fascism had arrived at a form of racial doctrine independently of German influence.

From the time of the Ethiopian campaign, some Italian women thus became outspoken accomplices of fascist militarism. At first they merely added nuanced and impassioned arguments to justify it. Later they furnished cadres to stiffen a spineless home front. At the end, as Mussolini's rump Republic of Salò was on the verge of collapse, a couple of thousand young fascists joined several hundred veterans of the women's *fasci* to assist as female auxiliaries of the fascist militia. From 1935 to the outbreak of World War II, no women's group was more activist than the several-thousand-member Fascist National Association of Women Artists and Degree Holders. Under the leadership of Maria Castellani, ANFAL was authorized to form squads of volunteers specialized in technical services, first aid, propaganda, transportation, and policing. But women "aspire to something more," Castellani affirmed, boasting of the numbers of women already employed in industry, the professions, and state administration. In particular they aspired to specialize in occupations traditionally described as male so as to assure that as many men as possible would be available for frontline duty![11]

With their belief that men and women became truly complementary, if not equal, in the cause of making war, women militarists created a rich imagery that was at once self-flagellating and hurtful to men, because so misleading about warfare's real nature. Their foremost struggle, to believe some, was to dominate their fickle female natures. "The only rival that a woman should tolerate is the nation," was the first principle the

Neapolitan artist Anna Dinella proposed for her Women's War Decalogue. Above all, women had to learn to "regiment sentiment." If they failed, Dinella's tenth principle affirmed, they were worse than deserters, because they knew they wouldn't be punished.[12] In 1937, when Dr. Mina Magri married a Roman military officer who had been blinded and lost an arm in Ethiopia, her mother, Maria Magri Zopegni, wrote in macabre detail of the wedding of the self-sacrificing home-front heroine to the sacrificed frontline hero: female wholeness regenerated male mutilation, the bride's bouffant white tulle gown offset the groom's limp-sleeved medal-bedecked dress uniform.[13] The plucky journalist Fanny Dini, a fascist of the first hour who at her return from touring Addis Ababa in 1937 won first prize in the Mussolini contest for her lyrical treatment of a dead soldier's mother's grief, privately and repeatedly entreated the Duce to allow her to enlist in the armed forces. Her special wish was to join the parachute corps to which her log of flying time qualified her. Moreover, "as a woman, having reached the ground, [she] could render more important services than a man, since she would more easily escape enemy detection."[14]

Fascist women thus shared in, and perhaps reinforced, the jejune militarism that fascist men practiced. This put sexual and military conquest on the same level and confused "demographic," "grain," and other domestic battles with those of the warfront. With its cock-of-the-walk aggressivity, fascist militarism was unthinking of means and costs, and it quailed the moment hostilities finally opened against France in June 1940. Then the privations and casualties of a real war brought home its terrible cruelty.[15] Ultimately, this militaristic culture also destroyed whatever legitimacy the fascist women's organizations had in the eyes of their female constituents.

As the euphoria of the Ethiopian campaign died away, it became obvious that militarism, far from clarifying gender lines, confused them. Soldiering and mothering were not analogous functions as Mussolini had claimed they were with his notorious dictum, "war is to man what maternity is to woman."[16] War making made women the main protagonists of civil society; it tempted the most self-aggrandizing ones to make claims of valor that diminished men and to delude themselves that wartime would tolerate the foundation of a "Herland" ruled by female sentiments and desires.[17] Not surprisingly, the militarization of Italian society during the late 1930s was accompanied by a redoubling of the attacks on feminism—although there had been no organized movement whatsoever since the early 1920s. Male ideologues railed against the "masculinization of customs" and the "obscuring of the limits set by nature and consecrated by tradition," calling them the "fruit of the economization of life and moral Jewishification."[18]

Worse, the new militarism taught that men had to make war to be men. The alliance with Hitler's Axis in the fall of 1936 put the slapdash authoritarianism of Mussolini's Italy before the seemingly perfected totalitarianism of the Third Reich. The image of the all-powerful NSDAP galvanized ambitious party cadres, though attempts to imitate it by saddling Italy with racial laws, centralizing party operations, and introducing choreographic touches like the goose step in military parades further distanced the regime from most Italians. After 1940 there were no battle victories to demonstrate male prowess, and the numerous losses—in Greece, North Africa, and Russia—Mussolini gratuitously laid to the ineptitude of the nation's multitude of inferior males.

In the end, the Nazi-fascist war to the finish put women as well as men beyond the old sexual conventions. The Italian militiamen of the Salò Republic, their cause besmirched by the Nazis' and their own atrocities against civilians, could no longer find female companionship to distract or comfort them. "The women no longer love us / because we wear black shirts. / To them we are all jail birds. / To them we're lost causes." In this song of the "last hour," the homoerotic pride of comrades-in-arms gives way to the pathos of men abandoned.[19] On April 14, 1944, as the Allied troops advanced northward, and partisan troops occupying mountain redoubts prepared for the spring offensive, the Italian Social Republic issued fascism's first call to enlist women in its armed forces. In the next several months, perhaps 6,000 enlisted in the Auxiliary Women's Service, or SAF, though probably no more than a couple thousand actually served. All told, their effort was as futile as that of the women's "Battalion of Death" which Alexander Kerensky's provisional government marshaled for the last-ditch defense of the Winter Palace. Still, the figure of the "woman-soldier" signaled a radical break with the past. If nothing more, fascist diehards could use the fact that these "enamored of the fatherland" volunteered to impugn the manhood of the ever-more numerous "rebels": the latter were "husbands, sons, lovers, brothers [who] desert their posts, throw down their arms, and have run off to hide under your skirts, under priests' garb, in the mountains, in the thick of the cities."[20]

Reconstructing the Home Front

Ultimately the conduct of the war distanced the majority of Italian women from the regime.[21] On June 5, 1940, the dictatorship suspended all quotas on women's work, and women began to be hired to substitute for some of the 1.63 million men called to arms. By 1943 women were prominent in the work forces of factories and public administrations. As early as 1935 the government had started to manipulate prices and the availability of food stocks in the name of autarchy. Already in September 1939, nine months before Italy entered the war, orders forbade the sale of meat two days a week. By November 1940 bakers were authorized to dilute wheat flour with corn meal. The following February, pasta began to be rationed; ten months later, in October 1941, bread, too. That winter many Italians were hungry. As women queued up for scarce goods, and black-market corruption further aggravated the normal inequities of daily life, they heard gossip about terrible setbacks. The first, in December 1941, was that Italy had declared war on the United States, which was generally regarded as invincible. By Christmas the Nazi crusade against the Soviet Union, though it had begun so auspiciously on June 22, 1941, accompanied by an enthusiastic if ill-equipped Italian expeditionary force and Church prayers for the salvation of Russian souls, was halted outside of Moscow. In the next year, rumors came back of German negligence and Soviet atrocities, the Italian troops freezing, starving, and deathly sick. In March 1943, eight months before the Allied armies landed in Sicily, thousands of Turin workers, mainly women, shouting "peace and bread," struck for overtime pay and cost-of-living increases. That Fiat, the major firm struck, capitulated and no party or police authorities stepped in was interpreted as a sign of the breakdown of the Duce's authority. The Allied landing in Sicily in early July convinced senior officials of the regime to convoke the Grand Council on July 24, 1943, and to oust Mussolini from power.

That women should have occupied a prominent role in the Resistance that spread after September 8, 1943, seems not at all surprising in retrospect. The brutality of the occupying Germans, the breakdown of services under Allied bombing, exploited work in the factories, and near starvation came on the top of long-standing disaffection with the dictatorship. By early 1944 the old parties were regrouping: the Communist party proved especially strong, capitalizing on tenacious clandestine networks and the fury of the working class and northern peasantry. The most formal organization through which women joined the Resistance were the Women's Defense Groups, founded at Milan in November 1943, under the loose control of the Committee of National Liberation. Their goal was twofold: to help the Resistance and to organize for women's emancipation. But planning for the latter was lost in the face of day-to-day exigencies. The heroine of the Resistance was the "staffetta" or courier. She was at once liaison and girl Friday: the jack-of-all-trades of partisan warfare, she carried messages and orders, kept lists of contacts, prepared safe houses, and transported news pamphlets and sometimes weapons. But most women were involved in more quotidian tasks around the home and neighborhood, sheltering and feeding, and garnering and transmitting information. The most basic task was to make the rounds of police headquarters and German military posts to locate prisoners, plead for their safekeeping, and provide for their upkeep. The saddest duty was to notify their kin and bury them in the event they were murdered in reprisals.

The breadth of women's activity testified, if nothing more, to the persistence of the family and community solidarities that, by later standards, might be called archaic. The big-city neighborhoods, in which eight-story buildings clustered around noisy courtyards, the walled centers of the small cities of the center and north, the village hill towns of Piedmont, which were almost entirely under partisan control by 1945, formed tight-knit communities. In the face of fascist attacks, and as survival became more arduous, their crowdedness and gossip fed solidarities. It came naturally for women to use the skills that patriarchal society attributed to them: intuition, cunning, protective motherly feelings, and the habit of gossip, as well as seductive wiles (*fascino femminile*), against which no man, not even the most truculent *repubblichino*, was immune.[22] All these qualities had been honed in the previous four years with the departure of the men for war, in the process of dealing with the black market and barter economy, in working outside the home, and in taking decisions previously not thought possible.

For women the decision to join the Resistance surely required a resolve greater than that required of men. Young men in particular were often forced to choose, on pain of being rounded up as deserters or conscripted as forced labor for the German *Lager*. By contrast, women stood to gain from staying put, if not from collaborating; they could earn supplies of cigarettes, coal, additional rationing cards, not to mention peace and tranquillity. Of the women interviewed, most of whom were working class, few motivated their decisions with book learning. Most referred to their family histories: the persecutions inflicted on their fathers, uncles, or grandfathers; the influence of their brothers or fiancés. Rightly or not, they perceived their determination to act as a fulfillment of their roles as mothers and wives: to provision the household, to preserve family unity, and to safeguard their children's lives.[23] Unlike partisan men, who justified their actions in terms of a cause—to drive out the Germans, to do as the Russians had done in 1917, to create a new world of peace and freedom—the women claimed that they were merely reacting to injustice. When Maria Peron of Padua, the daughter of small farmers, was questioned about her political beliefs, she insisted: "[I] never had a political idea, I'm only Catholic, a believer, a convinced one though." The persecution of the Jews, full knowledge of which was thrust upon her by requests for help, led her to join the Resistance.[24] Likewise, Amelia Maccarnelli of Treviglio, born 1906, said that Italy's treacherous invasion of France in June 1940 was her moment of awakening. But the idea-force behind her day-to-day action was her family: "I never said, 'I'm doing it for myself, for my future.' . . . At best I said . . . 'Let me save this one, he's a mother's son just like mine,' my hope being that somebody would treat my own with the same care."[25]

Once in the movement, women discovered unexpected resources and aptitudes. The younger ones especially were plunged into a new world of male-female camaraderie. Their tasks may not have been regarded as formally equal to the fighting forces, but they knew that theirs required equal skill and they enjoyed the men's grudging admiration. In the course of the war, "female consciousness," to use Temma Kaplan's term, which is to say the sense of collective obligations rooted in women's acceptance of the division of labor by sex, was joined to the "communal consciousness" of men and women as they struggled to liberate Italy from the Nazi-fascists.[26] To find what might be characterized as feminist aspirations is more difficult. As a political and social movement on behalf of freedom and social justice, the Resistance did not encourage critiques of male supremacy nor contemplate situations in which to confront complex issues of self-identity and gender reconstruction.

Partisan combatants were uneasy in the company of the emancipated young women, though they relied on them in order to conduct their operations. Women's presence at campsites, far from being a consolation, signaled the messiness of partisan warfare: this "female abundance" offended Partisan Johnny's "military puritanism," to recall the reactions of the novelist Beppe Fenoglio's hero; it was an anachronism "conceivable only in a late-seventeenth-century army." The fact that women chose battle names, like the men, provoked associations with "other women who used nicknames."[27] In the folk culture and art of the Resistance, women were reminders of the entrapping culture of domesticity, of the good life, of the cowardice of doing nothing which the sons of the middle class in particular had to repudiate in order to fight. Women were the anxious mothers whose worries about their sons' health and safety Dario Fo parodied in his comic Resistance song: "My mamma, she used to tell me, / Don't go up into the mountains, / You'll eat only bread and onions, / You'll die of a stomach ache." ("La mia mamma, / La mi diceva, / Non andare sulle montagne, / Mangerai sol polenta e castagne, / Ti verrà l'acidità.") The times were so catastrophic that, as so much of neorealist fiction tells us, mankind, which is to say men, yearned to find not love, but their humanity. Like Enne 2, the existentialist hero of Elio Vittorini's successful novel *Uomini e no* (1945), they longed for simplicity rather than complicated emotions; they sought comrades not a companion, engagement not commitment. Poor Enne 2 thus clings to the image of the dress his onetime lover left hanging behind his door, too numbed by the atrocities being perpetrated around him to seek her. In Roberto Rossellini's *Open City*, filmed in 1945 just after the Liberation, the heroic woman sacrifices herself for the cause, but in the name of her beloved. Embodied in the earthy working-class Pina, played by Anna Magnani, she is shot down by the Nazi fascists, less than halfway into the film, as she runs to stop German trucks from carting off her partisan husband. The bad woman in the film is stylishly modern: the blond Marina Mari plays a deracinated actress whose emotional turmoil, aggravated by her frustrated love of the Resistance leader Manfredi, causes her to seek solace in cocaine. Her addiction, fed by a lesbian Nazi, eventually leads her to betray her man to the gestapo.

Ultimately, the Resistance, insofar as it was designed as a military operation, could not garner full-fledged participation from women. Like any guerilla war, it counted on the support of civilian populations, yet it also endangered them. Female consciousness could not be ambivalent toward the armed teenaged males who, in the name of their cause, were indifferent to their own lives and endangered others as well. The story of Civitella della Chiana, the site of an SS massacre of Italian civilians in the last months of the war, is also the story of the town's divided consciousness about the dangers of partisan warfare. On June 18, 1944, with the Allied armies just days away, a tiny and wholly isolated local partisan group mounted an ill-conceived attack to snatch the weapons from four disbanded *Wehrmacht* soldiers who had straggled into the village's *dopolavoro*. They killed two of the Germans and wounded a third, who was helped to escape by his unscathed comrade. In fear of reprisals, most of the six hundred townspeople fled under a heavy rain. After three days, almost all returned. The children were dirty and tired, and several intermediaries satisfied the villagers that the German Army commanders were convinced of the town's good will. At daybreak on June 29, a Sunday and the feast day of Saints Peter and Paul, SS troops of the Hermann Göring Division, guided by local fascist militia, invaded the town. Moving from house to house, they shot down the men as they leaped from their beds. They then rounded up the several scores of men attending Mass, lined them up along with their priest, and machine-gunned them down five by five. That day and the following, the troops looted, mined, and burned the houses. At Civitella and the outlying villages of Cornia and San Pancrazio the massacre left 250 men dead. Of the handful of men who escaped, one was the partisan chief, Dr. Gambassini, a Florentine doctor who was the town's public health officer. He had decamped several days before. The rest were young draft dodgers who, fearful of capture, were roused by the first sound of ruckus and plunged over the city walls to flee.

In the wake of the liberation on April 25, 1945, the male image of the Resistance quickly canonized itself. To legitimate itself as a force capable of ruling Italian society, the left discouraged women in uniform from participating in the celebratory parades. For male activists, the postwar was the beginning of an era of progress. True, the radical hopes for a "Second Risorgimento" were disappointed, and never so much as when the Christian Democrats won the elections of April 1948. However, when the left began to advance once more in the 1960s, the Resistance's promises of a new social order seemed justified. In the late 1970s, Dr. Gambassini, who in 1950 had won a libel suit against a right-wing journalist who had accused the partisans of provoking the German massacre at Civitella, composed his memoirs.[28] He recalled how at the war's end, he returned to Florence. There he pursued his civic commitment by serving as City Health Commissioner. In 1963 he founded the Center for Social Medicine which in 1968 introduced the first scans for mammary cancer. By his account, his life history was coherent, unilinear, and full of satisfactions, much like conventional histories of postwar Italy's advance.

The women of Civitella tell a different story. Their "lament," transcribed in early 1946 by the Florentine Marta Chiesi and her companion, the writer Romano Bilenchi, a close friend of one of the men killed at Civitella, was the first testimony by Italian women of their experience of the war and the Resistance.[29] They testified in horrific detail to the seeming casualness of the events which had joined their own and their family's fates with the course of national history. For four years, the women said, Civitella had been a peaceful haven. In the summer of 1944, the townspeople were awaiting the arrival of the Allies and watching the Germans retreat on foot and by truck, car, and even oxen. Their anxiety calmed by the authorities, as well as by their spouses, the women went about their routines. They recalled the little details of the morning of June 29: Uliana Merini (the widow Caldelli) pleaded with the young soldier who had burst into her house to think of his own mother. But he shoved her aside, shouting "Raus, raus!" Her sick husband was too weak to dress himself; she would never have helped him had she known it was only to send him to his death in the piazza. Elda Morfini (the widow Paggi), with her four children and old mother underfoot, sought to rouse her mortally wounded husband with an injection of camphor while her old father was murdered outside the front door. A couple of women cursed the Germans forever. Several spoke of praying to divine providence for strength to survive, to comfort their children and one another, to bury the dead, and to go on. "We gathered up our dead ourselves, we built the caskets alone, we hoisted them by ourselves onto the wagon used to collect the town garbage and, three by three, we brought them down to the cemetery."[30]

Among the most vulnerable of the new Republic's citizens, the women of Civitella fell under the protection of the nearby Christian Democratic stronghold of Arezzo. Its chief patron, the up-and-coming young Catholic politician Amintore Fanfani, made sure that they were among the earliest beneficiaries of his party's family policies. In retrospect, the history of Civitella's women in the years since the fall of fascism resembles that of other Italian women. There is the history of the women as individuals and family heads. And there is the history tied to the tempo of national events. The former inevitably refers to the catastrophe of June 29. Time is dated "before the Front" and "after the Front." The episode is recalled with stoicism, as if in the face of an inexplicable destiny: "what happened, happened" (*A chi tocca, tocca*). The latter history refers to brighter times. Surviving the legacy of misery left by fascism, the women experienced the coming of the consumer revolution into their own homes during the 1960s, and in the 1970s the arrival of a more emancipated custom for women.

During the latter decade, especially, the rule of Mussolini began to seem as if it were another era altogether. That was a long time past when, the old ladies recall, families were huge, and everybody lived crowded together with chickens, pigs, rabbits, cats, and dogs. The peasants were so poor that they walked to town barefoot to save shoe leather. The party secretary was a decent enough fellow, though an opportunist. But the postal clerk, a spinster, ratted if someone said a bad word about Mussolini. The professor's charming son-in-law was a Jew, though given the times, nobody wanted to make much of the matter. His elegant wife's high heels click-clacked on the cobblestones until the very day the doctor arrived to deliver her fourth child. ONMI checked the weight of poor infants and doled out samples of powdered or canned milk if a hex had dried up the mother's. A few dishonest women got themselves up in rural housewives' outfits to cadge handouts, and the village's most ambitious girls aspired to be schoolteachers and to find beaux who were more worldly than the local boys.

Notes

CHAPTER 1

1. Irene Brin, *Usi e costumi, 1920–1940* (Palermo: Sellerio Editore, 1981), p. 11.

2. Diverse aspects of this contradictoriness have been captured by Marina Addis Saba in her exhaustive review and anthology of recent Italian studies on women under fascism: *La corporazione delle donne* (Florence: Vallecchi, 1989). See, too, three thoughtful English-language essays: Alexander De Grand, "Women under Italian Fascism," *Historical Journal* 19, no. 4 (1976): 947–68; Emiliana Noether, "Italian Women and Fascism: A Reevaluation," *Italian Quarterly* (Fall 1982): 69–80, and Lesley Caldwell, "Reproducers of the Nation: Women and the Family in Fascist Policy," in *Rethinking Italian Fascism*, ed. David Forgacs (London: Lawrence and Wishart, 1986), pp. 110–41.

3. John Maynard Keynes, *The Economic Consequences of the Peace* (1920; New York: Harper and Row, 1971), pp. 9–26.

4. Gunnar Myrdal, *Population: A Problem for Democracy* (Cambridge: Harvard University Press, 1940); as well as Alva Myrdal and Gunnar Myrdal, *Crisis in the Population Question* (Stockholm: Albert Bonniers Forlag, 1935). D. V. Glass's *Population Policies and Movements in Europe* (Oxford: Clarendon Press, 1940) draws a similarly broad European panorama, as does the succinct overview contained in C. F. McCleary, "Pre-War European Population Policies," *The Milbank Memorial Fund Quarterly* 19, no. 2 (Apr. 1941): 105–20.

5. Alva Myrdal, *Nation and Family: The Swedish Experiment in Democratic Family and Population Policy* (New York: Harper and Brothers, 1941), pp. 398ff.

6. Charles S. Maier, *Recasting Bourgeois Europe* (Princeton: Princeton University Press, 1975) provides an overview of the latter processes.

7. Michel Foucault, *The History of Sexuality*, vol. 1, *An Introduction*, trans. Robert Hurley (1976; New York: Pantheon, 1978), pp. 135–50.

8. Eli F. Heckscher, *Mercantilism*, trans. Mendel Shapiro, 2 vols. (1931; London: George Allen and Unwin, 1935), 2:145ff., 273ff.

9. Gunnar Myrdal, *Population: A Problem for Democracy*, p. 20.

10. Ibid., pp. 80, 190–91. The impact of policy is studied by Ann-Sophie Kälvemark, *More Children of Better Quality: Aspects on Swedish Population Policy in the 1930s*, Acta Universitatis Upsaliensis 115 (Uppsala, 1980).

11. George Mosse, *The Nationalization of the Masses* (New York: Howard Fertig, 1975). See, too, Eric Hobsbawm and Terence Ranger, eds., *The Invention of Tradition* (New York: Cambridge University Press, 1983).

12. This tendency, cutting across national borders, is analyzed in Martha Vicinus, ed., *Suffer and Be Still: Women in the Victorian Age* (Bloomington: University of Indiana Press, 1973); Bonnie G. Smith, *Ladies of the Leisure Class* (Princeton: Princeton University Press, 1981); and Karin Hausen, "Family and Role-Division: The Polarisation of Sexual Stereotypes in the Nineteenth Century," in Richard J. Evans and W. R. Lee, eds., *The German Family: Essays on the Social History of the Family in Nineteenth- and Twentieth-Century Germany* (London: Croom Helm, 1981), pp. 51–83.

13. Smith, *Ladies of the Leisure Class*, passim.

14. In addition to George Mosse's provocative *Nationalism and Sexuality: Respectability and Abnormal Sexuality in Modern Europe* (New York: Howard Fertig, 1985), esp. pp. 1–113, see Karen Offen, "Depopulation, Nationalism, and Feminism in Fin-de-Siècle France," *American Historical Review* 89, no. 3 (June 1984): 648–76, and Angus McLaren, *Sexuality and the Social Order: The Debate over the Fertility of Women and Workers in France, 1770–1920* (New York: Holmes and Meier, 1983); and on England, see Jeffrey Weeks; *Sex, Politics, and Society: The Regulation of Sexuality Since 1800* (New York: Longman, 1981), pp. 181–240.

15. Vera Zamagni presents compelling documentation of these trends in "Distribuzione del reddito e classi sociali nell'Italia fra le due guerre," in *La classe operaia durante il fascismo*, ed. Giulio Sapelli, Annali: Fondazione Giangiacomo Feltrinelli, vol. 20 (Milan, 1980), pp. 17–50. See too Mario Saibante, "Il tenore di vita del popolo italiano prima dell'ultima guerra, in confronto con quello degli altri popoli," appendix C of *Piano per le importazioni e le esportazioni*, vol. 5, ed. Centro di studi e piani tecnico-economici, Comitato interministeriale per la ricostruzione (Rome, 1947), pp. 193–213.

16. The nature of public "consensus" under fascism has been the subject of lengthy, often tedious debate in Italy. The best that can be said here is that the issue has been largely superseded by the publication, if

not acceptance, of more insightful methodologies and empirical findings that dispute the usefulness of the term. See in particular my *Culture of Consent: Mass Organization of Leisure in Fascist Italy* (New York: Cambridge University Press, 1981), pp. 3–23; also Luisa Passerini, *Torino operaio e socialista* (Bari: Laterza, 1984).

17. See Joseph V. Femia's persuasive presentation of this concept in *Gramsci's Political Thought* (Oxford: Clarendon Press, 1981), esp. pp. 38–45.

18. The role of fascism as a modernizing force in politics is underscored by the Marxist historian Ernesto Ragionieri in "Il partito fascista: Appunti per una ricerca," in *La Toscana nel regime fascista (1929–1936)*, 2 vols. (Florence: La Nuova Italia, 1971), 1:59–85. He draws on the Italian communist leader Palmiro Togliatti's intelligent assessment in *Lectures on Fascism*, trans. Daniel Dichter (1935; New York: International Publishers, 1976), esp. pp. 4–53. Although not dealing specifically with the organization of women, Togliatti makes the argument that fascist mass organizing generally performed a modernizing function. On the liberal side, see the massive biographies of Mussolini by Renzo De Felice, *Mussolini il Duce: Gli anni del consenso, 1929–1935* (Turin: Einaudi, 1974), and *Mussolini il Duce: Lo stato totalitario, 1936–1940* (Turin: Einaudi, 1981), esp. pp. 76–81.

19. For example, De Felice's seven-volume study of Mussolini (Turin: Einaudi, 1965–89) is organized according to the following periodization: "The Conquest of Power," 1921–25; "The Organization of the Fascist State," 1925–29; "The Years of Consensus," 1930–35; "The Totalitarian State," 1936–40; and "The Ally," 1940–43. See also Adrian Lyttelton, *The Seizure of Power: Fascism in Italy, 1919–1929* (New York: Scribner, 1973).

20. Vilfredo Pareto, "Il mito virtuista" (1914) in *Scritti sociologici*, ed. G. Busino (Turin: UTET, 1966), esp. pp. 484, 602.

21. Ferdinando Loffredo, *Politica della famiglia* (Milan: Bompiani, 1938).

CHAPTER 2

1. Good overviews of liberal Italy include Christopher Seton-Watson's detailed *Italy from Liberalism to Fascism, 1870–1925* (London: Methuen, 1967). See also Silvio Lanaro's engaging essay *L'Italia nuova* (Turin: Einaudi, 1988), as well as his *Nazione e lavoro: Saggio sulla cultura borghese in Italia* (Venezia: Marsilio, 1979), in addition to Raffaele Romanelli's workmanlike *L'Italia liberale (1861–1900)* (Bologna: Il Mulino, 1979).

2. Paolo Ungari, *Storia del diritto di famiglia in Italia, 1796–1942* (Bologna: Il Mulino, 1974), pp. 123–35.

3. Maria Vittoria Ballestrero, *Dalla tutela alla parità: La legislazione italiana sul lavoro delle donne* (Bologna: Il Mulino, 1979), pp. 11–56.

See also Annarita Buttafuoco, "Condizione delle donne e movimento di emancipazione femminile," *Storia della società italiana*. Pt. 5, vol. 20, *L'Italia di Giolitti* (Milan: Teti, 1981), pp. 154–85. Gaston Rimlinger's *Welfare Policy and Industrialization in Europe, America, and Russia* (New York: Wiley, 1971) offers an excellent basis for comparing Italy's experiences with those of Germany and Britain.

4. Donald Mayer, *Sex and Power: The Rise of Women in America, Russia, Sweden, and Italy* (Middletown, Conn.: Wesleyan University Press, 1987) offers a suggestive framework for comparing the character of diverse national women's movements. See also Richard J. Evans, *The Feminists: Women's Emancipation Movements in Europe, America, and Australasia, 1840–1920* (London: Croom-Helm, 1979).

5. On the rise of the Italian women's movement, see Franca Pieroni Bortolotti, *Alle origini del movimento femminile in Italia, 1848–1892* (Turin: Einaudi, 1963) and *Socialismo e questione femminile in Italia, 1892–1922* (Milan: Mazzotta, 1974) as well as Buttafuoco, "Condizione" and *Cronache femminili: Temi e momenti della stampa emancipazionista in Italia dall'unità al fascismo* (Arezzo: Dipartimento di studi storico-sociali e filosofici, Università di Siena, 1988).

6. In addition to Buttafuoco's forthcoming studies on the *Unione femminile nazionale*, see a pioneering work, Mariella Bartoli's unpublished thesis, "Il movimento di emancipazione femminile in Italia e il Consiglio Nazionale delle Donne Italiane, 1903–1923," 2 vols. (Florence: Università degli studi di Firenze, Facoltà di lettere e filosofia, 1987).

7. See Pieroni Bortolotti, *Socialismo e questione femminile*; also Maria Casalini, "Femminismo e socialismo in Anna Kuliscioff, 1890–1907," *Italia contemporanea* 143 (June 1981): 12–43, and Enzo Santarelli, "Donne e lotte di massa in Italia (il periodo 1890–1915)," *Critica marxista* 5, no. 16 (Sept.–Oct. 1978): 111–26.

8. See Paola Gaiotti de Biase, *Le origini del movimento cattolico femminile* (Brescia: Morcelliana, 1963); also Cecilia Dau Novelli, "Alle origini dell'esperienza cattolica femminile," *Storia contemporanea* 12, nos. 4–5 (Oct. 1981): 667–711, as well as *Società, chiesa e associazionismo femminile* (Rome: Societa A.V.E., 1988). See too F. M. Cecchini, *Il femminismo cristiano: La questione femminile nella prima democrazia cristiana* (Rome: Editori Riuniti, 1979).

9. Cited in Valeria Benetti Brunelli, *La donna nella civiltà moderna* (Turin: Fratelli Bocca, 1933), pp. 211–12.

10. On practical feminism, see Annarita Buttafuoco, "La filantropia come politica: Esperienza dell'emancipazionismo italiano del Novecento," in *Ragnatela di rapporti*, ed. Lucia Ferrante, Maura Palazzi, and Gianna Pomata (Turin: Rosenberg and Sellier, 1988), pp. 166–87. For comparable experiences elsewhere, see Nancy Black, *Social Feminism* (Ithaca: Cornell University Press, 1989). Nancy F. Cott highlights the varieties of "feminism" in "What's in a Name? The Limits of 'Social Feminism,' or Ex-

panding the Vocabulary of Women's History," *Journal of American History* 76, no. 3 (Dec. 1989): 809–29. Karen Offen refers specifically to the European context in "Defining Feminism: A Comparative Historical Approach," *Signs* 14, no. 1 (Autumn 1988); 119–57, and "Liberty, Equality, and Justice for Women: The Theory and Practice of Feminism in Nineteenth-Century Europe," in *Becoming Visible*, ed. Renate Bridenthal, Claudia Koonz, and Susan Stuard, 2d ed. (Boston: Houghton Mifflin, 1987), pp. 335–73.

11. Cited in Buttafuoco, "La filantropia come politica," p. 184.

12. The cult of virility as a general phenomenon in late nineteenth-century Europe is discussed in George Mosse, *Nationalism and Sexuality: Respectability and Abnormal Sexuality in Modern Europe* (New York: Howard Fertig, 1985), pp. 23–47, 153–80, and in Jeffrey Weeks, *Sex, Politics, and Society: The Regulation of Sexuality since 1800* (New York: Longman, 1981), pp. 96–121. On Italy, see Giovanni Papini, *Maschilità* (Florence: Libreria della Voce, 1915) (*Quaderni della voce*, vol. 3). See also Bruno Wanrooij, "Il 'casto talamo': Il dibattito sulla morale sessuale nel ventennio fascista," *Cultura e società negli anni del fascismo* (Milan: Cordani, 1987), pp. 534–35.

13. Scipio Sighele, *La donna e l'amore* (Milan: Treves, 1913), p. 28.

14. Cited in Luciano De Maria, ed., *Teoria e invenzione futurista* (Milan: Mondadori, 1983), p. 11.

15. Donna Paola [Paola Baronchelli Grosson], *La donna della nuova Italia: Documenti del contributo femminile alla guerra (maggio 1915–maggio 1917)* (Milan: R. Quintieri, 1917), pp. 240, 284.

16. On the impact of the war on feminist associations, see the innovating study of Stefania Bartoloni, "L'associazionismo femminile nella prima guerra mondiale e la mobilitazione per l'assistenza civile e la propaganda," forthcoming in *Donna lombarda (1860–1945)* (Milan: Franco Angeli, 1992). On the social effects of the war, see Temma Kaplan, "Women and Communal Strikes in the Crisis of 1917–1922," in *Becoming Visible*, ed. Renate Bridenthal et al., pp. 429–49. On Italy specifically, see Diego Leoni and Camillo Zadra, *La grande guerra: Esperienza, memoria, immagini* (Bologna: Il Mulino, 1986), as well as Franca Pieroni Bortolotti, *Femminismo e partiti politici in Italia, 1919–1926* (Rome: Editori Riuniti, 1978), pp. 84ff.

17. Cited in Pieroni Bortolotti, *Alle origini*, p. 275. For biographical references, see Luigi Dal Pane, "Antonio e Teresa Labriola," *Rivista internazionale di filosofia del diritto* 2d ser., 22 (Jan.–Feb. 1942): 48–79; also Enzo Santarelli, "Protagonisti femminili del primo Novecento: schede bibliografiche," *Problemi del socialismo* 17, no. 4 (Oct.–Dec. 1976): 248–50.

18. Laura Cabrini Casartelli, "Rassegna del movimento femminile italiano," *Almanacco della donna italiana, 1923*, pp. 178–79.

19. On the early fascist women's movement, see Denise Detragiache,

"Il fascismo femminile da San Sepolcro all'affare Matteotti, 1919–1924," *Storia contemporanea* 2 (Apr. 1983): 211–51, and Stefania Bartoloni, "Il fascismo femminile e la sua stampa: *La Rassegna femminile italiana* (1925–1930)" *Nuova DWF* 21 (1982): 143–69.

20. Cited in Elisabetta Mondello, *La nuova italiana* (Rome: Riuniti, 1987), p. 45; on women and futurism generally see Claudia Salaris, *Le futuriste* (Milan: Edizioni delle donne, 1982).

21. Archivio centrale dello stato, Segreteria particolare del Duce, Carteggio ordinario, fascicolo (ACS, SPD, CO. f.) 509509 Terruzzi, Regina; Denise Detragiache, "Du socialisme au fascisme naissant: formation et itinéraire de Regina Terruzzi," in *Femmes et fascismes*, ed. Rita Thälmann (Paris: Tiérce, 1986), pp. 41–66.

22. Detragiache, "Il fascismo femminile da San Sepolcro," p. 218–19; Bartoloni, "Il fascismo femminile e la sua stampa," pp. 145–49.

23. Emilia Carreras, "Ricordi di Ines Donati," *Lavoro e famiglia* 1, no. 1 (Mar. 23, 1938): 4; also *La donna italiana* 12, no. 11 (Nov. 1935): 498. See too Ivana Rinaldi, "Ines Donati: Realtà e mito di un 'eroina' fascista," *Quaderni di resistenza Marche* 13 (Jan. 1987): 48–89.

24. A judgment shared by foreign suffrage leaders; see *Jus Suffragii: The International Woman Suffrage News*, 17 (July 1923): 146.

25. Benito Mussolini, *Opera omnia*, ed. Edoardo Susmel and Duilio Susmel, 44 vols. (Florence: La Fenice, 1951–80), 19:215.

26. Cf. Pieroni Bortolotti, *Femminismo e partiti politici*, pp. 228–47; Renzo De Felice, *Mussolini il Duce II: Lo stato totalitario, 1936–1940* (Turin: Einaudi, 1981), pp. 78–81.

27. Cited in Bartoloni, "Il fascismo femminile e la sua stampa," p. 154.

28. PBA, "Una sconfitta," *Giornale della donna* 7, no. 2 (Jan. 15–31, 1925): p. 1.

29. *La donna italiana* 3, no. 4 (Apr. 1926): 332–33.

30. *Almanacco della donna italiana, 1925*, pp. 207, 213.

31. "Rassegna del movimento femminile italiano," *Almanacco della donna italiana, 1927*, pp. 275, 293.

32. Ibid., p. 297.

33. Cited in Bartoloni, "Il fascismo femminile e la sua stampa," p. 156.

34. ACS, SPD, CO, f. 110895, Majer-Rizzioli. Letter Niccolo Rizzioli-Mussolini, June 2, 1930.

35. Valeria Benetti Brunelli, *La Donna nella civiltà moderna*, p. 202.

CHAPTER 3

1. Benito Mussolini, "Discorso dell'Ascensione," May 26, 1927, *Opera omnia*, ed. Edoardo Susmel e Duilio Susmel, 44 vols. (Florence: La Fe-

nice, 1951–80), 22:360. For the context, see Luigi Salvatorelli and Giovanni Mira, *Storia d'Italia nel periodo fascista*, new ed. (Turin: Einaudi, 1964), pp. 416–23.

2. Giancarlo Fusco, *Le rose del ventennio* (Turin: Einaudi, 1958), p. 30.

3. Demographic politics was among the Duce's favorite themes of disquisition as his numerous comments on the subject suggest: "Rilievi demografici," Nov. 29, 1927, *Opera omnia*, 23:70–72; "Il numero come forza," Sept. 1, 1928, ibid., pp. 209–16, also published as an introduction to German racist Richard Korherr, *Regresso delle nascite, morte dei popoli* (Rome: Libreria del Littorio, 1928); "Discorso ai medici," Nov. 22, 1931, *Opera omnia*, 25:58–62; "Il numero è forza," Sept. 16, 1933, *Opera omnia*, 26:52–53; "Cifre," Dec. 20, 1933, ibid, pp. 124–25; "Cifre," Feb. 27, 1934, ibid., pp. 173–74; "Demografia e biologia," May 30, 1934, ibid., pp. 259–60; "Cifre in declino," Jan. 30, 1937, *Opera omnia*, 28:110–11; "Per il potenziamento della stirpe," Dec. 21, 1937, *Opera omnia*, 29:37. See also Emil Ludwig, *Talks with Mussolini*, trans. Eden and Cedar Paul (London: George Allen and Unwin, 1933), pp. 168–69.

4. On these aspects of normalization, see Adrian Lyttelton, *The Seizure of Power: Fascism in Italy, 1919–1929* (New York: Scribner, 1973), esp. pp. 269–363, Renzo De Felice, *Mussolini il fascista*, vol. 2, *L'organizzazione dello stato fascista, 1925–1930* (Turin: Einaudi, 1968); on labor and associational life, see Victoria de Grazia, *The Culture of Consent: Mass Organization of Leisure in Fascist Italy* (New York: Cambridge University Press, 1981), pp. 11–16, 33–50.

5. B. Mussolini, "Ai prefetti," Jan. 5, 1927, *Opera omnia*, 22:468.

6. Cited in Piero Meldini, *Sposa e madre esemplare* (Rimini-Florence: Guaraldi, 1975), p. 42.

7. B. Mussolini, *Opera omnia*, 23:216; Renzo De Felice, *Mussolini il fascista*, vol. 2, *L'organizzazione dello stato fascista*, p. 151.

8. The construction of the manliness of the "new fascist man" bears further study, taking account of George Mosse's insights on the thin boundary between homosocial and homoerotic behaviors in *Nationalism and Sexuality: Respectability and Abnormal Sexuality in Modern Europe* (New York: Howard Fertig, 1985), esp. pp. 153–80. See too Barbara Spackman's intriguing remarks on "The Fascist Rhetoric of Virility," *Stanford Italian Review* 8, nos. 1–2 (1990): 81–101.

9. Mussolini, "Discorso dell'Ascensione," in *Opera omnia*, 22:376.

10. Vasco Pratolini, *A Tale of Poor Lovers* (1947; New York: Monthly Review Press, 1988), p. 294.

11. Korherr, *Regresso delle nascite*, pp. 101–03; more generally on the history of regulating prostitution, see Mary Gibson, *Prostitution and the State in Italy, 1860–1915* (New Brunswick, N.J.: Rutgers University Press, 1986), p. 226.

12. D. V. Glass, *Population Policies and Movements in Europe* (1940; London: Frank Cass, 1967), pp. 219–68, gives a detailed overview of pronatalist measures in Italy and elsewhere, whereas Massimo Livi-Bacci, *A History of Italian Fertility during the Last Two Centuries* (Princeton, N.J.: Princeton University Press, 1972), pp. 176–273, seeks to ascertain their effectiveness. Denise Detragiache, "Un aspect de la politique démographique de l'Italie fasciste: La répression de l'avortement," *Mélanges de l'école française de Rome* 92, no. 2 (1980): 691–735, highlights the repressive measures. Lesley Caldwell relates demographic issues to fascist antifeminism and the development of the Italian welfare state in "Reproducers of the Nation: Women and the Family in Fascist Policy," in *Rethinking Italian Fascism*, ed. David Forgacs (London: Lawrence and Wishart, 1986), pp. 110–41.

13. Livio Livi, "Relazione," in *Atti della II riunione del comitato di consulenza per gli studi sulla popolazione, Firenze, 12 aprile 1938* (Florence: Facoltà di economia e commercio, scuola di statistica, 1938), 14:12–14; also Livi-Bacci, *A History of Italian Fertility*, p. 236.

14. Livio Livi, "Sulla attività del comitato di consulenza per gli studi sulla popolazione," in *Atti della III riunione della società italiana di demografia e statistica, Bologna, 13 novembre 1938* (Florence: Casa editrice Dott. Carlo Cya, 1939), p. 21.

15. Giorgio Gattei, "Per una storia del comportamento amoroso dei bolognesi: Le nascite dall'unità al fascismo," *Società e storia* 9 (1980): 627–28.

16. Libero Lenti, "Alcuni recenti aspetti della natalità milanese," in *Atti della II riunione*, pp. 140–43; more generally on population politics in Milan, see the recent study of David Horn, "The Goverment of the Social in Interwar Italy," (Ph.D. diss., Department of Anthropology, University of California, Berkeley, 1987).

17. See Detragiache, "Un aspect de la politique démographique de l'Italie fasciste," pp. 691–92; see also Livi-Bacci, *A History of Italian Fertility*, pp. 369ff.

18. The contemporaneous development of Italian population statistics, racialism, and demographic politics has not been studied sufficiently, although not for lack of contemporary sources. To start, see Claudio Pogliano's excellent "Scienza e stirpe: Eugenica in Italia (1912–1939)," *Passato e presente* 5 (1984): 61–97. For an example of the socio-biologist Nicola Pende's work, see "Costituzione e fecondita", *Atti del Congresso internazionale per gli studi della popolazione*, Rome, Sept. 7–10, 1931, ed. Corrado Gini, 7 vols. (Rome: Istituto poligrafico dello Stato, 1934), 3:77–86. Other research conditioned by the exaggerated biological positivism of the times includes Mario Tirelli and Alda Marasca, "Scopi e organizzazione della inchiesta antropologica e costituzionalistica sui genitori delle famiglie con 7 o piu figli nati vivi," ibid., 4:7–15; and the ludicrous

work of Carlalberto Grillenzoni, "I caratteri del fisico e del vestire considerati come fattori demografici," ibid., 2:261–69, which proved an unsurprisingly negative correlation between "fecundity" and "elegance." Cf. those investigators with a stronger social conscience, such as Umberto D'Ancona, "Indagine antropometrica e costituzionalistica sulle famiglie numerose," ibid., 245–60, and Elena Caroli-Saponaro, "Tenore di vita e psicologia delle famiglie numerose del Barese," ibid., 635–40.

19. See Nora Federici, *La riproduttività differenziale* (Rome: University of Rome, Istituto di Statistica, 1939); see also Pier Paolo Luzzatto-Fegiz, "La politica demografica del fascismo," *Annali di economia* 12 (1937), and Ugo Giusti, "L'andamento della natalità in Italia nel decennio 1931–1940 e i suoi aspetti ambientali," *Economia*, n.s. 19, vol. 27, nos. 3–4 (Mar.–Apr. 1941): 107–17.

20. Judged by sheer quantity of publications, demographics appears second only to labor issues as a topic of expert discourse. Nicola Pende, *Bonifica umana* (Bologna: Cappelli, 1933) and Giovan Battista Pellizzi, *Fecondità e potere* (Milan: Libreria d'Italia, 1929) exemplify the style of these "authoritative" summations.

21. In addition to Livi-Bacci, *A History of Italian Fertility*, pp. 249–83, see Glass, *Population Policies and Movements in Europe*; and Patrick Festy, *La fécondité des pays occidentaux de 1870 à 1970*, Travaux et Documents, no. 85 (Paris: Institut national d'études démographiques, 1979). For a more detailed discussion of some national characteristics, see Angus McLaren, *Sexuality and Social Order: The Debate over the Fertility of Women and Workers in France* (New York: Holmes and Meier, 1983).

22. The more complicated issue of reconstructing female motivation has been undertaken, with reference to the United States, by Linda Gordon, *Woman's Body, Woman's Right: A Social History of Birth Control in America* (New York: Penguin, 1977).

23. A good example is A. Molinari, "Un'indagine sulle motivazioni della diminuzione delle nascite," *Atti del Congresso internazionale* 7:473–512, based on a survey conducted in 1928–29.

24. Pier Paolo Luzzatto-Fegiz, "La politica demografica del fascismo," p. 121.

25. Jane Schneider and Peter Schneider, "Demographic Transitions in a Sicilian Rural Town," *Journal of Family History* (Fall 1984): 258–69.

26. This conclusion, shared by the Schneiders, was also reiterated in several inquiries in the *Atti della II riunione del comitato di consulenza per gli studi sulla popolazione* in 1938. See especially F. Livi, "La fecondità matrimoniale di operai della Spezia dal 1931 al 1937," 2:19–28; G. Golzio on Turin, "Qualche dato sulla relazione fra natalità e sviluppo industriale ed urbano in provincia di Torino," 2:122–29; and G. Tagliacarne on several big northern and southern port towns, "La diminuzione della fecondità legittima fra gli ultimi due censimenti della popolazione,

1931–1936," 3:105–17, esp. p. 107. Why the size of landless rural or subproletarian families should have stayed high or even increased in this period is unclear: the Schneiders' contention that poor women disrupted breast feeding to work, truncating the natural spacing between pregnancies, is debatable, though it adds fuel to the argument that having many children was increasingly associated with downward mobility.

27. Luigi Maccone, *Ricordi di un medico pediatra* (Turin: G. B. Paravia, 1936), p. 62.

28. See chapter 5.

29. Maccone, *Ricordi*, p. 67.

30. Cf. Luisa Passerini, *Torino operaio e fascismo* (Bari and Rome, 1984), pp. 189–91; 207–9.

31. Caroli-Saponaro, *Atti del Congresso internazionale*, 4:636–37.

32. The major work on this subject is Gisela Bock, *Zwangssterilisation im Nationalsozialismus: Studien zur Rassenpolitik und Frauenpolitik* (Opladen: Westdeutscher Verlag, 1986).

33. Cited in *Social Wellsprings*, ed. Joseph Husslein, 2 vols. (Milwaukee, Wis.: Bruce, 1942), *Eighteen Encyclicals of Social Reconstruction of Pope Pius XI*, pp. 148–49 (my translation).

34. Cited in Pogliano, "Scienza e stirpe: Eugenica in Italia (1912–1939)," pp. 79, 97.

35. Nicola Pende, "Nuovi orientamenti per la protezione e l'assistenza della madre e del fanciullo," *Medicina infantile* 7, no. 8 (Aug. 1936): 233.

36. Glass, *Population Policies and Movements in Europe*, pp. 231–32; also Detragiache, "Un aspect de la politique démographique de l'Italie fasciste," pp. 699–701; and esp. Passerini, *Torino operaio*, chap. 4, passim.

37. Nuto Revelli, *L'anello forte* (Turin: Einaudi, 1985).

38. On Italy, see Livi-Bacci, *A History of Italian Fertility*, pp. 336–39; on the United States, see James Reed, *The Birth Control Movement and American Society: From Private Vice to Public Virtue* (Princeton, N.J.: Princeton University Press, 1983); on England, see Angus McLaren, *Birth Control in Nineteenth-Century England* (London: Croom Helm, 1978); and on France, see McClaren, *Sexuality and Social Order*.

39. See especially Gisela Bock's English-language synthesis of her book, "Racism and Sexism in Nazi Germany: Motherhood, Compulsory Sterilization, and the State," *Signs* 8, no. 3 (1983): 400–21; and on the 1920s proper, various essays by Atina Grossmann, especially, "The New Woman and the Rationalization of Sexuality in Weimar Germany," in *Powers of Desire*, ed. Ann Snitow, Christine Stansell, and Sharon Thompson (New York: Monthly Review Press, 1983), pp. 153–71.

40. Whether true or not, the presumption that economic, occupational, and cultural differentials far outweighed the incidence of Catholic belief in determining fertility appears to have guided all inquiry. See, for

example, Pietro Carini, "Circa l'andamento della natalità in provincia di Cremona," *Atti della II riunione*, 50–54.

41. Gaetano Salvemini, "Do Italian Women Obey Mussolini?," *Birth Control Review* 17 (1933): 65.

42. Lalla Romano, *Una giovinezza inventata* (Turin: Einaudi, 1979), pp. 84–85. See also *Confessioni di una piccola italiana* (Verona: Essedue, 1983), pp. 120–21, 138.

43. Revelli, *L'anello forte*, pp. 58–59.

44. Passerini, *Torino operaio*, p. 189.

45. Diego De Castro, "Risultati di un'indagine preliminare sull'estensione dell'uso dei mezzi contraccettivi," *Atti della II riunione*, pp. 100–115. See too Aldo Masciotta, "L'operaio, donna e madre," *La ginecologia* 6, no. 12 (Dec. 1940): 633.

46. Gattei, "Per una storia del comportamento amoroso dei bolognesi," p. 629n37.

47. See Detragiache, "Un aspect de la politique démographique de l'Italie fasciste," pp. 702–9; and especially the recent fieldwork of Nancy Triolo, "The Angel-Makers: Fascist Pronatalism and the Professionalization of Midwives in Sicily" (Ph.D. diss., Department of Anthropology, University of California, Berkeley, 1989).

48. "La denuncia e il referto medico nei casi d'aborto," *Archivio di antropologia criminale, psichiatria e medicina legale*, ser. 4, vol. 57 (1937): 59–61.

49. Passerini, *Torino operaio*, pp. 201–8.

50. Passerini's oral histories are especially telling on this problem, ibid., pp. 194–213.

51. Jacques Donzelot, *The Policing of Families*, trans. Robert Hurley (1977; New York: Pantheon, 1979).

52. These trends in Great Britain are analyzed by Elizabeth Wilson, *Women and the Welfare State* (London: Tavistock, 1977) and Jane Lewis, *The Politics of Motherhood: Maternal and Child Welfare in England, 1900–1939* (London: Croom Helm, 1980). Comparative insights, highlighting the situation in Scandinavia, are found in Laura Balbo and Helga Nowotny, eds., *Time to Care in Tomorrow's Welfare System: The Nordic Experience and the Italian Case* (Vienna: European Centre for Social Welfare Training and Research, 1986); also Helga Maria Hernes, "Women and the Welfare State: The Transition from Private to Public Dependence," in *Patriarchy in a Welfare Society*, ed. Harriet Holter (Oslo: Universitetsforlaget, 1984), pp. 26–45.

53. Carlotta Grilli, "L'Opera nazionale maternità ed infanzia," *Almanacco della donna italiana, 1930*, pp. 152–63; ONMI, *Origine e sviluppo dell'ONMI, 1926(IV)–1935(XIII)* (Rome: Carlo Colombi, 1936), pp. 11–18. The major study of pre-twentieth-century foundling institutions

is Volker Hunecke, *Die Findelkinder von Mailand: Kindaussetzung und aussetzende Eltern von 17. bis 19. Jahrhundert* (Stuttgart: Klett-Cotta, 1987).

54. ONMI, *Origine e sviluppo,* pp. 22–48; see also Attilio Lo Monaco-Aprile, *La protezione della maternità e dell'infanzia* (Rome: Istituto nazionale fascista di cultura, 1934). There still has been no definitive study of ONMI, though several researchers, including Nancy Triolo and David Horn, are preparing books studying its local impact, and Maria S. Quine of St. Peters College, Oxford, is currently finishing a study of the national organization.

55. Lo Monaco-Aprile, *La protezione della maternità e dell'infanzia,* p. 11.

56. Marzio Barbagli, *Sotto lo stesso tetto: Mutamenti della famiglia in Italia dal XV al XX secolo* (Bologna: Mulino, 1984), p. 421. Barbagli cites an illegitimacy rate of just over 25 percent in 1933. In east-central Italy rates were also high, see Silvio Vianelli, "Sulla fecondità legittima ed illegittima nel comune di Bologna," *"Atti del Congresso internazionale,* 3:196; Giovan Battista Allaria, *Il problema demografico italiano visto da un pediatra* (Turin: Vincenzo Bona, 1935), p. 26. The problem of illegitimacy in fascist Italy bears study along the lines suggested by Gianna Pomata, "Madri illegittime tra Ottocento e Novecento: Storie cliniche e storie di vita," *Quaderni storici* 44, no. 8 (Aug. 1980): 497–542.

57. Anita Pensotti, *Rachele* (Milan: Bompiani, 1983), pp. 25–33, 43; also Rachele Mussolini, with Michael Chinigo, *My Life with Mussolini* (London: Robert Hale, 1959), pp. 23, 32, 57.

58. Stefano Somogyi, *La mortalità nei primi cinque anni di età in Italia, 1863–1963* (Palermo: Ingrana, 1967), p. 42, table 7; Gattei, "Per una storia del comportamento amoroso dei bolognesi," pp. 635–39.

59. Denise Detragiache, "Du socialisme au fascisme naissant: Formation et itinéraire de Regina Terruzzi," in *Femmes et fascismes,* ed. Rita Thälmann (Paris: Tiérce, 1986), pp. 45, 62. Also Archivio centrale dello stato, Segreteria particolare del Duce, Carteggio ordinario, fascicolo 509509, Regina Terruzzi: Sebastiani-Mussolini, July 19, 1935; Promemoria Terruzzi-Mussolini, Oct. 19, 1936; Terruzzi-Chiavolini, June 1, 1929; and ACS, SPD, CO, f. 509.817/3 Terruzzi-Sebastiani, June 27, 1937.

60. The staunchest defense of this position came from Doctor Attilio Lo Monaco-Aprile, "Il valore etico dell'assistenza alle madri illegittime," *Maternità ed infanzia* 5, no. 2 (Nov. 1930): 1111–18; and Doctor Sante De Sanctis, as cited in the anonymous article, "I figli di madri nubili," *Maternità ed infanzia,* 2, no. 2 (Feb. 1927): 29–34. See too the summary of the 1932 ONMI meetings by A. Lo Monaco-Aprile, "Il convegno nazionale dei delegati provinciali dell'ONMI," *Maternità ed infanzia* 7, no. 7 (July 1932): 631, as well as proposals from Daisy di Robilant in Archivio centrale dello stato, Segreteria particolare del Duce, Carteggio ordinario

(ACS, SPD, CO), f. 509.817/3 Memo-Duce: re di Robilant, May 1935; di Robilant: presentation to International Council of Women, September 23, 1937. See too Teresa Labriola, "Contributo agli studi della paternità" in *La donna e la famiglia nella legislazione fascista* (Naples: Edizione de la Toga, 1933), pp. 59–66.

61. Giorgio Quartara, *Le leggi del libero amore* (Turin: Bocca, 1931), pp. 425–66. This work gives a panorama of the changes in legislation regarding illegitimacy.

62. Lo Monaco-Aprile, *La protezione della maternità e dell'infanzia,* p. 21.

63. Olga Modigliani, *Lavoro sociale delle donne* (Rome: Fratelli Pallotta, 1935), p. 18.

64. Lo Monaco-Aprile, *La protezione della maternità e dell'infanzia,* pp. 26–27; ONMI, *Origine e sviluppo,* p. 99. Allaria, *Il problema demografico italiano visto da un pediatra,* p. 26.

65. See in particular Pius XI's *Casti connubi,* cited in Husslein, ed., *Social Wellsprings,* p. 170; Giorgio Quartara, *La femme et dieu* (Paris: Alcan, 1935), pp. 290–91; Passerini, *Torino operaio,* pp. 185–86.

66. Lo Monaco-Aprile, *La protezione della maternità e dell'infanzia,* p. 23.

67. Maccone, *Ricordi di un medico pediatra,* pp. 174–75.

68. Somogyi, *La mortalità nei primi cinque anni di età,* pp. 32–38. Cf. Caldwell, "Reproducers of the Nation," pp. 122, 130n31; also Allaria, *Il problema demografico italiano,* pp. 44–47. Whether larger families had higher infant mortality rates was the subject of medical debates and much obfuscation. See for example Prof. G. Frontali, "Mortalità infantile in generale e nelle famiglie numerose," *Minerva medica,* ser. 28, 46, 2 (Nov. 18, 1937): 541–44. On the causes of infant death, see also the various doctors' replies, "Risposta al questionario sul problema della mortalità infantile nel I biennio di vita," *Il lattante* 10, no. 3 (Mar. 1939).

69. Allaria, *Il problema demografico italiano,* p. 53; ONMI, *Origini e sviluppo,* p. 158.

70. Pensotti, *Rachele,* p. 49.

71. Nancy Triolo, "The Angel-Makers: Fascist Pronatalism and the Professionalization of Midwives in Sicily." Consulted by courtesy of the author.

72. Luigi Pirandello, *Donna Mimma: Novelle per un anno* (1917: Milan: Mondadori, 1951), pp. 4–5.

73. Triolo, "The Angel-Makers"; similar changes in midwifery are noted in Liliana Lanzardo, "Per una storia dell'ostetrica condotta," *Rivista di storia contemporanea* 1 (1985): 136–52.

74. The *podestà*'s injunctions, as summed up by an anonymous observer, are cited in Gattei, "Per una storia del comportamento amoroso dei bolognesi," p. 629. For Mussolini's views on D'Annunzio, see Gian-

carlo Fusco, "I 'play-boys' del regime," in *Playdux: Storia erotica del fascismo* (Rome: Tattilo, 1973), pp. 152–53.

75. Cited in Salvemini, "Do Italian Women Obey Mussolini?," p. 65.

76. See for example Ester Lombardo, "Rassegna del movimento femminile italiano," *Almanacco della donna italiana, 1928*, pp. 294–95; also Gina G. Alessandri, "Celibato: L'aumento della tassa sull'egoismo," *Donna fascista* 18, no. 5 (Mar. 1936): 2.

77. Bruno Rossi-Ragazzi, "Gli assegni familiari dal punto di vista demografico," in *Atti della III riunione*, pp. 231–32; Pier Paolo Luzzatto-Fegis, "Natalità e tributi," in *Atti della III riunione*, pp. 54–62; and Glass, *Population Policies and Movements in Europe*, pp. 99–142.

78. On German family policy under Hitler, see Tim Mason, "Women in Germany, 1925–1940," *History Workshop*, Pts. 1 and 2 (Spring 1976 and Autumn 1976): 74–113; 5–32.

79. Karin Hausen, "Mothers, Sons and the Sale of Symbols and Goods: The 'German Mother's Day' 1922–1933," in *Interest and Emotion: Essays on the Study of Family and Kinship*, ed. Hans Medick and David Warren Sabean (Cambridge: Cambridge University Press, 1984), pp. 371–413.

80. Luigi Salvatorelli and Giovanni Mira, *Storia d'Italia nel periodo fascista*, new ed. (Turin: Einaudi, 1964), pp. 519, 570; Margherita Sarfatti, "Italia d'oggi," *Augustea* 23 (1933): 655.

81. ONMI, *Origine e sviluppo*, pp. 101–3.

82. Passerini, *Torino operaio*, pp. 187–88.

83. See, for example, Paolo Ardali, *La politica demografica di Mussolini* (Mantua: Casa Editrice "Mussolinia" di Franco Paladino, 1929), pp. 29–31; also Stanis Ruinas, *Scrittori e scribacchine* (Rome: Accademia, 1930) and chapter 7 below.

84. Mussolini-Prefect of Bologna, June 29, 1934, cited in Renzo De Felice, *Mussolini il Duce: Gli anni del consenso, 1929–1936* (Turin: Einaudi, 1974), p. 155.

85. Alex, *Quello che deve sapere una giovane signora* (Milan: Istituto edizioni italiane, 1927), p. 19.

CHAPTER 4

1. "Elogio alle donne d'Italia," in *Opera omnia*, ed. Edoardo Susmel and Duilio Susmel, 44 vols. (Florence: La Fenice, 1951–80), 27:266.

2. Luigi Salvatorelli and Giovanni Mira, *Storia d'Italia nel periodo fascista*, new ed. (Turin: Einaudi, 1964), pp. 868–69; *La donna italiana*, 12, nos. 9–10 (Sept.–Oct. 1935): 449; 12, no. 11 (Nov. 1935): 491–92; 12, no. 12 (Dec. 1935): 538; 13, no. 1 (Jan. 1936): 3.

3. Luigi Chiarini, "Carattere retrivo della famiglia borghese," *Critica fascista* 11, no. 16 (Aug. 15, 1933): 305.

4. Sileno Fabbri, cited in ONMI, *Origine e sviluppo dell'ONMI, 1926(IV)–1935(XIII)* (Rome: Carlo Colombi, 1936), p. 98.

5. Mussolini, "Macchine e donna," Aug. 31, 1934, *Opera omnia* 20: 310–11.

6. See "Argo" (probably Guiseppe Bottai), "Compiti della donna," *Critica fascista* 11, no. 16 (July 15, 1933): 267; cf. other contributions that year by Mario Palazzi, "Autorità dell'uomo," vol. 11, no. 10 (May 15, 1933): 183–85; Manlio Pompei, "La famiglia e il fascismo: Un'inchiesta da fare," vol. 11, no. 9 (May 1, 1933): 163–66; Lince, "Gli uomini e le donne," vol. 11, no. 16 (Aug. 15, 1933): 303–4; Stefano Mario Cutelli, "Fasci e famiglia," vol. 11, no. 22 (Nov. 15, 1933): 436–38.

7. Indispensable, though diverse, insights into the problems of the family as it changed during the interwar years are found in the Frankfurt school of sociology's remarkable collection, *Autorität und Familie,* ed. and pref. Max Horkheimer (Paris: Felix Alcan, 1936) and in Horkheimer, "Authority and the Family," in *Critical Theory: Selected Essays* (New York: Seabury, 1972), pp. 47–128; in Alva Myrdal, *Nation and Family* (1941; Cambridge: MIT Press, 1968); and in British feminist Denise Riley, *War in the Nursery: Theory of the Mother and Child* (London: Virago, 1983).

8. Definitions of the range and types of family policy formulated in interwar Europe are found in Myrdal, *Family and Nation,* and Riley, *War in the Nursery.* See also John Macnicol, *The Movement for Family Allowances, 1918–1945* (London: Heinemann, 1980); Sheila Kammerman and A. J. Kahn, eds., *Family Policy: Governments and Families in Fourteen Countries* (New York: Columbia University Press, 1978). A theoretical overview is provided by Jacques Donzelot, *The Policing of Families,* trans. Robert Hurley (1977; New York: Pantheon, 1979).

9. The Nazis' treatment of the family bears many similarities with the projects of Italian fascists. See Tim Mason, "Women in Germany, 1925–1940: Family, Welfare and Work," *History Workshop* 1 (1976): 74–113, and 2 (1976): 5–32. Gisela Bock, in *Zwangssterilisation im Nationalsozialismus* (Opladen: Westdeutscher Verlag, 1986), rightly emphasizes Nazism's antifamily and antiprocreative racial politics. By contrast, Claudia Koonz, in *Women in the Fatherland* (New York: St. Martin's Press, 1987), argues that the Aryan family, by offering respite to men, legitimated their acts of violence against others and should thus be counted as a cause of the Third Reich's genocidal racism.

10. T. H. Marshall, *Social Policy in the Twentieth Century* (London: Hutchinson Education Series, 1985).

11. Analyses of the impact of welfare state politics on women in general help distinguish what was peculiar to fascist politics and what new gender distinctions and forms of dependency were common to all political systems. See Carole Pateman, "The Patriarchal Welfare State," Harvard

Center for European Studies Working Paper Series (Cambridge, 1987); Helga Hernes, "Women and the Welfare State: The Transition from Private to Public Dependence," in Patriarchy in a Welfare State, ed. Harriet Holter (Oslo: Universitetsforlaget, 1984), pp. 26–45; Jane Lewis, "Feminism and Welfare," in ed. Juliet Mitchell and Ann Oakley, What Is Feminism? (New York: Pantheon, 1986), pp. 85–100; and Elizabeth Wilson, Women and the Welfare State (London: Tavistock, 1977).

12. "Bardature della crisi," La riforma sociale (Sept.–Oct. 1932), collected in Luigi Einaudi, Saggi (Turin: La Riforma sociale, 1933), p. 515. See too Frederigo Nomi, Gli scambi non monetari e l'economia famigliare nell'Italia contemporanea (Padua: Cedam, 1935), who underscores the role of family in an autarchic economy.

13. See for example Ferruccio Lantini, La famiglia nella resistenza alle sanzioni (Rome: Società Editrice Novissima, 1937); also Francesca Ambrogi, "La donna e l'autarchia," Rivista di politica economica 30, no. 6 (June 1940): 469–78. At the same time, the fascist regime never conducted the family budget studies that other countries, at the urging of the International Labor Office and private firms, undertook beginning in the 1920s (and that the United States began at the turn of the century).

14. On Italy's internal migration, see Anna Treves, Le migrazioni interne nell'Italia fascista (Turin: Einaudi, 1976). Important insights into the new and old functions of the family in urban contexts are found in Stefano Mussu, "La famiglia operaia," in La famiglia italiana dall'Ottocento a oggi, ed. Pietro Melograni (Bari: Laterza, 1988), pp. 78–91, and Maurizio Gribaudi, Mondo operaio e mito operaio: Spazi e percorsi sociali a Torino nel primo Novecento (Turin: Einaudi, 1987).

15. Pompei, "La famiglia e il fascismo," p. 164. Figures on family composition are drawn from tables 13–14, "Famiglie residenti secondo i numeri dei membri residenti e la condizione sociale del capo famiglia, Censimento 21 aprile 1936," Compendio statistico italiano, 1938, p. 40.

16. Cesare Alessandri, "Punto di partenza: La nuzialità," Maternità ed infanzia 9, no. 6 (June 1934): 4–5.

17. Vera Zamagni, "Dinamica e problemi della distribuzione commerciale e al minuto tra il 1880 e la II Guerra Mondiale," in Mercati e consumi: Organizzazione e qualificazione del commercio in Italia dal XVII al XX secolo (Bologna: Edizioni Analisi, 1986), p. 598.

18. Marzio Barbagli, Sotto lo stesso tetto: Mutamenti della famiglia in Italia dal XV al XX secolo (Bologna: Il Mulino, 1984), pp. 428, 448–50. On the "patriarchal" family household, see Carlo Poni, "Family and 'podere' in Emilia Romagna," Journal of Italian History, 1, no. 1 (1978): 201–34, and Agopik Manoukian, "La famiglia dei contadini," in La famiglia italiana, ed. Melograni, pp. 13–34.

19. On ruralization, see Carl Schmidt's classic, The Plow and the Sword (New York: Columbia University Press, 1938), and the more recent overview by Domenico Preti, La modernizzazione corporativa: 1922–1940

(Milan: Franco Angeli, 1987), pp. 53–100. The gender distribution of labor in peasant households is vividly described in Donald Pitkin, *The House That Giacomo Built* (New York: Cambridge University Press, 1985); see also chapter 6, pp. 181–82.

20. *Le encicliche sociali dei papi*, ed. Igino Giordani, 4th ed. (Rome: Editrice Studium, 1956), p. 200.

21. Ferdinando Loffredo, *Politica della famiglia* (Milan: Bompiani, 1938), p. xviii.

22. Alva Myrdal, *Nation and Family*, p. 135.

23. Vera Zamagni, "Distribuzione del reddito e classi sociali nell'Italia fra le due guerre," in *La classe operaia durante il fascismo*, ed. Giulio Sapelli, Annali: Fondazione Giangiacomo Feltrinelli vol. 20 (Milan, 1980), pp. 25, 31–32.

24. Cutelli, "Fasci e famiglia," pp. 435–37.

25. Zamagni, "Distribuzione," pp. 33–43; on the privileges granted middle-class labor, see Victoria de Grazia, *The Culture of Consent: Mass Organization of Leisure in Fascist Italy* (New York: Cambridge University Press, 1981), pp. 127–50.

26. Bruno Biagi, "La madre e il fanciullo nell'impero fascista e nel lavoro," *Difesa sociale* 15, no. 12 (Dec. 1936): 957–58.

27. Paolo Ungari, *Storia del diritto di famiglia in Italia, 1796–1942* (Bologna: Il Mulino, 1974), p. 191. The Catholic position is summed up most ably by the jurist Ludovico Barassi, *La famiglia legittima nel nuovo codice civile*, 2d ed. (Milan: A. Giuffrè, 1941).

28. Frida Ceccon Marx and Graziella Ceccon Compagnoni, "La legislazione fascista intorno al matrimonio," in *La donna e la famiglia nella legislazione fascista intorno alla famiglia*, ed. Maria Laetitia Riccio (Naples: Edizione de la Toga, 1933), p. 1. See also Giorgio Quartara, *La riforma del Codice Civile: I libri I e III: La famiglia* (Milan: Bocca, 1938); as well as Paolo Ungari, *Storia del diritto di famiglia in Italia*, pp. 189–92.

29. Maria Laetitia Riccio, *Donna (diritto penale) donna (diritto privato e pubblico) donna maritata* (Turin: Unione Tip., 1938), pp. 209ff.; see also Teresa Labriola, "Per le nostre fanciulle," *Maternità ed infanzia* 2, no. 6 (June 1929): 77–82.

30. John A. Davis, *Conflict and Control: Law and Order in Nineteenth-Century Italy* (Atlantic Highlands, N.J.: Humanities Press International, 1988), pp. 217–22.

31. In the absence of studies of the relationship between liberal reform and fascist welfare bureaucracies, see Claudio Pogliano, "Scienza e stirpe: Eugenica in Italia (1912–1939)," *Passato e presente* 5 (1984): 61–97; also de Grazia, *Culture of Consent*, pp. 24–37; and the journals themselves, especially *Difesa sociale*.

32. "Per una carta della maternità," *Maternità ed infanzia* 7, no. 7 (July 1932): 651.

33. See Labriola's "Per la ricerca della paternità," *Maternità ed infanzia* 9, no. 1 (Jan. 1934): 2, and "Contributo agli studi sulla ricerca della paternità," in *La donna e la famiglia nella legislazione fascista*, ed. Maria Laetitia Riccio, pp. 61–66.

34. See Myrdal, *Nation and Family*; Macnicol, *The Movement for Family Allowances*; and Susan Pedersen's detailed study of family policy formulation, "The Failure of Feminism in the Making of the British Welfare State," *Radical History Review* 43 (1988): 86–110.

35. Archivio centrale dello stato, Presidenza consiglio dei ministri, 1934–36, fascicolo 3.2.2./577, Mussolini-Prefects, Jan. 25, 1933.

36. ACS, PCM, 1934–36, f. 3.2.2/577: *Premi demografici: elenco pratiche dei non aventi diritto*.

37. ACS, SPD, CO, f. 509.817/3. Fabbri-Chiavolini, Dec. 20, 1933; Fabbri–Sebastiani, Dec. 20, 1935.

38. ACS, SPD, CO, f. 509.817,1–2: "Elenco delle istanze presentate dalle madri prolifiche."

39. Loffredo's contributions, sometimes listing him with his middle name as E. or Enrico Loffredo, consisted mainly of well-informed reviews and review articles on books in five languages, for example, "Studi e attuazioni nel campo degli assegni familiari in Germania," *Rivista internazionale di scienze sociali* (hereafter *RISS*) 7 (May 1936): 286–96; "La Cina e i compiti del Kuo-Min-Tang," *RISS* 6 (1935): 622–40; and a book published by Gemelli's press, *La Cina e i compiti del Kuo-min-tang* (Milan: Vita e Pensiero, 1935). See too a sampling of his reviews, of A. Brucculeri, *Intorno al corporativismo*, *RISS* 6 (1935): 858–59; of André Corteano, *L'évolution de l'état*, *RISS* 6 (1935): 855–56; of Oreste Bellucci, *La medicina preventiva e la selezione professionale in rapporto alle assicurazioni sociali*, *RISS* 5 (1934): 149–50; of G. Ambrosini's *L'Unione sovietica nella sua formazione e struttura*, *RISS* 6 (1935): 785–86; of *Settimane sociali d'Italia*, *RISS* 5 (1934): 296–97.

40. Loffredo, *Politica della famiglia*, chap. 8 passim, pp. 230–31, 376, 412, 464.

41. Cited in Davis, *Conflict and Control*, p. 221.

42. Aldo Piperno, "La politica sanitaria," in *Welfare State all'italiana*, ed. Ugo Ascoli (Bari: Laterza, 1984), p. 162; see also Patrizia Davis, "Il sistema assistenziale in Italia," in *Welfare State all'italiana*, pp. 185–205. For a broad and careful overview, see Domenico Preti, "Per una storia sociale della Italia fascista: La tutela della salute nell'organizzazione dello stato corporativo (1922–1940)," in *Salute e classe lavoratrici in Italia*, ed. Maria Luisa Berti and Ada Gigli Marchetti (Milan: Franco Angeli, 1982), pp. 797–834.

43. Fanny Dessau, "Unità o specializzazione del servizio sociale?," *Difesa sociale* 9, no. 3 (Mar. 1930): 94–95; see also her "Contributo allo studio etico-sociale della struttura della famiglia: Saggio di elaborazione

delle monografie di 10 famiglie di operai in Roma," in *Atti del Congresso internazionale per gli studi della popolazione*, Rome, Sept. 7–10, 1931, ed. Corrado Gini, 7 vols. (Rome: Istituto poligrafico dello stato, 1934), 8: 40 and 37–63 passim.

44. Karin Hausen, "Unemployment Also Hits Women," in *Unemployment and the Great Depression in Weimar Germany*, ed. P. D. Stachura (New York: St. Martin's Press, 1986), p. 83; Chiara Saraceno, "La famiglia operaia sotto il fascismo," in *La classe operaia durante il fascismo*, p. 195.

45. The reforms in public health care are studied with exceptional detail and clarity in Domenico Preti, *La modernizzazione corporativa (1922–1940): Economia, salute pubblica, istituzioni e professioni sanitarie* (Milan: Franco Angeli, 1987), esp. pp. 127–92.

46. Marisa Ferro, "A Milano e in provincia tra i bimbi e le donne del popolo," *Giornale della donna* 14, no. 7 (Apr. 1, 1932): 5. The fight against tuberculosis is analyzed in Domenico Preti, "La lotta antitubercola nell'Italia fascista," in *Storia d'Italia, Annali, 7, Malattie e medicina* (Turin: Einaudi, 1985), pp. 995–1015.

47. Francesco Lo Presti Seminerio, "Sanità rurale: Risultati di un esperimento," *Giornale della donna* 9, no. 3 (Mar. 1934): 8.

48. Dessau, "Unità o specializzazione," p. 96. A similar phenomenon was observed in Great Britain during the 1930s, see Jane Lewis, "Dealing with Dependency: State Practices and Social Realities, 1870–1895," in *Women's Welfare, Women's Rights*, ed. Jane Lewis (London: Croom Helm, 1983), pp. 17–37.

49. "I lavori del convegno," *Maternità ed infanzia* 7, no. 7 (July 1932): 636.

50. Franca Pieroni Bortolotti, *Femminismo e partiti politici in Italia* (Rome: Editori Riuniti, 1978), pp. 125–26.

51. On the United States household reform movement, see Barbara Ehrenreich and Deirdre English, "The Manufacture of Housework," *Socialist Revolution* 5, no. 4 (Oct.–Dec. 1975): 5–40; and Ruth Swartz Cowan, "A Case Study of Technological and Social Change: The Washing Machine and the Working Wife," in *Clio's Consciousness Raised*, ed. Mary S. Hartman and Lois Banner (New York: Harper and Row, 1974), pp. 245–53. See too the works of Christine Frederick, *Household Engineer: Scientific Management in the Home* (Chicago: American School of Home Economics, 1919) and *The New Housekeeping: Efficiency Studies in Home Management* (Garden City, N.Y.: Doubleday and Pagge, 1923). This last work was translated by Diez Gasca as *La casa moderna: Come risparmiare tempo, fatica, denaro* (Rome: Enios, 1933); another of her works was translated by L. Tealdy as *La donna e la casa: Il taylorismo nella vita domestica: Libro destinato a tutte le donne d'Italia per facilitar loro il lavoro della casa* (Turin: C. ACCAME, 1928).

52. Helga [H. Jacky], "Come vorremmo la nostra casa," *Casa e lavoro* 1, no. 1 (1929): 11–12, cited in Bernardetta De Rossi, "Un progretto di razionalizzazione del lavoro domestico in Italia negli anni 30: La rivista *Casa e lavoro*" (Tesi di laurea, Dipartimento di storia, Facoltà di lettere e filosofia, Università degli studi di Bologna, 1978–79). See too the articles Diez Gasca published in ENIOS's monthly review, *L'organizzione scientifica del lavoro*, 1928–30.

53. Mario Saibante, "Il tenore di vita del popolo italiano prima dell'ultima guerra, in confronto con quello degli altri popli," Appendix C of *Piano per le importazioni e le esportazioni*, vol. 5, ed. Centro di studi e piani tecnico-economici, Comitato interministeriale per la ricostruzione (Rome, 1947), p. 287. Compare the Italian to other national experiences as illustrated, for example, in Theresa M. McBride, *The Domestic Revolution: The Modernisation of Household Services in England and France, 1820–1920* (London: Croom Helm, 1976).

54. Saibante, *Piano*, pp. 189, 281. See too Vanna Fraticelli, "*Parva sed apta mihi*: Note sulla cultura e sulla politica della casa negli anni venti in Italia," *Nuova DWF* 19–20 (Winter-Spring 1982): 39–47; and Alessandra Muntoni, "Cultura della casa nell'Italia del dopoguerra," ibid., 7–26.

55. Maria Albini, "L'arredamento come mezzo educativo," *Casa e lavoro* 5, no. 7–8 (1933): 240, cited in De Rossi, "Un progetto di razionalizzazione," p. 51.

56. Eugenia Montinari, *Dea vesta: il buon governo della casa* (Milan: Vallardi, 1933), pp. 9, 11ff. See also Erminia De Benedetti, *Il nostro nido: Consigli sul buon governo della casa—Nozioni di economia domestica* (Palermo: R. Sandron, 1928); Maria Pia and Ifigenia DeMichelis, *Manuale completo di economia domestica* (Turin: Società Editore Internazionale, 1929) and successive editions; Donna Clara, *Dalla cucina al salotto: Enciclopedia della vita domestica*, ed. Lidia Morelli, rev. ed. (Turin-Genoa: Lattes, 1925); and the popular Lidia Morelli, *Come sistemare e governare la mia casa* (Milan: Hoepli, 1928), and *Massaie di domani: Conversazioni di economia domestica* (Turin: Lattes, 1937, 1938); *Nuovo ricettario domestico: Enciclopedia moderna per la casa*, ed. L. Morelli, 10th ed. with addition by I. Ghezzi (Milan: Hoepli, 1941). There was also a special Catholic perspective in Chiara Bellati, *La nostra casa* (Milan: Vita e pensiero, 1930, 1937). See also Gabriella Turnaturi, *Gente perbene* (Milan: Sugar, 1988), and chapter 7, pp. 226–27.

57. Brin, *Usi e costumi, 1920–1940* (Palermo: Sellerio Editore, 1981), p. 195. See too chapter 6, pp. 190–91.

58. See Maristella Casciato, "L'abitazione e gli spazi domestici," in *La famiglia italiana*, ed. Melograni, pp. 525–87, and numerous publications from the period such as *Le case popolari: Norme e tipi di carattere generale* (Rome, 1937); Isidoro Andreani, *Le abitazioni moderne* (Milan:

Hoepli 1928); Renato Biasutti, *La casa rurale nella Toscana* (Bologna: Zanichelli, 1938); Bruno Moretti, *Case d'abitazione in Italia: Quartieri popolari, case operaie, case per impiegati* (Milan: Hoepli, 1929). On the changing fabric of town life, see the exemplary work on Turin by Stefano Musso, "Proletariato industriale e fascismo a Torino: Aspetti del territorio operaio," in *La classe operaia durante il fascismo*, pp. 511–66.

59. Istituto centrale di statistica, *Indagine sulle abitazioni al 21 aprile 1931*, pt. 1, with text by Alfredo Nicefero (Florence: A. Vallecchi, 1934–36). See also "Il problema delle abitazioni e l'industria edilizia in Italia," in *Piano per le importazioni e le esportazioni industriali dell'anno finanziario, 1947–1948* (Rome: Centro di studi e piani tecnico-economici, Comitato interministeriale per la ricostruzione, 1947), pp. 280–92.

60. Fernanda Momigliano, *Vivere bene in tempi difficili: Come le donne affrontano le crisi economiche* (Milan: Hoepli, 1933), pp. 6, 17ff., 85, 131. See also Piero Meldini, "A tavola e in cucina," in *La famiglia italiana*, ed. Melograni, pp. 454–56.

61. ACS, PCM, 1934–1936, f. 3.2.2/577, sf. 10.

62. Brin, *Usi e costumi*, p. 132.

63. Musso, "Proletariato industriale e fascismo a Torino." See also Giovanni Levi, Luisa Passerini, and Lucetta Scaraffia, "Vita quotidiana in un quartiere operaio di Torino fra le due guerre," *Quaderni storici* 35 (1977): 433–49.

64. Dessau, "Unità o specializzazione"; also Chiara Saraceno, "La famiglia operaia sotto il fascismo," in *La classe operaia durante il fascismo*; and Daniele Jalla, "The Working Class Family in Turin: Traditional Values and the Economy," in *Our Common History: The Transformation of Europe*, ed. Paul Thompson with Natasha Burchardt (London: Pluto Press, 1982), pp. 213–21. For experiences elsewhere, see Anna Davin's exhaustive treatment of British models of working-class uplift in "Imperialism and Motherhood," *History Workshop* 5 (1978): 9–66, and Ute Frevert, "The Civilizing Tendency of Hygiene: Working-Class Women under Medical Control in Imperial Germany," in *German Women in the Nineteenth Century: A Social History*, ed. John C. Fout (New York: Holmes and Meier, 1984), pp. 320–24.

65. "Il problema delle abitazioni e l'industria edilizia in Italia," in *Piano*, p. 282. See too the eloquent plea by the architect Giuseppe Pagano, "Case per il popolo," *Donna fascista* 12, no. 1 (Dec. 18, 1939):10.

66. Passerini, "Work Ideology and Working-Class Attitudes to Fascism," in *Our Common History*, ed. Paul Thompson with Natasha Burchardt, pp. 69–70.

67. Maria Mayo Faina, "La moglie dell'operaio," *Giornale della donna* 14, no. 13 (July 1, 1932):4.

68. Cf. Chiara Saraceno, "Percorsi di vita femminile nella classe

operaia: Tra famiglia e lavoro durante il fascismo," *Memoria* 2 (Oct. 1981): 64–75; also Jalla, "The Working Class Family in Turin" and Saraceno, "La famiglia operaia." The Italian case is consistent with Jane Humphries' contention that labor conflict reinforces family ties: see "Class struggle and the Persistence of the Working-class Family," *Cambridge Journal of Economics* 1 (1977): 241–58.

69. Anna Garin, *Esempi di lezioni di economia e di igiene domestica alle massaie rurali della Toscana* (Florence: PNF, Fasci femminili, sezione massaia rurale, 1935), p. 1.

70. Cesare Alessandri, "Maternità e natalità nelle campagne," *Maternità ed infanzia* 5, no. 10 (Oct. 1930): 1028–33, draws on a study called "Indagini sulle condizioni di vita dei contadini italiani" conducted by the *Confederazione nazionale dei sindacati fascisti dell'agricoltura*, which was apparently published with a preface by the union's head, Luigi Razza.

71. Franco Angelini, "La donna in agricoltura," *L'azione delle massaie rurali* 2, no. 2 (Feb. 1934): 1.

72. *L'azione delle massaie rurali* 2, no. 3 (Mar. 1934): 1. The takeover of the Lombard organization is alluded to in its periodical, *Domus rustica* (Milan) 1, no. 1 (issued on Jan. 1933 and continued through 1934). See too the brief, well-researched account of the *massaie's* origins and programs in Angela Amoroso, "Le organizzazioni femminili nelle campagne durante il fascismo," in *Storia in Lombardia: Il fascismo in Lombardia* 1–2 (1989): 305–16.

73. See *L'azione delle massaie rurali* 3, no. 2 (Feb. 1935): 1; 3, no. 3 (Mar. 1935): 2.

74. ACS, SPD, CO. f. 509509, Regina Terruzzi, Letter Terruzzi-Mussolini, Dec. 5, 1934.

75. For the hygienists' view of the colonies, see "La vita in colonia," *Maternità ed infanzia* 2, no. 4 (Apr. 1927): 78–84; also Archangelo Ilvento, "Colonie estive," ibid., 2, no. 5 (May 1927): 59–61.

76. *Donna fascista* 20, no. 17 (Sept. 10, 1938): 3.

77. "Attività assistenziale," *Maternità ed infanzia* 7, no. 2, (Feb. 1932): 142–43; "La Befana del Duce," *Giornale della donna* 16, no. 1 (Jan. 8, 1934):16.

78. Palazzi, *Autorità dell'uomo*, p. 182.

79. Luigi Maccone, *Ricordi di un medico pediatra* (Torino: G. B. Paravia, 1936), p. 67.

80. Unione fascista fra le famiglie numerose, *Istruzione per i fiduciari dei nuclei di famiglie numerose* (Padua: G. Gualtieri, 1938), pp. 6–10.

81. Pietro Capoferri, *Venti anni col fascismo e con i sindacati* (Milan, 1957), pp. 194–97. See too ACS, PCM, 1937–39, 1/3-1, f. 945, various letters and petitions.

82. Edward Banfield, *The Moral Basis of a Backward Society* (1958; New York: Free Press, 1967), p. 85.

83. Donald Pitkin, *The House That Giacomo Built*, pp. 7–12.

CHAPTER 5

1. Louise Diel, *La generazione di Mussolini* (Milan: Mondadori, 1934), pp. 202–3.

2. On Italian youth, almost exclusively on male Italian youth, see the insightful work by Edward Tannenbaum, *The Fascist Experience: Italian Society and Culture, 1922–1945* (New York: Basic Books, 1972), pp. 117–48. See also Tracy H. Koon's competent *Believe, Obey, Fight: Political Socialization of Youth in Fascist Italy, 1922–1943* (Chapel Hill: University of North Carolina Press, 1985). Bruno Wanrooij, "The Rise and Fall of Italian Fascism as a Generational Revolution," *Journal of Contemporary History* 22 (1987): 401–18, highlights generational conflicts. Statistics on the age composition of the Italian population are in *Annuario statistico italiano, 1944–48*, ser. 5, vol. 1 (Rome: Istituto poligrafico dello stato, 1949), pp. 31–34.

3. Zangrandi, *Il lungo viaggio attraverso il fascismo: Contributo alla storia di una generazione* (Milan: Garzanti, 1971). See too Luigi Preti's novel, *Giovinezza, giovinezza* (Milan: Mondadori, 1966).

4. Daria Banfi Malaguzzi, *Femminilità contemporanea* (Milan: Alpes, 1928), pp. 16–23.

5. For definitions of youth helpful to studying girlhood, see John Gillis, *Youth and History: Tradition and Change in European Age Relations, 1770 to the Present* (New York: Academic Press, 1974).

6. These include Rita Montalcini Levi, *Elogio dell'imperfezione* (Milan: Garzanti, 1987), translated as *In Praise of Imperfection: My Life and Work*, trans. Luigi Attardi (New York: Sloan Foundation Science Series/Basic Books, 1988); Susanna Agnelli, *Vestivamo alla marinara* (Milan: Mondadori, 1975); Iste Cagossi, *Da piccola italiana a partigiana* (Modena: Mucchi-S.T.E.M., 1976); G. Callegari, *Piccola borghese* (Milano: La Pietra, 1986); S. Fatta della Fratta, *Quando si cantava Giovinezza* (Palermo: La Luna, 1986); Anna E. Mellini, *Marionette bianche e nere* (Reggio Emilia: A.G.E. Grafica Editoriale, 1983); Marcella Olschki, *Terza liceo 1939* (Milan: Longanesi, 1950); and *Confessioni di una piccola italiana: Memorie anonime* (Verona: Essedue, 1983). See too the charming fictionalized account of Elena Canino, *Clotilde tra le due guerre* (Milan: Longanesi, 1957).

7. On prewar growing up, see Michela De Giorgio, "Signore e signorine italiane fra Otto e Novevento: Modelli culturali e comportamenti sociali regolati da uno stato civile," in *Ragnatela di rapporti*, ed. Lucia

Ferrante, Maura Palazzi, and Gianna Pomata (Turin: Rosenberg & Sellier, 1988), pp. 454–90.

8. Maria Diez Gasca, "La professione di madre," *Difesa sociale* 16, no. 8 (Aug. 1937): 1117–25.

9. On American girlhood in this period, see Peter Filene, *Him/her/self: Sex Roles in Modern America*, 2d ed. (Baltimore: Johns Hopkins University Press, 1986).

10. *Mezzadri di Val di Pesa e del Chianti*, vol. 14 of *Studi e monografie: Monografie di famiglie agricole* (Rome: INEA, 1931), p. 63. Evidence from these family monographs written under the direction of INEA suggests that peasant youths were less isolated than first impressions would indicate. For poignant oral histories of the most isolated peasant girls, those of the Piedmontese hill areas, nothing surpasses Nuto Revelli, *L'anello forte* (Turin: Einaudi, 1985). See too Charlotte Gower Chapman, *Milocca: A Sicilian Village* (Boston: Schenkman, 1971), esp. pp. 30–50, an anthropological study of Sicily in the 1920s.

11. Victor Margueritte, *La garçonne* (Paris: Flammarion, 1922); an Italian translation, called *La giovanotta* was published in Milan by Sonzogno in 1923. See too Ann-Marie Sohn, "La *Garçonne* face à l'opinion publique: Type littéraire ou type social des années 20?" *Mouvement social* 80 (1972): 3–27.

12. The novel was subsequently published in its entirety as *Mary, Mariù, Maria* (Milan: Sonzogno, 1930).

13. See, for example, the work of a young colleague of the Venetian educator Maria Pezzè Pascolato, Lina Passarella Sartorelli, *I bimbi: Esperienza di una mamma* (Bari: Laterza, 1932), which illustrates the rise of liberal models of child rearing in an authoritarian context.

14. Anna Garofalo, *L'italiana in Italia* (Bari: Laterza, 1956), p. 157.

15. The absence of a "children's culture" is noted by Vincenza Battistelli, *La letteratura infantile moderna: Guida bibliografica* (Florence: Vallecchi, 1923). On the pioneering experiments of Elena Agazzi and Maria Montessori, see their entries in *Enciclopedia biografica e bibliografica italiana*, ser. 37, *Pedagogisti ed educatori*, dir. Ernesto Codignola (Milan: Istituto editoriale italiano Bernardo Carlo Tosi, 1939), pp. 14–15, 299–300; see too *Enciclopedia Treccani* (Rome, 1949), 23: 758–59.

16. Anna Mellini, *Marionette bianche e nere*, p. 72.

17. Cited on p. 72 in Silvia Franchini, "L'istruzione femminile in Italia dopo l'Unità: Percorsi di una ricerca sugli educandati pubblici di elite," *Passato e presente* 10 (1986): 53–94.

18. Maria Maggi, "La donna del nostro tempo deve essere colta?" *Giornale della donna* 16, no. 2 (Jan. 15, 1934):5.

19. Rita Levi Montalcini, *In Praise of Imperfection*, pp. 27, 38 (*Elogio dell'imperfezione*, pp. 34, 44).

20. Massa's short story was published in the widely distributed house

magazine of the Istituto Nazionale Assicurazioni (INA), *Famiglia nostra* (May 1932): 9–11.

21. *Annuario statistico italiano, 1944–1948,* ser. 5, vol. 1 (Rome: Istituto poligrafico dello stato, 1949), p. 31. Cf. Maria Castellani, *Donne italiane di ieri e oggi* (Florence: Bemporad, 1937), p. 25.

22. Cesare Alessandri, "La nuzialità: Punto di partenza," *Maternità ed infanzia* 9, no. 6 (June 1934):4. Antonio Golini, "Profilo demografico della famiglia italiana," in *La famiglia italiana dall'Ottocento a oggi,* ed. Piero Melograni (Bari: Laterza, 1988), pp. 349–50.

23. Garofalo, *L'italiana in Italia,* pp. 50–51.

24. Revelli, *L'anello forte,* p. xxxix.

25. For listings of Catholic as well as other periodicals for women and female youth, see Emma Scaramuzza, "Repertorio dei periodici femminili della Biblioteca Comunale di Milano, 1919–1943," *Memoria* 2 (Oct. 1981): 122–27; "Riviste femminili italiane," *Almanacco della donna italiana, 1934,* pp. 103–4; and "Riviste femminili italiane," *Almanacco della donna italiana, 1938,* pp. 175–76.

26. On publishing in this period, see Michele Giocondi, *Lettori in camicia nera* (Florence: D'Anna, 1978) and Laura Lilli, "La stampa femminile," in AAVV, *La stampa italiana del neocapitalismo* (Bari: Laterza, 1976), pp. 267–78, though there is still no adequate study of the mass-circulation press for women.

27. Francesco Savio, *Ma l'amore no: Realismo, formalismo, propaganda e telefoni bianchi nel cinema italiano del regime, 1930–1943* (Milan: Sonzogno, 1975), pp. xii–xix.

28. Figures for radio subscribers in Italy are from 1939 as indicated in the *Annuario statistico italiano, 1941,* 4th ser., vol. 8, p. 311; comparative figures are drawn from David Landes, *Unbound Prometheus* (Cambridge: Cambridge University Press, 1969), pp. 427, 429. Figures for movie theaters are from 1938, cited in Lorenzo Quaglietti, *Storia economico-politica del cinema italiano, 1945–1980* (Rome: Editori Riuniti, 1980), p. 28.

29. J. P. Mayer, *British Cinemas and Their Audiences* (London: Oxford, 1948).

30. Diez Gasca, "La professione di madre," pp. 1123–24.

31. On the impact of American consumer models in Italy and in Europe more generally, see Chapter 7, pp. 207–10. See also Victoria de Grazia, "Mass Culture and Sovereignty: The American Challenge to European Cinemas, 1920–1960," *Journal of Modern History* 61, no. 1 (Mar. 1989): 53–87; also her "Puritan Minds/Pagan Bodies: Americanization and Models of Modern Womanhood in Interwar Europe" (paper delivered at the Rockefeller Foundation conference in Bellagio, Italy, "Women in Dark Times," Aug. 10–14, 1987).

32. Both Marxist and Marxist-influenced feminist positions have gen-

erally contended as much; see, for example, Stuart Ewen, *Captains of Consciousness* (New York: McGraw Hill, 1977) and Stuart Ewen and Elizabeth Ewen, *Channels of Desire: Mass Images and the Shaping of American Consciousness* (New York: McGraw Hill, 1982). Cf. recent work that treats the capacity of women to rework, as well as select and reject, styles and themes, notably Tania Modleski, *Loving with a Vengeance: Mass-produced Fantasies for Women* (New York: Routledge, Chapman and Hall, 1984); Kathy Peiss, *Cheap Amusements: Working Women and Leisure in Turn-of-the-Century New York* (Philadelphia: Temple University Press, 1986); also Janice A. Radway, *Reading the Romance: Women, Patriarchy, and Popular Literature* (Chapel Hill: University of North Carolina Press, 1984). The little Italian work dedicated to women's literature in this period subscribes to the view that mass culture is social control; see Pietro Cavallo and Pasquale Iaccio, "Ceti medi emergenti e immagine della donna nella letteratura rosa degli anni trenta," *Storia contemporanea* 15, no. 6 (Dec. 1984): 1149–70.

33. Garofalo, *L'italiana in Italia*, p. 161.

34. *Piccola* 3, no. 11 (Mar. 18, 1930):12.

35. *Piccola* 3, no. 13 (Apr. 1, 1930):14.

36. *Piccola* 4, no. 2 (Jan. 20, 1931):12.

37. Figures on cinema for 1934 are from *Statistica di alcune manifestazioni culturali italiane nel periodo, 1931–1935*, vol. 12 (Rome: Tipografia F. Failli, 1937), pp. 39, 42. For automobiles, see Mario Saibante, "Il tenore di vita del popolo italiano prima dell'ultima guerra, in confronto con quello degli altri popoli," Appendix C of *Piano per le importazioni e le esportazioni*, vol. 5, ed. Centro di studi e piani tecnico-economici, Comitato interministeriale per la ricostruzione (Rome, 1947), p. 209.

38. *Confessioni di una piccola italiana*, p. 120.

39. See Bruno P. F. Wanrooij, "The American Model in the Moral Education of Fascist Italy," *Ricerche storiche* 16, no. 2 (May–Aug. 1986): 407–23; also his "Il 'Casto talamo': il dibattito sulla morale sessuale nel ventennio fascista," *Cultura e società negli anni del fascismo* (Milan: Cordani, 1987), pp. 544ff., now integrated into his overview of changing male attitudes toward sexual morality, *Storia del pudore: La questione sessuale in Italia, 1860–1940* (Venice: Marsilio Editore, 1990).

40. Wanrooij, "Casto talamo," p. 539.

41. Irene Brin, *Usi e costumi, 1920–1940* (Palermo: Sellerio Editore 1981), p. 111.

42. Canino, *Clotilde tra le due guerre*, p. 619.

43. Cited in Anita Pensotti, *Rachele: Settant'anni con Mussolini nel bene e nel male* (Milan: Bompiani, 1983), p. 53. See also Antonio Spinosa, *I figli del Duce* (Milan: Rizzoli, 1983), pp. 60–64.

44. *Piccola* 3, no. 21 (May 27, 1930).

45. Banfi Malaguzzi, *Femminilità contemporanea*, esp. pp. 31–45, 89.

46. *Confessioni di una piccola italiana*, p. 118.

47. As in Canino, *Clotilde tra le due guerre*, p. 255.

48. Garofolo, *L'italiana in Italia*, p. 161.

49. Clara Calamai, "Decisi di diventare una diva," *Gente* 30, no. 31 (Aug. 1, 1986):102.

50. Koon, *Believe, Obey, Fight*, pp. 116–45, esp. 122, and 90–107.

51. On fascist male youth organizations, see n. 2 above. On Church-state relations under fascism, especially the role of Catholic Action, see Richard A. Webster, *The Cross and the Fasces: Christian Democracy and Fascism in Italy* (Stanford: Stanford University Press, 1960); also Sandro Rogari, "Come la Chiesa si difese da Mussolini," *Nuova Antologia* (Jan.–June 1978): 392–444. A still unsurpassed local history, focusing on the well-articulated Catholic networks of Turin, is Mariangiola Reineri, *Cattolici e fascismo a Torino 1925–1943* (Milan: Feltrinelli, 1978).

52. Tannenbaum, *The Fascist Experience*, p. 196.

53. Ibid.

54. Michela De Giorgio, "Metodi e tempi di un'educazione sentimentale: La Gioventù femminile cattolica italiana negli anni venti," *Rivista di storia contemporanea* 3 (1980):128. See also Paola Di Cori, "Storia, sentimenti, solidarietà nelle organizzazioni femminili cattoliche dall'età giolittiana al fascismo," *Nuova DWF* 10–11 (1979): 116, in addition to her "Rosso e bianco: La devozione al Sacro Cuore di Gesù nel primo dopoguerra," *Memoria* 5 (1982): 82–107. On Barelli, see her autobiographies *Incanto di un decennio: Episodi di vita e delle sezioni minori della Gioventù femminile di Azione Cattolica* (Milan: Vita e Pensiero, 1937) and *La sorella maggiore racconta* (Milan, 1948), in addition to Maria Sticco's fascinating *Una donna tra due secoli: Armida Barelli* (Milan: Edizione Or, 1983).

55. "The Motion Picture Production Code of 1930," cited in *The Movies in Our Midst*, ed. Gerald Mast (Chicago: University of Chicago Press, 1982) p. 324.

56. Cited in *Social Wellsprings*, ed. Joseph Husslein, 2 vols. (Milwaukee, Wis.: Bruce, 1942), vol. 1, *Eighteen Encyclicals of Social Reconstruction of Pope Pius XI*, p. 306.

57. Stefano Pivato, "L'organizzazione cattolica della cultura di massa durante il fascismo," *Italia contemporanea* 30, no. 132 (July–Sept. 1978): 3–25, esp. p. 17.

58. Carlo Canziani, *Rivista del cinematografo* 6, no. 3 (Mar. 1933):1.

59. Cited in *Rivista del cinematografo* 6, no. 8 (Aug. 1933): 189–90.

60. Mino Argentieri, *La censura nel cinema italiano* (Rome: Editori Riuniti, 1974), p. 50. Cf. Gian Piero Brunetta, who in *Cinema italiano tra le due guerre* (Milan: Mursia, 1975), pp. 60–66, highlights the intensely political and profascist tendencies within Church censorship.

61. French authors in translation included Victor Marchal, *La donna*

quale dev'essere (Turin: Società Edizioni Internazionali, 1934); Leopoldo Béaudenom, *La formazione religiosa e morale delle giovani,* 3d ed. (Milan: Vita e Pensiero, 1930); and Cécile Jéglot, *L'arte di essere se stessa* (Turin: Lega Italiana Cattolica, Editore R. Berruti, 1935).

62. Marianna Bettazzi Bondi, *Verso le nozze (dedicato alle fidanzate d'Italia)* (Rome: F. Ferrari, 1934).

63. These attitudes are especially visible in reader responses to "Problemi di vita femminile: Il nostro concorso," inaugurated in *Fiamma viva* 5, no. 8 (Aug. 1925): 506–7; see 5, no. 11 (Nov. 1925): 701–3; 5, no. 12 (Dec. 1925): 760–64; 6, no. 1 (Jan. 1926): 58–61; 6, no. 2 (Feb. 1926): 121–24; 6, no. 3 (Mar. 1926): 190–92; 6, no. 4 (Apr. 1926): 252–54; 6, no. 5 (May 1926): 315–17; 6, no. 11 (Nov. 1926): 697–98.

64. Maria Sticco, *Il dovere e il sogno,* 10th ed. (Milan: Vita e Pensiero, 1939), p. 117.

65. Cited in *Social Wellsprings,* ed. Husslein, p. 110.

66. Angelo Gaudio, "Scuola, Chiesa e fascismo: L'ente nazionale per l'insegnamento medio e superiore," *Rivista di storia contemporanea* 14, no. 2 (1985): 273, estimates that 104,711 students were enrolled in Catholic secondary schools in 1939–40, equal to 10.5 percent of the total secondary school population. As many as 200,000 of those enrolled in the elementary schools were in Catholic institutions, as well as at least half of the 800,000 children in *asili* or nurseries at the end of the 1930s. In the latter more than two-thirds of all caretakers (10,464 out of 15,262) were Catholic nuns according to 1928–29 figures. See *Annuario statistico italiano, 1930,* 3d ser., vol. 4 (Rome: Istituto poligrafico dello stato, 1930), p. 83; also *Annuario statistico italiano, 1939,* pp. 302, 304.

67. Paolo Bonatelli, *Lineamenti d'educazione e di storia dell'educazione femminile* (Florence: La Nuova Italia, 1942), pp. 541–42.

68. Bonatelli, *Lineamenti d'educazione,* p. 542.

69. *Giornale della donna* 12, nos. 10–12 (June 1–15, 1930): 1–2; 12, no. 18 (Oct. 1, 1930): 1.

70. Cited in Spinosa, *I figli del Duce,* p. 18.

71. Ibid, p. 19.

72. In *Carta della Scuola illustrata nelle singole dichiarazioni da presidi e professori dell'Associazione fascista della scuola* (Rome: Editore Pinciana, 1939), pp. 17–22.

73. Lucia Magrini Vinaccia, "La donna nuova," *Giornale della donna* 7, nos. 12–13 (Aug. 1, 1929):1.

74. Camila Bisi, "Steeple-chase delle dattilografe," *Giornale della donna* 11, no. 3 (Feb. 1, 1929): 1.

75. Sticco, *Il dovere e il sogno,* p. xvi.

76. "Plethora of learned misfits" are Gaetano Salvemini's words, the latter are of Augusto Monti in *La voce,* both cited in Marzio Barbagli's rightly acclaimed study, *Educating for Unemployment: Politics, Labor*

Markets, and the School System—Italy, 1859–1973, trans. Robert H. Ross (1974; New York: Columbia University Press, 1982), pp. 106–7.

77. Marzio Barbagli, *Educating for Unemployment,* pp. 102–30.

78. The causes, scope, and outcome of the Gentile Reform have been much debated topics whose terms and significance easily elude the outsider. L. Mineo-Paluello, *Education in Fascist Italy* (London: Oxford University Press, 1946) gives a clear account; so does Barbagli, *Educating for Unemployment,* pp. 102–86, whose argument that the reform was geared to reshaping the labor market is, however, much disputed. Luigi Ambrosoli, *Libertà e religione nella riforma Gentile* (Florence: Vallecchi, 1980) gives a persuasive account of Gentile's educational philosophy, as does Tina Tomasi, *Idealismo e fascismo nella scuola italiana* (Florence: La Nuova Italia, 1969). The last is especially good on the reform's implications for women.

79. Barbagli, *Educating for Unemployment,* pp. 130–35.

80. Cited in Simonetta Ulivieri, "La donna nella scuola dall'unità d'Italia a oggi: Leggi, pregiudizi, lotte e prospettive," *Nuova DWF* 2 (Jan.–Mar. 1977), pp. 116 ff.; see too Gentile's essay, "La donna e il fanciullo," in *Preliminari allo studio del fanciullo,* 9th ed., *Opere,* vol. 42 (Florence: Sansoni, 1969), pp. 75–138.

81. Zora Becchi, "Intorno ad alcune critiche della riforma Gentile," *Giornale della donna* 6, no. 1 (Jan. 1, 1924):2.

82. Emilia Siracusa Cabrini, "Di palo in frasca sulla riforma Gentile," *Giornale della donna* 6, no. 8 (Apr. 15, 1924):2.

83. Lucia Pagano, "L'ordine delle scuole femminili," in *Carta della Scuola illustrata nelle singole dichiarazioni da presidi e professori dell'Associazione fascista della scuola,* pp. 158–165; *Annuario statistico italiano, 1930,* pp. 90, 92.

84. Pagano, "L'ordine delle scuole femminili," pp. 153–58; Brunella Dalla Casa, "Istruzione professionale ed educazione femminile: L'Istituto 'Regina Margherita' di Bologna dalla guerra agli anni trenta," in Istituto regionale per la storia della resistenza in Emilia Romagna, *Annale 3, 1983 (Scuola e educazione in Emilia Romagna fra le due guerre),* ed. Aldo Berselli and Vittorio Telmon, pp. 501–35.

85. Calculated on the basis of figures supplied in *Annuario statistico italiano,* 2d ser., vol. 8, 1919–21 (Rome: Provvedorato Generale dello Stato, 1925), pp. 121–22; *Annuario statistico italiano 1930,* 3d ser., vol. 4, p. 90; *Annuario statistico italiano, 1939,* p. 305.

86. *Annuario statistico italiano, 1939,* p. 315. On middle-school percentages, see Ornello Vitali, *Aspetti dello sviluppo economico italiano alla luce della ricostruzione della popolazione attiva* (Rome: Istituto di demografia, 1970), p. 217.

87. Revelli, *L'anello forte,* pp. lx–lxi.

88. Mellini, *Marionette bianche e nere,* p. 100; Barbagli, *Educating for Unemployment,* pp. 158–76.

89. Enza Carrara, "Il presente problema dell'educazione femminile," R. Liceo-ginnasio Vittorio Emanuele II, Napoli, *Annuario dell'anno scolastico, 1930–1931* (Naples: Siem, 1931), p. 138. For statistics on women's progress, see *Annuario statistico italiano, 1939*, pp. 314–15. Dropout rates are estimated in Castellani, *Donne italiane di ieri e oggi*, p. 82.

90. Carrara, "Il presente problema dell'educazione femminile," p. 138.

91. Cited in *Carta della Scuola illustrata nelle singole dichiarazioni da presidi e professori dell'Associazione fascista della scuola*, p. 17.

92. Accounts of life in the public school system indicate that the degree of fascistization varied. Manlio Cancogni and Giuliano Manacorda (*Libro e moschetto*, Turin: ERI, 1979) argue that it was most thorough at the elementary level; Anna Mellini *(Marionette bianche e nere)* recalls the heavy-handed politicization of the middle schools that she eventually left for Catholic schooling, though neither she nor other family members were practicing Catholics. Marcella Olschki *(Terza liceo 1939)* attended the elite Liceo Michelangiolo of Florence. She recalls teachers who subtly promoted critical thinking, leading to antifascism, and those, like her chemistry professor, a fascist militia officer, whose martinet airs were the butt of student pranks. She also recalled the hilarity aroused by the new public address system. A workmanlike overview of the operations of the ONB is provided in Carmela Betti, *L'Opera Nazionale Balilla e l'educazione fascista* (Florence: La Nuova Italia, 1984).

93. Cited in Koon, *Believe, Obey, Fight*, p. 97.

94. Cited in Koon, *Believe, Obey, Fight*, p. 149.

95. Cagossi, *Da piccola italiana a partigiana*, pp. 21–22.

96. Mellini, *Marionette bianche e nere*, p. 113.

97. Cagossi, *Da piccola italiana a partigiana*, p. 22.

98. For information on these schools, see *Giornale della donna* 14, no. 9 (May 1, 1932): 1–4, and especially Rosella Isidori Frasca, *. . . E il Duce le volle sportive* (Bologna: Patron, 1983), pp. 55–74.

99. Cited in Marina Addis Saba, "Littoriali al femminile," in *Cultura a passo romano*, ed. Ugoberto Alfassio Grimaldi and Marina Addis Saba (Milan: Feltrinelli, 1983), p. 146.

100. Clara Valente, "Le giovani fasciste e la vita," *Giornale della donna* 13, no. 12 (June 15, 1931):4.

101. F. Catasta, "Studentesse d'Italia: GUF femminile e orientamento professionale," *Almanacco della donna italiana, 1935*, p. 158.

102. Cited in Marina Addis Saba, "Littoriali al femminile," p. 151.

103. Laura Conti, in Lydia Franceschi et al., *L'altra metà della Resistenza* (Milan: G. Mazzotta, 1978), p. 65.

104. Luce D'Eramo, *Deviazione* (Milan: Mondadori, 1979); Luce-D'Eramo, "Die Rhetorik der faschistischen Machtausübung oder: Opfern

ist Macht," in *Frauen und Macht,* ed.Barbara Schaeffer-Hegel (Berlin: Publica, 1984), pp. 75–80.

CHAPTER 6

1. Archivio centrale dello stato, Presidenza consiglio dei ministri (ACS, PCM), 1937–39, f. 1/3-1,945, letter: una donna fascista–amatissimo Duce, Oct. 10, 1938; also f. 954.4, petition: Rome, October 6, 1938–Duce, and others in file, including a memo from Regina Terruzzi, who, like "Pierina B.," insinuated that unemployed women, were they younger, would have no alternative but to prostitute themselves.

2. Figures on the sexual division of labor under fascism have not yet been reassessed systematically to take account of the new weights assigned census figures by Ornello Vitali in *Aspetti dello sviluppo economico italiano alla luce della ricostruzione della popolazione attiva* (Rome: Istituto di demografia, 1970), and *La popolazione attiva in agricoltura attraverso i censimenti italiani (1881–1961)* (Rome: F. Failli, 1968). This makes his work an indispensable reference, as testified by the recent work of Francesca Bettio, *The Sexual Division of Labor: The Italian Case* (Oxford: Clarendon Press, 1989), which relies on his figures. Earlier studies focusing on women's labor-force participation offer important insights into the impact of the regime on patterns of female employment. The most reliable, because informed by a thorough knowledge of international trends, is Franco Archibugi, "Recent Trends in Women's Work in Italy," *International Labor Review* 81 (1960): 285 –318. See too Nora Federici, "L'inserimento della donna nel mondo del lavoro," in *L'emancipazione femminile in Italia: Un secolo di discussioni, 1861–1961* (Florence: La Nuova Italia, 1963), pp. 87–128, and Rosa Anna Pernicone's cautious *L'inserimento della donna nelle attività economiche in Italia,* Società italiana di economia demografia e statistica, Collana di studi e monografie, n.s , 1, 1972. Franca Pieroni Bortolotti's "Osservazioni sull'occupazione femminile durante il fascismo," in *Sul movimento politico delle donne: Scritti inediti,* ed. Annarita Buttafuoco (Rome: Cooperativa Utopia, 1987), pp. 179–210, makes some telling points, though her use of statistics is faulty. The same holds true for the Catholic Lidia Fornaciari, "Osservazioni sull'andamento del lavoro femminile in Italia negli ultimi 50 anni," *Rivista internazionale di scienze sociali* 64, ser. 3, 27, no. 3 (May–June 1956): 222–240.

3. Good bases for comparisons between Italy and other countries are provided by Louise A. Tilly and Joan W. Scott, *Women, Work and Family* (New York: Holt, Rinehart and Winston, 1978), Laura Levine Frader, "Women in the Industrial Capitalist Economy," and Renate Bridenthal, "Something Old, Something New: Women between the Two World Wars,"

in *Becoming Visible: Women in European History,* ed. R. Bridenthal, C. Koonz, and S. Stuard, 2d ed. (New York: Houghton Mifflin, 1987), pp. 309–33, pp. 473–88, as well Archibugi, "Recent Trends in Women's Work in Italy," and Nora Federici, "L'inserimento della donna nel mondo del lavoro."

4. B. Mussolini, "Macchina e donna," Aug. 31, 1934, *Opera omnia,* ed. Edoardo Susmel e Duilio Susmel, 44 vols. (Florence: La Fenice, 1951–80), 26:311.

5. Zara Algardi, *La donna e la toga* (Milan: A. Giuffrè Editore, 1949), p. 25; Piero Addeo, *Eva togata* (Naples: Editrice Rispoli, 1939), p. 141.

6. Cesare Alessandri, "Il lavoro femminile nel regime fascista," *Rivista del lavoro,* 1938, no. 5:1.

7. Cited in Donna Paola [Paola Grosson Baronchelli], *La donna della Nuova Italia: Documenti del contributo femminile alla guerra (Maggio 1915–Maggio 1917)* (Milan: R. Quintieri, 1917), p. 240. On the wartime and postwar improvements in women's wages, see Bettio, *The Sexual Division of Labor,* pp. 112–17. See too Barbara Curli, "Effects of the First World War on Women's Employment in Italy," European University Institute, May 1990, provided by courtesy of the author and part of a sophisticated general analysis that is forthcoming, *La Grande Guerra e il lavoro femminile in Italia, 1915–1921.*

8. Franca Pieroni Bortolotti, *Femminismo e partiti politici in Italia, 1919–1936* (Rome: Riuniti, 1978), pp. 33, 179, 364–66; Ilva Vaccari, *La donna nel ventennio fascista (1919–1943)* (Milan: Vangelista, 1978), pp. 58–59, 72; Annarita Buttafuoco, *Le Mariuccine: Storia di un'istituzione laica—L'Asilo Mariuccia* (Milan: Franco Angeli, 1985), pp. 368–69. The Italian situation bears comparison with women's war experiences elsewhere. For an overview, drawing on the British case, see Gail Braybon and Penny Sumerfield, *Out of the Cage: Women's Experience in Two World Wars* (London: Pandora, 1987). See too *Behind the Lines,* ed. Margaret Higonnet et al. (New Haven: Yale University Press, 1987).

9. Pieroni Bortolotti, *Femminismo e partiti politici in Italia* (Rome: Riuniti, 1978), pp. 20, 33; Vaccari, *La donna nel ventennio fascista (1919–1943),* p. 58–59, 72.

10. For biographical information on Pertici Pontecorvo, see *Giornale della donna* 13, no. 11 (June 1, 1931); D.B.M., *Almanacco della donna italiana, 1933,* p. 303; Mario Gastaldi, *Panorama della letteratura femminile contemporanea* (Milan: Quaderni di Poesia, 1936), p. 494; *La donna italiana* 10, no. 1 (Jan. 1931): 22–23.

11. A cogent overview of changing labor market conditions during the interwar years is provided by Patrizia Sabbatucci Severini and Angelo Trento, "Alcuni cenni sul mercato del lavoro durante il fascismo," *Quaderni storici* 29–30 (May–Dec. 1975): 550–78.

12. B. Mussolini, "Macchina e donna," Aug. 31, 1934, *Opera omnia,* 26:311.

13. On the protective and exclusionary sides of fascist policy, see Maria Vittoria Ballestrero, *Dalla tutela alla parità: La legislazione italiana sul lavoro delle donne* (Bologna: Il Mulino, 1979), pp. 58–108.

14. On industry's triumph over the fascist trade unions, see Roland Sarti's cogently argued *Fascism and the Industrial Leadership in Italy, 1910–1940* (Berkeley: University of California Press, 1971). On the effects of corporate legislation on bargaining practices, see Giulio Sapelli's carefully documented study, *Fascismo, grande industria e sindacato: Il caso di Torino, 1929–1935* (Milan: Feltrinelli, 1975), as well as the several contributions on the subject edited by Giulio Sapelli in *La classe operaia durante il fascismo,* Annali Fondazione Feltrinelli, vol. 20, (Milan, 1980).

15. Archibugi, *Recent Trends in Women's Work in Italy,* pp. 306–7; Bettio, *The Sexual Division of Labor,* shows that this trend ran contrary to the experiences of women with collective bargaining elsewhere; see pp. 116–17. On the long-term impact of fascist corporatist politics in general, see Gino Giugni, "Esperienze corporative e post-corporative nei rapporti collettivi di lavoro in Italia," *Il Mulino,* Jan.–Feb. 1956.

16. Charles E. Maier, *Recasting Bourgeois Europe* (Princeton: Princeton University Press, 1976); Helga Hernes and Eva Hanninen-Salmelin, "Women in the Corporate System," in *Unfinished Democracy,* ed. Carolina Flaavio-Mannila et al. (London: Pergamon, 1985), pp. 106–33; also Helga Maria Hernes and Kirsten Voje, "Women in the Corporate Channel: A Process of National Exclusion," *Scandinavian Political Studies,* vol. 3, n.s., 2 (1980): 163–86.

17. On Pertici Pontecorvo, see note 10 above.

18. G. Napolitano, "La politica demografica tra le classi lavoratrici," *Critica fascista* 10 (Oct. 1934): 198.

19. Cited in Cesare Alessandri, "Il lavoro femminile nel regime fascista," p. 2.

20. Tullio Cianetti, cited in Cesare Alessandri, "Il lavoro femminile nel regime fascista," p. 2.

21. That the fascist union's ideal constituent was skilled, senior, and male is strikingly illustrated in the surveys and letter columns of *Il maglio,* the weekly newspaper of the well-organized Fascist Confederation of Industrial Workers of Turin; see especially the issues for 1938–40.

22. *Lavoro e famiglia: Per le sezioni operaie e lavoranti a domicilio dei fasci femminili* 1, no. 1 (Mar. 23, 1938): 1, edited by the Confederazione fascista dei lavoratori dell'industria e del commercio. Contributors included the liaison to the *fasci femminili,* Rachele Ferrari del Latte, labor experts Maria Guidi and Maria Gasca Diez, and writers A. B. Fassio and Rina Maria Pierazzi.

23. Ibid.

24. ACS, PCM, PNF, Direttorio, b. 344, f. 64f. Sezioni operaie e lavoranti a domicilio. Promemoria Franceschini–Ferrari del Latte, Mar. 21, 1938.

25. *Compendio statistico, 1938* (Rome: Istituto poligrafico dello stato, 1939), p. 16; *Compendio statistico, 1942*, p. 14.

26. Ballestrero, *Dalla tutela alla parità*, pp. 64–72.

27. Daisy di Robilant, "Previdenza materna in regime fascista," *Difesa sociale* 8, no. 4 (Apr. 1929): 144–46.

28. Robert C. Moeller, "Protecting Mother's Work: From Production to Reproduction in Postwar West Germany," *Journal of Social History* 22, no. 3 (Spring 1989): 413–37.

29. ACS, PCM, 1940–41, 1.1.10.1000, f. 582 and f. 586.

30. Archibugi, "Recent Trends in Women's Work in Italy," p. 305.

31. B. Mussolini, "Italia rurale," Dec. 8, 1936, *Opera omnia*, 28:87.

32. Vitali, *La popolazione attiva in agricoltura attraverso i censimenti italiani, 1881–1961* (Rome: F. Failli, 1968), pp. 170–73. Bridenthal, "Something Old, Something New," p. 476.

33. Francesco Coletti, *La proprietà rurale in Italia e i suoi caratteri demografici, psicologici, e sociali* (Piacenza: Federazione italiana dei consorzi agrari, 1925), p. 23.

34. Female farm labor was observed with varying insight during the early 1930s in the major study of farm life for the interwar period, that conducted by the Istituto Nazionale di Economia Agraria, Monografie di famiglie agricole, Studi e Monografie, 14 vols. (Rome, 1929–39). See especially no. 7, *Contadine della pianura livornese e pisana* (Rome, 1934); no. 5, *Mezzadri e piccoli proprietari coltivatori in Umbria* (Rome, 1933); and no. 14, *Mezzadri di Val di Pesa e del Chianti* (Rome, 1931), esp. pp. 46, 74, 94.

35. Francesco Omodeo-Zorini, "Lo sciopero delle mondine del giugno-luglio, 1927," *Ieri, Novara, oggi* 3 (1980): 134–54; Cesare Alessandri, "Donne e minorenni in risaia," *Maternità ed infanzia* 2, no. 3 (Mar. 1927): 32–35.

36. Giuseppe Giuffrida, *Condizioni di lavoro ed aborto, l'Ospedale Maggiore di Novara* no. 7 (Novara, 1935), pp. 1–15.

37. *La mondina: Settimanale della federazione provinciale pavese delle corporazioni sindacali fasciste* 1, no. 1 (June 16, 1925)–1, no. 3 (July 15, 1925).

38. "Quando il sole la risaia / tutta infuoca di calore / la mondina fresca e gaia / canta i canti dell'amore," *La mondina* 1, no. 3 (July 15, 1925).

39. *Giornale della donna* 12, nos. 12–13 (July 1–15, 1930); Guglielma Ronconi, "Le mondine," *L'azione delle massaie rurali* 2, no. 7 (July 1934); 3, no. 3 (Mar. 1935); 3, no. 7 (July 1935).

40. Camilla Ravera, *La donna italiana dal primo al secondo Risorgimento* (Rome: Riuniti, 1951), p. 127; also Vera Zamagni, "Distribuzione del reddito e classi sociali nell Italia fra le due guerre," in *La classe operaia durante il fascismo*, pp. 18–23. More specifically on the rice workers, see A. DeBernardi, "Il mondo rurale lombardo tra arretratezza e modernizzazione: Primi spunti di ricerca," in *Agricoltura e forze sociali nella Lombardia nella crisi degli anni trenta* (Milan: Franco Angeli, 1983), p. 162.

41. Maria Castellani, *Donne italiane di ieri e di oggi* (Florence: Bemporad, 1937), p. 102.

42. The percentage of women employed in industry increased by only a fraction of a percent from 1921 to 1936, from 23.6 percent to 24.1 percent, and it declined slightly as a percentage of the total work force, from 27.2 percent to 25 percent. Vitali, *La popolazione attiva in agricultura*, p. 221.

43. On the synthetics industry, which merits much further investigation, see Cesare Alessandri, "Il lavoro femminile nel regime fascista," p. 3. Giuseppe Tattara and Gianni Toniolo, "L'industria manifatturiera: Cicli, politiche e mutamenti di struttura (1921–1937)," in *L'economia italiana nel periodo fascista*, ed. P. Ciocca and G. Toniolo (Bologna: Il Mulino, 1976), pp. 158 ff., table A.3. In general, on the tendency of men to substitute women, see Archibugi, "Recent Trends in Women's Work in Italy," pp. 291–93.

44. *Giornale della donna* 13, no. 9 (May 1, 1931); Victoria de Grazia, *Culture of Consent: Mass Organization of Leisure in Fascist Italy* (New York: Cambridge University Press, 1981), pp. 84–87; Bruna Bianchi, "I tessili: Lavoro, salute, conflitti," in *La classe operaia durante il fascismo*, pp. 1048–50.

45. Bianchi, "I tessili: Lavoro, salute, conflitti," pp. 979–95, 1001, 1016–17.

46. Zamagni, "Distribuzione," p. 31; Bettio, *The Sexual Division of Labor*, p. 117.

47. Bettio, *The Sexual Division of Labor*, p. 117. See also A. Lorenzoni, "L'impiego delle donne nell'industria e le sue conseguenze sulla natalità," in *L'economia italiana* (1933), pp. 69–70. Fascist domestic ideology and a slight statistical increase in the numbers of households headed by a single breadwinner made it seem plausible that the opposite was true, as indeed an expert observer, Chiara Saraceno, has argued, "La famiglia operaia sotto il fascismo," in *La classe operaia durante il fascismo*, pp. 209–12.

48. Ballestrero, *Dalla tutela alla parità*, pp. 73–81; Luigi De Litala, "Contratti speciali di lavoro," in *Il contratto individuale di lavoro*, vol. 2, *Trattato di diritto del lavoro*, 2d ed. (Padova: Cedam, 1953), pp. 34–35,

323–27. On the lack of coverage for home workers, see Amalia Fassio, "Lavoro femminile, lavoro a domicilio, tubercolosi," *Politica sociale* 7, no. 4 (Apr. 1936).

49. Pieroni Bortolotti, "Osservazione sull'occupazione femminile durante il fascismo," p. 192.

50. The "servant problem" in fascist Italy merits a study in its own right. For background, see Riccardo Bachi, *La serva nell'evoluzione sociale* (Turin: Sacerdote, 1900), also various comments in Louise Diel, *La generazione di Mussolini* (Milan: Mondadori, 1934), p. 250; Pino, "Non è tutt'oro," *L'azione delle massaie rurali* 2, no. 3 (Mar. 1934). Statistics on marriage rates for the domestic service population are from the 1936 population census, in *Annuario statistico italiano, 1944–1948*, ser. 5, vol. 1, 1949, p. 24, table 20.51.

51. Buttafuoco, *Le Mariuccine*, pp. 456–67.

52. Vanessa Maher, "Sarte e sartine nella Torino fra le due guerre," in *Mezzosecolo 5: Materiali di ricerca storica* (Milan: Franco Angeli, 1985), pp. 249–77.

53. Aldo Masciotta, "L'operaia, donna e madre: Rassegna e considerazioni generali con contributo statistico," *La ginecologia* 6, no. 12 (Dec. 1940): 625–26.

54. Wanda Gorjux, "Il lavoro e il compito della donna nella società fascista," *La donna italiana* 11, no. 2 (Feb. 1934): 66–67.

55. Bridenthal, "Something Old, Something New," p. 436; T. Cole, "Italy's Fascist Bureaucracy," *American Political Science Review* 32, no. 3 (Dec. 1938): 1143–57, esp. p. 1148.

56. On the rationalization of office work, see William Henry Leffingwell's classic *Office Management: Principles and Practice* (Chicago: A. W. Shaw, 1925), as well as David Lockwood, *The Blackcoated Worker: A Study in Class Consciousness* (London: Allen and Unwin, 1958). The effects of office work on women are studied in several recent works, including Samuel Cohn, *The Process of Occupational Sex-typing: The Feminization of Clerical Labor in Great Britain* (Philadelphia: Temple University Press, 1985), Gregory Anderson, ed., *The White-blouse Revolution: Female Office Workers since 1870* (Manchester: Manchester University Press, 1988), and Margery W. Davies, *Women's Place Is at the Typewriter* (Philadelphia: Temple University Press, 1982).

57. "I patti di lavoro per le dattilografe," *Giornale della donna* 14, no. 19 (Oct. 1, 1932):3.

58. Luciana Peverelli, *Sogni in grembiule nero* (Milan: Archetipografia, 1940), p. 116.

59. Listings of professional women are contained in *Almanacco della donna italiana, 1938*, pp. 373–430. See also Mariella Tabellini, *La donna nelle professioni liberali* (Rome, 1942).

60. Emil Ludwig, *Talks with Mussolini*, trans. Eden and Cedar Paul (Boston: Little Brown, 1933), p. 168.

61. Anna Maria Speckel, "Architettura moderna e donne architette," *Almanacco della donna italiana, 1936*, pp. 121–34.

62. "Giornaliste d'Italia," *Almanacco della donna italiana, 1929*, pp. 111–18. Estimates of women journalists varied, with the 1921 census giving the figure 382, the 1931 census, 991, and the 1951 census, 939. The latter explicitly included translators and interpreters as well as writers and journalists; see Pernicone, *L'inserimento della donna nelle attività economiche in Italia*, pp. 39, 89. The *Almanacco della donna italiana, 1938*, pp. 395–408, lists 500 women, with addresses and the places where they published, suggesting that these numbers represent the women who actually practiced.

63. Vitali, *Aspetti dello sviluppo economico italiano*, p. 105 table 22.

64. Armando Michieli, "La donna nella scuola," *Almanacco della donna italiana, 1929*, pp. 100, 109.

65. Ester De Fort, "I maestri elementari italiani dai primi del novecento alla caduta del fascismo," *Nuova rivista storica* 68 (1984): 527–76, esp. p. 565.

66. To compare the German women's experience, see Jill McIntyre, "Women and the Professions in Germany," in *German Democracy and the Triumph of Hitler: Essays in Recent German History*, ed. Anthony Nicholls and Erich Mattias (London: George Allen and Unwin, 1971), pp. 175–213.

67. Maria Albini, "La donna e il lavoro," *Problemi del lavoro* (Sept. 1935): 17–18; see n. 70 below.

68. Wanda Gorjux, "Professioni della donna," *Giornale della donna* 15, no. 4 (Feb. 15, 1933).

69. Tabellini, *La donna nelle professionali liberali*, pp. 13–14.

70. Cited in Emma Scaramuzza, "Professioni intellectuali e fascismo: L'ambivalenza della Alleanza muliebre culturale italiana," *Italia contemporanea* (Sept. 1983): 111–33.

71. Il primo convegno nazionale del lavoro femminile commerciale, *Atti* (Rome: Tipografia Armani di M. Courrier, 1940).

CHAPTER 7

1. Luigi Preti, *Giovinezza, giovinezza* (Milan: Mondadori, 1964), p. 68.

2. The formation of modern notions of public space is studied in Jürgen Habermas, *Strukturwandel der Öffentlichkeit* (Neuwied: Hermann Luchterhand, 1962); see also Richard Sennett, *The Fall of Public Man*

(New York: Alfred A. Knopf, 1977). The destruction of private space and civil society by interwar dictatorships is conceptualized in Hannah Arendt, *The Origins of Totalitarianism* (New York: Harcourt Brace, 1951).

3. Vera Zamagni, "Alle origini della grande distribuzione in Italia," *Commercio* 4, no. 10 (1982): 71–95.

4. Cited in Gian Piero Brunetta, *Buio in sala* (Padua: Marsilio, 1989), p. 20.

5. Edmond Goblot, *La Barrière et les niveaux* (Paris: Alcan, 1925).

6. Corrado Alvaro, "I quarant'anni del cinema," *Nuova antologia*, ser. 7, 70, no. 1514 (Apr. 16, 1935):603.

7. Thorstein Veblen, *Theory of the Leisure Class* (1899; New York: Modern Library, 1934), esp. pp. 148–152, 167ff.

8. Cited in *Le donne italiane: Periodico quindicinale, organo del comitato nazionale per la correttezza della moda* 1, no. 16 (Dec. 31, 1927); 1, no. 17 (Jan. 15, 1928). Catholicism's traditionalist imagery of women is examined in Stefania Portaccio, "La donna nella stampa popolare cattolica, *Famiglia cristiana*, 1931–1945," *Italia contemporanea* 33, no. 143 (1981): 45–68.

9. Matteo Cuomo, *La donna nei proverbi*, 2d ed. (Salerno: Di Giacomo Editore, 1931), p. 131.

10. Victoria de Grazia, *The Culture of Consent: Mass Organization of Leisure in Fascist Italy* (New York: Cambridge University Press, 1981).

11. These attitudes are probed in Miriam Hansen, "Early Silent Cinema: Whose Public Sphere?" *New German Critique* 29 (Spring-Summer 1983), esp. pp. 174ff.; Andreas Huyssen, "Mass Culture as Woman: Modernism's Other," in *Studies in Entertainment: Critical Approaches to Mass Culture*, ed. Tania Modleski (Bloomington, Ind.: Indiana University Press, 1986), pp. 188–207; and Patrice Petro, *Joyless Streets: Women and Melodramatic Representation in Weimar Germany* (Princeton: Princeton University Press, 1989).

12. "Fondi di magazzino," *Il selvaggio* 4, no. 24 (Dec. 1929):57. On Americanization, see Victoria de Grazia, "Cinema and Sovereignty: The American Challenge to European Cinemas, 1920–1945," *Journal of Modern History* 61, no. 1 (Mar. 1989): 53–87, and Bruno Wanrooij, "The American 'Model' in the Moral Education of Fascist Italy," *Ricerche storiche* 16, no. 2 (May–Aug. 1986).

13. Mario Soldati, *America primo amore* (Florence: Bemporad, 1935).

14. Virgilio Lilli, "Americanismo ed europeismo," *Critica fascista* 9, no. 22 (Nov. 1931): 437–39; see also Emilio Cecchi, *America amara* (Florence, 1940), pp. 222–24.

15. Pietro Lanino, "Civiltà americana," *Nuova antologia* 65, no. 1403 (Sept. 1930): 234–48.

16. Cited in Soldati, *America primo amore*, pp. 70–71. See too Domenique Fernandes, *Il mito dell'America negli intellettuali italiani* (Rome-Caltanisetta: Salvatore Sciascia, 1969), p. 24.

17. Beniamino De Ritis, *Mente puritana in corpo pagano (saggio sulla civiltà negli Stati Uniti)* (Florence: Vallecchi, 1934).

18. See especially Catherine Gallagher, "The Body Versus the Social Body in the Works of Thomas Malthus and Henry Mayhew," in *The Making of the Modern Body*, ed. Catherine Gallagher and Thomas Laqueur (Berkeley: University of California Press, 1987), pp. 83–106.

19. Paule Herfort, *Chez les romains fascistes* (Paris: Revue des Deux Mondes, 1932), pp. 123–24.

20. Luigi Santini, "Cinematografo: Riflessioni tra un tempo e l'altro," *Cordelia, 1934*, p. 134.

21. "Una inchiesta fra i nostri lettori e le nostre lettrici," *Kines* 10, no. 23 (June 1, 1931): 13.

22. Margherita Sarfatti, *Dux* (1926; Milan: Mondadori, 1982), p. 312; V. J. Bourdeux, "La piacevole parentesi" (1927), cited in Maria Fraddosio, "La donna e la guerra: Aspetti della militanza femminile nel fascismo— Dalla mobilitazione civile alle origini del Saf nella Repubblica Sociale Italiana," *Storia contemporanea* 20, no. 6 (Dec. 1989): 1115–16; Herfort, *Chez les romains fascistes*, pp. 123–24.

23. Cited in Natalia Aspesi, *Il lusso e l'autarchia: Storia dell'eleganza italiana, 1930–1944* (Milan: Rizzoli, 1982), p. 43.

24. Gazzettino, "Donne," *Il selvaggio* 9, no. 7 (Aug. 1932): 42. In lieu of a proper social history of this extraordinary group, see Romano Bilenchi's "I silenzi di Rosai" (1971) in the same author's *Amici* (Milan: Rizzoli, 1988).

25. Cited in Giuseppe Poggi-Longostrevi, *Cultura fisica della donna (ed estetica femminile)*, 2d ed. (Milan: Hoepli, 1938), p. 248.

26. Luciano Folgore, in *Il travaso*, cited in Gianfranco Angelucci, "Le comiche," in *Playdux: Storica erotica del fascismo* (Rome: Tattilo Editrice, 1973), p. 45.

27. Preti, *Giovinezza, giovinezza*, p. 91.

28. Carlalberto Grillenzoni, "I caratteri del fisico e del vestire considerati come fattori demografici," *Atti del Congresso internazionale per gli studi della popolazione*, Rome, Sept. 7–10, 1931, ed. Corrado Gini, 7 vols. (Rome: Istituto poligrafico dello Stato, 1934), 2:261–69.

29. Antonio Faeti, preface to Gino Boccasile, *La signorina Grandi firme* (Milan: Longanesi, 1981), pp. ix–xii; Rjo MacKinnon-Raikes and Renzo Magoss, "Che cos è la letteratura?" in *Playdux: Storia erotica del fascismo*, pp. 348–49.

30. Maria Coppola, "La donna del millenovecento," *Cordelia, 1934*, p. 92.

31. Sergio Giuntini, "Agli albori della ginnastica femminile in Italia," *Ricerche storiche* 20, no. 3 (1989): 27–45.

32. Agostino Gemelli, *La educazione fisica della donna,* Collana della GCFI, vol. 3 (Milan, 1927), p. 28.

33. Cited in Sergio Giuntini, "La donna e lo sport in Lombardia durante il fascismo" (Paper delivered at the conference of the Istituto Lombardo per la storia del movimento di liberazione in Italia, "Donna Lombarda (1860–1945)," Milan, Apr. 1989), p. 8; cited by courtesy of the author.

34. Cited in Giuseppe Poggi-Longostrevi, *Cultura fisica della donna (ed estetica femminile),* 2nd rev. ed. (Milan: Ulrico Hoepli, 1938), p. 45.

35. Rosella Isidori Frasca, . . . *E il duce le volle sportive* (Bologna: Patron Editore, 1983), pp. 83ff., as well as Marina Addis Saba and Rosella Isidori Frasca, "L'angelo della palestra," *Lanciolotto e nausica* 1 (1986): 58–63.

36. Cited in Giuntini, "La donna e lo sport," pp. 10, 18; "Trebisonda (detta Ondina) Valle," Sandra Artom and Anna Rita Calabrò, *Sorelle d'Italia* (Milan: Rizzoli, 1989), pp. 278–79.

37. See Clara Valente, "La donna e lo sport: Le italiane alle Olimpiadi," *Almanacco della donna italiana,* 1937, pp. 221–31.

38. Amalia Musso, *Ginnastica ritmico-estetica femminile* (Turin: Sivestrelli e Cappelletto, 1927), p. 135.

39. Rosa Maria Miedico, *Ginnastica razionale femminile* (Milan: Archetipografia, 1935), pref.

40. Emilio Radius, *Usi e costumi dell'uomo fascista* (Milan: Rizzoli, 1964), p. 80. On fashion in this period, see especially Natalia Aspesi, *Il lusso e l'autarchia: Storia dell'eleganza italiana, 1930–1944* (Milan: Rizzoli, 1982). For comparisons with fashion changes elsewhere, see the stimulating study by Elizabeth Wilson, *Fashion and Modernity* (London: Virago Press, 1985).

41. Georg Simmel, "Fashion," in *On Individuality and Social Forms,* ed. Donald N. Levine (Chicago: University of Chicago Press, 1971), pp. 296–300.

42. Corrado Alvaro, *Tutto è accaduto* (1944–45; Milan: Bompiani, 1961), p. 7.

43. Lydia De Liquoro, *Le battaglie della moda, 1919–1933* (Milan, 1934), pp. 18, 38. For a comparable episode in response to the political leveling brought about by the French Revolution, see Philippe Perrot, "Simplicité et démocratisation: Quelques remarques," *Ethnologie française* 29, no. 2 (1989): 140–44.

44. *Lidel,* Jan. 15, 1927, p. 3; June 15, 1927.

45. Umberto Notari, *Autarchia contro xenolatria: A che gioco giochiamo?* (Milan: Società Anonima Notari, 1938), pp. 39–42, 62.

46. Cited in Antonio Spinosa, *Starace* (Milan: Rizzoli, 1981), p. 169.

47. ACS, PCM, 1937–1939, f. 1.7.7493. Grande adunata delle forze femminili, May 28, 1939, Agenzia Stefani, no. 25.

48. Ibid.

49. Telephone subscriber figures for 1924–25 are from *Annuario statistico italiano, 1922–1925*, p. 285, and for 1938, from *Annuario statistico italiano, 1939*, p. 121. Statistics on radio subscribers, estimated for 1925 on the basis of 1940 figures (1.3 million) are from Antonio Papa, *Storia politica della radio in Italia*, 2 vols. (Naples: Guida Editori, 1978), 1:26, 2:114.

50. Irene Brin, *Usi e costumi, 1920–1940* (Palermo: Sellerio Editore, 1981) p. 31.

51. Maria Coppola, "La donna nel millenovecento," *Cordelia, 1934*, pp. 93–94.

52. Luciana Peverelli, *L'amore del sabato inglese* (Milan: Rizzoli, 1934), p. 45.

53. F. T. Marinetti e Fillìa, *La cucina futurista* (1931; Milan: Longanesi, 1986); trans. Susan Brill as *The Futurist Cookbook* (San Francisco: Bedford Arts, 1989).

54. Cited in Raffaello Barbiera, *Il salotto della contessa Maffei*, 15th ed. (Milan: Treves, 1925), pp. 34–35, 343. See too the well-crafted work of Maria Iolanda Palazzolo, *I salotti di cultura nell'Italia dell'Ottocento: Scene e modelli* (Milan: Franco Angeli, 1985).

55. Cited in Barbiera, *Il salotto della contessa Maffei*, p. 345.

56. Sarfatti, *Acqua passata* (Bologna: L. Cappelli, 1955), pp. 39, 67ff.

57. On Sarfatti, see chapters 2 and 8 in this book, as well as her memoir, *Acqua passata*, and her numerous art essays. Aspects of her activity as cultural promoter are examined in Anna Nozzoli, "Margherita Sarfatti, organizzatrice di cultura: *Il popolo d'Italia*," in *La corporazione delle donne*, ed. Marina Addis Saba (Florence: Vallecchi, 1988), pp. 227–72, and in Rossana Bossaglia, *Il Novecento italiano: Storia documenti, iconografia* (Milan: Feltrinelli, 1979), esp. pp. 128–54, 210–11. On her activities in Rome, see the informers' reports in ACS, Ministero dell'Interno, Direzione generale della pubblica sicurezza, Divisione polizia politica, f. Margherita Sarfatti. By far the most vivid account of her person, albeit a fictionalized one, is Corrado Alvaro, *Tutto è accaduto* (Milan: Bompiani, 1961), in which Sarfatti appears, thinly disguised as Sofia Pitagliano, as seen through the eyes of a half-corrupted young male with artistic pretensions. See too the fawning contemporary portrait by Orazia Belsito Prini, *Figure del tempo mussoliniano: Margherita Sarfatti* (Piacenza: Tipografia de "La Scure," 1934).

58. Sarfatti, *America, ricerca della felicità* (Milan: Mondadori, 1937), pp. 192, 199.

59. Alba De Cespedes, *Nessuno torna indietro* (1938; Milan: Mondadori, 1966), p. 114.

CHAPTER 8

1. "Congressi internazionali a Parigi: Luglio 1922–Luglio 1934," *La donna italiana* 12, no. 1 (Jan. 12, 1935): 72–75. See also International Council of Women, *Women in a Changing World: The dynamic story of the International Council of Women since 1888* (London: Routledge and Kegan Paul, 1966), pp. 66–67, 234–36.

2. Monica Miniati, "Tra emancipazione ebraica ed emancipazione femminile: Il dibattito della stampa ebraica dall'unità alla grande guerra," *Storia contemporanea* 20, no. 1 (Feb. 1989): 45–78.

3. Olga Modigliani, *Lavoro sociale delle donne: Le grandi organizzazioni femminili in Italia e all'estero, conferenze* (Rome: Fratelli Pallotta, 1935), p. 22. Biographical information is culled from Olga Modigliani Flaschel, "Anime moderne," *Almanacco della donna italiana, 1923*, pp. 81–91. See also *Enciclopedia italiana*, s.v. "Enrico Modigliani."

4. Marziola Pignatari, *La partecipazione delle donne fasciste alla vita dell'impero* (Rome: Fratelli Palombi, 1937), p. 22.

5. Nancy Cott, *The Grounding of Modern Feminism* (New Haven: Yale University Press, 1989), p. 274.

6. *Giornale della donna* 12, no. 8 (Apr. 15, 1930): 1.

7. Denise Detragiache, "Fascismo femminile da San Sepolcro all'affare Matteotti (1919–1925)" *Storia contemporanea* 14, no. 2 (Apr. 1983): 251n250.

8. Margherita Armani, "Fascismo e la donna," *La civiltà fascista illustrata nelle dottrine e nelle opere*, ed. G. B. Pomba (Turin: Unione Tipografica Torinese, 1928), pp. 617–19.

9. Albert Hirschman, *Shifting Involvements* (Princeton: Princeton University Press, 1982), p. 102.

10. Michela De Giorgio, "La fin du féminisme: Organisations catholiques de femmes et faisceaux féminins" (unpublished paper, 1987, courtesy of the author), p. 4.

11. Brin, *Usi e costumi, 1920–1940* (Palermo: Sellerio, 1981), p. 110; Stefano Somogyi, *Il suicidio in Italia, 1864–1962*, Collana di studi demografici, no. 2 (Rome, 1967), p. 23.

12. *Giornale della donna* 16, no. 2 (Jan. 15, 1934):1.

13. *Bulletin: International Council of Women* 2, no. 37 (Mar. 1933): 68–69. For biographical information on di Robilant, see *Almanacco della donna italiana, 1933*, p. 361; also *Almanacco della donna italiana, 1935*, p. 37, as well as her various contributions, for example, *Le cause e profilassi del traviamento femminile*, written on behalf of the Federazione provinciale dei fasci femminile dell'Urbe (Rome: Fratelli Pallotta, 1938).

14. Fiorenza Taricone, "La FILDIS (Federazione Nazionale Laureate e Diplomate) e l'associazionismo femminile (1920–1935)," in *La corpora-

zione delle donne, ed. Marina Addis Saba (Florence: Vallecchi, 1989), pp. 127–69.

15. Cited in "Società femminili italiane," *Almanacco della donna italiana, 1930,* p. 355; Archivio centrale dello stato, Ministero dell'Interno, Affari generali e riservati, G1, Associazioni, B. 38, f. Federazione italiana del suffragio e i diritti civili e politici delle donne.

16. ACS, MI, AAGGRR, G1, Associazioni, B. 38, f. Federazione italiana del suffragio e i diritti civili e politici delle donne. Citation is from the petition circulated Jan. 26, 1932. The accommodation of feminist groups is touched on in Sara Follacchio, "Conversando al femminismo: *La donna italiana,*" in *La corporazione delle donne,* pp. 211–20.

17. Cited in Giancarlo Fusco, *Le rose del ventennio* (Turin: Einaudi, 1958), pp. 30–31.

18. On the Catholic women's movement, see above, chapter 2, note 8 and chapter 5, note 54, as well as De Giorgio, "La fin du féminisme." On the leaders, see A. Barelli, *Incanto di un decennio: Episodi di vita delle sezioni minori della Gioventù femminile di Azione Cattolica* (Milan, 1937). For the names of the organizations, see *La Sorella Maggiore racconta* (Milan: Vita e Pensiero, 1948), p. 161, and Maria Sticco's fascinating *Una donna tra due secoli: Armida Barelli* (Milan: Edizione Or, 1983). The relations between Catholic women and fascist women's groups needs study along the lines of Laura Gellott and Richard Phayer's essay on Central Europe, "Dissenting Voices: Catholic Women in Opposition to Fascism," *Journal of Contemporary History* 22, no. 1 (Jan. 1987): 91–114.

19. Renato Moro, "La 'modernizzazione' cattolica tra fascismo e post-fascismo come problema storiografico," *Storia contemporanea* 19, no. 4 (Aug. 1988): 625–716.

20. M.-Z., "Conciliazione," *La donna italiana* 6, no. 3 (Mar. 1929): 132–33.

21. Maria Pezzè Pascolato, "I fasci femminili," *Gerarchia* 12, no. 2 (Feb. 1932): 116.

22. As in Valeria Benetti Brunelli, *La donna nella civiltà moderna* (Turin: Fratelli Bocca, 1933), pp. 215ff.

23. Annarita Buttafuoco, *Le Mariuccine: Storia di un'istituzione, l'Asilio Mariuccia* (Milan: Franco Angeli, 1985), pp. 412–14, 433.

24. Moro, "La 'modernizzazione' cattolica," p. 713. See also Cecilia Dau Novelli, " 'Daremo sei milioni di voti': Il movimento delle donne cattoliche nei primi anni delli Repubblica," *Memoria* 21 (1987): 45–55.

25. *Giornale della donna* 13, no. 11 (June 1, 1931):1.

26. On Ester Lombardo, born Giovanna Mogavero at Trapani in 1892, see Mario Gastaldi, *Donne, Luce d'Italia: Panorama della letteratura femminile contemporanea* (Milan: Ed. Quaderni di Poesia, 1936), p. 406; Maria Bandini Buti, *Poetesse e scrittrici,* 2 vols., series 6, *Enciclopedia biografica e bibliografica italiana* (Rome: Bernardo Carlo Tosi, 1941–42),

p. 342; as well as Franca Pieroni Bortolotti, *Femminismo e partiti politici in Italia, 1919–1926* (Rome: Editori Riuniti, 1978), p. 37.

27. *Giornale della donna* 16, no. 6 (Mar. 15, 1934), *Almanacco della donna italiana, 1936*, p. 57.

28. Maria Pezzè Pascolato, the distinguished Venetian educator, was called on to give the first description of the *fasci femminili's* functions for official consumption, "I fasci femminili," *Gerarchia* 12, no. 2 (Feb. 1932): 113–17.

29. Augusto Turati, *Giornale della donna* 10, no. 12 (Apr. 8–15, 1930): 1.

30. Quotations are from T. Labriola, "Il nostro programma," *La donna italiana* 6, no. 12 (Dec. 1929): 654–55, and "Nell'orbita del femminismo," *La donna italiana* 7, no. 10 (Oct. 1930): 544–49. See also "Per la donna fascista," *La donna italiana* 12, no. 8 (Sept.–Oct. 1935): 450–51. On Labriola, see Luigi Dal Pane, "Antonio e Teresa Labriola," *Rivista internazionale di filosofia del diritto*, A. 22, ser. 2 (Jan.–Feb. 1942): 47–89; and "Teresa Labriola," in "Protagonisti femminili nel primo novecento," *Problemi del socialismo* 17, no. 4 (Oct.–Dec. 1976): 248–50.

31. Labriola, "Il nostro programma," *La donna italiana* 6, no. 12 (Dec. 1929): 655.

32. On the new stratifications in Italian national culture under fascism, see Victoria de Grazia, *The Culture of Consent: Mass Organization of Leisure in Fascist Italy* (New York: Cambridge University Press, 1981), esp. pp. 187–224. For Gentile's views, see "La donna nella coscienza moderna," in *La donna e il fanciullo* (Florence: Sansoni, 1934), pp. 3–28.

33. Archivio centrale dello stato, Segreteria particolare del Duce, Carteggio ordinario (ACS, SPD, CO), f. 516.214, Fanny Dini.

34. See Sandra Artom and Annarita Calabrò, *Sorelle d'Italia* (Milan: Rizzoli, 1989), pp. 156–57.

35. Mario Gastaldi, *Donne, luce d'Italia* (Pistoia: G. Grazzini, 1930), revised and enlarged as *Donne, luce d'Italia: Panorama della letteratura femminile contemporanea* (Milan: Editore Quaderni di Poesia, 1936). Maria Bandini Buti, *Poetesse e scrittrici*, 2 vols., ser. 6, *Enciclopedia biografica e bibliografica italiana* (Rome: Istituto Editoriale Italiano B. C. Tosi, 1941–42).

36. Daria Banfi Malaguzzi, "Rassegna letteraria: Scrittrici d'Italia," *Almanacco della donna italiana, 1938*, pp. 178–81.

37. Studies of Italian literature have conventionally studied male literary figures: see Sergio Pacifici, *The Modern Italian Novel*, 3 vols. (Carbondale, Ill.: Southern Illinois University Press, 1969–72), vols. 2 and 3. Michele Giocondi, *Lettori in camicia nera* (Florence-Messina: D'Anna, 1978) gives a cursory examination of new genres and reading publics in the interwar years. Alberto Asor Rosa's important *Scrittori e popolo: Il populismo nella letteratura italiana contemporanea* (1969; Turin: Ei-

naudi, 1988) touches on the revival of the populist tradition under fascism and the origins of neorealism.

38. Italian translations of the novels of Carlisle are *La felicità conquistata* (1935) *(The Wife)*, *Il grido della madre* (1933) *(Mother's Cry)*; of Földes, *Prendo marito* (1932), *Si comincia domani* (1937); of Mansfield *Preludio e altri racconti* (1931) and *Diario* (1933).

39. Banfi Malaguzzi, "Rassegna letteraria: Scrittrici d'Italia," p. 181.

40. Liliana Scalero, "Le donne che scrivono," *Almanacco della donna italiana, 1937*, pp. 212–13.

41. Maria Maggi, "Rassegna letteraria: Scrittrici d'Italia," *Almanacco della donna italiana, 1930*, p. 182.

42. Ester Lombardo, *Lettore d'amore*, 2d ed. (Florence: Bemporad, 1928), p. 15.

43. Lombardo, *La donna senza cuore*, 2d ed. (Milan: Corbaccio, 1929), p. 268.

44. Tania Modleski, *Loving with a Vengeance* (New York: Methuen, 1982), pp. 38, 45.

45. Maria Maggi, "Rassegna letteraria: Scrittrici d'Italia," *Almanacco della donna italiana, 1930*, p. 182. On Maggi, see M. A. Loschi, "Donne italiane: Profili, Maria Maggi," *La donna italiana* 4, no. 5 (Apr. 1927): 328.

46. Teresa Labriola, "Di voi, con voi, per voi," *La donna italiana* 10, no. 12 (Dec. 1933): 659.

47. Lina Pietravalle, *Le catene* (Milan: Mondadori, 1930), pp. 23, 311.

48. Cited in Ilva Vaccari, "La donna nel ventennio fascista (1919–1943)" in *La donna e resistenza in Emilia-Romagna*, 3 vols. (Milan: Vangelista, 1978), 1:11/; see also Stanis Ruinas, *Scrittrici e scribacchine* (Rome: Accademia, 1930).

49. Margherita Sarfatti, *Il palazzone* (Milan: Mondadori, 1929), pp. 14, 214, 236, 238.

50. Daria Banfi Malaguzzi, "Rassegna letteraria: Scrittrici d'Italia," p. 185.

51. On Sarfatti's designs for this novel, see her own account, "Lebensskizze," in *Führende Frauen Europas*, ed. Elga Kern, new ed. (Munich: Verlag von Ernst Reinhardt, 1930), pp. 113–14; see also Victoria de Grazia, "Il fascino del priapo: Margherita Sarfatti," *Memoria* 4 (1982): 149–54. Sarfatti expresses her attitudes toward American women in *America, ricerca della felicità* (Milan: Mondadori, 1937), p. 210, chaps. 14–15, passim.

52. Galeazzo Ciano, *Ciano's Hidden Diary, 1937–1938*, translation and notes by Andreas Mayor (New York: E. P. Dutton, 1953), p. 10.

53. Emma Scaramuzza, "Professioni intellettuali e fascismo: L'ambivalenza della Alleanza muliebre culturale italiana," *Italia contemporanea*, nos. 151–52 (Sept. 1983): 111–33, esp. pp. 121–23.

54. D.B.M., "Attività intellettuali femminili," *Almanacco della donna*

italiana, 1933, pp. 322–25; "Società femminili italiane,"*Almanacco della donna italiana, 1935*, pp. 385–87; "Società femminili italiane," *Almanacco della donna italiana, 1938*, pp. 341–48. On Castellani, see, in addition to D.B.M., "Attività intellettuali femminili," p. 324, "La nuova fiduciaria provinciale dei fasci femminili dell'Urbe," *La donna italiana* (Feb. 1937):59.

55. Mussolini, "Alle donne fasciste," *Opera omnia*, ed. Edoardo Susmel and Duilio Susmel, 44 vols. (Florence: La Fenice, 1951, 1951–80), 17: 204–5.

56. Francesco Orestano, preface, *Enciclopedia biografica e bibliografica*, ser. 7, *Eroine, ispiratrici, e donne d' eccezione*, directed by Francesco Orestano (Milan: B. C. Tosi, 1940).

57. See Detlev Peukert's insightful comments in *Inside Nazi Germany: Conformity, Opposition and Racism in Everyday Life*, trans. Richard Deveson (1982; New Haven: Yale University Press, 1987).

58. Wanda Bruschi, "In tema di educazione," *Giornale della donna* 15, no. 10 (May 15, 1933):5; Elisabetta Mondello, *La nuova italiana* (Rome: Editori Riuniti, 1987), p. 78.

59. D.B.M., "Attività intellettuali femminili," *Almanacco della donna italiana, 1931*, p. 304.

60. Teresa Labriola, "Lo spirito dell'assistenza in regime fascista," *Giornale della donna* 13, no. 12 (June 15, 1931): 1.

61. ACS, SPD, CO. f. 100895, Elisa Majer Rizzioli–Mussolini, Dec. 23, 1925.

62. *Giornale della donna* 12, no. 23 (Dec. 1, 1930).

63. Pezzè Pascolato, "I fasci femminili," pp. 116–17.

64. On Itta (Giuditta) Stelluti Scala Frascara, see *La donna italiana* 10, no. 12 (Dec. 1933): 98–99, also ACS, SPD, CO, f. 516.216.

65. ACS, SPD, CO, f. 509.504/3 Moretti, Angiola.

66. See David Graves Horn's thoughtful study of Milan, *The Government of the Social in Interwar Italy* (Ph.D. diss., Department of Anthropology, University of California, Berkeley, 1987), esp. chap. 4.

67. Irene Giunti di Targiani, *La donna nella famiglia, nel lavoro, nella vita sociale*, Corso per visitatrici fasciste (Rome: Federazione dei fasci di combattimento dell'Urbe, delegazione provinciale fasci femminili, 1935), pp. 6–7, 27.

68. Modigliani, *Lavoro sociale delle donne*, pp. 19–20. See also Marziola Pignatari, *Beneficenza, assistenza, previdenza in Italia* (Rome: Fratelli Palombi, 1936). Cf. Ugo Manunta, *Previdenza e assistenza sociale negli stati totalitari* (Rome: Istituto nazionale fascista della previdenza sociale, 1939).

69. Giulia Boni, *Il lavoro sociale della donna, le grandi organizzazioni in Italia e all'estero* (Pisa: Tipografia Pellegrini, 1935), pp. 9, 4.

70. Boni, *Il lavoro sociale della donna*, p. 4.

71. Mussolini, "Alle donne fasciste," June 20, 1937, *Opera omnia*, 28:205.

72. Renzo De Felice, *Mussolini il Duce, 1936–1940* (Turin: Einaudi, 1981), pp. 76–81; ACS, SPD, CO, f. 525.997; Clara Franceschini, *La donna fascista* 19, no. 1 (Jan. 1, 1937).

73. On Wanda Bruschi Gorjux, see "Protagoniste femminili del primo Novecento," *Problemi del socialismo* 17, no. 4 (Oct.–Dec. 1976): 236–37; on Teresita Ruata Menzinger, see ACS, SPD, CO, f. 539.328. On Olga Medici Del Vascello, see ACS, SPD, CO, f. 184.815, as well as her daughter Elvina Pallavicini's memoir in *Sorelle d'Italia*, eds. Sandra Artom and Annarita Calabrò (Milan: Rizzoli, 1989), pp. 236–40.

74. For listings of the fiduciaries, see *Almanacco della donna italiana, 1932*, pp. 324–27; *Almanacco della donna italiana, 1933*, pp. 357–60; *Almanacco della donna italiana, 1935*, pp. 379–80. On Angiola Moretti, see ACS, SPD, CO, f. 509.504/3.

75. ACS, SPD, CO, f. 548.001: Rachele Ferrari del Latte. Letter, Ferrari del Latte–Sebastiani, Feb. 23, 1939.

76. ACS, PNF, Direttorio, B. 244: f. 64 D. See too *La donna fascista* 17, no. 11 (June 5, 1935); *La donna fascista* 19, no. 1 (Jan. 1, 1937).

77. RFD, "La difesa della razza," *Lavoro e famiglia* 1, no. 10 (Dec. 1938):3.

CHAPTER 9

1. Archivio centrale dello stato, Segreteria particolare del Duce, Carteggio riservato (ACS, SPD, CR), b. 142, Ada De Morvi–Eccellenza, Aug. 24, 1938.

2. Several studies attest to the volatility of public opinion on the eve of the war and in the wake of the declaration of hostilities, including Victoria de Grazia, *Culture of Consent: Mass Organization of Leisure in Fascist Italy* (New York: Cambridge University Press, 1981); Renzo De Felice, *Mussolini il Duce: Gli anni del consenso*, 1929–1935 (Turin: Einaudi, 1974); and Renzo Martinelli, ed., *Il fronte interno a Firenze, 1940–1943* (Florence: Università degli studi di Firenze, Dipartimento di storia, fonti 1, 1989). On public attitudes toward anti-Semitism, see Renzo De Felice's excellent *Storia degli ebrei italiani sotto il fascismo*, 3d rev. ed. (Milan: Mondadori, 1977) and Meir Michaelis, *Mussolini and the Jews* (Oxford: Oxford University Press, 1978).

3. The standard English-language work on the Resistance is Charles F. Delzell, *Mussolini's Enemies* (Princeton: Princeton University Press, 1961). Since Bianca Guidetti Serra published her oral history, *Compagne: Testimonianze di partecipazione politica femminile*, 2 vols. (Turin: Einaudi, 1977), several histories, also using oral testimony, have highlighted women's involvement in Resistance activities; see Mirella Alloisio

and Giuliana Beltrami, *Volontarie della liberta* (Milan: Mazzotta, 1981); Annamaria Bruzzone and Rachele Farina, *La resistenza taciuta: Dodici vite di partigiane piemontesi* (Florence: La Pietra, 1976); and Laura Mariani, *Quelle della idea* (Bari: De Donato, 1982).

4. See Detlev Peukert, *Inside Nazi Germany: Conformity, Opposition and Racism in Everyday Life*, trans. Richard Deveson (1982; New Haven: Yale University Press, 1987). Luisa Passerini, *Torino operaio e socialista* (Bari: Laterza, 1984) develops this approach using oral histories. See too the discussion in Victoria de Grazia and Luisa Passerini, "Alle origini della cultura di massa: Cultura popolare e fascismo in Italia," *Ricerca folklorica* 7 (Summer, 1983): 19–25; also Dianella Galiani, Luigi Casali, et al., "Cultura popolare negli anni del fascismo," *Italia contemporanea* (Dec. 1984): 63–90.

5. Film studies has thus far produced the most insightful readings of gender and other forms of oppositional politics under fascism. See James Hay, *Popular Film Culture in Fascist Italy: The Passing of the Rex* (Bloomington: Indiana University Press, 1987), and Marcia Landy, *Fascism in Film: The Italian Commercial Cinema, 1931–1934* (Princeton: Princeton University Press, 1986). More generally, on the usefulness of textual analysis for analyzing the construction of gender, see Joan Wallach Scott, *Gender and the Politics of History* (New York: Columbia University Press, 1988).

6. Michael Geyer, "The Militarization of Europe, 1914–1945," in *The Militarization of the Western World*, ed. John Gillis (New Brunswick: Rutgers University Press, 1989), pp. 65–102. A similar argument is made for both Italy and Germany in MacGregor Knox, "Conquest, Foreign and Domestic, in Fascist Italy and Nazi Germany," *Journal of Modern History* 56 (1984): 1–57.

7. The first work to study the impact of fascist militarization on women is Maria Fraddosio, "La donna e la guerra: Aspetti della militanza femminile nel fascismo—dalla mobilitazione civile alle origini del Saf nella Repubblica Sociale Italiana," *Storia contemporanea* 20, no. 6 (Dec. 1989): 1105–81, which is the core of a forthcoming book.

8. Marziola Pignatari, *La partecipazione delle donne fasciste alla vita dell'impero: Conversazione tenuta alle donne fasciste di Littoria*, Apr. 1937 (Rome: Fratelli Palombi, 1937), p. 5.

9. Olga Medici del Vascello, *I compiti e le responsabilità della donna nell'ora presente della vita nazionale: Conversazione tenuta alle donne e giovani fasciste di Venezia*, Mar. 18, 1936 (Genoa: S. A. Imprese tipografiche, 1936), p. 14.

10. Cited in Laura Marani, "Preparazione della donna alla vita coloniale," *Congresso mondiale lavoro e gioia* (Rome, 1938), p. 4. See too Mercedes Astuto, "La donna italiana e le nostre colonie," *Almanacco della donna italiana, 1936*, pp. 115–33.

11. Maria Castellani, "La nazione armata: Le donne professioniste e laureate ausiliarie civili," *Almanacco della donna italiana, 1936*, pp. 52, 54. The same themes are rehearsed in "La donna e il servizio militare," *Almanacco della donna italiana, 1937*, pp. 89–94.

12. Anna Dinella, *Italiane d'oggi: Commento al decalogo delle donne fasciste di Berlino* (Naples: SIEM, 1936), pp. 8–9.

13. *La donna italiana* 14, nos. 7–8 (July–Aug. 1937): 209–10.

14. ACS, SPD, CO. f.516.124. Fanny Dini–Mussolini, June 3, 1939.

15. Virgilio Ilari and Antonio Sema analyze this military culture in *Marte in Orbace: Guerra, esercito e milizia nella concezione fascista della nazione* (Ancona: Edizioni Nuove Ricerche, 1988). See too MacGregor Knox, *Mussolini Unleashed, 1939–1941* (New York and Cambridge: Cambridge University Press, 1980).

16. Benito Mussolini, Speech to the Chamber of Deputies, May 26, 1934, *Opera omnia*, ed. Edoardo Susmel and Duilio Susmel, 44 vols. (Florence: La Fenice, 1951–80), 9:98.

17. On the aspiration of middle-class women to create a "Herland," see Sandra M. Gilbert, "Soldier's Heart: Literary Men, Literary Women, and the Great War," reprinted in *Behind the Lines: Gender and the Two World Wars*, ed. Margaret Randolph Higonnet et al. (New Haven: Yale University Press, 1987), pp. 197–226. The false but noteworthy analogy between birthing and making war is analyzed with acumen by Nancy Huston, "The Matrix of War: Mothers and Heroes," in *The Female Body in Western Culture: Contemporary Perspectives*, ed. Susan Rubin Suleiman (Cambridge: Harvard University Press, 1985), pp. 119–36.

18. Ellevì, "Femminismo borghese," *Gerarchia* 19, no. 6 (June 1939):405.

19. Cited in Lamberto Mercuri, "Brevi note per una storia del fascismo canoro," *Il protagora*, 26–27 (Apr.–June 1963): 112.

20. Cited from the SAF's broadsheet, *Donne in Grigioverde* by Maria Fraddosio, "Donne nell'esercito di Salò," *Memoria* 4 (June 1982):70. See too Fulvia Giuliani, *Donne d'Italia: Le ausiliarie della RSI* (Rome: Arnia, 1952), p. 118.

21. Women's experience of the war is skillfully evoked by Miriam Mafai, *Pane nero* (Milan: Rizzoli, 1988).

22. Alloisio and Beltrami, *Volontarie della liberta*, p. 25. Also Daria Banfi Malagazzi, *A Milano nella resistenza* (Rome: Riuniti, 1964) p. 149.

23. These attitudes are documented in Bruzzone and Farina, *La resistenza taciuta: Dodici vite di partigiane piemontesi*, and Bianca Giudetti Serra, *Compagne: Testimonianze di partecipazione politica femminile*. In English, see Anna Maria Bruzzone, "Women in the Italian Resistance," in *Our Common History*, ed. Paul Thompson with Natasha Burchhardt (London: Pluto Press, 1983), pp. 272–96.

24. "Donne e resistenza nel Verbano," *Ieri, Novara, oggi* 4 (1980):479.

25. Ibid., p. 491.

26. Temma Kaplan, "Female Consciousness and Collective Action: The Case of Barcelona, 1910–1918," *Signs* 7 (Spring 1982): 545–66. The term "communal consciousness" is suggested by Nancy F. Cott, "What's In a Name? The Limits of 'Social Feminism'; or, Expanding the Vocabulary of Women's History," *Journal of American History* 76, no. 3 (Dec. 1989): 827.

27. Beppe Fenoglio, *Partigiano Johnny* (Turin: Einaudi, 1968), p. 118.

28. Luciano Gambassini, *Medico fra la gente* (Florence: Vallecchi, 1981).

29. First published in 1946 in the Florentine journal *Società*, edited by Bilenchi, some selections were almost immediately published in French translation in Jean-Paul Sartre's *Les temps modernes*, Aug.–Sept. 1947, pp. 345–70. Subsequently, they were republished in Romano Bilenchi, *Cronache degli anni neri* (Rome: Riuniti, 1984), pp. 254–89.

30. "La strage di Civitella," *Cronache degli anni neri*, p. 259.

Index

Compositor: Maple-Vail Book Mfg. Group
Text: 10 / 13 Aldus
Display: Aldus
Printer: Malloy Lithographing, Inc.
Binder: Malloy Lithographing, Inc.